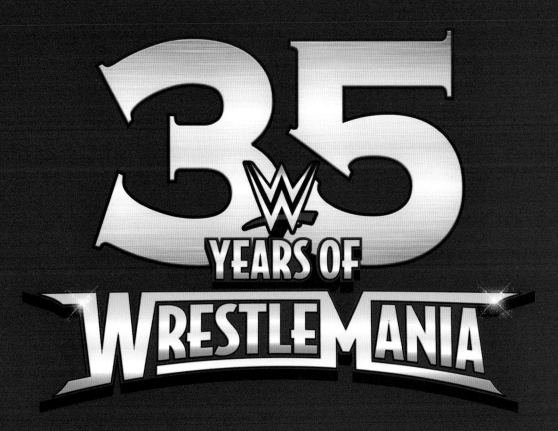

35

WWE

YEARS OF

WrestleMania

Written by Brian Shields and Dean Miller

FOREWORD

You never forget your first *WrestleMania*. It doesn't matter if you are a fan, an employee, or a WWE Superstar, you NEVER forget your first *WrestleMania*. Mine was *WrestleMania V* in Atlantic City, where I teamed with Marty Jannetty as part of "The Rockers." While we were not on the winning end of our match, the fact that we were on the card was a major accomplishment for us, and the highlight of my career up to that point.

Throughout my WWE career, I witnessed first-hand how *WrestleMania* became a pop-culture phenomenon and a spectacle that no rock concert or sporting event can compare to. Performing in front of sold-out stadiums with more than 70,000 people in attendance and being a part of the week-long series of events where fans from all over the world come to celebrate every year has been nothing short of an honor. It is an event that is just as special for the WWE Superstars as it is for the WWE Universe.

In the pages of this book, you have the opportunity to relive many classic *WrestleMania* moments, from *WrestleMania 1* at Madison Square Garden, to *WrestleMania 35* at MetLife Stadium, and everything in between. All WWE fans around the world have their own special *WrestleMania* memories, and I am humbled that many of my matches are included on their lists.

"Mr. WrestleMania" is not just a nickname for me; it is something that I take great pride in. I worked hard to give my best in every *WrestleMania* match that I was part of. When my in-ring career ended against Undertaker at *WrestleMania XXVI*, I was completely at peace, knowing that there was no better place than *WrestleMania* for it to happen. Since that time, I have enjoyed watching the next generation of WWE Superstars create their own *WrestleMania* moments for the legions of passionate WWE fans around the world.

Sit back and enjoy 35 years of *WrestleMania*. I can't wait to see what's in store for the next 35 years. I know I will be watching.

182	188	194	200	210
XXVI	XXVII	XXVIII	29	30
220	226	232	238	246
31	32	33	34	35

CONTENTS

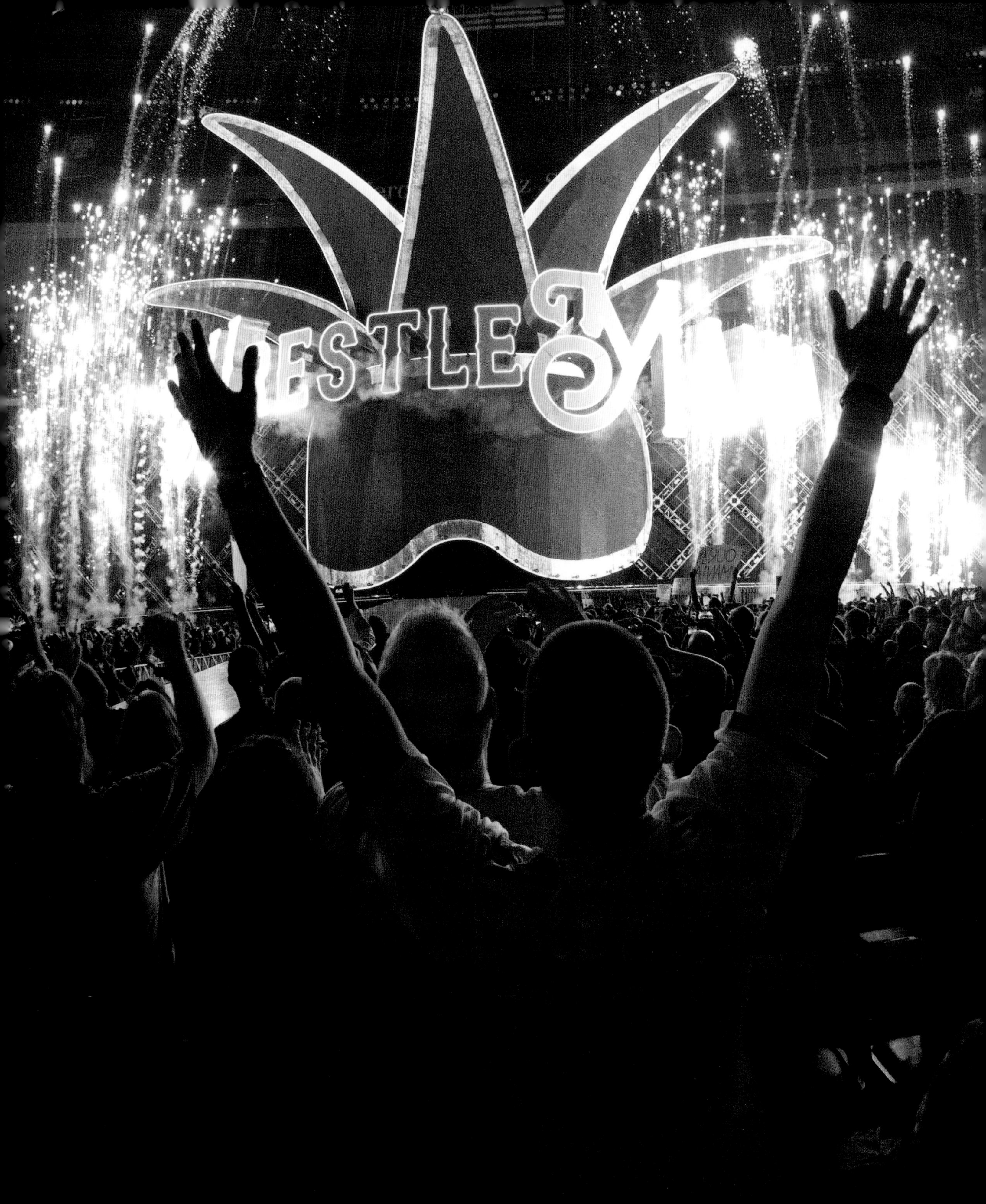

DEVELOPMENT EDITOR Jennifer Sims **BOOK DESIGNER** Dan Caparo

PRODUCTION DESIGNER Tracy Wehmeyer **VICE PRESIDENT & PUBLISHER** Mike Degler

EDITOR-IN-CHIEF H. Leigh Davis **LICENSING MANAGER** Christian Sumner

DIGITAL PUBLISHING MANAGER Tim Cox **MARKETING MANAGER** Katie Hemlock

OPERATIONS MANAGER Stacey Beheler

2019 update: Project Editor Pamela Afram, Senior Editor Alastair Dougall,
Editor Julia March, Senior Designer Nathan Martin, Senior Pre-Production Producer Jennifer
Murray, Producer Louise Daly, Managing Editor, Paula Regan, Managing Art Editor Jo Connor,
Art Director Lisa Lanzarini, Publisher Julie Ferris,
Publishing Director Simon Beecroft

The publisher would like to give a special thanks to Marc Staples
at DK and Dean Miller for their work on this updated edition.

First American Edition, 2019
Published in the United States by DK Publishing
1450 Broadway, Suite 801, New York, NY 10018

Page design copyright ©2019 Dorling Kindersley Limited
DK, a Division of Penguin Random House LLC

21 22 10 9 8 7 6 5 4 3 2

002-312631-Sept/2019

A catalog record for this book is available from the Library of Congress.

ISBN: 978-1-4654-7974-7

DK books are available at special discounts when purchased in bulk for sales promotions,
premiums, fund-raising, or educational use. For details, contact:
DK Publishing Special Markets
1450 Broadway, Suite 801,
New York, NY 10018
SpecialSales@dk.com

Some photographs on pages 76, 77, 79, and 80 by Pro Wrestling Illustrated.

Printed and bound in China

Consumer Products

GLOBAL PUBLISHING MANAGER Steve Pantaleo

VICE PRESIDENT, INTERACTIVE MEDIA Ed Kiang

SENIOR VICE PRESIDENT, CONSUMER PRODUCTS Sarah Cummins

Photo Department
Brad Smith, Josh Tottenham, Frank Vitucci, Georgiana Dallas,
Jamie Nelson, Melissa Halladay, Mike Moran, and JD Sestito

Archivist
Ben Brown

Creative Services
SENIOR VICE PRESIDENT, CREATIVE SERVICES Stan Stanski

CREATIVE DIRECTOR John Jones

COVER DESIGNER Franco Malagisi

Legal
VICE PRESIDENT, INTELLECTUAL PROPERTY Lauren Dienes-Middlen

About the Authors

Brian Shields is a New York Times Bestselling Author. Since 1998, he has worked
with WWE on special projects, and partnered with Mattel, 2K Games, and Topps.
Brian has written books for WWE and writes at the Friars Club in New York City
where he enjoys membership.

Dean Miller is an author and editor who has built hundreds of fiction and non-fiction
books in the areas of sports, wrestling, computer technologies, and education. He is
the author of DK's *The WWE Book of Top 10s* and a co-author of *WWE: Everything You
Need to Know*, *WWE RAW: The First 25 Years*, and *WWE SmackDown: 20 Years and
Counting*. He has served as editor for several books by sports entertainment
personalities such as Mick Foley, Shawn Michaels, Eddie Guerrero, and Eric Bischoff.

THE ROAD TO WRESTLEMANIA

In the midst of the 1980s home entertainment boom, Vince McMahon saw WWE's fan base converging with the audiences of mainstream rock 'n' roll, primetime television, and pop culture like never before. Sensing a captivating opportunity, McMahon envisioned the future of his company with younger fans and their families filling large venues. He knew that, as in rock 'n' roll culture, electrifying music, colorful attire, and sensational entrances were essential to providing a singular entertainment experience. If he could devise creative, well-executed cross promotions to combine the strengths of WWE with the burgeoning MTV craze, the results could propel both companies to unprecedented notoriety.

Happenstance yielded the initial alliance of these two juggernauts. On an airplane flight, legendary WWE personality Captain Lou Albano met pop music mega-star Cyndi Lauper. Lauper's then-boyfriend and manager David Wolfe was a huge WWE fan and suggested the two find a way to work together. This had to be handled delicately. During these years, professional wrestling was still shrouded in secrecy to uphold the personalities and storylines portrayed on television. "Good Guys" and "Bad Guys" were forbidden to be seen together in public. If a Superstar so much as went to a restaurant and an adversary was already there, one of them would have to leave.

As a first step, Albano was cast as Lauper's father in the music video for her smash hit, "Girls Just Want to Have Fun." The combined popularity of the video and Albano's famous WWE persona planted the seeds of "The Rock 'N' Wrestling Connection," and Lauper prepared for her debut on WWE programming. Because Albano was considered a WWE "villain," he would have to extend his appalling behavior toward Lauper in front of WWE fans. It was arranged for Albano and Lauper to engage in a heated dispute on "Rowdy" Roddy Piper's combative talk show, Piper's Pit. On July 23, 1984, American television featured these two popular genres coming together as one. The event was WWE's The Brawl to End It All, broadcast nationally on MTV. Millions tuned in to see Captain Lou's Fabulous Moolah defend her undefeated Women's Championship reign against rising star Wendi Richter, who was aligned with Lauper. In a harbinger of WWE success to come, the special event was an overwhelming hit in live attendance and set a Nielsen television rating record of 9.0, or an estimated 10 million viewers for MTV.

▶ *Vince McMahon at Madison Square Garden*

The next big inspiration came at an unexpected time. At year's end, Vince McMahon and his wife, Linda, enjoyed a Caribbean vacation. There, Vince McMahon conceived the nucleus of an idea: a yearly destination event where WWE Superstars would share the stage with iconic figures from the arts, entertainment, and professional sports worlds, and it would be broadcast live on closed-circuit television. Vince McMahon recalls, "I just thought it was the next logical step for us. Hollywood had the Oscars, the NFL had the Super Bowl, and so forth. … Why not have a WWE annual spectacular?" Vince asked Linda to assemble a meeting of his inner circle. At that time, his cabinet consisted of industry luminaries such as George Scott, Jim Barnett, Pat Patterson, Ed Cohen, and relative newcomer Howard Finkel. Vince told them WWE would create an annual spectacular. It didn't have a name yet, but it was already booked for Sunday, March 31, 1985, at Madison Square Garden in New York City.

THE CABINET

From the late 1940s through the early 1970s, George Scott, with his brother Sandy, comprised the famous team aptly named, "The Flying Scotts." Revered for his work behind the scenes creating matches, George arrived in WWE's front office in 1983.

Jim Barnett broke into the wrestling business during the golden age of the DuMont Network. The grappler turned promoter was considered the forefather of "studio wrestling," matches broadcast weekly from a television studio. A trusted friend, Barnett became a senior adviser to Vince McMahon in 1984.

Pat Patterson was known as a prolific in-ring performer and captivating storyteller. His work with partner Ray "The Crippler" Stevens as "The Blond Bombers" was groundbreaking. He was brought to WWE by Vince McMahon, Sr., and was crowned WWE's first Intercontinental Champion in 1979. Patterson was regarded as a savant in the areas of character development, storyline creation, and ring psychology.

The first time many heard the name Ed Cohen was when he appeared on an episode of *Rogers' Corner* as WWE's Charity Coordinator. Ed was responsible for scheduling WWE's massive live event calendar. With an incredible Rolodex of contacts, he booked celebrity talent including Liberace, The Rockettes, and Billy Martin.

Through WWE's national television syndication and home video line, Howard Finkel became known as the voice of WWE. Howard handled a myriad of roles, from columnist for WWE's *Victory* magazine to arranging talent travel and recording voice-overs. Finkel is also distinguished as the first full-time employee hired by Vince and Linda McMahon.

WRESTLEMANIA I

MADISON SQUARE GARDEN – NEW YORK, NY

March 31	
1985	
Attendance	
19, 121	

ANNOUNCERS
Gorilla Monsoon
Jesse "The Body" Ventura

RING ANNOUNCER
Howard Finkel

LOCKER ROOM CORRESPONDENTS
"Mean" Gene Okerlund
Lord Alfred Hayes

SPECIAL GUEST RING ANNOUNCER FOR MAIN EVENT
Billy Martin

SPECIAL GUEST TIME KEEPER
Liberace

SPECIAL GUEST REFEREE FOR MAIN EVENT
Muhammad Ali

SPECIAL GUESTS FOR MAIN EVENT
The Rockettes

Event Card

MAIN EVENT
- Hulk Hogan & Mr. T w/ Jimmy "Superfly" Snuka def. "Rowdy" Roddy Piper & "Mr. Wonderful" Paul Orndorff w/ Cowboy Bob Orton

WOMEN'S CHAMPIONSHIP MATCH
- Wendi Richter w/ Cyndi Lauper def. Leilani Kai w/ Fabulous Moolah to become new Champion

WORLD TAG TEAM CHAMPIONSHIP MATCH
- Nikolai Volkoff & Iron Sheik w/ "Classy" Freddie Blassie def. Mike Rotundo & Barry Windham w/ Capt. Lou Albano to become new Champions

INTERCONTINENTAL CHAMPIONSHIP MATCH
- Junkyard Dog def. Greg "The Hammer" Valentine w/ "Mouth of the South" Jimmy Hart

BODYSLAM CHALLENGE
- André the Giant def. Big John Studd w/ Bobby "The Brain" Heenan

OTHER MATCHES
- King Kong Bundy w/ "Mouth of the South" Jimmy Hart def. "S.D." Special Delivery Jones
- Ricky Steamboat def. Matt Borne
- David Sammartino w/ Bruno Sammartino vs. Brutus Beefcake w/ Luscious Johnny Valiant went to a no contest
- Tito Santana def. The Executioner

"We hocked everything we owned for *WrestleMania*."

—Linda McMahon

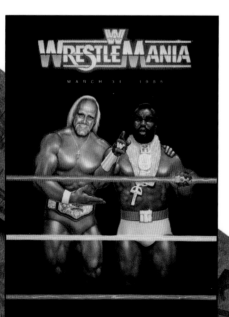

The Strategy

McMahon and his brain trust had just two months to create the WWE spectacular they envisioned. With the ground still shaking from the formation of "The Rock 'N' Wrestling Connection," Hulkamania running wild, and Brawl to End It All's success, McMahon recognized time was of the essence. To launch WWE into the stratosphere, he needed to use the promoter's savvy that dated back to the days of his grandfather, Jess McMahon. McMahon knew fans were familiar with annual events. Many territories hosted yearly happenings often billed as "Super Cards," a collection of high profile contests presenting famous rivalries, never-before-seen matches, and top attractions. By and large, they were marketed in the traditional NWA fashion of a legitimate sport, not entertainment.

To realize his vision, Vince McMahon needed to implement a more diverse promotional approach, distinguishing WWE from other brands across the country. His signature was operating, marketing, and promoting WWE like an entertainment company whose primary focus was professional wrestling or "sports-entertainment." McMahon explains, "We didn't want to be 'pro wrestling' like everybody else. How do we label this? How do we sell this? My dad was always more entertainment oriented than most of the other promoters anyhow, hence the phrase 'sports' in terms of the athleticism, and 'entertainment' because that's what we do."

It was important to satisfy the loyal WWE fan, and McMahon was confident that Madison Square Garden would sell out. However, with the star-studded assembly of celebrities scheduled to illuminate the stage, it was crucial to entice casual and prospective new fans. This event needed to be an exciting, accessible point of entry for people to get acquainted with the WWE product.

▶ *Liberace gave this signed poster to the McMahons as thanks for being invited to appear at WrestleMania*

The Celebrities

Billy Martin was most famous for managing the New York Yankees. Known as "NY's #1," Martin's explosive personality eminently qualified him as guest ring announcer for *WrestleMania*'s main event.

▶ *"Mean" Gene Okerlund with Billy Martin*

As one of early television's first stars, **Liberace** epitomized show business. Known as "Mr. Showmanship," he combined piano prowess with the spectacle of live theatre.

Mr. T achieved pop-culture status after his performance as Clubber Lang in Rocky III. Leading up to *WrestleMania*, he was promoted as an ally of Hulk Hogan in the unwavering battle against "Rowdy" Roddy Piper, "Mr. Wonderful" Paul Orndorff, and Cowboy Bob Orton.

Muhammad Ali first formed a relationship with the McMahon family in the 1970s when Vince, Sr. and his son promoted Ali's "Boxer v. Wrestler" match. Vince McMahon believed that the man known as "The Greatest" was the ultimate Special Guest Referee to expand the appeal of *WrestleMania*.

Setting the Stage

The event's framework was taking shape but the question was, would people buy a ticket to watch the event on closed-circuit? Vince McMahon remembers, "[It] wasn't cable TV as we know it today; it wasn't pay-per-view. It was in an arena with a giant television screen and a projector. It didn't work for the Indianapolis 500 and a number of other things. It was the biggest gamble I've ever been involved with. Who knew that WWE fans would pay their money in an arena and watch television?"

Many wrestling "purists" derided the notion of including such heavy celebrity involvement. Even within WWE, some had difficulty accepting it. Then-agent Gerry Brisco recalls, "I think the biggest resentment was … not so much having them as a part of WWE, but when you inserted them in the ring and told them, 'This is our business. This is what we do in there.' Many of the guys asked, 'Why are you showing these people what we do in the ring? Because we work so very hard to keep what we do in the ring professional.'"

Vince McMahon and George Scott looked at the roster of WWE Superstars. By this time, WWE had personalities and rivalries that received national attention: André the Giant, Jimmy "Superfly" Snuka, Iron Sheik, Hulk Hogan, "Rowdy" Roddy Piper, and others. The *WrestleMania* card had to heighten the tension of WWE's existing conflicts, select the right mixture of celebrity interaction, and make sure newer match-ups thrilled the crowd. This set the stage for The War to Settle the Score. Using the same format as The Brawl to End It All, the event did exactly what it had to do—it exacerbated the bitter quarrels and rivalries between WWE personas. Once Mr. T asserted himself as Hulk Hogan's "blood brother," the main event for *WrestleMania* was established, and all of entertainment was talking about it. Roddy Piper remembers, "I had kicked the most popular woman in music in the head; I slapped the biggest television star in the world … I tormented Hogan and chased poor Dick Clark to the dressing room. I couldn't go anywhere. I'm with my family and I'm fighting my way in and out of restaurants, if they'd even serve me."

One of the greatest remaining obstacles in ushering *WrestleMania* into the light of day was money. Linda McMahon remembers, "In 1976, Vince and I went bankrupt. We had spent years rebuilding. To take a risk like this again was quite scary. But Vince truly believed in this concept. It hadn't been done before. Offering something on closed-circuit meant you had to broker individual deals with the venues themselves all around the country. You had to rent all of the equipment necessary to carry the event. We didn't have that kind of cash. So then to convince a bank to give us a letter of credit to do all of this. … You just knew that letter of credit would be due the morning after *WrestleMania*, and it was tense that whole night. We hocked everything we owned for *WrestleMania*."

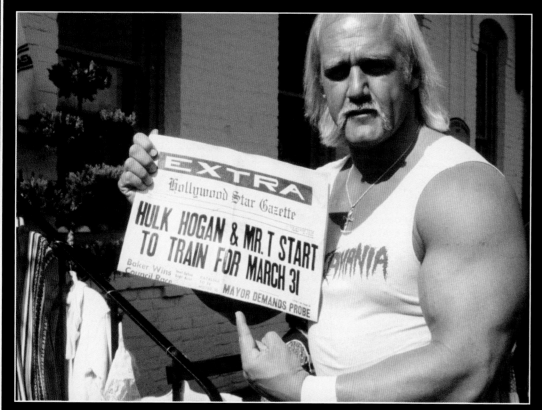

▶ *Mr. T and Hulk Hogan on the Observation Deck of the Empire State Building*

Vince McMahon and his new concept were often met with arrogance and anger from regional promoters. At times, hostilities escalated to actual threats on his life. For as many people who wanted *WrestleMania* to succeed, an equal number outside WWE rooted for it to go down in flames. Many Superstars felt if *WrestleMania* didn't succeed they would be out of a job—WWE would be out of business, and they'd be blackballed by the promoters in other territories. Pat Patterson remembers, "Everyone was excited but also very nervous. This was the biggest event of everyone's lives. You had a sold out Madison Square Garden; celebrities and everyone wanted to … showcase their abilities."

McMahon knew the best chance to reach new viewers was to do something almost unheard of as a wrestling promoter: open the door to mainstream media. Until this point, the industry was a bit of an anomaly and not welcoming to outsiders. Furthermore, the mainstream press often took any opportunity to criticize the industry. "Vince told me," recalls Patterson, "We're going to issue press passes … We're going to allow photographers who are not WWE employees to shoot at ringside, and WWE Superstars are going to do press interviews. He wanted to get rock 'n' roll fans, sports fans, boxing fans, and young people to know about what we were doing and want to see it. And he did."

Hulk Hogan and Mr. T appeared on CBS Morning News, The Today Show, and late night talk shows. Reaching the apex of television entertainment at that time, they hosted Saturday Night Live on the eve of *WrestleMania*. But keeping Mr. T on the right path proved challenging at times. As Ed Cohen remembers, "He was, as I liked to describe at the time, 'more show than go.' After a long day of travel and press appointments, WWE Superstars make a point to train in the gym. Mr. T rarely accepted the invitations to work out with [them]. I received a call from a colleague. The person said, 'Mr. T fired one of our employees.' So, we kept that employee away from Mr. T to give him the illusion that person was no longer an employee."

Unfortunately, Mr. T did not get along with one of WWE's biggest stars—someone he was scheduled to work with in the main event. Roddy Piper recalls, "Everything started with T and me at the first press conference. The press was there taking pictures, and T flexes his arm and says, 'Feel that; it's pretty hard.' So, I looked at him and squeezed his head and said, 'Pretty soft.' I didn't know we were not allowed to touch him. He traveled in a limousine, had an entourage with him, and had his own dressing room. I felt he didn't have respect for our business. We dislike each other to this day."

"At first, *WrestleMania* was a vision I didn't understand. There was a buzz around the entire country. It was something I had never felt before."

—Hulk Hogan

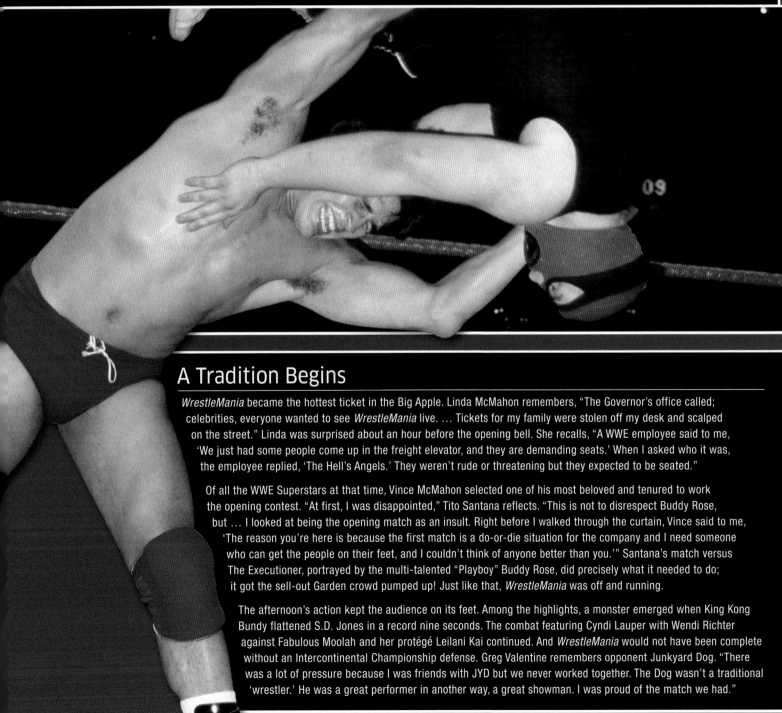

A Tradition Begins

WrestleMania became the hottest ticket in the Big Apple. Linda McMahon remembers, "The Governor's office called; celebrities, everyone wanted to see *WrestleMania* live. … Tickets for my family were stolen off my desk and scalped on the street." Linda was surprised about an hour before the opening bell. She recalls, "A WWE employee said to me, 'We just had some people come up in the freight elevator, and they are demanding seats.' When I asked who it was, the employee replied, 'The Hell's Angels.' They weren't rude or threatening but they expected to be seated."

Of all the WWE Superstars at that time, Vince McMahon selected one of his most beloved and tenured to work the opening contest. "At first, I was disappointed," Tito Santana reflects. "This is not to disrespect Buddy Rose, but … I looked at being the opening match as an insult. Right before I walked through the curtain, Vince said to me, 'The reason you're here is because the first match is a do-or-die situation for the company and I need someone who can get the people on their feet, and I couldn't think of anyone better than you.'" Santana's match versus The Executioner, portrayed by the multi-talented "Playboy" Buddy Rose, did precisely what it needed to do; it got the sell-out Garden crowd pumped up! Just like that, *WrestleMania* was off and running.

The afternoon's action kept the audience on its feet. Among the highlights, a monster emerged when King Kong Bundy flattened S.D. Jones in a record nine seconds. The combat featuring Cyndi Lauper with Wendi Richter against Fabulous Moolah and her protégé Leilani Kai continued. And *WrestleMania* would not have been complete without an Intercontinental Championship defense. Greg Valentine remembers opponent Junkyard Dog. "There was a lot of pressure because I was friends with JYD but we never worked together. The Dog wasn't a traditional 'wrestler.' He was a great performer in another way, a great showman. I was proud of the match we had."

▶ *King Kong Bundy defeats S.D. Jones in a record nine seconds*

▶ *Wendi Richter and Cyndi Lauper celebrate their victory*

A Battle of Giants

The inaugural *WrestleMania* featured a spectacular Bodyslam Challenge. The rivalry between Big John Studd and André the Giant captivated WWE fans everywhere. Despite being 6'10" to André's 7'4", Studd long boasted that he was the only true giant in WWE. He took great pride in proclaiming that he had never been, and could never be, slammed. During the preceding November, Studd, stable mate Ken Patera, and leader Bobby "The Brain" Heenan had cut André's hair. This presaged André's triumphant WWE return at *WrestleMania*, seeking redemption in a "$15,000 Body Slam Challenge." The crowd roared as André, the Eighth Wonder of the World, lifted his enemy over his head, slammed him, and ultimately claimed victory.

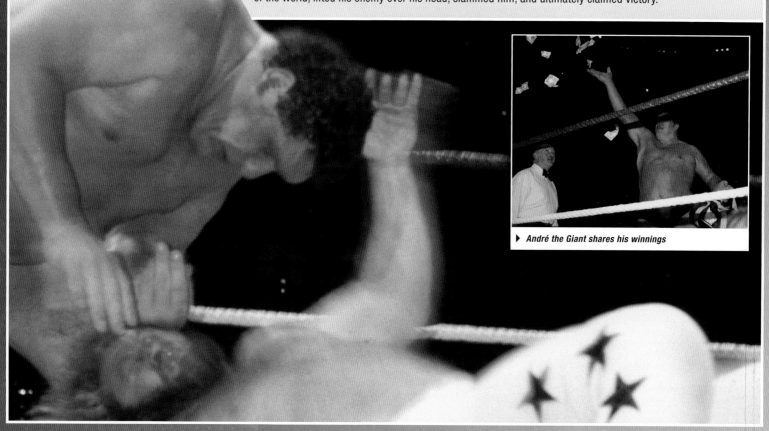

▶ *André the Giant shares his winnings*

A Cold War Upset

Leading into the World Tag Team Championship Match, many truly considered the trio of Iron Sheik, Nikolai Volkoff, and their manager, the legendary "Classy" Freddie Blassie, to be public enemy number one. The Iron Sheik explains, "I was not a character like other wrestlers. I loved this country. When I moved here, I was an assistant coach for the U.S. Olympic wrestling team. But my anti-U.S. comments were for business. I am Iranian. During those days, the people really hated me because of the Iranian hostage crisis. People waited in the back of the buildings to fight me … They felt they were defending America." Nikolai Volkoff remembers, "I hated communism. I escaped Russia when I was a young man. I didn't want to be a Russian sympathizer. Freddie Blassie told me the best way for me to fight communism was to show how evil it was. He suggested to Vince to put Sheik and I together. It worked right away. We had people jump in the ring and try to attack us … It was dangerous and very real in those days."

Audiences couldn't wait for Mike Rotunda and Barry Windham, The U.S. Express, to bring Sheik and Volkoff to justice. All four were accomplished athletes, intensifying their competition during the Cold War of the 1980s. Mike Rotunda reflects, "Sheik was an Olympic wrestler and Nikolai was so strong and an accomplished boxer. Barry and I were not only close friends, but we were brothers-in-law. He played college football and I wrestled at Syracuse University. With Iran and Russia being America's mortal enemies, it was a match made in heaven, especially at *WrestleMania*."

The Main Event

The evening's action whipped the fans into a frenzy for *WrestleMania*'s final headline match. A "mano-a-mano" clash for the WWE Championship between Hogan and Piper had already taken place at *The War to Settle the Score*. This conflict became more about a way of life than championship accolades. When Vince McMahon witnessed the crowd's reaction to Mr. T, he knew it was time to raise the stakes; a tag team match would headline his first sports-entertainment spectacular. Each team would have the representative of their choice in its corner. To no one's surprise, "Ace" Orton would shadow the Piper camp. Given the history he had with the opposition, Hogan and Mr. T had Jimmy "Superfly" Snuka by their side.

Leading up to the main event, Pat Patterson remembers, "Vince instructed me, 'When Muhammad Ali arrives, let him know what he's going to do as the referee.' I kept talking to Ali and just got a feeling that he wasn't 100%. So I said to Vince, 'I don't know if Muhammad Ali can referee the match.' Vince asked what I suggested. I told him, 'I'll referee the match and we'll have Ali as a referee on the outside of the ring.' At the last minute, that's what we did."

As Mr. T and Roddy Piper went nose-to-nose, the decibel level at Madison Square Garden skyrocketed. Even the celebrity guests were compelled into the action. "At one point, Ali jumped into the ring to get at Paul Orndorff," Pat Patterson remembers. "That wasn't expected. Orndorff then goes at Ali and threatens him. So, when Billy Martin heard that, he started to take his tuxedo jacket off, and we almost had a real brawl on our hands." In the final moments, a "miscue" from Bob Orton led to Hulk Hogan's victory for his team and Piper knocking out Pat Patterson.

"Roddy wrestled my dad when he was coming up. *WrestleMania*, Hogan, Mr. T, Snuka—we were hated everywhere we went. My favorite time in my career was my time with Roddy. There was never a dull moment."

—Bob Orton, Jr.

When the event came to a close, the backstage atmosphere was exuberant. As a live event at Madison Square Garden, *WrestleMania* was an overwhelming success. With worries about the bank's letter of credit hanging over the McMahons like Damocles' sword, questions weighed on their minds: how did the rest of the country do? Attendance figures started to come in from closed-circuit operators across North America. Says Linda McMahon, "We got a call around three o'clock in the morning, and I went into Vince and said we just broke even." The inaugural *WrestleMania* was viewed by more than one million fans on closed-circuit! According to Vince McMahon, "The success of *WrestleMania 1* really put us on the map. It coined the phrase 'sports-entertainment' because we were trying to figure out, 'Okay, who are we?' I mean, the kitchen sink was thrown into what we normally did (laughs). And it caught the imagination of media and people all over the world."

As Vince and Linda McMahon enjoyed their final celebratory moments, they realized that Vince's dream for a national sports-entertainment entity had been realized. Time would prove that, while there were challenges ahead, the best was yet to come.

WRESTLEMANIA 2

NASSAU COLISEUM, UNIONDALE, NY; ROSEMONT HORIZON, ROSEMONT, IL; LOS ANGELES MEMORIAL SPORTS ARENA, LOS ANGELES, CA

April 7
1986

Attendance
40,085

NEW YORK TEAM

ANNOUNCERS
Vince McMahon,
Susan St. James

RING ANNOUNCER
Howard Finkel

SPECIAL GUEST RING ANNOUNCER
Joan Rivers

SPECIAL GUEST TIMEKEEPER
Herb

CHICAGO TEAM

ANNOUNCERS
Gorilla Monsoon,
"Mean" Gene Okerlund,
Cathy Lee Crosby

RING ANNOUNCER
Chet Coppock

LOS ANGELES TEAM

ANNOUNCERS
Jesse "The Body" Ventura,
Lord Alfred Hayes, Elvira

RING ANNOUNCER
Lee Marshall

SPECIAL GUEST RING ANNOUNCER FOR MAIN EVENT
Tommy LaSorda

SPECIAL GUEST TIME KEEPER FOR MAIN EVENT
Ricky Schroder

SPECIAL GUEST REFEREE FOR MAIN EVENT
Robert Conrad

Event Card

WWE CHAMPIONSHIP STEEL CAGE MATCH
- Hulk Hogan (Champion) def. King Kong Bundy w/ Bobby "The Brain" Heenan

WORLD TAG TEAM CHAMPIONSHIP MATCH
- The British Bulldogs (Dynamite Kid & Davey Boy Smith) w/ Captain Lou Albano and Ozzy Osbourne def. The Dream Team (Brutus Beefcake & Greg "The Hammer" Valentine) w/ Luscious Johnny Valiant to become new Champions

WWE AND NFL BATTLE ROYAL MATCH
- André the Giant def. Jimbo Covert (Chicago Bears), Pedro Morales, Tony Atlas, Ted Arcidi, Harvey Martin (Dallas Cowboys), Dan Spivey, Hillbilly Jim, King Tonga, Iron Sheik, Ernie Holmes (Pittsburgh Steelers), Big John Studd, B. Brian Blair, Jumpin' Jim Brunzell, Bill Fralic (Atlanta Falcons), Bret "Hit Man" Hart, Jim "The Anvil" Neidhart, Russ Francis (San Francisco 49ers), Bruno Sammartino, and William "The Refrigerator" Perry (Chicago Bears)

FLAG MATCH
- Corporal Kirchner def. Nikolai Volkoff w/ Classy Freddie Blassie

WOMEN'S CHAMPIONSHIP MATCH
- Fabulous Moolah def. Velvet McIntyre to become new Champion

BOXING MATCH
- Mr. T w/ Joe Frazier and the Haiti Kid def. "Rowdy" Roddy Piper w/ Cowboy Bob Orton by disqualification

INTERCONTINENTAL CHAMPIONSHIP MATCH
- Randy "Macho Man" Savage w/ Elizabeth def. George "The Animal" Steele to retain Championship

OTHER MATCHES
- Jake "The Snake" Roberts def. George Wells
- "Mr. Wonderful" Paul Orndorff vs. "Magnificent" Don Muraco w/ Mr. Fuji went to a double count-out
- Terry & Hoss Funk w/ "Mouth of the South" Jimmy Hart def. Junkyard Dog & Tito Santana
- "Adorable" Adrian Adonis w/ "Mouth of the South" Jimmy Hart def. Uncle Elmer
- Ricky "The Dragon" Steamboat def. Hercules

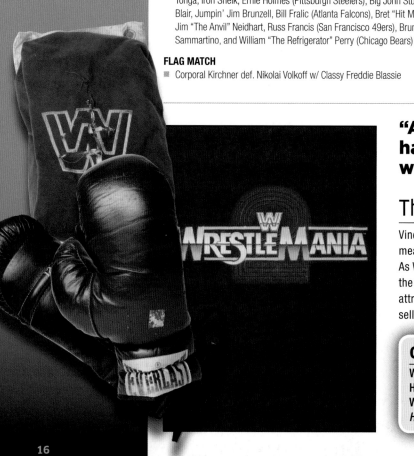

"After having had the success we had of *WrestleMania 1*...we thought we could do most anything."

—Vince McMahon

The Idea

Vince McMahon knew that *WrestleMania*'s critical and commercial success meant that a follow-up *WrestleMania* effort in the spring of 1986 was vital. As WWE approached *WrestleMania 2*, they began to consider how to make the event special. The initial *WrestleMania* had been a wonderful, tremendous attraction, showcasing incredible icons of sports and entertainment—even selling out Madison Square Garden. What could WWE do to top that?

GOING MAINSTREAM

WWE's mainstream acclaim continued to expand. *Sports Illustrated* featured Hulk Hogan on its cover. *Saturday Night's Main Event* solidified a diverse WWE television portfolio, which even included a Saturday morning cartoon, *Hulk Hogan's Rock 'n' Wrestling*.

Vince McMahon's concept for *WrestleMania 2* was ground-breaking: three events—each as monumental as the first *WrestleMania*—located, staged, and billed separately. McMahon recalls, "We wanted to have a presentation for the New York area, Chicago, and then the Southern California area in Los Angeles: a three-hour event with one hour in each segment." Three separate event sites meant WWE would shoulder three times the risk and would need a trifecta of Superstars and celebrities. Howard Finkel remembers, "There were many logistical challenges in topping the inaugural *WrestleMania*. For a three-location event, Point 'A' had to flow into Point 'B,' which had to flow into Point 'C.' If one thing went wrong, it could have a domino effect on the entire evening."

After an exhaustive location search, WWE selected the venues for *WrestleMania 2*: the Nassau Coliseum in New York, the Rosemont Horizon outside Chicago, and the Los Angeles Sports Arena. McMahon explains, "Each site would have its own respective main event. We began on the east coast at the Nassau Coliseum, where fans in the other two venues watched the action via closed-circuit. When the show in New York ended, giant projector screens descended from the arena ceiling and projected what was taking place at the other *WrestleMania* sites. It was a technological feat for that era."

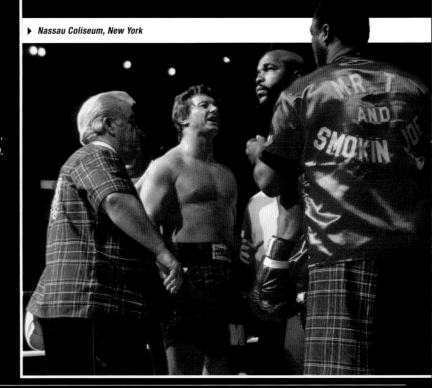

▶ *Nassau Coliseum, New York*

The Strategy

In addition to having to do everything in triplicate to manage an event in three separate venues, the marketing and advertising efforts to promote *WrestleMania 2* were the most challenging, and possibly the most crucial in WWE history. They had to communicate that *WrestleMania 2*, for most people, would be enjoyed via closed-circuit in theaters and arenas. Each of the 200-plus stations that aired WWE received customized videotapes for their specific market, right down to the phone number and ordering information. It as a machine that no other entity had.

▶ *Rosemont Horizon, outside of Chicago*

As a viable communication system among the three venues was established, modifications had to be implemented in a timely fashion. In those days, large-screen televisions were not considered standard equipment. The screens would have to be purchased or rented, and then installed and lowered from the roof in every arena. It was a massive undertaking. The match-making duo of Vince McMahon and George Scott evaluated the Superstars and celebrities who would be paramount for each site. For *WrestleMania 2* to validate its predecessor's success, its marketing, in-ring performances, and ticket sales had to be phenomenal.

▶ *Los Angeles Sports Arena, Los Angeles*

THE CELEBRITIES

WWE dialed up the celebrity involvement for *WrestleMania 2*, beginning with Ray Charles performing his world famous rendition of "America the Beautiful."

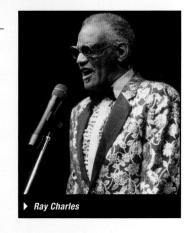
▶ *Ray Charles*

Celebrity Judges, Referees, and Corner Men

The boxing match between Roddy Piper and Mr. T utilized several celebrities. Cab Calloway, G. Gordon Liddy, and Darryl Dawkins all served as celebrity judges for the match. "Smokin'" Joe Frazier and Lou Duva lent their expertise as corner men for Mr. T and Piper, respectively. Ozzy Osbourne backed his Union Jack brethren as a corner man for the British Bulldogs during their match. Actor Robert Conrad served as special guest referee during the Hulk Hogan versus King Kong Bundy main event.

▶ *"Smokin" Joe Frazier*

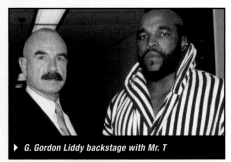
▶ *G. Gordon Liddy backstage with Mr. T*

Guest Timekeepers, Commentators, and Ring Announcers

Susan St. James showed her guest commentator chops alongside Vince McMahon. Elvira, Mistress of the Dark, served as a guest commentator with Jesse "The Body" Ventura. Comedienne Joan Rivers and baseball legend Tommy Lasorda brought their signature styles to *WrestleMania* as special guest ring announcers. Young actor Ricky Schroeder and Herb, of Burger King's "Where's Herb?" ad campaign, both served as guest timekeepers.

▶ *Elvira, Mistress of the Dark*

NFL Battle Royal

Dick Butkus and Ed "Too Tall" Jones both served as special guest referees for the NFL Battle Royal, which featured NFL stars Bill Fralic, Ernie Holmes, Harvey Martin, Jimbo Covert, Russ Francis, and William "The Refrigerator" Perry. Clare Peller, of Wendy's "Where's the Beef?" fame served as a guest timekeeper.

▶ *William "The Refrigerator" Perry*

Marketing to the Masses

A critical component to promoting *WrestleMania 2* was the build-up across WWE programming. In particular, Saturday Night's Main Event produced enough electricity to cement *WrestleMania 2*'s card in the public's mind. The program reopened old wounds between Mr. T and "Rowdy" Roddy Piper. Although WWE's partnership with Mr. T caused some unrest backstage, fans loved seeing Mr. T in the WWE environment. Piper displayed his infamously odious behavior when he began whipping Mr. T with his leather belt. This walked a delicate line of storytelling, but it was ultimately successful in building a one-on-one match between Mr. T and his nemesis.

▶ *Mr. T at Saturday Night's Main Event*

The second conflict Saturday Night's Main Event established was between King Kong Bundy and Hulk Hogan. An assault on the Hulkster perpetrated by Bundy, Bobby "The Brain" Heenan, and the Magnificent Muraco resulted in Hogan being driven away in an ambulance. Thus, the rivalry between Hogan and Bundy was aflame, establishing *WrestleMania 2*'s main event for the L.A. Sports Arena.

With the two marquee matches set, WWE's promotional machine continued to roll. As with *WrestleMania*, sometimes WWE had to do whatever was necessary for the show to go on. WWE Executive, Basil DeVito recalls, "We didn't realize, because the boxing match between Mr. T and Roddy Piper would take place in New York, that WWE was bound by New York State Athletic Commission rules. The commission insisted on an official weigh-in with physicals. So, weeks before *WrestleMania*, I'm in a chartered plane with Mr. T and Roddy en route to Albany, New York. There was a weigh-in at a Holiday Inn for [another] fight the next day. We told Mr. T that many important press members would be there, and this would be a great opportunity to hype the match and himself. I went down to the ballroom a little early and my heart stopped; there was one lone member of the press. WWE's presence was a last-minute decision, and word didn't get out to the media. I explained the situation to Roddy. He looked at me and said, 'I know what to do.' Roddy banged and yelled at Mr. T's door—remember, these two legitimately could not stand one another. Roddy got Mr. T fired up the way only he could. Roddy pushed Mr. T through the door, and I took him through the weigh-in as fast as possible. Roddy then came in and put on this incredible show, yelling at Mr. T, taunting him like every major news outlet in the country was there. Mr. T kept asking how important it could have been because there was only one reporter. Roddy looked at me and smiled. I could always count on Roddy."

To generate excitement in Chicago, WWE put on a media blitz. Because the Bears had won the Super Bowl weeks prior, the Chicago portion of *WrestleMania 2* had a gridiron theme, and the Rosemont's main event would be a WWE/NFL Battle Royal. WWE hosted a staged weigh-in at a popular Chicago sports bar, using a cattle scale. DeVito remembers, "With WWE Superstars and the NFL pros all on the scale together, it made for great pictures." But not all of the participants were pleased with the event. DeVito adds, "Big John Studd came to my hotel room that night. Imagine there's an unexpected knock at your door and it's someone who's almost seven feet tall and 400 pounds. He wasn't at the weigh-in, but he was angry that it was held at a bar. He felt I was mocking the business. He saw a *WrestleMania* ad in a paper on the bed, and it featured the NFL players. Studd lifted me in the air and put me against the wall. He said, 'Don't you know who sells the tickets? We do! Not them!' Many of the Superstars back then weren't sure what they were—Wrestlers? Entertainers? Athletes? The idea of 'sports-entertainment' was new, and not everyone was ready to embrace it."

For the Los Angeles market, the focus was on the return of the WWE Champion, Hulk Hogan. Hulkamania was approaching its zenith, and while the stars from Hollywood and the sports world shined, the priority was hyping the main event. WWE programming featured interviews from doctors on the condition of Hogan's ribs. Workout sessions furthered the aura of a showdown between WWE's iconic hero and his assailant, the almost 500-pound King Kong Bundy.

New York

WrestleMania 2 began at the Nassau Coliseum. The festivities kicked off after Vince McMahon's now famous salutation, "Welcome to the greatest sports-entertainment spectacular of all-time. Welcome, to *WrestleMania*." From there, Ray Charles stunned the audience with his compelling rendition of "America the Beautiful."

The first match of the evening was between "Mr. Wonderful" Paul Orndorff and The Magnificent Muraco. This was followed by a WWE rivalry whose popularity came as a surprise to many: Randy "Macho Man" Savage versus George "The Animal" Steele.

▶ *"Mr. Wonderful" Paul Orndorff versus The Magnificent Muraco*

George Steele spent much of his career as one of the most feared and bizarro villains in wrestling. As Steele recalls, "My character becoming a 'good guy' was not planned. I thought being in the six-man with Sheik and Volkoff on Saturday Night's Main Event was going to be my exit. They beat me up for losing the match, and the fans started to cheer because I went at them, the anti-American villains. Captain Lou [Albano] comes in … I put my head in his stomach, like he's consoling me, and people blew the roof off the place. I think Vince saw something in that."

At that time, Randy "Macho Man" Savage was one of the newest and most hated villains in WWE. His on-air manager, Miss Elizabeth, was also Randy's real-life wife. Steele remembers, "The matches with Randy were a natural fit. People felt such sympathy for my character. I never won a match against Randy, and it became so strong, after a while I didn't need to win. It was more about getting distracted by Elizabeth. Randy was very protective of Elizabeth backstage. I would do things to get him worked up. Those practical jokes helped our matches because Randy, who was a phenomenal talent, really got angry with me."

"Welcome to the greatest sports-entertainment spectacular of all-time. Welcome, to *WrestleMania*."

—Vince McMahon

CAN WE TALK?

After fans witnessed the *WrestleMania* debut of Jake "The Snake" Roberts and his snake, Damien, someone backstage would meet the pair for the first time. Linda McMahon recalls, "I was rehearsing with Joan Rivers, reminding her to say her signature line, 'Can we talk?' Joan walks to the curtain and is about to go out … [and] who does she end up standing next to? Jake "The Snake" Roberts—and he had the snake around his neck. Joan's this little thing and was beside herself. We made it to the ring and the crowd starts chanting her name. I'm not on camera but I was at ringside yelling, 'Can we talk, Can we talk.' She hit the line, but I'll always remember the look on her face seeing that snake." Rivers recalls, "*WrestleMania 2* was great. It's not every day you bump into a man with a 12-foot python around his neck before you go on stage. It was a big reunion—I was carrying the python's cousin as a bag. I made money for my charity and I came out of it the winner by pinfall."

The crowd eagerly awaited the start of the Mr. T and "Rowdy" Roddy Piper boxing contest. Having a celebrity participate in a WWE match requires careful arrangement. The objective is to use the figure's star power without hurting them physically or tarnishing their image. With Mr. T's persona, he had to look like a credible opponent. However, Piper was a WWE Superstar who appeared on television every week, so he needed to finish strong and burnish his reputation. Piper recalls, "I ended up throwing a chair at Mr. T in between rounds. I felt like I was representing wrestling and everyone in the locker room."
The match ended when Piper reverted to his WWE move set and bodyslammed Mr. T, disqualifying himself.

"I felt he didn't have respect for our business. We dislike each other to this day."
—"Rowdy" Roddy Piper

BEHIND THE SCENES

A "main event" of sorts took place backstage when the closed-circuit feed had to switch from Nassau Coliseum to the Rosemont Horizon. George Steele remembers, "When that feed transferred, it was tense. No one knew if it would switch over. When it did, it looked like Vince jumped ten feet in the air he was so excited. The event was going to work. I had a new respect for him that day as a business man."

Vince McMahon explains, "Just the technology alone today would be extraordinary if you could pull that off, but this was way back when, 1986. Lady Luck has always been a part of my personal life, as well as my professional one with WWE."

▶ *Fabulous Moolah defends her Championship*

Chicago

At the Rosemont Horizon, the event began with Fabulous Moolah defending her Women's Championship against Velvet McIntyre. The Windy City crowd then rose to its feet as the Cold War battle continued with a flag match featuring Corporal Kirschner versus Nikolai Volkoff.

▶ *Corporal Kirschner versus Nikolai Volkoff in a flag match*

The 20-Man WWE/NFL Battle Royal was the Rosemont Horizon's main event. George Scott and Pat Patterson were on-site in Chicago to make sure the match went smoothly. Patterson remembers, "The NFL players were really good guys and respected what we did. They understood the concept of the match in that you would be eliminated by being thrown over the top rope. That match was a lot of fun." Jim Neidhart recounts, "All the NFL players were great. I remember how fast 'Refrigerator' Perry was. He was over 300 pounds and moved like a cat. He loved being in the ring. They all couldn't believe how big André the Giant was."

When it came to the WWE Superstar roster, a change was made a couple of weeks before, in Boston. Bret Hart recalls, "George Scott told me they were putting Steamboat and I together so we could get used to each other's styles for *WrestleMania*. Afterward, Chief Jay Strongbow told me the plan had changed. I was really disappointed because I respected Ricky so much and knew we would tear the house down. But I felt better about it when I was told we'd be working with André [the Giant] in the Battle Royal."

It was obvious the special guest referees Dick Butkus and Ed "Too Tall" Jones would have their hands full. Jim Neidhart recalls, "Russ Francis had some experience in the ring. His dad was a promoter in Hawaii, and for some reason Russ had a problem being thrown over the ropes. He insisted it had to be done a certain way. We tried to tell him the way he wanted to go was the most dangerous, but he wouldn't let up. André told Bret and me to keep Russ away … so the Hart Foundation took care of him."

The Battle Royal ended in grand fashion, thanks to a last-minute suggestion. Bret Hart remembers, "I got to the dressing room and I had an idea. By that point, André and I had become good friends. I worded it carefully because nobody changed an ending to a match with André or told him what to do. I just said, 'What if we did this instead …' André pictured it in his head and said, 'That would be okay. I like that.' It was the move where I whipped Jim [Neidhart] into the corner, and he'd reverse it and send me in for a tackle. But instead of tackling André, André stuck his boot up. He eliminated Jim, then pressed me over his head and threw me onto Jim, and he won the match."

William "The Refrigerator" Perry thinks back, "Winning the Super Bowl, scoring a touchdown in the Super Bowl, and being in *WrestleMania* all in the same season? It was incredible. It's like someone wrote a Hollywood script for The Fridge. Today, I do a lot of public appearances and still, after all these years *WrestleMania* is all the fans want to talk about. It's unbelievable and I love it."

Los Angeles

At the LA Sports Arena, the crowd eagerly anticipated the main event. Before the final clash, WWE audiences saw one of their heroes, Ricky "The Dragon" Steamboat, continue to shine. Another bout saw two of WWE's favorite heroes, Junkyard Dog and Tito Santana, battle against the famous Funk Brothers. Dory Funk recalls, "The relationship between the Funks and the McMahons goes back to when my dad used to work with Vince, Sr. When we got to *WrestleMania*, I had no idea of the size of the production. The locations, the celebrities—it was spectacular. JYD and Tito were so popular with the fans that when we cheated to beat them, people hated us even more. It was great."

The capacity crowd stared in amazement as the 15-foot-high steel cage was assembled around the ring. King Kong Bundy represented a new type of opponent for Hulk Hogan. It was uncommon in those years for the Hulkster to be at a physical disadvantage. Bundy's ferocity made people believe that he was on a mission to end Hulk Hogan's career.

> ## "When you were in a Battle Royal with André the Giant, everybody was small."
> —Hillbilly Jim

During this era, the Steel Cage Match was billed as the last resort, a situation no one wanted their rivalry to reach. But when Superstars had no other choice, they set foot inside the ultimate battleground. This aura of peril made the headline match a "must see." Both Superstars knew it would be a hard-hitting contest. Hogan explains, "Vince built this new cage that had iron squares. A chain-link fence cage is very forgiving. You can get hurt, but it has some give to it. When I got back to the locker room, I had lumps all over my head from this new cage. We used that design for a long time."

The stage was set for incredible theater. Hogan recalls, "I've always said if you're going to be a main event guy, you have to have something different. King Kong Bundy had everything. He was a monster. When Bundy dropped an elbow or body slammed you, the whole arena would explode. He was easy to work with as far as crowd reaction, but if he kicked you, it was like his boot was going through your chest. Whenever I knew I was going in there with him, I knew I would come out in different physical shape than when I went in. He was a great guy, but just very, very strong." Though Bundy made a ferocious opponent, Hogan surmounted incredible odds and left *WrestleMania* victorious.

> ## "Whenever I knew I was going in there with King Kong Bundy, I knew I would come out in different physical shape than when I went in."
> —Hulk Hogan

TAG TEAM CHAMPIONSHIP

The WWE World Tag Team Championship continued to gain prestige during this era. Mean Gene remembers, "Having tag teams like The British Bulldogs, The Hart Foundation, The Killer Bees, The Dream Team, Sheik and Volkoff—they could do so much." Greg Valentine adds, "Tag teams can be great, but they can also be hard. Earlier in my career, Ric Flair and I had a successful tag team. But it was difficult at times. We both wanted to be in charge. When I found out I was going to team with Brutus [Beefcake] and have a run with the tag belts, it was fabulous. The matches with the Bulldogs were just as good as any match I had during my singles career."

WRESTLEMANIA III

PONTIAC SILVERDOME, PONTIAC, MI

March 29
1987

Attendance
93,173

ANNOUNCERS
Gorilla Monsoon
Jesse "The Body" Ventura

RING ANNOUNCER
Howard Finkel

LOCKER ROOM CORRESPONDENTS
"Mean" Gene Okerlund
Lord Alfred Hayes
Vince McMahon

SPECIAL GUEST RING ANNOUNCER
Bob Uecker

SPECIAL GUEST TIME KEEPER
Mary Hart

SPECIAL MUSICAL GUEST
Aretha Franklin

Event Card

MAIN EVENT – WWE CHAMPIONSHIP MATCH
- Hulk Hogan (Champion) def. André the Giant w/ Bobby "The Brain" Heenan to retain the Championship

INTERCONTINENTAL CHAMPIONSHIP MATCH
- Ricky "The Dragon" Steamboat w/ George "The Animal" Steele def. Randy "Macho Man" Savage (Champion) w/ Elizabeth to become new Champion

FAREWELL, "HAIR VS. HAIR" MATCH
- "Rowdy" Roddy Piper def. Adorable Adrian Adonis w/ "The Colonel" Jimmy Hart

SIX-MAN TAG MATCH
- The Hart Foundation (Bret "Hit Man" Hart & Jim "The Anvil" Neidhart) & "Dangerous" Danny Davis w/ "The Colonel" Jimmy Hart def. The British Bulldogs (Dynamite Kid & Davey Boy Smith) & Tito Santana

THE CROWN MATCH
- King Harley Race w/ Bobby "The Brain" Heenan & Fabulous Moolah def. Junkyard Dog

THE BATTLE OF THE FULL-NELSON'S
- Billy Jack Haynes vs. Hercules Hernandez w/ Bobby "The Brain" Heenan resulted in a double count-out

SIX-MAN MIXED TAG TEAM MATCH
- Hillbilly Jim, Little Beaver & The Haiti Kid def. King Kong Bundy, Little Tokyo & Lord Littlebrook

OTHER MATCHES
- The Dream Team (Greg "The Hammer" Valentine & Brutus Beefcake) w/ Luscious Johnny Valiant & Dino Bravo def. The Rougeau Brothers (Jacques & Raymond)
- "The Natural" Butch Reed w/ Slick def. Koko B. Ware
- Can-Am Connection (Rick Martel & Tom Zenk) def. The Magnificent Muraco & Cowboy Bob Orton w/ Mr. Fuji
- Honky Tonk Man w/ "The Colonel" Jimmy Hart def. Jake "The Snake" Roberts w/ Alice Cooper
- Nikolai Volkoff & Iron Sheik def. Killer Bees (B. Brian Blair & Jim Brunzell) by Disqualification

"The irresistible force meeting the immovable object."

—Gorilla Monsoon

Preparing For A Quantum Leap

In preliminary discussions for the third *WrestleMania*, Vince McMahon was adamant that WWE make the event a bigger, more grandiose production than *WrestleMania 2*. Given the success of the previous two events, for WWE the question was, "How do we make *WrestleMania* better?" The first step was returning *WrestleMania* to one location. Marketing was also key. During an early meeting to brainstorm taglines, the WWE team threw around different possible catchphrases until someone said, "This one's going to be bigger, it's going to be better, and it's going to be badder." Vince McMahon jumped from his chair and said, "Stop right there." He began to draw it in the air with his hand, "*WrestleMania III*: Bigger, Better, Badder."

The "Better" and "Badder" aspects were an accepted mission statement in a company that hosted live events 52 weeks a year. The "Bigger" component required additional work. *WrestleMania* sold out Madison Square Garden. *WrestleMania 2* emanated from three locations and drew over 40,000 fans, along with hundreds of thousands more via closed-circuit. What could WWE do to make *WrestleMania III* "Bigger?"

WWE wanted *WrestleMania III* to be as close to the east coast as possible. While WWE was a national company by then, their strongest fan base was in the eastern half of the United States. The Pontiac Silverdome was quickly selected as first choice. Ed Cohen remembers, "The phone rang at two in the morning. I was asleep, so my answering machine picked up. Vince started talking fast, saying, 'Wake up! Ed, wake up!' I got on a plane to Michigan that morning with a check for $50,000 in my hand to hold the date for the Silverdome." Selling 60,000 seats would have produced the largest crowd in WWE history, but the Silverdome could hold more than 90,000 spectators. To fill its seats, WWE needed the best talent combined with a breakthrough promotional campaign.

The Pontiac Silverdome could be configured for various seating arrangements. When asked which configuration he wanted to use, Vince McMahon replied, "The whole way, we are going to break the all-time indoor attendance record. It's going to be over 90,000 people."

Hulk Hogan added, "Haven't you heard who's in the main event, brother?"

"We were doing things that no one had ever done in this type of business. So why not go for the biggest venue we could possibly find?"

—Vince McMahon

▶ *Preparing the Silverdome*

▶ *This specially decorated cart was used to ferry Superstars to the ring*

The Blueprint For History

WrestleMania III rested on the public's connection with Hulk Hogan and André the Giant. Crossing into 1987, Hogan became a household name and the industry's most recognizable ambassador.

Throughout his career, André the Giant was the greatest attraction the industry had ever known. But heading into the mid-1980s, André's body started to suffer the rigors of the business. He felt it was time to wind down his in-ring career. For *WrestleMania III* to fulfill its mission, André would have to agree to participate. Vince McMahon remembers, "Right after *WrestleMania 2*, I flew to England to visit André. He was filming *The Princess Bride*. He was suffering from excruciating back pain and needed surgery. Originally, he wasn't going to have the surgery but I convinced him to have it and be a part of this one last thing. I told him, 'You and Hogan will draw the biggest crowd ever for an event like this.' And he agreed." To account for André's post-surgery absence, WWE issued a statement saying that he had been suspended for not fulfilling certain contractual obligations. Very few people knew at the time that André was recovering at the McMahon family home in Greenwich, Connecticut.

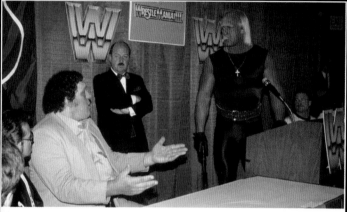

▶ *WrestleMania pre-show press conference*

"It was everyone contributing to the storyline, and you could feel right away this was going to be special. You just knew it."

—"Rowdy" Roddy Piper

The buildup to *WrestleMania III*'s main event started on the January 17, 1987, episode of Piper's Pit. Hogan and André received awards from then-WWE President Jack Tunney. André took the first step toward the historic encounter by leaving in the midst of Hogan's acceptance speech. Roddy Piper remembers, "The André and Hogan segments were done in the Pit because WWE needed the three biggest properties—André, Hogan, and Piper—together to get the storyline over with the fans. I needed the crowd to focus because this was serious."

Over the next two weeks, WWE personalities who had credibility with the audience as "knowing" André speculated on his uncharacteristic behavior. On February 7, the Piper's Pit audience gasped when André appeared with Bobby "The Brain" Heenan. Staring at Hulk Hogan, André challenged the Hulkster to a match at *WrestleMania III*. To dramatize André's transformation to a life of evil, he tore off Hogan's shirt and cross, and blood ran down the WWE Champion's chest. The segment ended with Piper consoling Hogan in one of sports entertainment television's most memorable moments.

▶ *"Look at me when I'm talking to you! I'm here for one reason, to challenge you for the World Championship Match in WrestleMania!"*

Turning André into a villain created the ultimate showdown and maximized *WrestleMania III*'s drawing power.

It took Hulk and André a long time to reach a point of mutual friendship and respect. Hulk Hogan recalls, "I'd be on the way to the building, knowing I had to wrestle [André], and I was so scared that I would pull the car over and vomit." However, André gained respect for Hogan in Japan. Hogan faced a tough situation with a wrestler named Tatsumi Fujinami who would have seriously injured Hogan if he could. When the Hulkster claimed the victory despite the challenging circumstances, André saw the skill Hogan displayed in the ring. Hogan said of his relationship with André, "I think, after that night, things changed."

▶ *Piper to Hogan, "You're bleeding."*

► *Little Beaver and The Haiti Kid lock down Lord Littlebrook and Little Tokyo in the Six-Man Mixed Tag Team Match*

► *Hard rock pioneer Alice Cooper made the perfect corner man for Jake "The Snake" Roberts*

A SPECIAL MESSAGE

WWE had its final production meeting for the event. Vince McMahon was quoted as saying, "Tomorrow night's attraction, André, has been in this business his whole life, and he is an icon known the world over. When the main event goes on, everybody needs to understand how hard these people are working for all of our benefit. When that main event goes on, if anybody in this room leaves this stadium before that main event is over, just keep going." It was poignant, it was direct, and it was correct and it also reminded the WWE production crew why they were here.

Unique Challenges

Because the 20'x20' ring would essentially be in the middle of a football field, WWE needed to ensure an exciting fan experience from any seat in the Silverdome. Engineers installed four giant television screens, one on each side of the ring. Because of the Silverdome's natural light and translucent roof, images on the giant screens wouldn't be visible until approximately 5:30 P.M., 90 minutes after the event's start. WWE talked about moving the start time, but it was too close to the event date. They even considered painting the roof before finding out that if it were a dark, cloudy day, everything would be fine. Upon hearing this, Vince McMahon slapped the table and said, "Done! It'll rain. End of discussion." Luckily, the day of *WrestleMania* was overcast, making the giant TV screens easy for fans to see.

Bigger, Better, Badder

On March 29, a surprise awaited WWE's caravan when it arrived at the parking lot. Gerry Brisco thinks back, "We pulled up to the Silverdome and people in the parking lot were tailgating, like what you see at the Super Bowl. ... It was such a festive atmosphere."

"All you could hear was one, singular roar from the crowd."
—Linda McMahon

WrestleMania III featured the most diverse *WrestleMania* card to date. The lineup had singles, tag team, six-man, mixed midget tag, a "Hair vs. Hair" farewell match, a battle of Finishing Moves, and WWE Championships on the line. WWE Hall of Famer Harley Race remembers, "You have more than 90,000 people looking at you, responding to what you do. If that doesn't make it one of the top moments of a career, what the hell else would?"

The match between Jake "The Snake" Roberts and Honky Tonk Man finalized a role reversal for the two opposing characters. Roberts thinks back, "I had sustained a neck injury when Honky Tonk hit me with the guitar on Piper's Pit ... Our match at *WrestleMania* was the first time in the history of the business that both guys switched. I went from a bad guy to a good guy, and he went from a good guy to a bad guy. I wrestled for a year and a half with those two discs blown out of my neck."

The Retirement Match between Roddy Piper and Adrian Adonis surprised many when Piper assumed the unfamiliar good guy role. Piper recalls, "I go back to what guys from the Gorgeous George era taught me; you leave a territory when it almost peaks, not when it peaks. Toward the end of the second round at *WrestleMania 2*, the fans made me a good guy by cheering for me, and I refused to take a dive. To stay on top, I needed to get out of the business completely. So, I went and did They Live with director John Carpenter. I needed to do something in another form and then walk back in [through] the front door."

The Iron Sheik and Nikolai Volkoff defeated the Killer Bees, thanks to interference from "Hacksaw" Jim Duggan. Upset at Volkoff's singing of the Soviet National Anthem, Duggan came out swinging his infamous 2x4, this time with an American flag attached. During the match, Duggan continued to interfere, finally hitting the Iron Sheik with his iconic weapon, unwittingly giving the Sheik and Volkoff the victory by disqualification.

"My dad passed away prior to the first *WrestleMania*. He would have so much appreciated that accomplishment. And then *WrestleMania 2* and *WrestleMania III*. I was walking to the ring ... I couldn't think of anything but my dad. Stepping through the ropes, I could feel his presence. I still feel it today. Whenever you have an appreciation for someone like that, you can feel that moment ... it's one of the greatest things in the world that so few people experience. That was an extraordinary moment for me, because my dad was there."

—Vince McMahon

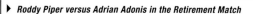

▶ *Roddy Piper versus Adrian Adonis in the Retirement Match*

"Steamboat-Savage ... It's one of the matches that gave *WrestleMania* its roots to grow to what it is today."
—George Steele

The Steamboat-Savage story was deeply rooted in reality. Savage's attack on Steamboat, crushing his larynx with the ring bell, brought Steamboat incredible fan sympathy and branded Savage as one of the WWE's most denounced men. The fast-paced, brutal action stunned the audience, making this match a fan favorite for years to come.

Steamboat remembers, "We wanted to steal the show. We knew that Hogan and André drew it, but we had a big part in it also, but let's be real. We stole the night. I'll never forget that night. At the *WrestleMania* party afterwards, everybody started coming up and congratulating myself. Then I looked over at Randy, and everybody was congratulating him. It actually started a line of guys. It was Gorilla Monsoon and guys that were icons in our business that actually came up to shake my hand. Then I looked over at Hogan's table and there was nobody."

Irresistible Force meets Immovable Object

Despite the collaboration the main event required from Hulk Hogan and André the Giant, there was uncertainty up until the last minute. It was crucial that André allow two things: the bodyslam and the ultimate defeat. Vince McMahon reflects, "It's funny because Hogan was scared to death. Hogan had been in the ring with [André] before, but not like this. André had this habit with anyone of consequence as far as size was concerned; he had to show them who was boss. [Hogan] wasn't too sure if the result would come out like he thought it would. I knew what André was going to do; Hogan knew what André could do. Big difference."

"I couldn't function.
I couldn't eat.
I couldn't sleep.
I'd break out in a sweat just thinking about the match."

—Hulk Hogan

Hulk Hogan entered the Silverdome to the deafening roar of his Hulkamaniacs. The Hulkster and André the Giant traded displays of power and dominance, each move eliciting outcries from the record crowd. Then Hulk Hogan performed the unimaginable. He slammed "The Eighth Wonder of the World" and pinned him with his famous Leg Drop. In the act of defeat, André the Giant showed his love for the business that made him an icon. McMahon recalls, "That was the highest moment that André would ever have in the business. He was so proud of that. Even in his later days, when he could hardly move in the ring, he lived off of that, and he should have."

WrestleMania III sold more tickets than the Super Bowl, and WWE was now the undisputed owner of the indoor attendance record. As the show came to a close, WWE, Hulk Hogan, and André the Giant crossed the threshold of entertainment immortality together.

WRESTLEMANIA IV

TRUMP PLAZA HOTEL AND CASINO AND ATLANTIC CITY CONVENTION CENTER – ATLANTIC CITY, NJ

March 27
1988

Attendance
19,199

ANNOUNCERS
Gorilla Monsoon
Jesse "The Body" Ventura

RING ANNOUNCER
Howard Finkel

LOCKER ROOM CORRESPONDENT
"Mean" Gene Okerlund

SPECIAL GUEST PRESENTER OF THE

WWE CHAMPIONSHIP
Robin Leach

SPECIAL GUEST RING ANNOUNCER
Bob Uecker

SPECIAL GUEST TIME KEEPER
Vanna White

SPECIAL MUSICAL GUEST
Gladys Knight

Event Card

WWE CHAMPIONSHIP TOURNAMENT
- Randy "Macho Man" Savage def. "Million Dollar Man" Ted DiBiase in the main event of the 14-Man Single Elimination Tournament that also featured Hulk Hogan, André the Giant, "Hacksaw" Jim Duggan, Don Muraco, Dino Bravo, Ricky "The Dragon" Steamboat, Greg "The Hammer" Valentine, "The Natural" Butch Reed, Bam Bam Bigelow, Jake "The Snake" Roberts, and Ravishing Rick Rude

WORLD TAG TEAM CHAMPIONSHIP MATCH
- Demolition w/ Mr. Fuji def. Strike Force (Champions) to become new Tag Team Champions

INTERCONTINENTAL CHAMPIONSHIP MATCH
- Honky Tonk Man (Champion) w/ "Mouth of the South" Jimmy Hart & Peggy Sue def. Brutus "The Barber" Beefcake to retain the Championship

20-MAN BATTLE ROYAL
- Bad News Brown def. Bret "Hit Man" Hart, Jim "The Anvil" Neidhart, Jim Powers, Paul Roma, Sika, "Dangerous" Danny Davis, Sam Houston, Hillbilly Jim, B. Brian Blair, Jumpin' Jim Brunzell, Ray Rougeau, Jacques Rougeau, Junkyard Dog, Ken Patera, Ron Bass, King Harley Race, Nikolai Volkoff, Boris Zhukov, and George "The Animal" Steele

OTHER MATCHES
- The Islanders (Haku & Tama) & Bobby "The Brain" Heenan def. The British Bulldogs (Dynamite Kid & Davey Boy Smith) & Koko B. Ware w/ Matilda & Frankie
- Ultimate Warrior def. Hercules w/ Bobby "The Brain" Heenan

> **"Of all the different old school promoters I worked for during my career, all the different things I saw, one of the major things that separated Vince McMahon from anyone else was that he took the money he made and put it back into the business."**
>
> —George "The Animal" Steele

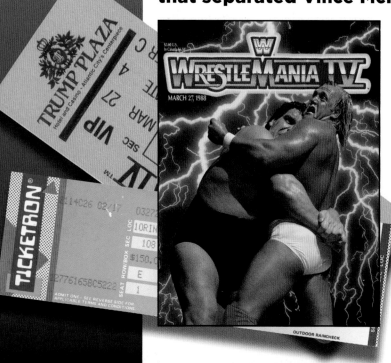

Following History

Cataloging and identifying the components of *WrestleMania III*'s watershed moment triggered a palpable internal struggle on how to surpass it. Accommodating a larger crowd than the Silverdome's was not possible, and having a more momentous main event match didn't appear feasible either.

Just as WWE's behind-the-scenes team believed that every door they tried to open was bolted shut, opportunity knocked. WWE was given the chance to bring *WrestleMania* to Atlantic City and Trump Plaza. WWE initially had some concerns that it was not the best venue for the family friendly crowd WWE attracted. However, Mark Etess, then-President of Trump Plaza Hotel and Casino, convinced them otherwise. He proposed that WWE host a festival in the days leading up to *WrestleMania*. The Fan Axxess of today can be directly traced back to the events held at Trump Plaza for *WrestleMania IV*.

In its mere fourth year of existence, *WrestleMania* had evolved from an annual show to an entire weekend of themed events. This concept attracted a wider array of fans than previous *WrestleMania*s. For those looking for family-friendly entertainment, a weekend package was the perfect complement to the *WrestleMania* event itself.

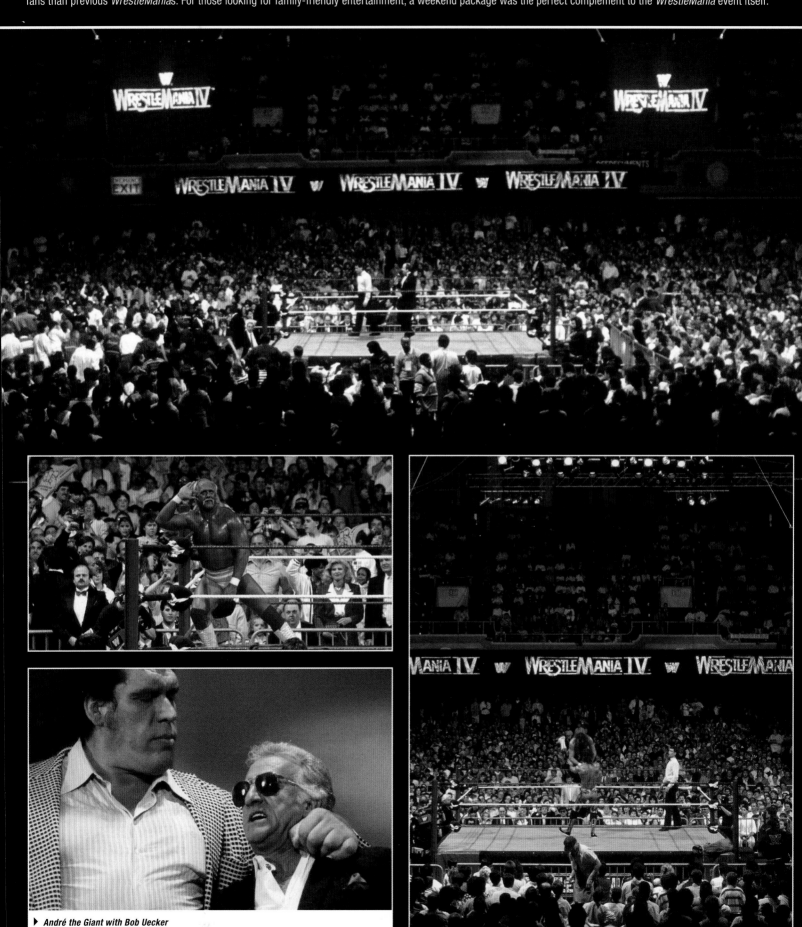

▶ *André the Giant with Bob Uecker*

Continuing to Set the Trend

WWE's marketing and television production components continued to evolve exponentially. These groups remained industry leaders and models for how sports and entertainment organizations reached, engaged, and inspired their audiences.

When it came to celebrities, WWE maintained its belief that the right celebrity pairing could extend an invitation to the general sports and entertainment fan. WWE sustained the same philosophy it promoted for *WrestleMania III*: A-List stars, but fewer of them involved in the show. Gladys Knight, Robin Leach, Vanna White, and Bob Uecker were all on hand to lend their star power to the event.

▶ *Gladys Knight performs her rendition of "America the Beautiful" at Trump Plaza*

▶ *Special Guest Timekeeper Vanna White with the WWE Championship Tournament Bracket*

Turmoil Surrounds WWE's Crown Jewel

Hulk Hogan was approaching three and a half years as WWE Champion, one of the longest championship reigns in recent history. Behind the scenes, the world's most iconic wrestler wanted to take a break from full-time WWE action and explore opportunities in Tinseltown. The idea was that Hogan could capitalize on his mass media star power on the silver screen and return in time to drive WWE and Hulkamania into the 1990s.

Before that could happen, it was necessary for a WWE Superstar to show he was ready to assume the responsibility of being the 11th WWE Champion. One Superstar's connection with the audience, strength of character, and performance in the ring made him a prime candidate as the next man to carry the richest prize in sports entertainment around his waist—Randy "Macho Man" Savage.

During *Saturday Night's Main Event*, Hulk Hogan saved Savage from a vicious attack by the Hart Foundation and Honky Tonk Man. The act thrilled audiences who saw the one-time enemies shake hands, forming "The Madness" and "The Mania". This act instantly elevated Savage to the role of the hero. The overwhelming positive fan reaction meant Vince McMahon had found the next white knight WWE fans could proudly stand behind.

The greatest hero is only as great as his most loathsome villain. With Savage now taking on the hero role, a larger than life nemesis must be found. Ted DiBiase was primed to bring to life Vince McMahon's villainous vision of greed and excess. Through an underhanded conspiracy involving André the Giant and twin referees, DiBiase was able to strip Hulk Hogan of the WWE title during *The Main Event*.

Hogan's Championship defeat received national media coverage. As fans turned to WWE programming, they learned that the WWE Championship, for the first time in history, would be vacated—and a new Champion crowned at *WrestleManina IV*.

Tournament Time

WrestleMania IV kicked off with a Twenty-Man, Over-The-Top-Rope Battle Royal that featured five prominent tag teams and top contenders to WWE Championship gold.

A grudge match versus a powerhouse served as the *WrestleMania* debut for the Ultimate Warrior. Fans of regional wrestling may have recognized him from his days in World Class Championship Wrestling. But when he arrived in WWE, the "Warrior" became "Ultimate," garnering immediate favorite status with WWE audiences.

▶ *Battle Royal*

The British Bulldogs returned to six-man tag action and the Tag Team Championship made its return to *WrestleMania* for a title defense.

▶ *Davey Boy Smith of the British Bulldogs*

▶ *Honky Tonk Man versus Brutus Beefcake*

As Intercontinental Champion, the Honky Tonk Man was one of the WWE Superstars fans loved to greet with a sea of boos. The longer his Intercontinental Championship reign lasted, and the more songs he sang, the more enraged the fans became. Brutus Beefcake remembers, "My matches with Honky were always fun, especially our match at *WrestleMania IV*. That was the year it was being discussed that I'd have a run with the Intercontinental Title."

Macho Man Triumphs

The story of the vacated WWE Championship unfolded like a Shakespearian drama. In a *WrestleMania* rematch, fans would have to wait until the beginning of the second round to see Hulk Hogan attempt to avenge his controversial loss to André the Giant. When both Superstars were counted out, the crowd stood in awe. This end result, which no one expected, meant that a new Champion, neither Hulk Hogan nor André the Giant, would be crowned at Trump Plaza.

After three courageous performances from hero Randy "Macho Man" Savage, and two victories from the villain-extraordinaire "Million Dollar Man," Ted DiBiase stood in the way of "Macho Man's" capturing the WWE Championship. Added suspense came in the final round when Ted DiBiase was seconded to the ring by the imposing André the Giant. Another turn in the road to the championship came after Miss Elizabeth returned to ringside with Hulk Hogan.

▶ *"Macho Man" Savage defeats Butch Reed*

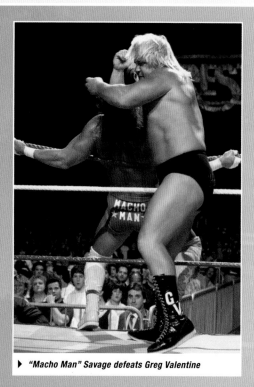

▶ *"Macho Man" Savage defeats Greg Valentine*

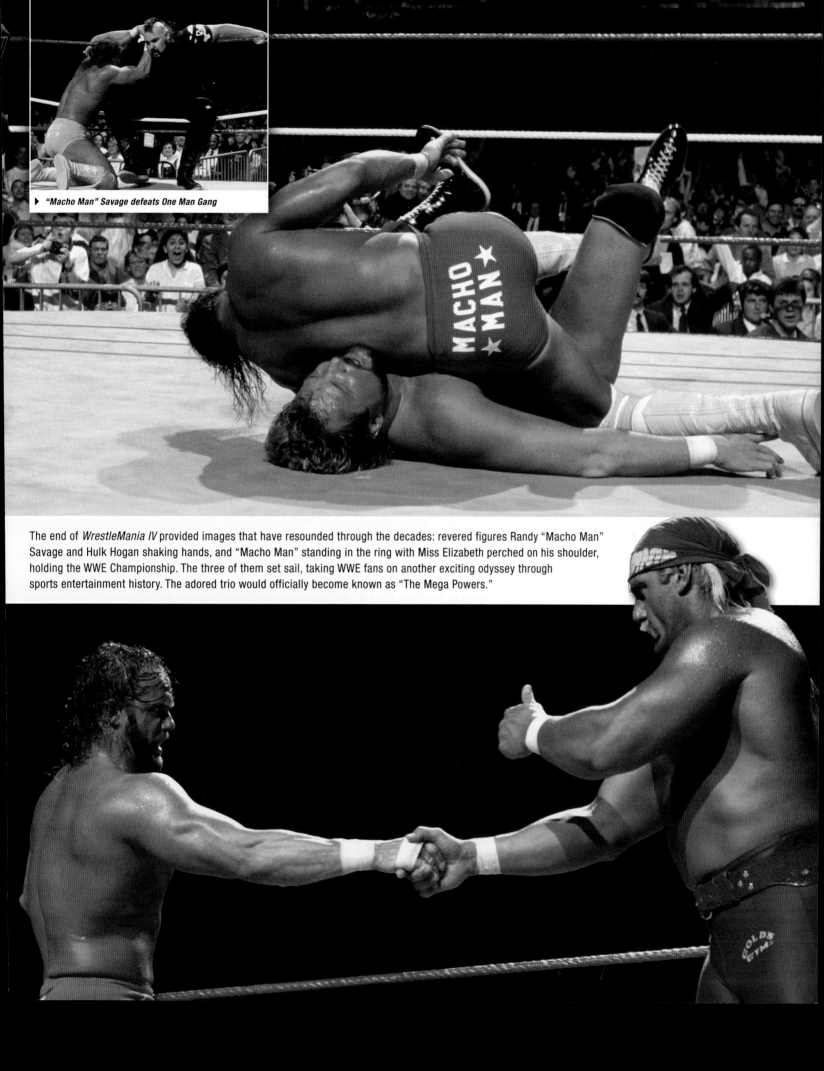

▶ *"Macho Man" Savage defeats One Man Gang*

The end of *WrestleMania IV* provided images that have resounded through the decades: revered figures Randy "Macho Man" Savage and Hulk Hogan shaking hands, and "Macho Man" standing in the ring with Miss Elizabeth perched on his shoulder, holding the WWE Championship. The three of them set sail, taking WWE fans on another exciting odyssey through sports entertainment history. The adored trio would officially become known as "The Mega Powers."

TRUMP PLAZA HOTEL AND CASINO AND ATLANTIC CITY CONVENTION CENTER –
ATLANTIC CITY, NJ

April 2
1989

Attendance
20,369

ANNOUNCERS
Gorilla Monsoon
Jesse "The Body" Ventura

RING ANNOUNCER
Howard Finkel

LOCKER ROOM CORRESPONDENTS
"Mean" Gene Okerlund
Tony Schiavone

ON-LOCATION CORRESPONDENT
Sean Mooney

SPECIAL CELEBRITY GUEST
Morton Downey, Jr.

SPECIAL MUSICAL GUEST
RUN-DMC

Event Card

WWE CHAMPIONSHIP MATCH
- Hulk Hogan def. Randy "Macho Man" Savage (Champion) to become new Champion.*
  *Miss Elizabeth was at ringside in a neutral corner

INTERCONTINENTAL CHAMPIONSHIP MATCH
- Ravishing Rick Rude w/ Bobby "The Brain" Heenan def. Ultimate Warrior to become new Champion

WORLD TAG TEAM CHAMPIONSHIP MATCH
- Demolition (Ax & Smash) (Champions) def. The Powers of Pain (Warlord & Barbarian) w/ Mr. Fuji

OTHER MATCHES
- The Hart Foundation (Bret "Hit Man" Hart & Jim "The Anvil" Neidhart) def. Greg "The Hammer" Valentine & Honky Tonk Man w/ "Mouth of the South" Jimmy Hart
- Jake "The Snake" Roberts def. André the Giant w/ Bobby "The Brain" Heenan via disqualification*
  *Special Guest Referee Big John Studd

- The Brain Busters (Arn Anderson & Tully Blanchard) w/ Bobby "The Brain" Heenan def. Strike Force (Tito Santana & Rick Martel)
- Dino Bravo w/ Frenchy Martin def. Rugged Ronnie Garvin
- Mr. Perfect def. The Blue Blazer
- The Bushwhackers (Luke & Butch) def. The Fabulous Rougeau Brothers (Jacques & Raymond) w/ "Mouth of the South" Jimmy Hart
- "The Million Dollar Man" Ted DiBiase w/ Virgil and Brutus "The Barber" Beefcake fought to a double count out
- The Twin Towers (Big Boss Man & Akeem) w/ Slick def. The Rockers (Shawn Michaels & Marty Jannetty)
- Hercules def. King Haku w/ Bobby "The Brain" Heenan
- Bad News Brown vs. "Hacksaw" Jim Duggan went to a no contest
- Red Rooster def. Bobby "The Brain" Heenan

"We did so well in Atlantic City with *WrestleMania IV* that our customers demanded that we bring WWE back for *WrestleMania V*."

—Donald Trump

A New Champion is Established

The Mega Powers trio of Hogan, Savage, and manager Miss Elizabeth took sports entertainment by storm, becoming WWE's top attraction. Behind the scenes, their relationship sometimes required careful management. Vince McMahon recalls, "[Randy Savage and Hulk Hogan] both wanted the spotlight and would do a number of things to edge the other one out, which I thought was humorous. But that also needed to be managed because otherwise you could have a real problem … You had the woman between the two guys, and that always led to one thing or another, which made it a far more interesting scenario."

Lighting the Fuse

The inaugural *SummerSlam* provided a pivotal chapter in the Mega Powers story when Savage disapproved of Hogan's post-match celebration. Months later, at the second *Survivor Series*, The Macho Man once again looked with disdain at Hogan's post-match behavior toward Miss Elizabeth, sowing the discord which would lead to the eventual destruction of the Mega Powers.

The Mega Powers Break

The speculated rift between the Mega Powers became a talking point throughout WWE programming. The scenario beckoned fans to Milwaukee's Bradley Center for the second broadcast of NBC's *The Main Event*. It took a final turn when "Macho Man" was thrown outside the ring and landed on Miss Elizabeth, knocking her unconscious. Torn between bringing Elizabeth to medical attention and helping his partner, Hulk Hogan carried Elizabeth to the locker room, leaving Savage alone to fend off the Twin Towers. After the match, "Macho Man" went ballistic on his former partner and manager. What began as a subtle show of disapproval at SummerSlam '88 helped develop the Mega Powers' story into the marquee match at *WrestleMania V*.

> **"You had the woman between the two guys, and that always led to one thing or another, which made it a far more interesting scenario."**
>
> **—Vince McMahon**

▶ *Hogan picks up the unconscious Miss Elizabeth*

> **"Randy was so incredibly jealous of anyone who would do or say anything to Elizabeth."**
>
> **—Vince McMahon**

The Mega Powers' narrative was a different form of drama involving Hulk Hogan and, for that matter, WWE. It contained a layer of complexity that previous Hulkamania storylines did not possess. McMahon adds, "The subject matter was a bit adult in terms of the love triangle, but the way it was executed really wasn't. If you're writing well, there are double entendres that can mean one thing to a younger audience and something else to an older audience. ... Part of the dynamic was [that] Randy was so incredibly jealous of anyone who would do or say anything to Elizabeth. It was a natural, evolving, real-life story."

Return to Atlantic City

By this time, *WrestleMania* was so successful that cities began submitting bids to host the extravaganza. Ideally, WWE wanted to enter a new city every year and cultivate new fans and relationships with that area's business community. However, a fateful phone call caused a change in plans. Donald Trump affirms, "We did so well in Atlantic City with *WrestleMania IV* that our customers demanded that we bring WWE back for *WrestleMania V*." After hearing the pitch, it was evident to WWE that Trump knew their needs. The venue added another 2,000 seats to accommodate more than 20,000 people, breaking the all-time attendance record at the Atlantic City Convention Center.

> **"I believe I've had more Mike Tyson fights than anybody, and he was a monster in terms of his draw. I would say that *WrestleMania* was at least as good and maybe in certain ways even better.**
>
> **—Donald Trump**

WRESTLEMANIA THE VIDEO GAME

WWE's first-ever licensed video game for home console systems was released prior to *WrestleMania V* for the Nintendo Entertainment System. Only one name was appropriate for this historic product: *WrestleMania*.

Sold Out Show

In promoting *WrestleMania V*, WWE expanded the television, live event, and local advertising efforts that proved successful for *WrestleMania IV*. The strategy worked. More than 20,000 fans filled the sold-out Trump Plaza and Atlantic City Convention Center to witness the explosion of the Mega Powers. Donald Trump remembers, "I believe I've had more Mike Tyson fights than anybody, and he was a monster in terms of his draw. I would say that *WrestleMania* was at least as good and maybe in certain ways even better. It was just a very, very big event."

Hercules vs. King Haku

For years, Hercules was a member of Bobby "The Brain" Heenan's stable. Things went sour when Heenan sold Hercules' contract to "The Million Dollar Man" Ted DiBiase, who only wanted his own personal "slave." This decision angered Hercules and he turned his sights on Heenan's charges, including King Haku.

Hercules got off to a great start, dominating King Haku throughout the early parts of the match, but he then turned his attention to Heenan outside the ring. Hercules' thirst for revenge backfired, as it allowed Haku to nail him with a powerful clothesline. Rolling Hercules back into the ring, the King started to take Hercules apart, getting several two-counts. Hercules was able to regain momentum, avoiding a Haku clothesline and pinning the King after a suplex.

▶ *Hercules regains momentum against King Haku*

Brutus Beefcake vs. "The Million Dollar Man" Ted DiBiase

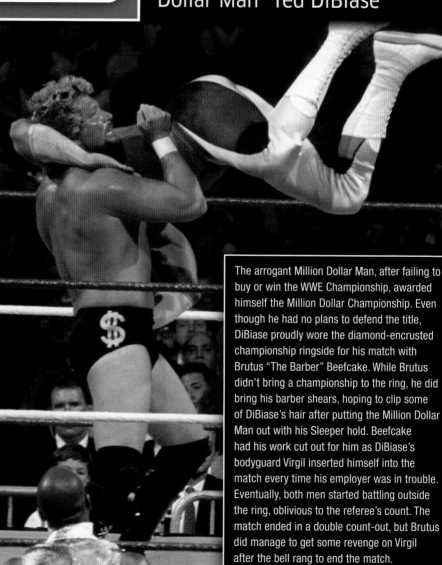

The arrogant Million Dollar Man, after failing to buy or win the WWE Championship, awarded himself the Million Dollar Championship. Even though he had no plans to defend the title, DiBiase proudly wore the diamond-encrusted championship ringside for his match with Brutus "The Barber" Beefcake. While Brutus didn't bring a championship to the ring, he did bring his barber shears, hoping to clip some of DiBiase's hair after putting the Million Dollar Man out with his Sleeper hold. Beefcake had his work cut out for him as DiBiase's bodyguard Virgil inserted himself into the match every time his employer was in trouble. Eventually, both men started battling outside the ring, oblivious to the referee's count. The match ended in a double count-out, but Brutus did manage to get some revenge on Virgil after the bell rang to end the match.

International Competition

Two international teams competed against each other at *WrestleMania V* when New Zealand's Bushwhackers made their *WrestleMania* debut competing against Jimmy Hart's French Canadian charges, the Rougeau Brothers. Fans loved the brawling and licking shenanigans of the Bushwhackers, and cheered every move by the burly Kiwis. The Rougeau brothers entered the match confident that their mat expertise would make this an easy victory, but the Bushwhackers took advantage of a distracted referee to execute their battering ram move, as well as a double-team move to pin Raymond, earning the surprising victory.

Tag Team Handicap Match

Demolition was in the midst of a lengthy reign as World Tag Team Champions, a title they had won at the previous year's *WrestleMania*. At the time, they were managed by the devious Mr. Fuji, but Fuji betrayed the duo at 1988's *Survivor Series* and aligned himself with Demolition's biggest rivals, the Powers of Pain. Warlord and Barbarian were hoping that Mr. Fuji could guide them to championship gold just as he had done with Demolition. He did help the Powers of Pain attack the champions on several occasions, enraging Demolition to the point of accepting a Handicap Match for the titles at *WrestleMania*.

While Fuji was not the powerhouse wrestler like the other four men in the ring, he still was an asset to his team, having won the World Tag Team Championship as a competitor five times. Still, he was smart enough to let Warlord and Barbarian do most of the work in the ring, but when they had worn down Ax and Smash enough, Fuji did tag in to attack his former team. At one point, while the referee was preoccupied with the Barbarian, Fuji tried to throw ceremonial salt in the eyes of Demolition's Smash, but he ducked and Warlord was hit with it instead. Demolition was then able to target Mr. Fuji, hitting him with their Demolition Decapitation, winning the match and continuing their reign as World Tag Team Champions.

▶ *Fuji turns on Demolition in the Tag Team Handicap Match*

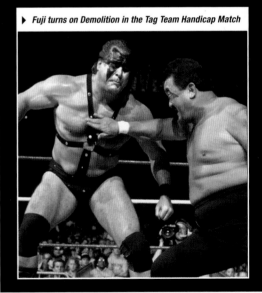

The Blue Blazer vs. Mr. Perfect

Shawn Michaels was not the only Superstar making his *WrestleMania* debut... future WWE Hall of Famer Mr. Perfect made his debut against the Blue Blazer, also in his first *WrestleMania* match. There was a tremendous amount of pressure on Mr. Perfect, as he had yet to lose a match in WWE, and certainly didn't want his first blemish to be on the big stage of *WrestleMania*. The high-flying Blue Blazer was doing everything he could to be the first Superstar to defeat Perfect. After the two men traded offensive moves, the Blazer almost pulled off a stunning move when he put Mr. Perfect into a crucifix and came close to a three-count. But Mr. Perfect managed to kick out at the last minute and execute his Perfect Plex to win the match and remain undefeated.

Red Rooster vs. Bobby "The Brain" Heenan

The time had come for Red Rooster to take out his frustrations on his former manager. The Red Rooster avenged public humiliation by "The Brain" in one of the quickest victories in *WrestleMania* history.

Strike Force vs. the Brain Busters

Arn Anderson and Tully Blanchard were the first two members of the original Four Horsemen to compete in a *WrestleMania* match. After jumping from WCW in 1988, the two joined the Heenan Family and looked to continue to dominate tag team wrestling. Making their *WrestleMania* debut, they were facing former World Tag Team Champions, Strike Force. While Rick Martel and Tito Santana had won gold in the past, their teamwork was a bit rusty, and Santana, looking to hit Blanchard with a flying forearm, accidently hit his own partner, knocking Martel off the ring apron. The Brain Busters were then able to dominate Santana while Martel tried to recover from the blow. Santana finally made it back to his ring corner, but Martel refused to tag back in, leaving the ring and heading back to the dressing room.

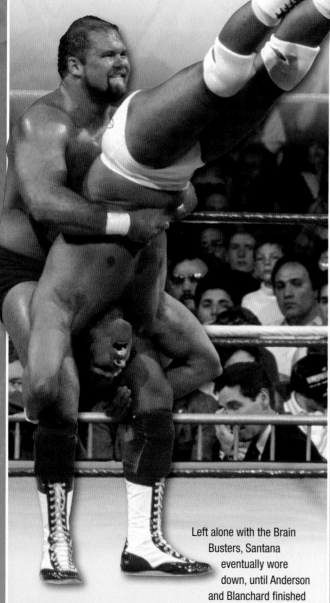

Left alone with the Brain Busters, Santana eventually wore down, until Anderson and Blanchard finished him off with a spike Piledriver. When confronted about his actions by "Mean" Gene Okerlund, Martel claimed he was tired of Santana riding his coattails, and that their tag-team partnership was over.

Ronnie Garvin vs. Dino Bravo

The French Canadian powerhouse Bravo was looking to make a name for himself in singles competition at the expense of "Rugged" Ronnie Garvin. The two had a short, yet intense, battle at *WrestleMania V*, with Garvin coming close to a victory with a sleeper hold and a rolling cradle, but Bravo used his strength to power out of a piledriver attempt and was able to pin Garvin after a side suplex. A bitter Garvin dumped the victorious Bravo out of the ring and gave Martin the Garvin Stomp.

Bad News Brown vs. "Hacksaw" Jim Duggan

Bad News Brown, an Olympic Bronze Medalist in Judo, and "Hacksaw" Jim Duggan, a former NFL Atlanta Falcon, unleashed chaos in Atlantic City. After "Hacksaw's" Three Point Stance Clothesline, his 2x4 clashed with Bad News' steel chair. Referee Tim White was forced to disqualify both men.

Mr. WrestleMania's Debut

The second match of the night featured the Rockers taking on the Twin Towers. Shawn Michaels recalls, "Marty [Jannetty] and I worked really hard trying to make the absolute most of that opportunity, and I'd like to think we had a real good match with the Twin Towers … To get acceptance with the fans and have them consider you somebody that they liked and wanted to see more of was incredibly important."

While the Rockers never captured a Tag Team Championship in WWE, Shawn Michaels would see his career reach dizzying heights once he broke off on his own. The WWE's first Grand Slam Champion gave the WWE Universe a taste of what was to come in his match against the Twin Towers, hitting some impressive double-team maneuvers

with partner Marty Jannetty, which included a double missile drop kick on the Big Boss Man. Michaels did take the loss for his team when Akeem splashed him with the Air Africa finisher, but the WWE Universe had to know Michaels was destined for bigger things on WWE's grandest stage.

Ophidiophobia

At 7'4" and 520 pounds, André the Giant feared no man. Snakes, on the other hand, were a completely different matter. Jake Roberts used this phobia to his advantage at every opportunity. WWE officials knew that a match between the two Superstars would be difficult to manage, so they appointed future Hall of Famer "Big" John Studd as the special guest referee. Remembering their rivalry leading into the first *WrestleMania*, André the Giant was not happy with the choice.

André gained an early advantage in the match by slamming Jake's head into an exposed turnbuckle that left Roberts woozy and André on the offensive. Eventually, André got tied up in the ring ropes and Jake was able to grab the upper hand. Jake considered grabbing his trusty bag and unleashing Damien. His hesitation cost him though, as André freed himself and grabbed Roberts in a chokehold. Roberts was finally able to take control of the match and knock the Giant down by ramming André's head into the same exposed turnbuckle that Roberts had been victimized by at the beginning of the match. The match devolved into chaos as Ted DiBiase and Virgil came to the ring to steal Damien's bag and André attacked the referee, Studd. When Jake got the bag back and let his pet snake free in the ring, André bailed and Jake collected the disqualification victory.

The Hart Foundation vs. Greg "The Hammer" Valentine and The Honky Tonk Man

The Hart Foundation had once been under the tutelage of Jimmy Hart, but since they split off on their own, the fans had embraced the former rule-breakers. The Mouth of the South, meanwhile had paired two of his former champion singles competitors, Valentine and Honky Tonk Man, looking for the next great tag team. Their lack of cohesion as a team hurt them at first, as the Hart Foundation took early control of the match. Valentine and Honky then gained control by isolating Hart from his partner and working over the Hit Man with some quick tags and powerful offense. The Honky Tonk Man had Bret in a world of hurt, but instead of going for the pin, he tagged in Valentine, who tried to further punish the Hit Man with the Figure 4 submission move. Bret was able to get out and tag in his partner. Both teams came close to getting the victory, when "The Mouth of the South" tried to get his trademark megaphone to the Honky Tonk Man, but the Hart Foundation had the move scouted out, and Neidhart was able to intercept the object and give it to the Hit Man, who used it on the Honky Tonk Man to get the pinfall victory.

▶ *Valentine feels the wrath of the Hart Foundation*

Favorites Return

For Superstar comebacks, WWE did not disappoint. Jimmy "Superfly" Snuka, who left WWE shortly after the first *WrestleMania*, enjoyed a hero's welcome as he announced to the *WrestleMania* crowd that he was ready to take flight in WWE once again.

The last time fans saw "Rowdy" Roddy Piper in a WWE ring was his Farewell Match at *WrestleMania III*. *WrestleMania V* would serve as "The Hot Rod's" homecoming. A special installment of *Piper's Pit* set Morton Downey, Jr., an outspoken "trash TV" talk show trailblazer, against Piper. Piper remembers, "Brother Love, Morton Downey, Jr., and I are on, and I immediately say to Downey, 'Don't blow smoke in my face anymore.' When I used the fire extinguisher [on him], he went low and grabbed behind my ankle … it's going to be a single-leg take down. Oh, Downey let go and that was the end of it. If it hadn't been for that, the fire extinguisher would have accidentally landed on his head."

Bruce Prichard (Brother Love) adds, "In those days, Morton Downey was the hottest thing on TV. So you take the biggest mouth that we had at the time, which was me; you take the biggest mouth from the past that everybody was compared to, which was Piper; and then you take the single biggest, hottest mouth on television at the time. It was perfect because Morton Downey felt he was the king and no one could touch him. Obviously, Morton hadn't met Roddy before."

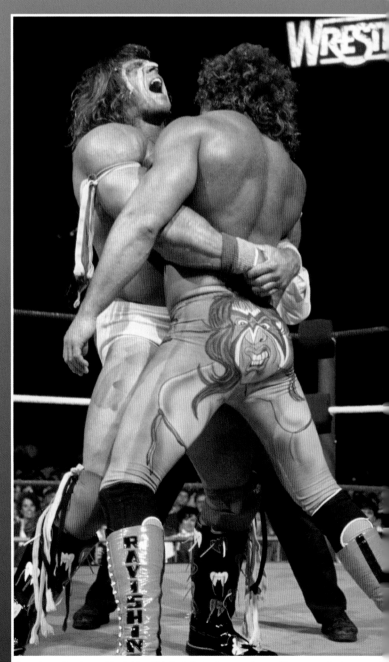

Setting up the Intercontinental Championship match, *WrestleMania V* marks one of the first times a Royal Rumble event foreshadowed a major *WrestleMania* matchup. The "Super Posedown" between Ultimate Warrior and Rick Rude at *Royal Rumble* in January 1989 did exactly that. Ultimate Warrior's popularity continued to increase, while Ravishing Rick Rude's on-screen arrogance, bodybuilder physique, and way of berating WWE crowds made him a Superstar that fans loved to hate. Many felt this match showcased each man's potential to rise to WWE's upper-echelon event cards.

▶ *Ultimate Warrior and Ravishing Rick Rude in the Intercontinental Championship Match*

The Mega Powers Explode

The main event truly was a blurring of the lines between art, entertainment, and real life. The fans became so invested in the Mega Powers' love triangle storyline that additional security was requested. Randy Savage wasn't comfortable with Elizabeth walking to the ring alone. Pat Patterson remembers, "I knew if a fan somehow touched her that would've been it." Randy might have lost control and gone after the fan. Patterson continues, "I told Vince and Randy I was going out there with her because this was the main event; it was *WrestleMania*; everything needed to go as planned."

This was "Macho Man's" second consecutive *WrestleMania* main event. It was the Hulkster's first main event since *WrestleMania III*, and his first as the championship challenger. Despite the tumultuous relationship they had at times away from the ring, Randy Savage and Hulk Hogan were pure magic when it was time to perform. Following the scripted story, "Macho Man" unleashed a relentless attack. But as Hogan began to "Hulk up," he was suddenly impervious to any pain inflicted on him. The crowd reacted as if they had been waiting for their hero to return to the top of the mountain. It was clear that Hulkamania was back.

WrestleMania's fifth event was a significant achievement for Vince McMahon and WWE. Over the course of those five years, the one-time experiment had been seen by nearly 200,000 fans live, and by millions via closed-circuit and pay-per-view.

RUN-DMC

Popular group, RUN-DMC, was the special musical guest for *WrestleMania V*. Darryl "DMC" McDaniels of RUN-DMC remembers, "I was a huge WWE fan as a kid. I used to get the wrestling magazines and draw Bruno Sammartino. I started working out because of Hulk Hogan. Performing at *WrestleMania V* was better than winning a Grammy, an American Music Award, or being at the Super Bowl. We were the first musical act to perform at *WrestleMania*. It was a privilege for RUN-DMC to step in the squared circle. It's one of the top five events of my life."

▶ WrestleMania V The Rockers vs. The Twin Towers

▶ WrestleMania VI The Rockers vs. The Orient Express

▶ WrestleMania VII The Rockers vs. The Barbarian and Haku

WrestleMania VIII vs. El Matador

MR. WRESTLEMANIA

"I will give you a show like you have never, ever seen before."

—Shawn Michaels

▶ WrestleMania XIX vs. Chris Jericho

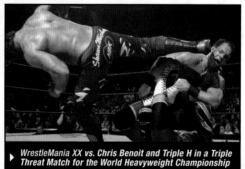

▶ WrestleMania XX vs. Chris Benoit and Triple H in a Triple Threat Match for the World Heavyweight Championship

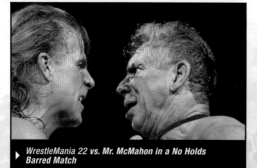

▶ WrestleMania 21 vs. Kurt Angle

▶ WrestleMania 22 vs. Mr. McMahon in a No Holds Barred Match

▶ WrestleMania 23 vs. John Cena for the WWE Championship

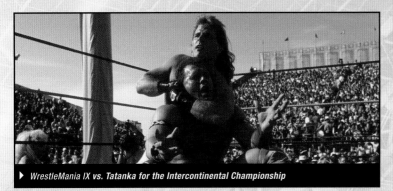

WrestleMania IX vs. Tatanka for the Intercontinental Championship

WrestleMania X vs. Razor Ramon in a Ladder Match for the Intercontinental Championship

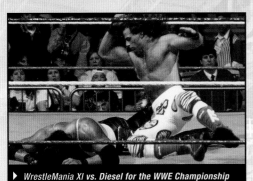

WrestleMania XI vs. Diesel for the WWE Championship

WrestleMania XII vs. Bret "Hit Man" Hart in a 60-Minute Iron Man Match for the WWE Championship

WrestleMania XIV vs. Stone Cold Steve Austin for the WWE Championship

Shawn Michaels first thrilled *WrestleMania* audiences at WWE's fifth annual spectacular. Along with his partner Marty Jannetty, Michaels brought fans to their feet for the next two years at the Show of Shows as part of The Rockers.

In his winning effort as a singles Superstar at *WrestleMania VIII*, Michaels, dubbed "The Heartbreak Kid," showed he was destined for greatness. He continued to evolve as a competitor and a storyteller, taking WWE audiences on an exhilarating ride. His indissoluble bond with the audience allowed them to share a visceral connection with their hero—the infinite thrill of his triumphs, and the excruciating agony of his defeats.

When WWE's brightest lights illuminated the Grandest Stage of Them All, Shawn Michaels, with each awe-inspiring performance, reimagined the art of storytelling and cemented his legacy as one of the greatest in-ring performers in the history of WWE. Michaels' phenomenal career spanned 17 *WrestleMania* matches, coming to an end at *WrestleMania XXVI*.

Michaels' boundless abilities enabled him to exhibit unmatched artistry and achieve amazing performances. He was enshrined in the WWE Hall of Fame in 2011 and continues to be celebrated and revered today. The man who transformed an industry enjoyed several monikers: The Showstopper, The Icon, The Main Event, and most notably, Mr. WrestleMania, a name that indisputably belongs to him.

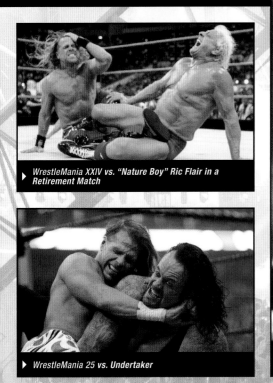

WrestleMania XXIV vs. "Nature Boy" Ric Flair in a Retirement Match

WrestleMania 25 vs. Undertaker

WrestleMania XXVI vs. Undertaker in a Streak vs. Career Match

WRESTLEMANIA VI

TORONTO SKYDOME – TORONTO, ONTARIO, CANADA

April 1
1990

Attendance
67,678

ANNOUNCERS
Gorilla Monsoon
Jesse "The Body" Ventura

RING ANNOUNCER
Howard Finkel

LOCKER ROOM CORRESPONDENTS
"Mean" Gene Okerlund
Sean Mooney

SPECIAL MUSICAL GUEST
Robert Goulet

SPECIAL INTERVIEW CORRESPONDENT
Rona Barrett

Event Card

TITLE VERSUS TITLE – WWE CHAMPIONSHIP & INTERCONTINENTAL CHAMPIONSHIP MATCH
- Ultimate Warrior (Intercontinental Champion) def. Hulk Hogan (WWE Champion) to become new WWE Champion

TAG TEAM CHAMPIONSHIP MATCH
- Demolition (Ax and Smash) def. Colossal Connection (André the Giant & Haku) (Champions) w/ Bobby "The Brain" Heenan

MILLION DOLLAR CHAMPIONSHIP MATCH
- "Million Dollar Man" Ted DiBiase w/Virgil def. Jake "The Snake" Roberts

OTHER MATCHES
- Big Boss Man def. Akeem w/ Slick
- "The American Dream" Dusty Rhodes & Sapphire w/ Miss Elizabeth def. "Macho King" Randy Savage and Queen Sherri

- "Hacksaw" Jim Duggan def. Dino Bravo w/ "Mouth of the South" Jimmy Hart
- "Rowdy" Roddy Piper and Bad News Brown fought to a double countout
- The Hart Foundation (Bret "Hit Man" Hart & Jim "The Anvil" Neidhart) def. The Bolsheviks (Nikolai Volkoff & Boris Zhukov)
- The Orient Express (Sato & Tanaka) w/ Mr. Fuji def. The Rockers (Shawn Michaels & Marty Jannetty) via countout
- Brutus "The Barber" Beefcake def. Mr. Perfect w/ The Genius
- Ravishing Rick Rude w/ Bobby "The Brain" Heenan def. Jimmy "Superfly" Snuka
- The Barbarian def. Tito Santana
- "The Model" Rick Martel def. Koko B. Ware
- Earthquake w/ "Mouth of the South" Jimmy Hart def. Hercules

> ## "I've been to the Super Bowl, I've been to the World Series, I've even been to The Rolling Stones. But there is one event that surpasses them all, and that's *WrestleMania*."
>
> —Jesse "The Body" Ventura

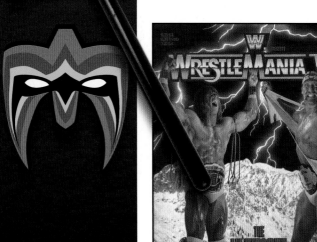

Passing the Torch

As Hulk Hogan cemented his position as undisputed champion, Ultimate Warrior's legions of fans were expanding rapidly. The frenzy he created with his physical intensity was thrilling. Warrior emerged from a series of matches with Ravishing Rick Rude as the Intercontinental Champion. Now a two-time Intercontinental Champion, Ultimate Warrior was on the fast track to the main event.

As still holds true today, the WWE Champion shouldered the burden of embodying success for the entire company: drawing crowds for live events, attracting viewers for television and pay-per-view, and driving the sales of WWE merchandise. Hulk Hogan carried this torch for the better part of six years, an impressive feat. Behind the scenes, questions loomed surrounding who would be future opponents for both Hulk Hogan and Ultimate Warrior.

WrestleMania Heads North

The decision was made; *WrestleMania VI* would be held in a dome, but not in the continental United States. This time, Vince McMahon would export WWE's annual sports entertainment spectacular north of the border. The Toronto SkyDome was a dynamic facility boasting all the amenities of the day. This made it the perfect location for a production of *WrestleMania*'s magnitude.

Another factor made the SkyDome compelling. Dating back to the 1930s, wrestling cnjoyed remarkable popularity in Toronto and across Canada's coast-to-coast wrestling territories. Since the days of Vince McMahon, Sr., WWE Superstars were well received in the Great White North.

Making A National Media Splash

WWE was pleasantly surprised at how the Canadian media embraced *WrestleMania*. Like Mexico and Japan, Canada could suspend disbelief and appreciate the qualities that defined sports entertainment. Canada's respect translated into favorable media coverage all over the country. WWE never promoted *WrestleMania* as a legitimate sporting event, but the media's enthusiasm presented a wonderful opportunity. Suddenly, sports reporters began attending WWE press conferences and asking Superstars serious questions such as, "What is your strategy going into the match? How do you plan to win?" WWE was very grateful for that kind of media support.

Unexpected Resistance

Ecstatic at *WrestleMania*'s reception throughout Canada, the company was eager to begin its collaboration with SkyDome. As President of WWE Canada, Jack Tunney arranged a meeting with SkyDome executive teams. WWE told them *WrestleMania VI* would be the biggest event of the year, promoted on 200 television stations across the United States and the 20 they worked with in Canada at the time. WWE intended to set the all-time attendance record at SkyDome. They let the Skydome team know that they wanted to work with them to develop integrated sponsorship and co-promotional programs. Not a single one of the Skydome teams would work with WWE. A WWE executive remembers, "One of our team members said, 'Thank you for listening to us. WWE will set an attendance record here with or without your help.'" WWE never knew why they were so uncooperative, even forcing WWE to configure its own box office within the SkyDome.

WWE did exactly what they said they would do. Within three months, WWE created and launched a multi-faceted promotional campaign. It engaged Toronto, from local television and print media, to placement on the mass transit bus fleet and giant billboards.

A New Approach

WrestleMania VI marked many firsts for WWE: it was the first *WrestleMania* held outside the United States, the first to present a hero-versus-hero main event, and the first to have both the WWE and Intercontinental Championship titles on the line. Within WWE, the idea of a hero-versus-hero main event at *WrestleMania* intrigued many and concerned some. Longtime pros remembered the Pedro Morales versus Bruno Sammartino main event at 1972's *Showdown at Shea*. Because it was an exhibition match with no title at stake, both men's personas were preserved. McMahon carefully orchestrated events to create tension between Hogan and Warrior. This was not a story of "Good versus Evil." Rather, the focal point was who was more powerful: Hulk Hogan or Ultimate Warrior? Care was required, as both would retain their good-guy personas after *WrestleMania*.

First, the two heroes formed a team on *Saturday Night's Main Event* against Mr. Perfect and The Genius. After Warrior hit the Hulkster with an "accidental" clothesline, the two became embroiled in a face-to-face altercation. Audiences then watched Hogan and Warrior "save" one another from the attacks of WWE villains to set up an evenly matched *WrestleMania* battle. For the first time in WWE history, the WWE Champion and the Intercontinental Champion would put their respective titles on the line in *WrestleMania*'s main event.

Preparing For a Challenge

During this era, pitting one "babyface," or good guy, against another was considered a major risk. A key concern was dividing the crowd. Normally, a hero versus a villain would generate almost unanimous audience support for the hero. Thrusting two good guys into conflict could fragment the audience, damage the Superstars' heroic appeal, and produce a disappointing *WrestleMania* main event. Nevertheless, a dream match featuring powerhouse heroes Hulk Hogan and Ultimate Warrior posed a compelling opportunity. Vince McMahon had to introduce the concept to his audience carefully.

An experimental "face-versus-face" confrontation involving Hogan and Ultimate Warrior was conducted at 1990's *Royal Rumble*. WWE reasoned that the audience might embrace the concept within *Royal Rumble*'s every-Superstar-for-himself format; babyfaces could end up fighting one another. If it wasn't well received, the scenario could die there and everyone would move on. However, once Hogan and Warrior cleared the ring of opposition, the audience came unglued as the two collided in battle. The crowd's decibel level confirmed that this Royal Rumble would jumpstart *WrestleMania* storylines.

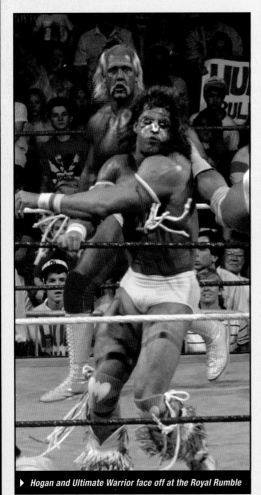

▶ *Hogan and Ultimate Warrior face off at the Royal Rumble*

The Model vs. Koko B. Ware

Ever since turning his back on Tito Santana at *WrestleMania V*, Rick Martel had shown a distasteful new attitude. Calling himself "The Model," Martel displayed an arrogance that was also the fitting name of the cologne he constantly sprayed from the oversized atomizer he carried to the ring. For his singles *WrestleMania* debut, Martel faced the challenge of future WWE Hall of Famer Koko B. Ware, who also brought his pet bird Frankie to the ring.

Martel may have initially underestimated Ware, as Koko managed to level Martel with some powerful moves. Slowly, the Model began to take control of the match, and after one failed attempt, finally locked Koko in Martel's Boston Crab submission maneuver. With the move cinched in the center of the ring, Ware had no choice but to tap out.

Million Dollar Championship

This battle saw a combination of technical grappling and brawling. Roberts shocked DiBiase when he attempted the DDT minutes into the match. This seesaw fight saw Virgil's interference produce dividends. DiBiase won the match via count out and reclaimed his Million Dollar Championship.

The Colossal Connection vs. Demolition

Two of the larger and more powerful members of the Heenan Family had combined to win tag team gold. For André the Giant, it was his longest championship reign in WWE, and he and his partner Haku had every intention of keeping their championship through *WrestleMania VI* and beyond. They had their work cut out for them, as they were facing Demolition, who had left the last two *WrestleMania* events as Tag Team Champions.

Few tag teams in WWE could handle a combination like André and Haku, but Demolition quickly demonstrated they had the power needed to hang with the champions. But the Colossal Connection

was able to take control of the match by isolating Ax from his partner and working him over and beating him down. When Ax was finally able to tag out, the match became a more even affair and the Connection tried to resort to illegal double-team movements to finish off Ax and Smash. Unfortunately the plan backfired and Haku kicked André into the ring ropes, and Demolition was able to pin Haku and win their third World Tag Team Championship.

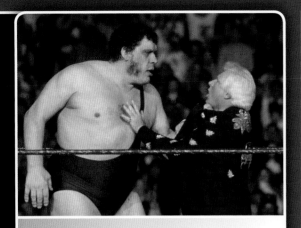

ENDING A GIGANTIC CAREER

It was clear to the WWE Universe that André's in-ring career would soon be coming to an end, and many hated to see him still accompanied to the ring by the hated weasel, Bobby "The Brain" Heenan. After Heenan's charges lost their match at *WrestleMania VI*, The Brain got right in André's face and started berating him. While it was a tense situation, it may have blown over if Heenan hadn't gone a bit further, slapping André's face. The Giant struck back, repeatedly hitting Heenan to the delight of the crowd, who were even happier when André also took out his former partner Haku. It would be André's last *WrestleMania* match, and the WWE fans were happy to cheer him once again.

A Natural Disaster

A natural disaster struck *WrestleMania VI*—a Richter-scale-busting phenomenon known as Earthquake. The massive new Superstar had been crushing the competition and he was looking to add Hercules to his list of victims. Although Hercules was in the unusual position of facing a competitor bigger and stronger than him, he took up the challenge. Hercules had to be surprised that his flying shoulder tackles seemed to have no effect on the massive Earthquake, but a pair of clotheslines weakened Earthquake until he was down on one knee. Hercules tried to press his advantage by going for the Backbreaker, but he couldn't get Earthquake up and the massive monster took advantage and leveled Hercules with the Earthquake Splash to gain the pinfall victory. To send a message to the Superstars of WWE, Earthquake inflicted additional injury by hitting a second splash on Hercules, or as he and his manager Hart called it, an "aftershock."

▶ *Hercules prepares to take on Earthquake with Jimmy Hart*

The Hart Foundation vs. The Bolsheviks

After an extended championship drought, the Hart Foundation was looking to get back in the World Tag Team Championship picture, and had already declared their intentions by challenging the winner of the *WrestleMania VI* Championship bout to a match. Heading to the ring for their match with the Bolsheviks, Bret "Hit Man" Hart and Jim "The Anvil" Neidhart already knew they would have to face long-time rivals Demolition if they wanted to regain the gold. But first, they had to deal with a pair of powerful Soviet grapplers.

A painful memory for many WWE fans of the late '80s was being subjected to the Bolsheviks' singing of the Soviet National Anthem, and that was how they started their *WrestleMania VI* match. Jim Neidhart had no interest in listening, so he attacked Volkoff mid-song and dumped him out of the ring. The Anvil and the Hit Man then set up Zhukov for their Hart Attack maneuver, gaining the Foundation a pinfall victory in less than 20 seconds. This strengthened their case as #1 contenders for the title, and reminded the Bolsheviks that they should have been more focused on wrestling, and less on singing.

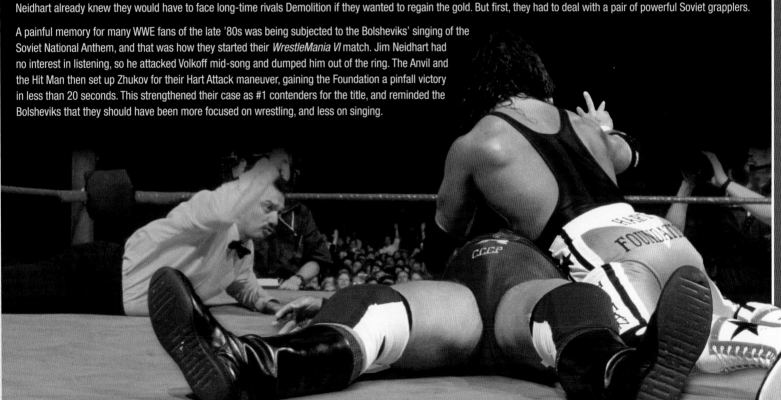

Tito Santana vs. the Barbarian

After the breakup of the Powers of Pain, the Barbarian joined the Heenan Family where Bobby "The Brain" Heenan looked to guide the powerful Barbarian to greater heights as a singles competitor. To prove his mettle, the Barbarian challenged two-time Intercontinental Champion Tito Santana. Tito proved to be strong competitor for the massive Barbarian, even coming close to winning the match when he took down the Barbarian with a flying forearm. He managed a two-count, but Heenan managed to prevent a three-count when he put the Barbarian's foot on the rope. The near-miss seemed to energize the Barbarian, as he came roaring back with a series of power moves on Tito, ending with a clothesline off the top turnbuckle to put Santana down for the three-count.

▶ *The Barbarian pins Tito Santana for the win*

The American Dream

This match was the *WrestleMania* debut of "The American Dream," Dusty Rhodes. After nearly 12 years away, Rhodes returned to WWE in 1989. Some felt that Rhodes' WWE persona was created at his expense, but Rhodes recalls, "I remember Vince telling me, "'You've been so involved in this war. You need to relax and have some fun.' Pat Patterson said, 'What if you wore polka dots?' It wasn't like they said, 'You've got to do this.' … A year and a half later, one of my biggest years in the industry was in my bank, so it didn't bother me."

Vince McMahon adds, "People thought that I wasn't serious about the character. And that wasn't true. We did some vignettes of Dusty, who's just so entertaining. At that juncture, he was no longer a spring chicken, so I wanted to go with more fun, rather than the athleticism.

Rhodes was a favorite of the WWE Universe and a hated rival of Randy Savage. Not only did the Macho King do everything he could to make Rhodes' career miserable, Savage's queen, former WWE Women's Champion Sensational Sherri, would also attack Dusty, drawing the ire of his manager, Sapphire. To settle this unusual rivalry, *WrestleMania* would see its first-ever match featuring intergender teams.

With Sherri having far more ring experience, Dusty and Sapphire seemed to be at a bit of a disadvantage, until Dusty revealed his team's secret weapon—they had Savage's former manager, Miss Elizabeth, in their corner. The shocking revelation worked at first, as Savage and Sherri were clearly thrown for a loop. The two were able to cheat in order to regain the upper hand, particularly Savage, who used his scepter as a weapon to take down Rhodes.

Although the men were only supposed to battle each other, and the same with the women, all four competitors broke that rule. Elizabeth had enough of Sherri's antics and got involved in the match, allowing Sapphire to roll up Sherri for a stunning pinfall victory for her team.

▶ *Big Boss Man finally gains the advantage against Akeem*

Big Boss Man vs. Akeem

After a successful tag-team partnership as the Twin Towers, Big Boss Man decided to go off on his own. "The Million Dollar Man" Ted DiBiase had tried to buy off Big Boss Man, but he refused to be bought off by anyone, redeeming the former rule breaker in the eyes of the WWE Universe. His former manager Slick and partner Akeem were already looking to take Big Boss Man out, but DiBiase provided them with an additional financial incentive.

Before Big Boss Man could even get into the ring, DiBiase, who'd been hiding under the ring, attacked Big Boss Man, hitting devastating punches to soften him up and then rolling him into the ring so Akeem could make quick work of him. The match was quick, but the result was not what DiBiase expected. Big Boss Man was able to recover and hit Akeem with his patented side slam to get the pinfall victory over his former tag-team partner.

Watch Out for the 2x4

It was a testament to the popularity of "Hacksaw" Jim Duggan with the WWE Universe that the Skydome crowd cheered wildly for the patriotic Superstar as he came to the ring with his 2x4 and his American flag. Duggan needed all the help he could get, as facing French Canadian strongman Dino Bravo was already enough of a challenge, but having to deal with the outside interference of both Earthquake and Jimmy Hart made the task seem almost impossible.

The two men started brawling right from the opening bell. Bravo thought no one in WWE could match his strength, but Duggan was able to counter Bravo's attacks and take the advantage. Duggan was setting up for his Football Tackle Clothesline, but Earthquake tried to involve himself in the match. While the referee was focused on Earthquake, Jimmy Hart tried to give Bravo an unfair advantage by tossing Hacksaw's 2x4 into the ring. Unfortunately for Dino, Hacksaw got to the board first and cracked it over Bravo's back to pin him. Duggan may have won the match, but he came out on the losing end of a post-match confrontation, as Earthquake devastated Hacksaw with three Earthquake Splashes.

"Superfly" Jimmy Snuka vs. "Ravishing" Rick Rude

Former Intercontinental Champion "Ravishing" Rick Rude had bigger goals on his mind in 1990. The Heenan Family member was after the WWE Championship. His opponent at *WrestleMania VI*, "Superfly" Jimmy Snuka, was making his in-ring *WrestleMania* debut.

Rude didn't even wait for the bell to ring, attacking Snuka with clubbing blows. But Snuka reversed the momentum, taking control with several moves, including a headbutt and back body drop that sent Rude crashing to the mat. But Snuka went for one move too many, and Rude was able to take the Superfly down with a suplex and then taunt the crowd with his patented gyrations. The two evenly matched Superstars traded moves until Snuka missed one of his high-flying moves and Rude took advantage by nailing Superfly with his Rude Awakening, picking up the pinfall victory.

The Rockers vs. The Orient Express

After breaking up the Powers of Pain, Mr. Fuji was looking for a new tag team to share his championship experience with. He found a perfect pair of clients from his home country of Japan in the Orient Express. To begin their path up the championship ladder, the duo challenged the Rockers at *WrestleMania VI*. Shawn Michaels and Marty Jannetty were also looking to make a statement about why they should be considered championship contenders.

Sato and Tanaka gained an early advantage with some powerful kicks, but Jannetty was able to turn things around with a Powerbomb that led to some effective double-team moves by the Rockers. Mr. Fuji was able to turn the tide by hitting Jannetty with his cane, but over time the momentum swung back in the Rocker's favor, as they energized the crowd with double drop kicks and other moves. Fuji tried to become involved again, and a fed-up Jannetty stalked the manager out of the ring, allowing Sato to throw ceremonial salt in Marty's face, blinding the Rocker and giving the count-out victory to the Orient Express.

Bad News for the Hot Rod

One of the more intense rivalries heading into *WrestleMania VI* was between Bad News Brown and "Rowdy" Roddy Piper. Piper had eliminated Brown from the 1990 Royal Rumble Match, but Bad News did not take that well. Brown got his revenge by leaping onto the ring apron and pulling Piper out of the ring, eliminating him. The two continued to brawl outside and all the way back to the locker room. The animosity continued to build over the next few weeks, with Brown taunting Piper for wearing a kilt. It became clear to the WWE Universe that the two needed to settle matters in the ring, and a match was set for *WrestleMania VI*.

Brown was already in a foul mood and the crowd's support for Piper did nothing to improve that fact. Piper tried to work Bad News into more of a frenzy by dancing and playing to the crowd. The official twice separated the competitors at the beginning of the match, but he soon lost control over the proceedings. Piper stunned Brown with an early high-cross body for a two count. As the official once again tried to separate the competitors, Brown took advantage, clocking the Rowdy with a punch. He punched Piper a few more times then slammed Piper into two turnbuckles. Brown tried to sap Piper's energy with a painful trapezius hold, but Piper broke out with a few well-placed elbows to Brown's midsection. The two stood toe-to-toe, trading punches and elbows with neither able to keep his opponent down for a three count. Each man was not above skirting the rules, as both Piper and Brown delivered thumbs to their rival's eyes and Brown stripped the padding off a turnbuckle. This latter plan backfired when Piper tossed Brown into the exposed turnbuckle.

Eventually the competitors started battling outside the ring, ignoring the official's count. He had no choice but to count out both competitors, leaving the match without a decisive winner. Neither Piper nor Brown seemed to care, as they were only focused on inflicting punishment on each other.

Ending Perfection

One highly anticipated match was Brutus "The Barber" Beefcake's showdown against the then-undefeated "Mr. Perfect," Curt Hennig. Though Mr. Perfect put up a good defense, The Barber was the first person to pin Hennig in a televised match. Brutus remembers, "We had a great chemistry in the ring. We could walk in the ring without speaking and get in the ring have a real classy, *WrestleMania* match anytime, anywhere. I remember leading up to *WrestleMania VI* we'd be performing at live events. We were put on early in the card and we'd just tear the house down wherever we went. When we got to SkyDome it was awesome. I ended Perfect's undefeated streak."

INSPIRING A FUTURE SUPERSTAR

One *WrestleMania VI* audience member was encouraged to raise his dream to a new level. WWE Hall of Famer Edge remembers, "I was a huge WWE fan growing up in Canada. The first *WrestleMania* that I actually got to see was *WrestleMania IV*. I went to the Guelph Memorial Gardens and watched it on closed-circuit. I remember listening to *WrestleMania III* on the radio. When my mom found out that *WrestleMania* would be in Toronto, she knew I had to be there. It was a neat time to be a fan because the crowd was so split, and that was the first time something like that happened. I didn't experience a feeling of tangible electricity like that again until I performed in *WrestleMania* as a WWE Superstar."

REMEMBERING THE ULTIMATE WARRIOR

Over the next few years following *WrestleMania VI*, the Ultimate Warrior made sporadic appearances in WWE, until he disappeared from WWE shortly after *WrestleMania XII*, with many thinking he would never return. But his legacy was properly honored the weekend of *WrestleMania 30*, when the world was treated to powerful appearances by the Warrior at his induction into the WWE Hall of Fame, *WrestleMania 30*, and *RAW* the following night. The weekend cemented the Warrior's legacy as one of the all-time greats, but were sadly his final appearances ever, as Warrior passed away the next day. While the world lost one of the most colorful characters of all time, without a doubt Warrior will forever be in the hearts of all WWE fans—past, present, and future.

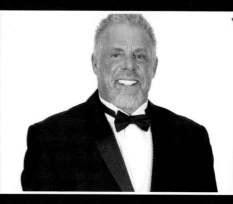

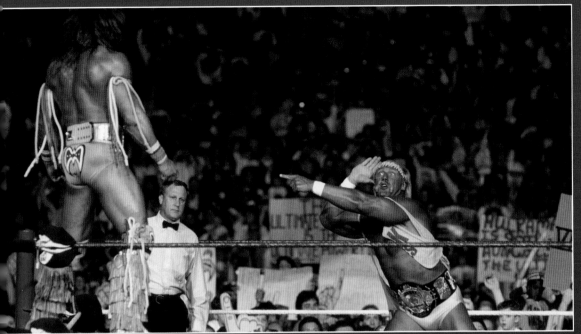

The Ultimate Challenge

It seemed an eternity had passed from the first time Hulk Hogan and Ultimate Warrior met at the *Royal Rumble* until their main event clash at the SkyDome. In its opening minutes, the Hogan-Warrior match reestablished both Superstars' equal power. The fans cheered for each competitor—at no point did they turn on either champion. Both men displayed similar determination, even down to the final three-count. Hogan first kicked out of Warrior's finishing move. The Warrior eluded Hogan's famous Leg Drop, one of the only times in Hogan's career that he missed his signature finishing move. Ultimately, the Warrior pinned the Hulkster, defeating him in a clean victory. The Ultimate Warrior was the new WWE Champion.

In a tremendous show of respect, Hogan relinquished the WWE Championship and the two embraced in the center of the ring. Pat Patterson reflects, "I remember telling Vince I wanted to see the end by being in the crowd. As I watched the match, I began to cry. I looked over and had no idea Vince was standing next to me. I see him and he has tears in his eyes. It was such a powerful moment."

The postmatch embrace between Hulk Hogan and the Ultimate Warrior remains one of the most emotional scenes in WWE history. When Hogan got back into the ring after being pinned, the stadium held its collective breath to see what was going to happen, but Hulk showed grace and class, handing the Warrior the title and raising his hand in victory. The event closed with the potent image of Warrior holding up both the Intercontinental and WWE Championships, and the WWE Universe no doubt believed that the Warrior would be a long-reigning champion and standard-bearer in WWE, just like Hogan had been for years. It wasn't to be. Warrior didn't even make it to *WrestleMania VII* as champion, and the Hulkster regained the title at that event.

▶ *Ultimate Warrior wins the Championship*

WRESTLEMANIA VII

LOS ANGELES SPORTS ARENA – LOS ANGELES, CA

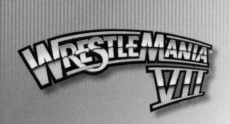

March 24
1991

Attendance
16,158

ANNOUNCERS
Gorilla Monsoon, "Hacksaw" Jim Duggan, Lord Alfred Hayes, Bobby "The Brain" Heenan

RING ANNOUNCER
Howard Finkel

LOCKER ROOM CORRESPONDENTS
"Mean" Gene Okerlund
Sean Mooney

SPECIAL MUSICAL GUEST
Willie Nelson

SPECIAL GUEST COMMENTATOR FOR MAIN EVENT
Regis Philbin

SPECIAL GUEST TIMEKEEPER FOR THE MAIN EVENT
Marla Maples

SPECIAL GUEST RING ANNOUNCER FOR THE MAIN EVENT
Alex Trebek

Event Card

MAIN EVENT – WWE CHAMPIONSHIP MATCH
- Hulk Hogan def. Sgt. Slaughter (Champion) w/ General Adnan to become new Champion

RETIREMENT MATCH
- Ultimate Warrior def. Randy "Macho Man" Savage w/ Queen Sherri

WWE TAG TEAM CHAMPIONSHIP MATCH
- The Nasty Boys (Brian Knobbs & Jerry Sags) w/ "Mouth of the South" Jimmy Hart def. The Hart Foundation (Bret "Hit Man" Hart & Jim "The Anvil" Neidhart) (Champions) to become new Champions

INTERCONTINENTAL CHAMPIONSHIP MATCH
- Big Boss Man def. Mr. Perfect (Champion) w/ Bobby "The Brain" Heenan by disqualification

BLINDFOLD MATCH
- Jake "The Snake" Roberts def. "The Model" Rick Martel

OTHER MATCHES
- Legion of Doom (Animal & Hawk) def. Power & Glory (Hercules & Paul Roma) w/ Slick
- Genichiro Tenryu & Koji Kitao def. Demolition (Smash & Crush) w/ Mr. Fuji
- The Mountie w/ "Mouth of the South" Jimmy Hart def. Tito Santana
- Virgil w/ "Rowdy" Roddy Piper def. "The Million Dollar Man" Ted DiBiase
- Earthquake w/ "Mouth of the South" Jimmy Hart def. Greg "The Hammer" Valentine
- Texas Tornado def. Dino Bravo w/ "Mouth of the South" Jimmy Hart
- Undertaker w/ Paul Bearer def. Jimmy "Superfly" Snuka
- British Bulldog def. Warlord w/ Slick
- The Rockers (Shawn Michaels & Marty Jannetty) def. The Barbarian & Haku w/ Bobby "The Brain" Heenan

"The F.B.I. came to Madison Square Garden and told me they thought it was a good idea if I wear a bullet proof vest when I performed."

—Sgt. Slaughter

Sgt. Slaughter Returns

Immediately following *WrestleMania VI*, Vince McMahon began planning his next spectacular. It all started with a handwritten letter from a Superstar who had not set foot in a WWE ring in over six years—Sgt. Slaughter.

In the 1980s, Sgt. Slaughter was one of the biggest stars in wrestling. Initially a villain, his battles with the Iron Sheik garnered mainstream media attention and transformed this former United States Marine Corps drill instructor into an American hero. To his fans' dismay, Slaughter disappeared from WWE programming at the end of 1984.

Slaughter remembers, "Right before the first *WrestleMania* [Vince and I] parted ways. I went to wrestle in the AWA and worked with Hasbro as an ambassador for G.I. Joe. I didn't watch *WrestleMania*s 1 through V. I couldn't watch them, but I decided to watch *WrestleMania VI*. I was so impressed with the event from a production standpoint that I wrote Vince a letter telling him so."

Slaughter recalls, "My phone rang and on the other end I hear, 'Sarge, it's Vince.' He said, 'Are you ready to go back to work?' I said, 'Yes, yes I am.' So he told me to meet him the next day and that he had an idea."

Current events had always helped shape characters, create storylines, and promote events. Characters like the villainous German and Japanese sympathizers in the post World War II television era, the American hero dressed in military attire, and the brave Native American, were traditionally incorporated into sports-entertainment's storylines. The same was true during the summer of 1990, when tensions began to rise in the Middle East after then-Iraqi President Saddam Hussein announced the invasion and occupation of neighboring nation, Kuwait.

Slaughter looks back, "I go to Vince's house and it was like we never missed a day. Vince said, 'I'm ready to bury the hatchet if you are,' and I was … So I'm ready to hear all about Sgt. Slaughter coming back to WWE, the red, white, and blue. Vince sits me down and says, 'I have this idea about the situation in Iraq and Saddam Hussein overtaking Kuwait …' I said, 'Ok,' waiting to hear about a big patriotic campaign. And Vince says, 'I want you to be on the side of Saddam Hussein.' I couldn't believe it. I just couldn't believe it. He said, 'I want you to go home and think about it and talk to your family about it.' I went home and spoke to my family about it. My wife said, 'You can't do that. It'll be dangerous.' After I thought about it, that's what made it fun. The challenge, could I do this? So I called Vince back and said, 'Let's do it.'"

A week later, Sgt. Slaughter was on the set of a secret WWE film shoot. WWE wanted to create a series of vignettes to reintroduce Slaughter to its audience. Slaughter recalls, "Even the cameramen, who I knew from my early days with WWE, were shaking their heads. They couldn't believe what we were doing."

Slaughter's scenarios were strategically rolled out. Footage featured the sergeant eviscerating Americans for "becoming soft." The new Sgt. Slaughter explained that, as a Marine, he was disgusted by the behavior of Americans. Each week another vignette assaulted viewers, slowly building the storyline. The ultimate objective was to develop a Slaughter-led crusade culminating in a showdown against "The Real American" Hulk Hogan at *WrestleMania VII*.

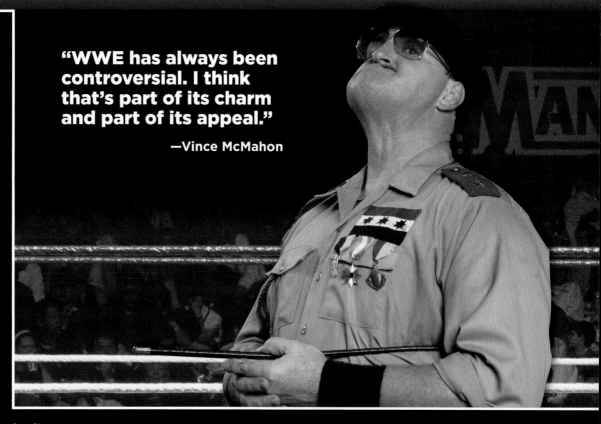

"WWE has always been controversial. I think that's part of its charm and part of its appeal."

—Vince McMahon

Sgt. Slaughter was energized by the progressing storyline. This veteran performer sensed the escalating anger rising from the crowd each week. Slaughter recalls, "We were at Madison Square Garden and the F.B.I. was there and asked to meet with me. They said every arena I appeared in received a threat of some sort, and a threat was made at me. Every place. So the F.B.I. came to Madison Square Garden and told me they thought it was a good idea if I wore a bullet-proof vest when I performed. So I did. I wore it every night. If you watch the match against Hogan, you can see I'm wearing it."

Sgt. Slaughter's experience with encountering serious anger from fans continued throughout the country. Slaughter recounts, "After I won the WWE Championship at the *Royal Rumble*, Hulk and I stayed at the arena until 2 a.m. taking promotion pictures for *WrestleMania*. I leave with my agent and we stop at a Denny's. We're the only ones in the restaurant and no one is coming over to greet us or take our order. My agent asks if someone can take our order. The grill cook had a Marine Corps tattoo on his arm. He points at me and says to my agent, 'You can eat. He's not.' The next day I get to Philadelphia and … I speak with Vince and he says, 'After you won the title I got back to the office and we received some death threats. Someone called up and said they were going to kill you, me, our families, the WWE office, the TV studio, and anyone that is associated with us.' We then had 24-hour security for my family for the next ten weeks."

A Change of Venue

A proud performer, Slaughter reveled in the effect he had on the audience. His excitement skyrocketed when he reviewed plans for the Los Angeles Memorial Coliseum. Slaughter recalls, "I remember being in Vince's office and he showed me the seating charts and plans for the Coliseum. It was incredible. It had giant video screens in the stadium with a seating capacity that could hold over 100,000 people. It was awesome and motivated me to keep doing what we were doing."

Vince McMahon remembers, "Again, the ego being what it is, it was like, 'Wow, we have to go to the Los Angeles Coliseum, we have to sell it out.' Because that would have been the largest crowd ever. Then the war breaks out. We felt it was not the right patriotic thing to do, in terms of going to the large venue. We decided this is a little too close to reality. We better bring it back indoors and control it better, tone it down some because it was … art imitating life. Again, always being extraordinarily patriotic, you had to be careful how you portrayed it. There's good guys and bad guys in the WWE and also in the real world. So you can't cross those two worlds all that often. If you do, you have to do it with a great deal of sensitivity. Sometimes when you come too close to reality you can actually hurt the audience. Because there were United States soldiers that didn't make it, some came back wounded and things of that nature, and you have to be careful what you do."

For WWE, their enthusiasm for promoting the event changed in late January. Once American servicemen and women began to lose their lives in war, what was once regarded as a well-placed promotion for an entertainment event turned into something that bordered on poor taste. For the 1991 Super Bowl in Tampa, Florida, the NFL had terrorist threats that resulted in a significant increase in security, including metal detectors at each gate. WWE was hosting an outdoor event with an expected crowd of 90,000 starring a U.S. Marine turned Iraqi-sympathizer. After the NFL's Super Bowl experience, WWE made the difficult decision to change the venue.

Deciding to change an event venue is not a trivial matter. For WWE it was a necessary nightmare. They were well into the promotions campaign and in the first month sold about 17,000 tickets. Thankfully, the LA Sports Arena was right next door.

▶ *Vince McMahon poses next to a billboard for the sold out event*

Slaughter recounts, "I remember when Vince told me the news. It was devastating. To not be at the first *WrestleMania* was hard to accept. To now, all these years later, be WWE Champion, in the main event, and have the pursuit of a new indoor attendance record taken away … It hurt a lot. I understood why it had to happen. I understood, but it hurt." Mean Gene Okerlund recalls, "Everyone in the locker room was aware of the death threats to Vince and Sarge and their families. It was a difficult time. Security became an issue for our events and for *WrestleMania*. When Sgt. Slaughter burned a poster of Hulk Hogan, and then the following week on television a Hulk Hogan t-shirt, the storyline became very real for people around the county."

The Texas Tornado vs. Dino Bravo

▶ *Bravo starts the fight before Von Erich could remove his ring robe*

When he debuted in the WWE, Kerry Von Erich aka The Texas Tornado made quite an opening impression by being in the right place at the right time. When Brutus "The Barber" Beefcake was unable to challenge Mr. Perfect for the Intercontinental Championship at *SummerSlam 1990*, the Texas Tornado stepped in and shocked Perfect by winning the title and successfully defending it for months. Eventually Mr. Perfect reclaimed the title and so the Tornado entered *WrestleMania VII* looking to re-establish himself in singles competition by defeating the Canadian powerhouse Dino Bravo.

Bravo took the fight to Von Erich before he could even take off his ring robe, but the Texas Tornado was soon able to reverse the momentum. The two men battled back and forth until the Tornado was able to slap the famous Von Erich claw on Bravo and then follow it up with his Spinning Discus Punch to drop Bravo to the mat and pin Dino for the victory.

The Streak Begins

After a dominant six months in WWE since his debut at the 1990 *Survivor Series*, *WrestleMania VII* was the *WrestleMania* debut of Undertaker, who was set to take on Jimmy "Superfly" Snuka. Snuka made the mistake of taking his eyes off Undertaker at the start of the match, giving The Deadman the opportunity to take an early advantage with hits and kicks. The WWE Universe was astounded to see the future WWE Hall of Famer dominated in a match the way Undertaker took it to Superfly. Even when Snuka was able to fire blows back at The Deadman, nothing Snuka did could keep Undertaker down. A flying high-cross body, normally a powerful move by Snuka, backfired as Undertaker caught him and eventually turned his momentum into a Tombstone Piledriver. Undertaker quickly defeated Snuka to begin his epic 21 win *WrestleMania* streak. The WWE Universe was impressed by the match, but they had no idea that it was the start of the most impressive run in the history of sports-entertainment, extending almost a quarter of a century.

Bret Hart remembers, "I didn't know a lot about Undertaker coming into WWE before his debut. I worked with him in his first match at *Survivor Series*. You could tell right away Undertaker had great size, agility, and control. Every once in a while there's a character that becomes an overnight sensation and that was Undertaker."

Davey Boy Smith vs. The Warlord

Smith and Warlord both claimed to be the most powerful Superstars in WWE. The Warlord believed no man could break his Full Nelson, while Smith was convinced he could get any Superstar up on his shoulder to administer his Running Powerslam. The two men were destined to clash at *WrestleMania VII* to determine whose claim was valid.

Both men were seconded, Warlord by his manager, Slick, and the British Bulldog by his mascot, Winston the Bulldog. From the start, it was clearly not about wrestling holds, but pure power moves. At first neither man was able to get a significant advantage, but the Warlord eventually got Smith into the Full Nelson. Commentator Gorilla Monsoon correctly pointed out that Warlord had not locked his fingers behind Smith's head, so wasn't applying the move's maximum pressure. This may have been the reason the Bulldog powered out of the Full Nelson, to the shock of both Warlord and Slick. To the delight of the crowd, Smith hoisted Warlord onto his shoulder and delivered a Running Powerslam for the three count.

▶ *Smith breaks out of Warlord's loose Full Nelson, enabling Smith to deliver a Running Powerslam*

Blindfold Match

On an episode of *The Brother Love Show* in October 1990, "The Model," Rick Martel, sprayed Jake Roberts' snake with Arrogance in order to improve its odor. When Roberts realized what was happening, he lunged at Martel and the Model "accidentally" sprayed Jake in the eyes with his pungent cologne. Roberts was blinded for weeks, and the WWE Universe worried that he'd never regain his sight. Even when blinded, Roberts had a singular focused vision—get revenge on Rick Martel at *WrestleMania*.

Roberts wanted The Model to know what it was like to be without sight, so he proposed a Blindfold Match. To open the match, each man had a hood placed over his head, making it impossible for either of them to see. The crowd did everything it could to help Roberts, cheering whenever the Snake was heading toward Martel. The two missed each other several times, building the crowd's anticipation for when Roberts would finally get his hands on The Model. Things almost went south for the Snake when Martel got a hold of a steel chair outside of the ring, but his blind swing missed Roberts completely and hit the ring post instead. Both men made their way back into the ring where Martel briefly cinched a Boston Crab, but Jake worked his way out of it, nailed The Model with a DDT for the pinfall victory, and further humiliated Martel by crushing his Arrogance atomizer and draping his pet snake Damien on The Model's body.

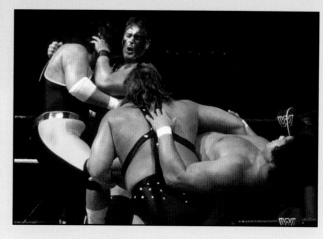

Genichiro Tenryu & Koji Kitao vs. Demolition

One of the special attractions of *WrestleMania* was a pair of Japanese Superstars making their *WrestleMania* debut. They faced a tall order, battling the team that had competed for the World Tag Team Championship at each of the last three *WrestleMania* events, Demolition.

Demolition proved to be rude hosts, attacking Kitao right from the start. Smash and Crush isolated Kitao, keeping the Japanese Superstar off balance with quick tags and power moves. Eventually Kitao was able to tag in Tenryu, but after a quick start by Tenryu, Demolition gained an advantage again through the use of illegal double teams. The Japanese Superstars dumped Crush out of the ring, and Tenryu nailed Smash with a kick to the back of his head, and Kitao delivered a Powerbomb to score the pin for the visiting tag team.

The Intercontinental Championship

▶ *Heenan delivers some sneaky attacks to Big Boss Man*

Bobby "The Brain" Heenan had continually disparaged Big Boss Man's mother while providing commentary and interviews. The unprovoked remarks enraged the Superstar and he set about getting his revenge on each member of the Heenan Family, taking them out until only one member remained, Intercontinental Champion, Mr. Perfect. At *WrestleMania VII*, Big Boss Man would have an opportunity to get his hands on Perfect, as well as the championship.

At the opening bell, Perfect tossed his towel in Boss Man's face, and each slapped the other before the action began in earnest. Mr. Perfect's in-ring abilities were some of the finest in WWE, and Boss Man showed surprising speed and agility for a man his size. The Superstars appeared evenly matched, but Perfect soon gained an advantage thanks to some sneaky attacks by his manager, Heenan. Things got a bit more equal when Andre the Giant came to ringside to chase Heenan, as well as to distract Mr. Perfect by taking his Intercontinental Championship. With the tide turning in Big Boss Man's favor, Heenan Family members Haku and the Barbarian came to the ring to attack Boss Man, causing the Disqualification of Mr. Perfect. Unfortunately, the title could not change hands on a Disqualification, so Mr. Perfect left *WrestleMania* as champion.

Greg "The Hammer" Valentine vs. Earthquake

Greg Valentine had been a long-time client of Jimmy Hart, but recently the Hammer had gone off on his own, to the delight of the WWE Universe. Hart decided to gain a measure of revenge by pitting his most powerful client, the massive Earthquake, against Valentine at *WrestleMania VII*. Valentine showed he was up for the challenge by matching Earthquake blow for blow, and even managed to get Earthquake off his feet in order to set him up for the Figure Four Leglock. Hart's annoying antics were enough of a distraction that Earthquake was able to slam Valentine to the mat and crush The Hammer with the Earthquake Splash, claiming the victory.

The Rockers vs. The Barbarian and Haku

The speed, continuity, and determination of Jannetty and Michaels were on a collision course with the power, evil strategy, and physical cruelty of Barbarian and Haku. This struggle began with Shawn Michaels and Haku going move-for-move. Michaels avoided the Tongan's crushing power while Haku displayed his impressive agility. When Barbarian interfered, The Rockers showed they would not be intimidated.

▶ *Virgil assists Piper after he was attacked by DiBiase with his own crutch*

Michaels and Jannetty continued to keep their adversaries off-balance with their signature quick tags and double-team attacks. Haku and Barbarian's power ripped the advantage from The Rockers. The villain's strength and ring presence kept them dominant as they continued ruthlessly beating on Marty Jannetty. The tide turned when Jannetty avoided Barbarian's top rope headbutt. The roar from the crowd intensified and The Rockers high-powered tandem offense set up what would be the final flight of their *WrestleMania* careers as a team. Jannetty nailed Haku with a top rope missile dropkick, and Shawn Michaels sealed the deal with a flying crossbody, scoring the victory.

A Disgruntled Employee

Never did "Million Dollar Man" Ted DiBiase think that he'd lose his bodyguard, Virgil. After years in DiBiase's employ, Virgil had enough of the demeaning tasks he had to perform. DiBiase constantly said that everyone had a price for the Million Dollar Man, but Virgil decided his dignity could no longer be bought. DiBiase was looking forward to handling his former employee in the ring, but when Virgil revealed that "Rowdy" Roddy Piper was training him, the match became much more intriguing.

As the match started, Virgil showed some impressive moves and it took some time for Ted DiBiase to recalibrate his strategy. To further aid his friend, "Rowdy" Roddy Piper accompanied Virgil to the ring, despite being on crutches as the result of a motorcycle accident. Piper shouted instructions and encouragement as DiBiase and Virgil traded moves and blows. On a few occasions, DiBiase found his focus split between his in-ring opponent and Piper, and that distraction proved costly. DiBiase rolled out of the ring and attacked the Hot Rod. This caused DiBiase to be counted out, giving the victory to Virgil. An enraged DiBiase, joined at ringside by Sensational Sherri, attacked Piper with his own crutch, further injuring Piper's knee.

The Legion of Doom vs. Power & Glory

From the moment they jumped from WCW to WWE, the Legion of Doom had one goal on their minds—win the World Tag Team Championship. They were set to grab the #1 contenders' spot and a shot at the title at *WrestleMania*, but Power & Glory interfered and created the opening for the Nasty Boys to grab the challenger spot. Without a title match at *WrestleMania VII*, the Legion of Doom decided gaining revenge on Hercules and Roma would be the next best thing.

Power & Glory tried to gain the early advantage by dumping Animal out of the ring and double-teaming Hawk. The plan quickly failed, as Hawk delivered a double clothesline to the team. Animal made his way back into the ring as all four men started brawling. The official had no control of the action as Hawk and Animal dumped Hercules out of the ring and then set Roma up for the Doomsday Device, and a pinfall victory in just under a minute.

The Hart Foundation vs. The Nasty Boys

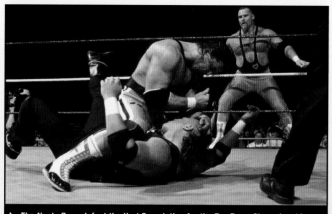

▶ *The Nasty Boys defeat the Hart Foundation for the Tag Team Championship*

The Hart Foundation entered *WrestleMania VII* as the World Tag Team Champions. Their opponents, the Nasty Boys, may have been new to the WWE, but their manager, "The Mouth of the South" Jimmy Hart, knew the champions well and planned to use his knowledge to give The Nasty Boys an advantage in the match.

Jimmy Hart, wearing an airbrushed motorcycle helmet in addition to his outrageous jacket, led his charges to the ring amidst a chorus of boos. The Nasty Boys used illegal double teams and moves to keep Bret "Hit Man" Hart in the ring, switching in and out to maximize their advantage. Even when Bret finally tagged The Anvil in, Jimmy Hart and The Nastys distracted the referee enough for him to miss the legal tag, so he forced Neidhart out of the ring. Bret finally hit an explosive clothesline, and tagged in the powerful Neidhart. The Anvil cleaned house and Bret recovered enough for the duo to hit Knobbs with their finishing Hart Attack, but while the official escorted Bret out of the ring, Sags hit The Anvil with Jimmy Hart's helmet, and The Nasty Boys won the World Tag Team Championship.

WrestleMania VII would be the final *WrestleMania* where the Hart Foundation appeared as a team. Bret Hart reflects, "Dropping the titles at *WrestleMania VII* was bittersweet. I figured we were approaching the end of the Hart Foundation because … I was going to start a solo push. I was looking at this great opportunity that presented itself but was proud of what Jim and I accomplished as a team, and we were close, and have always been close friends."

Macho Man vs. Ultimate Warrior

The rising conflict between Ultimate Warrior and "Macho King" Randy Savage produced one of the most anticipated matches of *WrestleMania VII*. Many people were unaware of the close, real-life friendship between the Warrior and Savage. Having this "Career Ending Match" at *WrestleMania* meant a great deal to both of them. This was confirmed in no uncertain terms by the wording around a painted WWE Championship on the back of Warrior's trunks, "Means Much More Than This."

Howard Finkel remembers, "The build-up to the Warrior-"Macho Man" match was exceptional. Ultimate Warrior had a tremendous fan base, and Randy really had the best of both worlds. Elizabeth, she was demure and sweet, and when Randy was a villain he was very overbearing towards her, and when he was a hero they were a great couple. When Randy was with Sherri, they pushed each other's buttons. Sherri was so talented and played the role of diabolical manager so well. The way the crowd reacted at the end of that match showed how much people loved Randy and Elizabeth together. They were truly WWE royalty."

To bring additional drama to what was to be the "Final Chapter," the camera glimpsed Miss Elizabeth in the crowd; it was her first appearance on WWE programming in nine months. She was there to watch Savage, and it was evident by the look of concern on her face that she wasn't sure if he would make it.

Together, Warrior and Randy Savage created one of the most memorable performances in WWE history. While Savage lost the match when his manager Queen Sherri attacked him in anger, Miss Elizabeth rushed to the ring. With tears streaming down her face, Elizabeth opened her arms and embraced the "Macho Man." An outpouring of emotion came from the capacity crowd. Once again, Randy Savage and Miss Elizabeth created a memorable moment, reaffirming their enduring love affair with the WWE audience.

Tito Santana vs. The Mountie

New to the WWE, The Mountie had little regard for his American neighbors and even less respect for his in-ring competition. Claiming that he always got his man, The Mountie often dispensed his own brutal brand of justice, using an electric cattle prod to shock his downed opponents. In his *WrestleMania VII* match with Tito Santana, The Mountie found himself in trouble as Tito rolled on offense, hitting The Mountie with a variety of hard-hitting maneuvers. With the referee distracted, Jimmy Hart handed The Mountie the electric cattle prod, which he used to shock a hard-charging Tito Santana. With Santana on the mat, The Mountie picked up the easy (but not earned) pinfall victory.

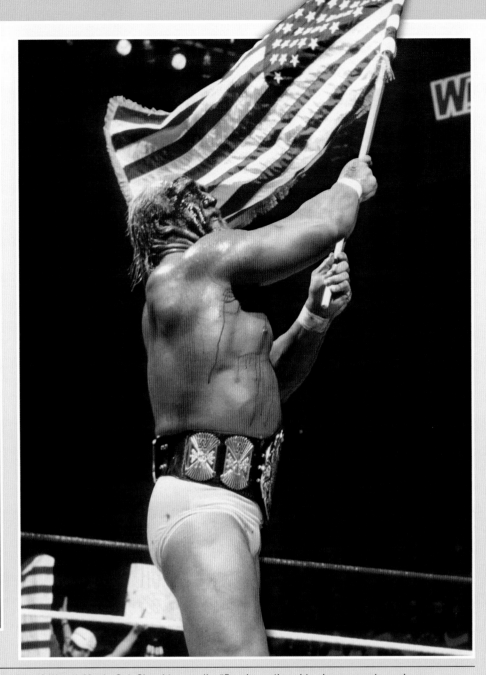

Turncoat vs. American Hero

Fan hostility directed against Sgt. Slaughter continued to the day of *WrestleMania*. Sgt. Slaughter recalls, "People continued to show anger towards me. I knew even some of the wrestlers in the locker room were not happy about the storyline. When I got to the building the day of *WrestleMania*, Alex Trebek came up to me backstage. I never met him before. He came up to me and said, 'I hope Hulk Hogan kicks your ass.' And he was serious."

When Sgt. Slaughter crossed the threshold of the Los Angeles Sports Arena, months of death threats, sneaking into venues, wearing bullet-proof vests, all culminated in this moment. Slaughter's disappointment in watching *WrestleMania*'s unprecedented ascent without him vanished. In sports-entertainment, the opponent you battle in the ring defines the work you've done and the performer you are. Slaughter made it to the main event of *WrestleMania*, and his adversary was a cultural icon synonymous with WWE. That said it all.

As the familiar anthem "Real American" introduced their hero, the audience united in a singular roar. With the stars and stripes of the American flag in his hand, Hulk Hogan was poised to play a role with which he was very familiar, the national hero. With crowd chants of "USA, USA" Hogan incorporated his tried and true offense with thrilling new moves. Not since the Hulkster's wars with Andre the Giant had WWE fans seen him climb to the top rope.

Slaughter remained steadfast in his assault. The final insult came after Slaughter draped Hogan in the Iraqi flag. Mounting another celebrated battle from the brink of defeat, the Hulkster rose from the canvas and ripped the Iraqi flag, successfully concluding the story of Turncoat versus American Hero and becoming the first three-time WWE Champion in the company's history.

WRESTLEMANIA VIII

HOOSIER DOME – INDIANAPOLIS, IN

April 5
1992

Attendance
62,167

ANNOUNCERS
Gorilla Monsoon
Bobby "The Brain" Heenan

RING ANNOUNCER
Howard Finkel

LOCKER ROOM CORRESPONDENTS
"Mean" Gene Okerlund

SPECIAL MUSICAL GUEST
Reba McIntyre

SPECIAL GUEST COMMENTATOR FOR MAIN EVENT
Ray Combs

Event Card

FIRST MAIN EVENT – WWE CHAMPIONSHIP MATCH
- Randy "Macho Man" Savage w/ Elizabeth def. "Nature Boy" Ric Flair (Champion) w/ Mr. Perfect to become new Champion

SECOND MAIN EVENT
- Hulk Hogan def. Sid Justice w/ Harvey Wippleman by DQ

WORLD TAG TEAM CHAMPIONSHIP MATCH
- Natural Disasters (Earthquake & Typhoon) def. Money Inc. ("Million Dollar Man" Ted DiBiase & Irwin R. Schyster) w/ "Mouth of the South" Jimmy Hart

INTERCONTINENTAL CHAMPIONSHIP MATCH
- Bret "Hit Man" Hart def. "Rowdy" Roddy Piper (Champion) to become new Champion

OTHER MATCHES
- "Hacksaw" Jim Duggan, Sgt. Slaughter, Virgil & Big Boss Man def. The Mountie, Repo Man, & The Nasty Boys (Brian Knobbs & Jerry Sags) w/ "Mouth of the South" Jimmy Hart
- Owen Hart def. Skinner
- Tatanka def. "The Model" Rick Martel
- Undertaker w/ Paul Bearer def. Jake "The Snake" Roberts
- Shawn Michaels w/ Sensational Sherri def. El Matador

> **"The match between Ric Flair and Hulk Hogan was supposed to be the big one. To this day, it is unknown why the match did not take place."**
> —"Mean" Gene Okerlund

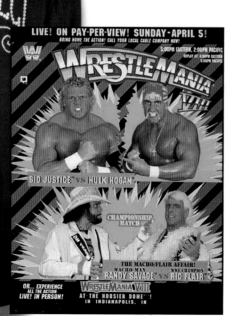

The Dream Match

In September of 1991, the sports-entertainment industry stopped dead in its tracks. On an episode of *The Funeral Parlor*, Bobby "The Brain" Heenan appeared holding the NWA World Heavyweight Championship. Heenan's remarks seemed like something from a "Dream Match" mode in a video game— "The Brain" announced that "Nature Boy" Ric Flair was on his way to WWE.

WWE programming initially portrayed Flair as being under contract to another organization, with Flair's arrival to the WWE pending. In actuality, Flair was already under contract to WWE.

After much anticipation, "Nature Boy" Ric Flair walked through the curtain and graced *Prime Time Wrestling*'s stage. It was a sight many thought they would never see. To the delight of fans everywhere, Flair talked about the match people debated for almost a decade—Flair versus Hogan. The NWA Champion versus the WWE Champion.

To the Heartland

In considering where the eighth sports-entertainment spectacular should originate, Vince McMahon felt it was time *WrestleMania* go to America's Heartland—Indianapolis. In addition to the allure of the Hoosier Dome as a venue, presenting a live event in Indianapolis gave the host organization proximity to other major cities, like Chicago, St. Louis, and Cincinnati.

The Path to Indianapolis

In October of 1991, the "Nature Boy" and the Hulkster began their main event match appearances at non-televised WWE live events around the country. To further exploit this epic legend and sustain the strength of both men's characters, the matches ended in a variety of controversial, indecisive outcomes.

After the WWE Championship was vacated, Flair won the 1992 *Royal Rumble* to be crowned the new WWE Champion.

In his on-air victory speech, Flair said to "Mean" Gene Okerlund, "This is the only title in the wrestling world that makes you number 1. When you're the king of the WWE, you rule the world."

The '92 *Rumble* was a historic evening for one of Flair's greatest on-screen rivals, and one of his closest friends outside the ring, "Rowdy" Roddy Piper. That night, Piper won what would be his only singles championship in WWE—the Intercontinental Championship. The title victory put Piper on a path to *WrestleMania* against one of WWE's brightest stars-on-the-rise of that time, "The Excellence of Execution," Bret "Hit Man" Hart.

WWE promoted the Flair-Hogan main event at its televised press conference with the five top contenders present—Hulk Hogan, "Rowdy" Roddy Piper, Randy "Macho Man" Savage, Undertaker, and Sid Justice. President Jack Tunney named Hulk Hogan the number one contender for the WWE Championship and Flair's opponent at *WrestleMania*.

But then the creative focus for *WrestleMania* somehow changed. In one of the most debated occurrences in sports-entertainment history, Hulk Hogan was no longer facing Ric Flair in the main event at *WrestleMania*. This change in direction meant that for the first time in its history, *WrestleMania* would feature a "Double Main Event."

Soon after, it was announced that Hulk Hogan would face Sid Justice. On-air, it was explained that Justice, a one-time ally of Hogan, turned on "The Real American" in a tag match against Ric Flair and Undertaker on *Saturday Night's Main Event*. To add a sense of concern about the new rivalry, speculation on WWE television underscored the fact that this could be Hogan's last WWE match.

The other main event would pit the WWE Champion Ric Flair against the newly reinstated Randy "Macho Man" Savage. The hype for the match came from Flair doctoring Miss Elizabeth's personal photos and swapping out the "Macho Man" for himself. Flair persisted in this charade by claiming to have been romantically involved with Elizabeth.

El Matador vs. Shawn Michaels

In the early 1990s, Tito Santana decided to explore his heritage, and started calling himself El Matador, wearing impressive bullfighting garb to the ring. At *WrestleMania VIII*, he faced the arrogant Shawn Michaels, who was making his singles debut after competing as a tag-team specialist over the past three *WrestleMania* events. Accompanied by Sensational Sherri, the Heartbreak Kid quickly annoyed the live crowd with his arrogant antics.

As the bell rang, the two started with some shoves, which quickly led to punches. Michaels was one of the most talented high flyers in the WWE at the time, but El Matador was one of the few Superstars that could match him move for move, evidenced by Santana tossing the Heartbreak Kid out of the ring early in the match. Sherri helped Michaels regroup and the two traded the advantage. HBK thought he was in control until Santana surprised him with a flying forearm that may have led to a pin, but Michaels rolled out of the ring. Back in the ring, Santana continued his assault, until Michaels rolled out of the ring again to once again break the momentum. El Matador looked to scoop slam Michaels off the apron and back into the ring, but Shawn held on to the ring rope and then pinned Santana for the surprise three-count.

Tatanka vs. "The Model" Rick Martel

The Native American Superstar Tatanka was making his *WrestleMania* debut after less than two months in WWE. To date, no one had been able to pin this member of the Lumbee Tribe. However, the quality of his opponents was about to be raised significantly, as he was set to face "The Model" Rick Martel at *WrestleMania VIII*.

The veteran savvy of Martel allowed The Model to jump out to an early advantage, but Tatanka's youthful strength and powerful knife-edge chops allowed him to work over Martel. The two Superstars battled back and forth, both in and out of the ring, with neither man able to enjoy a sustained advantage. Martel briefly had Tatanka down on the mat and was looking to finish him off with a top-rope move, but Tatanka shook the ropes until Martel fell, catching his groin on the ring post. Martel made one more attempt to launch offense, but Tatanka was able to hit The Model with a flying high-cross body move that led to a pinfall, and a continuation of Tatanka's undefeated streak.

Undertaker vs. Jake "The Snake" Roberts

For his second appearance at *WrestleMania*, The Deadman faced former ally Jake "The Snake" Roberts. The Snake had been up to his typical devious tricks leading into *WrestleMania*, even locking Undertaker's hand in a coffin on an episode of Paul Bearer's *Funeral Parlor*. With Undertaker incapacitated, Roberts set his sights on Paul Bearer and crushed The Deadman's manager with a brutal DDT.

What few people knew was when Roberts became Undertaker's second *WrestleMania* victim in Indianapolis, he also arranged it to be his last WWE match at the time. Roberts recalls, "I wanted to write; it's my dream. Pat Patterson had stepped down. I went to Vince and said, 'Pat's gone—now's the time.' He said, 'Out of due respect to Pat, we're not going to hire anybody.' I felt jilted, conned. No disrespect to Pat; I was upset about the whole situation. My father went to WCW. Kip Frey talked to my Dad. For a very large amount of money ... I did something I thought I'd never do. I held somebody up at *WrestleMania*. I said, 'I get released, or I don't wrestle the Undertaker.' I'm ashamed of that."

Entering the ring, Undertaker was looking for revenge for both him and Bearer. Roberts however, proved to be a worthy opponent, dodging Undertaker's early attacks and countering with body blows, even knocking The Deadman out of the ring. That proved to be a mistake, as Undertaker pulled The Snake out of the ring and threw him into the ring post. Back in the ring, Roberts recovered, and hit Undertaker with two of his patented DDT moves. Instead of attempting the pin, Roberts, thinking that Undertaker was down for the count, rolled out of the ring and tried to wrest the urn from Paul Bearer. To the delight of the crowd, Undertaker sat up, followed Jake outside the ring, grabbed him, and performed a Tombstone Piledriver on his wily opponent. The Deadman rolled Roberts back into the ring and covered him for the pinfall, his second victory at *WrestleMania*.

Friends Face Off

Roddy Piper had been a long-time fixture in WWE, but he'd never held a championship until the 1992 *Royal Rumble*, when he defeated the Mountie for the Intercontinental Championship. Former champion Bret "Hit Man" Hart wanted the title back, and was named the #1 Contender heading into *WrestleMania VIII*. It was tough for the two friends to go after each other, but the lure of the championship trumped the bond of their friendship, so the rare match pitting two fan favorites was set.

From the start of the match, each man showed a more vicious side than they typically would, with Piper actually spitting on his friend when he got frustrated that Hart was able to flip him out of the ring. Most assumed that Hart would have a significant advantage in the technical wrestling arena, but Piper held his own, taking Hart down with some arm drags and an impressive bulldog. Hart was able to sucker Piper in on two opportunities, lulling the Hot Rod into thinking Bret was down and out, only for him to attack when Roddy got close. Both men came close to winning the match on several exchanges, securing two-counts. One heated exchange led to the referee getting knocked down, and without the official to stop him, Piper got the ring bell to use as a weapon versus the Hit Man. The crowd pleaded with Roddy to not win in such a devious manner, and they got to Piper, who tossed the bell out of the ring and looked to finish Hart off with a sleeper hold. In an ingenious counter, Bret kicked his feet off the middle turnbuckle and turned it into a pin of Piper, regaining the Intercontinental Championship.

While disappointed with the loss, Piper showed great sportsmanship, shaking Hart's hand, and helping to put the championship around Bret's waist. Roddy Piper remembers, *"I didn't have the chance to wrestle with anybody. All my matches started with a bang. Every one was always a feud; that's what I did. The match with Bret Hart, I was the champion. That's a completely different match. Plus, we were both fan favorites. So it's a completely different psychology."*

Bret Hart adds, "This match was a good opportunity for both Roddy and I to show our skills—me working with a top guy, and for Roddy, to show he could wrestle with the best of them as far as having a hard-fought match with a technical wrestler. Roddy was the genius behind most of that match and that match really started to pave the way for me."

Eight-Man Tag Team Match

▶ *Virgil and Big Boss Man win the Tag Team Match*

Fans were treated to an eight-man tag team matchup featuring four unique Superstars, Sgt. Slaughter, "Hacksaw" Jim Duggan, Virgil, and Big Boss Man, uniting to deal with clients of Jimmy Hart, including former World Tag Team Champions The Nasty Boys (Brian Knobbs and Jerry Sags), former Intercontinental Champion The Mountie, and the sneaky Repo Man. The match began chaotically, with all eight men slugging it out. Slaughter's team dumped all four of their opponents out of the ring, and while they regrouped with their manager Hart, Duggan led the Indianapolis crowd in a spirited "USA!" chant that no doubt infuriated The Mountie.

It was nearly impossible for the referee to keep control of the action, as both sides refused to stick to one man in the ring at a time, and each side periodically grabbed control of the match. Finally, all eight men were in the ring. The Nasty Boys targeted Virgil, looking to take him out with an illegal object. But Virgil ducked and Sags accidentally hit his partner Knobbs instead. Virgil took advantage of the mistake and pinned The Nasty Boy, claiming the victory for his team.

Owen Hart vs. Skinner

WrestleMania VIII was already a great night for the Hart Family, Canada's wrestling royalty. With Bret winning the Intercontinental Championship earlier in the event, his younger brother could make it a clean sweep for the family by taking out the rugged Skinner in their *WrestleMania VIII* encounter. Owen looked to energize the crowd by doing a backflip off the top rope into the center of the ring, but Skinner was waiting, and spat in Hart's face. Skinner then followed up the offensive act by pounding on Owen and tossing him out of the ring. But Owen held on to the ropes and flipped himself back in. Skinner saw none of this as he had started antagonizing the crowd after he thought he had tossed out Hart. While Skinner was arguing with some fans at ringside, Hart sneaked back into the ring and pinned Skinner with a flip.

The World Tag Team Championship

"The Million Dollar Man" Ted DiBiase knew how to use his fortune to advance his WWE career. Jimmy Hart had a contract for a tag team championship match, and the Natural Disasters, Earthquake and Typhoon, assumed that they would be getting the opportunity. Unfortunately, Hart betrayed his charges and sold the shot to Ted DiBiase and I.R.S., known as Money, Inc., who won the World Tag Team Championship. The Disasters were furious at the double cross, so they fired Hart as their manager and set their sights on the new champions with a match at *WrestleMania VIII*.

The teams were polar opposites, as DiBiase and I.R.S. were best known for their scientific wrestling abilities, while the Disasters used their massive girth to punish opponents with power moves. DiBiase and I.R.S. tried to use Typhoon's size against him by wearing him down with physical moves, but he was able to tag in his partner Earthquake, who brought I.R.S. and DiBiase down with clotheslines and slams. Earthquake was set to give a prone I.R.S. the Earthquake Splash, but Hart pulled I.R.S. out of the ring and the members of Money, Inc. lost due to a countout. The Disasters were unhappy with the victory as they knew the title could not change hands unless there was a pinfall or submission.

"We had a really good match. We gave them a hell of a show and it was awesome. That was my first *'Mania* and one of the finest memories of my career."

—Ric Flair

Macho Madness Overcomes the Nature Boy

The first part of "The Double Main Event" was for the WWE Championship. In his *WrestleMania* debut, "Nature Boy" Ric Flair would face Randy "Macho Man" Savage. This match provided another example of the intensity and audience involvement that resulted when the lines of reality and entertainment blurred. "Nature Boy's" slanderous accusations and doctored photos of himself and Elizabeth in "private" moments captured the audience's attention. People felt the pain of WWE's most beloved couple and their struggle to defend their honor.

Ric Flair recalls, "It was just a tremendously well-written program. It was like Randy was married to Liz back then and she was a huge commodity and a huge star with the WWE. And the thing was, 'She was mine before she was yours.' We had a really good match. We gave them a hell of a show and it was awesome. That was my first *Mania* and one of the finest memories of my career."

The "Nature Boy" delivered. His dastardly acts and audacious self-adulation triggered deep-rooted feelings of hatred from the capacity crowd. In the end, "Macho Madness" overcame Ric Flair. Savage became WWE Champion for the second time in his illustrious career. The Hoosier Dome faithful hailed the new champion. This was the last time fans would see the "Macho Man" and the lovely Elizabeth in the ring together at a *WrestleMania*.

The question of why "Nature Boy" Ric Flair and Hulk Hogan did not meet in the main event remains unanswered. Over the years, sports-entertainment luminaries have shared their thoughts on why the match did not take place.

"Mean" Gene Okerlund reflects, "I thought Ric was a great addition to WWE. The match between Ric Flair and Hulk Hogan was supposed to be the big one. Someone put the brakes on that one, and I always wondered if it were one of the talents involved in the match. But, especially after all these years, anyone's guess is as good as mine."

Gerry Brisco speculates, "This is strictly my opinion on why Flair and Hogan didn't take place. It was a creative difference, it was an ego difference, it was a professional difference. And I don't think Ric Flair was accepted into the WWE Universe like we all thought he would be. We thought it'd be a natural flow. Ric was a different style than Hogan, a different character than Hogan. And when he came to the WWE, I know there were several pre-matches with Hogan and Ric Flair together, and none of them seemed to be the attraction that we thought it was going to be. So I think there was a lot of creative thought put into it by Vince and the powers-to-be at the time, and I think it really just came down to, 'I don't think this will be the quality match, and I don't think it will be the attraction everybody figured it would be in the beginning.'"

Sports-entertainment media personality Bill Apter states, "For years at the *Pro Wrestling Illustrated* family of magazines, we teased matches between Hulk Hogan and Ric Flair. WWE started having matches between them at live events, so we thought WWE was preparing to have it on a big stage. To this day, it shocks me that match did not take place on a *WrestleMania* platform."

Hogan vs. Justice

WrestleMania VIII's final contest featured Sid Justice versus Hulk Hogan. In the weeks leading up to *WrestleMania*, one question was on everyone's mind: would this be Hogan's last match? To further emphasize the notion of Hogan's retirement, Vince McMahon hosted a private interview with Hulk Hogan for WWE television. The two discussed Hogan's WWE career, past triumphs, the threat of the new villain Sid Justice, and if, indeed, this would be the Hulkster's final match. Hogan ended the interview with the perfect cliffhanger, claiming he didn't know if *WrestleMania VIII* would be his last match.

When Hogan and Justice finally clashed, they unloaded their high-powered offenses. Fans were stunned as they watched Hulk Hogan lifted and thrown to the canvas in Justice's Chokeslam, and then hoisted in the Power Bomb. But the tide turned and Hogan rallied. He delivered a powerful Leg Drop to Justice and attempted the pin. Justice kicked out, and because of outside interference, the match ended in a disqualification.

In the match's aftermath, Hulk Hogan was assaulted by Sid Justice and accomplice Papa Shango. But the abuse didn't last long, as the Ultimate Warrior sprinted to the ring and Hogan's aid. Using indoor pyrotechnics for the first time since *WrestleMania VI*, the broadcast ended in sheer excitement with the Hulkster and the Warrior celebrating in the ring together.

"The match between Ric Flair and Hulk Hogan was supposed to be the big one."
—"Mean" Gene Okerlund

WRESTLEMANIA IX

CAESARS PALACE – LAS VEGAS, NV

April 4
1993

Attendance
16,891

ANNOUNCERS
Bobby "The Brain" Heenan, Jim Ross, Randy "Macho Man" Savage, Todd Pettengill

RING ANNOUNCER
Finkus Maximus

LOCKER ROOM CORRESPONDENT
"Mean" Gene Okerlund

WRESTLEMANIA HOST
Gorilla Monsoon

Event Card

MAIN EVENT – WWE CHAMPIONSHIP MATCH
- Yokozuna w/ Mr. Fuji def. Bret "Hit Man" Hart (Champion) to become new Champion

WORLD TAG TEAM CHAMPIONSHIP MATCH
- Money Inc. ("Million Dollar Man" Ted DiBiase & Irwin R. Schyster) def. The Mega-Maniacs (Brutus "The Barber" Beefcake & Hulk Hogan) w/ "Mouth of the South" Jimmy Hart by disqualification

INTERCONTINENTAL CHAMPIONSHIP MATCH
- Tatanka def. Shawn Michaels (Champion) w/ Sensational Sherri by count out

OTHER MATCHES
- Undertaker def. Giant Gonzales w/ Harvey Wippleman
- "The Narcissist" Lex Luger def. Mr. Perfect
- Steiner Bros. (Rick & Scott) def. The Headshrinkers (Fatu & Samu)
- Doink def. Crush
- Razor Ramon def. Bob Backlund

> ## "You had to deliver a good match, not just look the part."
>
> —Bret "Hit Man" Hart

The World's Largest Toga Party

Searching for a new venue that would appeal to a different segment of the entertainment audience, the WWE team was intrigued by Caesars Palace. Caesars had experience with grand events; plus, they held WWE's reputation for brilliant event promotion in high esteem. WWE's only hesitation was that Caesars was an outdoor venue. Even though WWE had held outdoor events in the past, an outdoor venue for *WrestleMania* would be a first. However, since the bid from Caesars was so compelling, and included a guarantee that *WrestleMania IX* would surpass its predecessor's revenue, any concerns over weather-related issues were quickly dismissed. *WrestleMania* was going to Las Vegas.

An outdoor *WrestleMania* generated both excitement and anxiety within WWE's production team. This was the first time in *WrestleMania* history that the event had a theme. WWE spent hundreds of thousands of dollars converting a banal stadium into a magnificent Roman Coliseum. To complete the motif, WWE had the event announcers dress in togas. *WrestleMania IX* became known as "The World's Largest Toga Party."

▶ *In grand style, Bobby "The Brain" Heenan enters Caesars Palace riding backwards on a camel*

The New Generation

By the end of 1992, plans for *WrestleMania IX* were well underway. WWE decided to move forward without incorporating Hulk Hogan into its plans. Hogan had been in and out of WWE for the last couple of years as he looked into other interests. Because of this, WWE did not plan to include the Hulkster in their strategy for marketing and promoting *WrestleMania IX*.

It was agreed that *WrestleMania IX* would proudly feature Superstars who were being advertised as "The New Generation"—Superstars who incorporated more technical ring prowess in their performances and excelled in a different form of storytelling.

A Hero Returns

When plans changed and WWE announced that Hulk Hogan would be a part of *WrestleMania IX*, people at Caesars believed WWE had been secretly withholding information from them. Basil DeVito adds, "They thought we were sandbagging them, that this was the plan all along, that Hulk was part of *WrestleMania* from the beginning and we were hiding it from them. My friend who worked at Caesars then became very vocal about how there was no way Hulk Hogan was leaving Caesars Palace without the WWE Championship. I told him Hulk wasn't even in the WWE Championship match, but there was no convincing him."

The announcement of the Hulkster's return hit like a bolt of lightning. This would be Hogan's ninth consecutive *WrestleMania*—a great achievement in itself. Hogan's return to what had become his signature event altered the show's marketing materials to reflect that *WrestleMania IX* would have a "Double Main Event."

As excited as the fans were for Hogan's return, members of the locker room were curious what it would mean in the larger WWE picture. Bret Hart remembers, "From what I remember, everyone in the locker room was a big supporter of mine and I was proud of that. It was tough being asked to essentially fill Hulk Hogan's shoes, which Warrior had trouble doing, and even "Macho Man" had trouble doing. I think it was a surprise to everybody when Vince picked me to be the guy to turn things around. I felt I was doing a good job as champion and was looking forward to my match with Yokozuna. I was told when Hulk came back that he was coming back to be in a tag match with Beefcake to help promote a movie he was in, and that it had nothing to do with me. I felt really confident and was told not to expect anything, so I didn't. The only thing I was thinking about was working to figure out how to get the Sharpshooter on Yokozuna. I had no idea what was waiting for me there."

The World Tag Team Championship

As WWE stood poised to take over Las Vegas with *WrestleMania*, an unexpected issue arose. Hulk Hogan suffered a jet ski accident near his home in Florida, badly injuring the left side of his face. It was uncertain if the Hulkster would be able to perform. Though Hogan was a late addition to the program, WWE worried about the effect of pulling him from the event. After all, Hogan was the biggest name in the history of the company. Because of his drawing power, WWE decided to announce the possible change to their pay-per-view audience and ticket holders, offering refunds if necessary. They felt it was the only correct thing to do for the fans and for their event partner, Ceasars Palace.

An injured Hulk Hogan at the press conference

From the morning of *WrestleMania* until the middle of the day, WWE did not know if Hulk Hogan was going to be able to perform. When WWE informed the Caesars Palace staff, they didn't believe it. They were convinced this was the latest happening in the Hulk Hogan-*WrestleMania* saga."

Word came down that Hulk Hogan was able to perform. In WWE's tradition of turning a negative into a positive, Hogan's real-life injury was embellished to enhance the Money Inc. storyline. The audience was told that a group of ruthless thugs, hired by DiBiase and I.R.S., attacked Hogan after a pre-*WrestleMania* workout at a Las Vegas gym.

Upon the Mega-Maniacs' entrance, the crowd reaction indicated that the fans were elated that Hulk Hogan was part of *WrestleMania*. Because of Hogan's serious injury, he was cautious regarding how much time he spent in the ring and careful about the physicality. To protect his own face, previously injured in an accident, Brutus Beefcake wore a specially designed mask. More fan interest existed concerning the Hulkster, as he sported a black eye and a bruised face.

Money, Inc. tried to attack the Mega-Maniacs during their opening ring entrance, but Hogan and Beefcake dumped the duo out of the ring to the delight of the fans. As the consummate villains, Money Inc. did a phenomenal job of employing illegal tactics and infuriating the crowd. The early momentum in the match shifted between the two teams, but sensing they were in trouble, Money, Inc. decided to head to the back, figuring that if they lost by count-out, they would still retain their championship. However, Howard Finkel informed the crowd that the referee decided if Money, Inc. did not return to the ring, they would forfeit their championship. The duo raced back to meet the deadline, and used cheating tactics to wear down Hulk Hogan. Hogan was finally able to tag in Beefcake, but the official was knocked down in all the in-ring chaos. I.R.S. tried to hit Hogan with Beefcake's mask, but Hogan grabbed it and hit both members of Money, Inc. Unfortunately, an official saw what Hogan did, and disqualified the Hulkster, giving the victory to Money, Inc.

While the Hulkster and Brutus Beefcake did not win the match, Hogan's signature post-match celebration thrilled the audience. Most were unaware that they would see Hulk Hogan in the ring again later in the event.

A Legendary Hero Faces The Bad Guy

Other than the great Bruno Sammartino, no one had a longer continuous reign as WWE Champion than Bob Backlund, but he had left WWE before the *WrestleMania* era began. His return to WWE allowed him to finally compete in a *WrestleMania* match, but he would face one of WWE's biggest upcoming Superstars, "The Bad Guy," Razor Ramon.

At the beginning of the match, Backlund tried to offer Ramon a handshake in a show of sportsmanship, but the Bad Guy just laughed and flicked his toothpick in Backlund's face. The combatants locked up twice before Ramon was able to throw Backlund into the corner and then hammer him with several blows and consecutive slams. Backlund turned the tide with a pair of hip tosses, a double underhook suplex, and a devastating Atomic Drop that showed Backlund's impressive strength. Backlund looked to further punish Ramon by getting ready to scoop Razor up for another slam, but Ramon countered the move into an inside cradle, stunning the accomplished wrestler by beating him with a wrestling move.

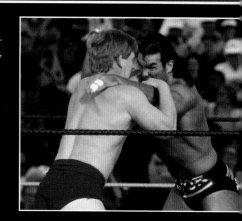

The Intercontinental Championship

The Native American Superstar Tatanka, appearing in his second *WrestleMania*, was still undefeated in his time at WWE. He was looking to turn his winning streak into championship gold when he challenged Intercontinental Champion Shawn Michaels at *WrestleMania VIII*. The champion's former manager, Sensational Sherri, accompanied Tatanka to the ring. The champion was then accompanied to the ring by the deranged Luna Vachon, and while the action occurred in the ring between champion and challenger, the two managers outside the ring seemed destined for a physical confrontation as well.

Leading into their match, Tatanka had to feel some confidence in his title chances, as he had previously pinned the Heartbreak Kid in both a non-title match and a six-man tag match. Michaels took control early with a standing headlock, but Tatanka eventually turned the move into a suplex, and was able to chop Michaels out of the ring. He then used a series of chops to knock the champion off the ring apron every time Michaels tried to get back into the ring. Michaels eventually used an illegal thumb to Tatanka's eye to get back in, and then the match became a close series of moves and counter moves. Tatanka, slamming the Heartbreak Kid off a top-rope move, came very close to obtaining a three count, but Michaels kicked out at the last minute. Michaels tried to hit Tatanka with a high-risk move outside the ring, but missed and hit his head on the ring steps, leading to Michaels being counted out. Tatanka continued with his undefeated streak, but did not win the title. Things got even worse for Tatanka when his ring escort Sherri was brutally attacked by Luna, who continued the assault later in the night.

▶ *Tatanka attempts to pin Shawn Michaels for the win*

The Steiner Brothers vs. the Headshrinkers

The Steiner Brothers, Rick and Scott, had already made their names in the world of professional wrestling as one of the great tag teams of all time, but they were finally making their *WrestleMania* debut. Their opponents, also making their first appearance at *WrestleMania*, were descendants of tag team royalty, as both were related to WWE Hall of Famers, The Wild Samoans. Afa, one half of that duo, served as their manager. With their wild brawling style and willingness to inflict, as well as receive, pain, Samu and Fatu of The Headshrinkers were going to be a tough challenge for the Michigan All-Americans.

▶ *Scott Steiner gains the upper hand on Samu*

While the Steiners grabbed early control with their unique Steiner Line attacks, eventually The Headshrinkers managed to toss Scott outside the ring, where Fatu and Afa attacked him with illegal moves and blows. Rolling Scott back into the ring, the two Samoans punished him repeatedly, and almost gained a three-count on several occasions. Scott finally managed to avoid a top-rope headbutt from Samu and tagged his brother in to change the flow of the match. Scott then hit a Frankensteiner to pin Samu and get the victory for his team.

Crush vs. Doink

In the months leading to *WrestleMania IX*, newcomer Doink had been giving clowns everywhere a bad name, playing mean tricks on the young fans of WWE. Crush had enough of the abusive clown, so he sought to stop Doink by beating him in a match. Doink begged off the confrontation, showing up with his arm in a sling. But when Crush turned his back, Doink revealed the injured arm was in fact a fake and he beat Crush with the phony limb. Crush looked for revenge at *WrestleMania IX*, but Doink ominously warned that after their *WrestleMania* clash, Crush would be "seeing double."

Crush took early control of the match, using his strength to punish Doink for all his recent misdeeds. Several times Doink tried to hit Crush with knife-edge chops, but they seemed to have no effect on the massive Hawaiian Superstar. While Doink did manage to hit Crush with some wrestling maneuvers, Crush locked the demented clown in his head-crushing vice grip, but Doink's thrashing knocked out the referee. Realizing he couldn't get the pin until the ref came to, Crush decided to further injure Doink with another vice grip. That's when Doink's "seeing double" prediction became clear—a second Doink made his way to the ring, and he nailed Crush again with the fake arm. As the referee woke up, the second Doink hid under the ring, and the original clown obtained the pinfall victory.

Undertaker vs. Giant Gonzales

Part of Undertaker's mystique is the way he towers over his opponents. In Giant Gonzales, The Deadman faced an opponent almost a foot taller than him. Brought to the WWE by Harvey Wippleman to gain revenge on Undertaker, Gonzales had first made an impression on the WWE Universe when he eliminated Undertaker from the 1993 *Royal Rumble*. From that moment their clash at *WrestleMania IX* was inevitable.

As the two faced each other in the ring, Gonzales used his height advantage to rain clubbing blows down on Undertaker. Although the attacks did not seem to affect Undertaker at first, the continued blows eventually brought him down to a knee. Undertaker was able to recover and take control of the match, cornering Gonzales and punching and kicking the Giant. Gonzales eventually nailed Undertaker with an impressive kick and took control of the match. But after every powerful move knocked Undertaker down, The Deadman would sit right back up. Realizing that typical wrestling moves would not allow his client to beat Undertaker, Wippleman tossed Gonzales a chloroform-soaked rag. While the Giant used the rag to knock out Undertaker, the referee saw what Gonzales had done and disqualified the enormous Superstar, giving Undertaker the victory. WWE officials took Undertaker out of the ring on a stretcher while Gonzales paraded around the ring gloating. The Giant's joy ended when Undertaker came racing back and attacked him, knocking Gonzales out of the ring.

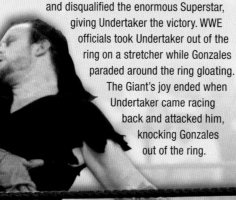

Mr. Perfect vs. Lex Lugar

Lex Lugar had been in a motorcycle accident requiring doctors to place a metal plate in his arm to help the broken bones heal. Unfortunately for the rest of WWE, that metal plate made Luger's forearm smash, already an impressive move, a knockout blow. Several Superstars felt the force of the metal plate, but Mr. Perfect was determined to become the first man to avoid the knockout and pin The Narcissist.

Their match at *WrestleMania IX* was a clash of styles. Perfect was a master of scientific wrestling, while Luger relied on power moves that took advantage of his amazing physique. After an opening exchange of traded wristlocks, the two men traded offense, with Luger focusing on Perfect's lower back, exploiting an injury that had kept Perfect out of competition for months. Luger got Mr. Perfect in a backslide, but Mr. Perfect managed to get his feet on the ring ropes. The official, missing that detail, counted the pin and awarded the victory to Lex Luger. Mr. Perfect went to argue with the official, but Luger took advantage of a distracted Mr. Perfect and nailed him with his steel-plated forearm. When he came to, an enraged Mr. Perfect raced backstage to confront Luger, but Shawn Michaels attacked Perfect from behind, launching a heated rivalry between the two Superstars.

A NEW RUMBLE RULE

The *Royal Rumble* had become famous for helping to set the stage for *WrestleMania*. The 1993 *Royal Rumble* was the first to stipulate that the WWE Superstar who won was entitled to a WWE Championship Match at *WrestleMania*. When Yokozuna eliminated Randy Savage at the *Royal Rumble*, the main event of *WrestleMania IX* was set: WWE Champion Bret "Hit Man" Hart would defend his prized title against the gargantuan Sumo wrestler, Yokozuna.

Standing at 6'4" and weighing more than 500 pounds, Yokozuna was a tremendous athlete who was known for his agility, strength, and balance in the ring. As a merciless villain, Yokozuna, along with his manager Mr. Fuji, struck fear in the hearts of WWE fans.

Bret Hart remembers, "Yoko and I had a really good chemistry. One of the keys to a match with him was pacing. You wanted to make sure there were points along the way he could catch his breath. Yoko worked really hard in the ring and could move so fast for someone his size. He was a great athlete."

Reclaiming the Title

As the "Hit Man" prepared to walk through the curtain of his first *WrestleMania* main event, he still couldn't believe the phone call he had received 48 hours earlier. Bret Hart thinks back, "Vince asked me to come to his room at Caesars. He then explained to me what was going to happen with Hulk, that there was a change in the main event and Hogan was going to leave *WrestleMania* the champion. I was just shocked."

While on paper the match clearly did not favor "The Hit Man," Hart worked hard to collaborate with Yokozuna to tell a thrilling story. The combination of Yokozuna's crushing offense and Hart's unmatched skills resulted in a battle that kept the audience on the edge of their seats from the moment the bell rang.

The sight of the "Hit Man" putting Yokozuna in the Sharpshooter was unbelievable. The events that followed, which began with Mr. Fuji throwing salt in the champion's face, resulting in a pinfall, were astonishing.

Hulk Hogan entered the ring to explain to the referee what happened and come to the aid of a "blinded" Bret Hart. A boastful Mr. Fuji challenged Hogan to a match on the spot. Once Hogan received the okay from the "Hit Man," the crowd erupted. When Fuji's plan of blinding Hogan with his ceremonial salt backfired, Hogan sent Yokozuna down with a clothesline followed by the famous Leg Drop. With the audience's deafening roar behind him, Hulk Hogan became the WWE Champion for the fifth time.

Bret Hart left Las Vegas disappointed. He explains, "If Vince said to me, 'We're bringing Hulk back and we need to put the title back on him,' and explain to me what they had in mind rather than letting me think I was doing a great job, I wouldn't have had a problem with it. While Hulk was back we didn't speak until it was time to go over the finish for the match. Everything was very friendly. He thanked me and said he'd be happy to return the favor. And I said, again in a friendly way, 'I'm going to remember that and hold you to it.' It never happened. I think that set the stage for a lot of things."

The title victory was part of a Hulk Hogan story that once again sent massive roars through the *WrestleMania* crowd. Whether the deafening response from the capacity crowd was partly out of shock, or partly due to their hero wearing WWE gold for the fifth occasion, the moment reaffirmed that in the magic of *WrestleMania*, anything can happen.

HALL OF FAME

In March of 1993, a touching video tribute to André the Giant aired on WWE programming. This wonderful career retrospective, shown days after the legend passed away, heralded the creation of WWE's own Hall of Fame. As the ultimate reflection of admiration, the "Eighth Wonder of the World" would be its first inductee.

Sixteen months later, the premier WWE Hall of Fame ceremony was held on June 18, 1994, the night before the King of the Ring pay-per-view in Baltimore, Maryland. As Regis Philbin served as Master of Ceremony, distinguished figures like "Classy" Freddie Blassie, "Nature Boy" Buddy Rogers, Arnold Skaaland, Bobo Brazil, Chief Jay Strongbow, Gorilla Monsoon, and James Dudley took their rightful places alongside André. The next two years saw Hall of Fame induction ceremonies before the event went into hiatus.

Since 2004, on the eve of the Showcase of the Immortals, WWE has enshrined sports entertainment's most revered figures in its Hall of Fame. Today, with more than 190 sports entertainment icons immortalized, even including a Celebrity Wing, the WWE Hall of Fame induction ceremony is one of the most eagerly anticipated traditions of *WrestleMania* Week's thrilling events.

CLASS OF 1993

▶ *André the Giant*

CLASS OF 1994

Buddy Rogers was the original "Nature Boy" and the first WWE Champion. Rogers is credited with inventing the Figure-Four Grapevine, which later became the Figure-Four Leglock. He is one of the few men to hold both the NWA World Heavyweight Championship and the WWE Championship.

▶ *"Nature Boy" Buddy Rogers*

▶ *Arnold Skaaland*

▶ *Bobo Brazil*

▶ *"Classy" Freddie Blassie*

▶ *Gorilla Monsoon*

▶ *Chief Jay Strongbow*

▶ *James Dudley*

CLASS OF 1995

A television star, Rocca was sports entertainment's first high-flyer. He invented the dropkick, and his acrobatic style endeared him to wrestling fans all over the world. Rocca's popularity was so great that he appeared on the cover of DC Comics' "The Downfall of Superman" in 1962 opposite the Man of Steel.

During a 50-year career, the Fabulous Moolah's 28-year reign as Women's Champion is the longest title reign in history. She was later honored as the "Queen of WWE," and fittingly became the first female Hall of Fame inductee.

▶ *The Grand Wizard*   ▶ *Ivan Putski*

▶ *Ernie Ladd*   ▶ *Pedro Morales*

◀ *Fabulous Moolah*

▶ *George "The Animal" Steele*   ▶ *Antonino "Argentina" Rocca*

CLASS OF 1996

With his unique concept of professional wrestling, Vincent J. McMahon embraced the advent of television in the 1950s as a way to draw larger crowds to his live events. In 1963, McMahon did the unthinkable and broke away from the National Wrestling Alliance to form the company known today as WWE.

▶ Baron Mikel Scicluna

▶ "Captain" Lou Albano

▶ Jimmy "Superfly" Snuka

▶ Johnny Rodz

▶ Killer Kowalski

▶ Pat Patterson

▶ The Valiant Brothers

▶ Vincent J. McMahon

CLASS OF 2005

Paul Orndorff was despised by fans because of his intensity and arrogance. The master of the Piledriver was part of the main event at the first *WrestleMania*. He set an attendance record when 70,000 fans packed Toronto's CNE Stadium to see "Mr. Wonderful" battle Hulk Hogan for the WWE Championship.

CLASS OF 2004

"The Brain" engineered some of the most memorable careers in sports entertainment and referred to the Superstars under his tutelage as members of "The Heenan Family." Along with Gorilla Monsoon, he subsequently achieved fame as a broadcast journalist on WWE programming. "The Brain" is regarded as the greatest manager of all time, but don't ever call him "Weasel."

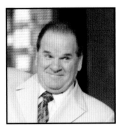
▶ Pete Rose

▶ Big John Studd

▶ Don Muraco

▶ Sgt. Slaughter

▶ Bobby "The Brain" Heenan

▶ Harley Race

▶ Tito Santana

▶ Junkyard Dog

▶ Greg "The Hammer" Valentine

▶ Jesse "The Body" Ventura

▶ "Superstar" Billy Graham

▶ "Cowboy" Bob Orton

▶ Hulk Hogan

▶ The Iron Sheik

▶ "Mr. Wonderful" Paul Orndorff

▶ Nikolai Volkoff

▶ "Rowdy" Roddy Piper

▶ "Mouth of the South" Jimmy Hart

CLASS OF 2006

Trained by the Fabulous Moolah, Sensational Sherri dominated the ring and held the AWA and WWE Women's Championships. She excelled as a manager for Randy Savage, Ted DiBiase, Shawn Michaels, and Ric Flair, among others. Sherri redefined women's roles in sports entertainment and paved the way for today's WWE Divas.

▶ The Blackjacks

▶ Bret "Hit Man" Hart

▶ "Sensational" Sherri

▶ Eddie Guerrero

▶ "Mean" Gene Okerlund

▶ Tony Atlas

▶ Verne Gagne

▶ William Perry

CLASS OF 2007

"The American Dream" first rose to fame as one-half of the Texas Outlaws. Rhodes was a force in front of the camera as a three-time NWA World Heavyweight Champion, and behind the scenes creating events for the NWA and WCW. "The Dream"'s magnetism drew fans into arenas. His famous WWE rivalries included "Superstar" Billy Graham, Randy Savage, and Ted DiBiase.

▶ Jim Ross

▶ Dusty Rhodes

▶ The Sheik

▶ Mr. Fuji

▶ "Mr. Perfect" Curt Hennig

▶ Nick Bockwinkel

▶ The Wild Samoans

▶ Jerry "The King" Lawler

CLASS OF 2008

"The greatest compliment I ever received was from Ed "Strangler" Lewis. He was a World's Champion and he said, 'I don't like girl wrestlers. But after seeing you wrestle, you were born to be a wrestler.'" — Mae Young

▶ Mae Young

▶ The Brisco Brothers

▶ "Nature Boy" Ric Flair

▶ Eddie Graham

▶ Gordon Solie

"High Chief" Peter Maivia

▶ "Soulman" Rocky Johnson

CLASS OF 2009

"My rewards are not measured in wins and losses. It was about the performance. The match. To know you left everything you had in that ring." — Ricky "The Dragon" Steamboat

▶ Ricky "The Dragon" Steamboat

▶ Cowboy Bill Watts

▶ The Funks

▶ Howard Finkel

▶ Koko B. Ware

▶ Stone Cold Steve Austin

▶ The Von Erich Family

CLASS OF 2010

One of the original stars of American television, Gorgeous George enraged audiences with his platinum blonde hair, lavish robes, and manservant. In addition to inspiring generations of wrestlers, "The Sensation of the Nation" was considered an idol by Muhammad Ali, James Brown, and Bob Dylan. George also made the "Wrestling Wedding" and the Hair Match famous.

▶ Antonio Inoki

▶ Bob Uecker

▶ Wendi Richter

▶ Gorgeous George

▶ "Million Dollar Man" Ted DiBiase

▶ Stu Hart

▶ Maurice "Mad Dog" Vachon

CLASS OF 2011

The Road Warriors' reign of terror began in Georgia Championship Wrestling in the early 1980s and tore through the NWA, AWA, and Japan. In 1991, Animal and Hawk cemented their position as the most dominant tag team in sports entertainment when they won the WWE Tag Team Championship. They are the only team to win tag team gold in the NWA, AWA, Japan, and WWE.

▶ Shawn Michaels

▶ Abdullah the Butcher

▶ "Bullet" Bob Armstrong

▶ Drew Carey

▶ Sunny

▶ "Hacksaw" Jim Duggan

▶ The Road Warriors w/ Paul Ellering

CLASS OF 2012

"There was a day about 25 years ago when four exceptional athletes held all the major championships. Somebody said they should all go out for a TV interview together. The sun and all the planets and the moon and the stars were in perfect alignment that day because something truly magical happened. The Four Horsemen were born." — J.J. Dillon

▶ The Four Horsemen

▶ Yokozuna

▶ Mil Mascaras

▶ Edge

▶ Mike Tyson

▶ Ron Simmons

CLASS OF 2013

Bruno Sammartino was the first true WWE Superstar. The Italian Superman headlined Madison Square Garden 211 times with 187 sell-out events. Sammartino is considered the greatest WWE Champion of all time, with two reigns combining for an unprecedented 11 years. The Living Legend is a hero without equal.

▶ Bob Backlund

▶ Booker T

▶ Trish Stratus

▶ Donald Trump

▶ Mick Foley

▶ Bruno Sammartino

CLASS OF 2014

"I am Warrior. That is my name. I am the creator and performer of the Ultimate Warrior, the one and only Ultimate Warrior. You are the Ultimate Warrior fans. Ultimate Warrior is a legend and the Ultimate Warrior fans; you are legendary. I'm here tonight because of you." — Ultimate Warrior

▶ Ultimate Warrior

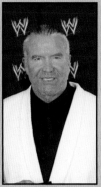
▶ Razor Ramon

▶ Lita

▶ Mr. T

▶ Jake "The Snake" Roberts

▶ Carlos Colón

▶ Paul Bearer

CLASS OF 2015

The Madness finally came to the WWE with the induction of two-time WWE Champion "Macho Man" Randy Savage. In addition, the WWE created the Warrior Award, which honors individuals that have overcome adversity and demonstrated the strength reminiscent of The Ultimate Warrior. The first honoree was Connor "The Crusher" Michalek, who had passed away in April of the previous year.

▶ Randy Savage

▶ Rikishi

▶ Alundra Blayze

▶ Larry Zbyszko

▶ Tatsumi Fujinami

▶ Kevin Nash

▶ The Bushwhackers

▶ Arnold Schwarzenegger

CLASS OF 2016

A year after making his WrestleMania debut, WCW's franchise Superstar Sting made his way to the WWE Hall of Fame. The six-time WCW World Champion was joined by tag team innovators The Fabulous Freebirds; the trio that introduced the "Freebird Rule" to tag team competition that The New Day uses to this day.

▶ Fabulous Freebirds

▶ Snoop Dogg

▶ Jacqueline

▶ Stan Hansen

▶ Big Boss Man

▶ Sting

▶ Godfather

CLASS OF 2017

Kurt Angle returned to WWE after a more than 10 year absence. The Olympic gold medalist and six-time World Champion celebrated his induction into the Hall of Fame by chugging two bottles of milk. Former Rutgers University football star Eric LeGrand was honored with the Warrior Award for his motivational work since he was paralyzed on the football field.

▶ Beth Phoenix

▶ DDP

▶ Kurt Angle

▶ Rick Rude

▶ Rock 'N' Roll Express

▶ Teddy Long

CLASS OF 2018

f the question "who's next?" was being asked about the WWE Hallof Fame, the answer in 2018 was "Goldberg." One of the most dominant Superstars in WCW history, Goldberg amassed an unthinkable 173-0 winning streak to start his career, a run that included winning the WCW World Heavyweight Championship. The Hall of Fame also welcomed the most decorated tag team in history, The Dudley Boyz, the only team to win the ECW, WCW, and WWE Tag Team Championships.

▶ Goldberg

▶ Hillbilly Jim

▶ Ivory

▶ Kid Rock

▶ Dudley Boyz

▶ Mark Henry

▶ Jeff Jarrett

CLASS OF 2019

After helping WWE win the Monday Night Wars and making the McMahons' life a living hell, D-Generation X finally took their place among the all-time greats. The inclusion of DX made Shawn Michaels a two-time Hall of Famer, joining Ric Flair, but Michaels wasn't the only one that night. Harlem Heat's induction also made Booker T a two-time Hall of Famer, as well as Bret "Hit Man" Hart who was inducted as one-half of the Hart Foundation.

▶ D-Generation X (with Chyna)

▶ Harlem Heat

▶ Torrie Wilson

▶ The Honky Tonk Man

▶ The Hart Foundation

▶ Brutus "The Barber" Beefcake

WRESTLEMANIA X

MADISON SQUARE GARDEN – NEW YORK, NY

April 4
1994

Attendance
16,891

ANNOUNCERS
Jerry "The King" Lawler, Vince McMahon

RING ANNOUNCERS
Bill Dunn, Howard Finkel

LOCKER ROOM CORRESPONDENT
Todd Pettengill

SPECIAL GUEST RING ANNOUNCERS
Donnie Wahlberg, Burt Reynolds

SPECIAL GUEST TIME KEEPERS
Rhonda Shear, Jennie Garth

SPECIAL HAIR CONSULTANT
Sy Sperling

WWE RADIO ANNOUNCERS
Chet Coppock, Gorilla Monsoon

Event Card

MAIN EVENT – WWE CHAMPIONSHIP MATCH
- Bret "Hit Man" Hart def. Yokozuna (Champion) w/ Mr. Fuji & Jim Cornette to become new Champion*
  *Special Guest Referee "Rowdy" Roddy Piper

WWE CHAMPIONSHIP MATCH
- Yokozuna (Champion) w/ Mr. Fuji & Jim Cornette def. Lex Luger*
  *Special Guest Referee Mr. Perfect

INTERCONTINENTAL CHAMPIONSHIP – LADDER MATCH "CHAMPION VERSUS CHAMPION"
- Razor Ramon (Champion) def. Shawn Michaels (Champion) w/ Diesel to become new Champion

PINFALLS COUNT ANYWHERE, LAST MAN STANDING MATCH
- Randy "Macho Man" Savage def. Crush

TAG TEAM CHAMPIONSHIP MATCH
- Men On A Mission (Mabel & Mo) w/ Oscar def. The Quebecers (Jacques & Pierre) w/ Johnny Polo

MIXED TAG TEAM MATCH
- Bam Bam Bigelow & Luna Vachon def. Doink & Dink

WOMEN'S CHAMPIONSHIP MATCH
- Alundra Blayze (Champion) def. Leilani Kai

OTHER MATCHES
- Owen Hart def. Bret "Hit Man" Hart
- Earthquake def. Adam Bomb w/ Harvey Wippleman

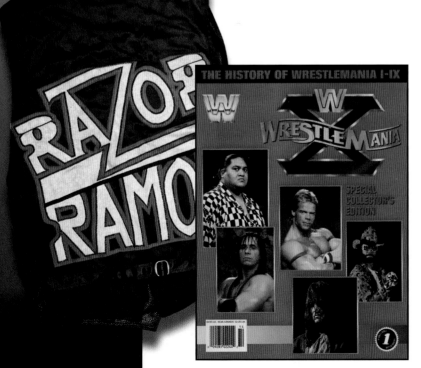

"The Garden is the Garden!"

—Vince McMahon

Chaos at the Rumble

The 1994 *Royal Rumble* proved to be a busy night for Bret Hart, and WWE Officials. After months of trying to make amends with his brother Owen, Bret had his injured leg kicked-in by his younger sibling, setting the stage for a match at *WrestleMania X*.

Later in the card, controversy filled the Civic Center in Providence, Rhode Island. A new kind of history was made when Lex Luger, who would receive a WWE Championship Match at *WrestleMania* if he won the *Rumble*, was one of two remaining participants along with Bret Hart. The two heroes fought for the chance to go to *WrestleMania* when suddenly, they eliminated each other. After referees deliberated, it was announced that for the first time in *Royal Rumble* history, there were two co-winners.

President Jack Tunney decided that both Bret Hart and Lex Luger would get title shots at *WrestleMania X*, but they would each need to wrestle two matches at the event. Lex Luger won a coin toss which gave him the right to face Yokozuna first. The "Hit Man" was required to wrestle Owen.

Preparing for a New Era

WWE sought to honor *WrestleMania*'s past, while also celebrating its future. "The Fan Festival" was one of the initial concepts created to achieve just that. WrestleMania X was a very special weekend for WWE and its fans. They wanted to add something to the weekend that furthered the WrestleMania experience. WWE hosted autograph sessions, video game booths, product displays, and that was the first time fans could have their voice recorded announcing a classic WWE match. Fans could also interact with WWE personalities, something which had never been done before.

In the final hours leading up to the event, the new Fan Festival was the perfect way to ensure The Big Apple was ready for *WrestleMania*. Tickets for *WrestleMania X* sold out in less than one hour— all of Madison Square Garden. WWE opened the Paramount Theater and people could pay $20 to watch what was going on live upstairs on closed-circuit; those 5,000 seats were soon sold out. The Fan Festival drew more than 30,000 people, so by the time *WrestleMania* Sunday arrived and the fans were in their seats, Madison Square Garden was rocking.

▶ *Randy Savage signing autographs at the Fan Festival*

The fans who attended the closed-circuit screening got a surprise: an impromptu meet-and-greet with Randy "Macho Man" Savage. WWE realized the Paramount had sold out and wanted to give those people a little something special. The company knew that those fans could've just ordered *WrestleMania* on pay-per-view, but they wanted to come to the building. So when Randy Savage came out from behind the giant screen, the fans went absolutely nuts. Savage was always very happy to sign autographs and meet the fans, even in a situation like this one where it was a last minute decision after his *WrestleMania* match.

Brother Against Brother

No contest could have provided a bigger opening bang than the battle between two brothers. The match between the "Hit Man" and his brother Owen continued to thrill the crowd as these two glorious storytellers wove their tale. Vince McMahon elaborates, "The Owen-Bret situation was very interesting because in a lot of respects Owen was as good as Bret, but again living in the shadow of his brother, I don't think that was the easiest thing for Owen to do in this business. ... You could see the rivalry, and it wasn't something like brother hates brother, it wasn't like that at all, and it wasn't even portrayed like that. It was more of a natural rivalry between two brothers. I don't think that Owen and Bret had a cross word between the two of them. Bret was always Owen's brother, yet in the ring the two of them had such great technical skills and storytelling skills that they could make you believe anything in the world."

Bret Hart reflects, "I remember saying to Owen, 'We're old school. We don't ride together, we don't sit in the bar, we don't talk to each other. If we do this, we don't insult anybody's intelligence. If we do this right, it will work really well.' We were not on the same planes, we never rode together, we didn't talk to each other. We'd be the only two guys in the airport and wouldn't talk to each other. I remember the customs people flagged us down and we were being detained and searched. Owen said something to me and I leaned over nonchalantly and said something to him and the lady came out and said, 'I caught you.' I think that's why they stopped us. They wanted to see if what they saw on TV was true. They set us up to see if we could talk. They got such a big charge out of it. It just goes to show you how serious we took this stuff. There is a certain beauty carrying that off and doing it as well as we did."

Climbing the Ladder

By 1994, Shawn Michaels, "The Heartbreak Kid," was considered one of the top performers in all of sports-entertainment. He was recognized as a top singles performer and a main attraction as Intercontinental Champion.

Razor Ramon, portrayed by Scott Hall, took WWE by storm upon his arrival in 1992. While the 6'8", 280-pound powerhouse had made a name for himself in wrestling circles before coming to WWE, it was his portrayal of Razor Ramon in WWE which made him a star.

Shawn Michaels was in the midst of a thrilling series of matches with Razor Ramon for the Intercontinental Championship when Michaels was suspended. Vince McMahon ordered Michaels to return the title, but he refused. HBK remembers, "This was when I was going into my 'Nobody's going to tell me what to do' phase." Since Michaels refused to return it, WWE made another title. After serving his suspension, Michaels returned, title in hand. This created a question of who was the real Intercontinental Champion—a question that could only be settled in a Ladder Match at *WrestleMania*.

▶ **Shawn Michaels with the Intercontinental Championship**

Both Shawn Michaels and Razor Ramon knew that having the first-ever Ladder Match at *WrestleMania* meant giving the crowd a great show, but neither viewed it as an opportunity to write history. Shawn Michaels recalls, "I never once went into it thinking, 'This is the one.'"

From the start, the match was truly a spectacle. The two Intercontinental Championships were suspended 15 feet above the ring, and the 10-foot aluminum ladder stood in the Superstars' entrance aisle. Once the ladder made it into the action, the crowd reacted like they were on the receiving end of every blow. And as the Superstars began to climb the ladder, the tension heightened with every rung.

Michaels remembers, "There's nobody else I could've done that match with on that night but Scott Hall. He's a 6'8", 280-pound stud that went out there and worked his tail off for me. We knew each other like the back of our hands; he trusted me and I trusted him. ... I think Scott and I did a great job. It was one of those situations where everything aligned."

▶ **Razor Ramon with the Intercontinental Championship**

Though Ramon claimed the victory, the performances from both "The Heartbreak Kid" and Razor Ramon displayed some of the most exhilarating athletic ability and palpable drama ever seen in sports-entertainment history. The Ladder Match at *WrestleMania X* inspired generations of future performers. Jerry "The King" Lawler recalls, "For a lot of people this was the first Ladder Match they were seeing. No one, including Vince and myself, really knew what to expect. It seemed like every step Shawn and Razor took in that match was revolutionizing the business."

Mixed Tag Team Match

In the year since *WrestleMania IX*, the WWE Universe had come to embrace Doink the Clown, particularly after Doink stopped playing pranks on young WWE fans and instead targeted some WWE Superstars. Doink started bringing a smaller clown to the ring with him. This sidekick was known as Dink, who helped Doink play his tricks and jokes. Bam Bam Bigelow had enough of Doink and his companion and wanted to get his hands on both, so a unique mixed tag match was set for *WrestleMania X*, where Doink and Dink would team up to face Bam Bam Bigelow and Luna Vachon.

To protect Dink, the match had specific rules. Doink could only face Bam Bam, and Dink could square off against Luna, so if one side tagged in, the other had to as well. Doink and Bam Bam started off, with Doink getting the better of the Beast from the East at first. Just when Bam Bam was going to get some revenge, Doink tagged in Dink, which forced Bigelow out of the match. Luna tried to get her hands on Dink, but he proved to be quick and slippery, dodging her attacks. She finally got a hold of him and slammed the miniature clown. Doink and Bam Bam re-entered the match, and even though Doink nailed Bigelow with an impressive DDT, the clown couldn't keep the Beast from the East down. He pinned Doink after a top-rope diving headbutt.

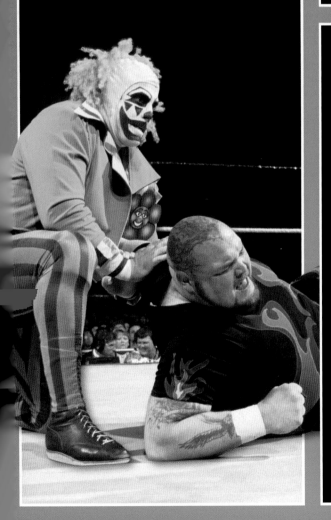

A Betrayal Avenged

After an enduring friendship between Crush and Randy Savage, Crush turned his back on the Macho Man as well as the entire WWE Universe by aligning himself with Mr. Fuji. The former friends' enmity was so great that they decided to settle things at *WrestleMania X* with a Falls Count Anywhere Match. The unique rules of the bout stated that once a man was pinned, he had to make it back to the ring within 60 seconds or he'd lose.

Savage wasted no time, choosing to attack Crush before the Hawaiian Superstar could even make it to the ring. It was an unwise choice as Crush countered Savage's early attacks and slammed the Macho Man on the concrete and then dropped him on a guard rail. Gaining the pin, it looked like the match would be over soon, but Savage made it back to the ring with seconds to spare. Crush looked to finish Savage by throwing salt in the Macho Man's face, but the plan backfired and Savage pinned Crush outside the ring. Crush barely made it back in time. Then things got even more brutal as the match spilled out of the ring and into the arena. Savage pinned Crush again and tied Crush's legs so he couldn't return to the ring, giving Savage the unique victory.

The WWE Women's Championship

After being inactive for three years, WWE revived the WWE Women's Championship in 1993 with a tournament to crown a new champion. WWE newcomer Alundra Blayze won the tournament and was set to battle all comers. At *WrestleMania X*, Blayze was set to defend the championship against the woman that defended the title at the inaugural *WrestleMania* event, also held at Madison Square Garden, Leilani Kai. Kai had lost the title at that first event, but she had every intention of leaving *WrestleMania X* as the WWE Women's Champion.

While Blayze was the better technical wrestler, Kai had an advantage in the power department, and used it to trap Alundra in an illegal choke move. Blaze then slammed Kai and nailed the challenger with an overhead suplex into a bridge pin, obtaining the three-count and successfully defending her championship at *WrestleMania X*.

The World Tag Team Championship

Since the middle of 1993, the Quebecers were the dominant tag team in WWE. With the exception of a seven-day reign by Marty Jannetty and the 1-2-3 Kid, the Canadian pair was in the midst of a six-month reign as the World Tag Team Champions heading into *WrestleMania X*. Their opponents were perhaps the largest pair they would face during their reign. Men on a Mission (or MOM) were made up of Mo, a massive competitor, and Mabel, who dwarfed his partner in size. The duo came to the ring with their rapping manager, Oscar, who was an effective counter to the Quebecer's manager, Johnny Polo.

Mo and Mabel got off to an effective start against Pierre, and the two effectively made quick tags and hit some double-team moves. Eventually this led to a change of momentum, as while the referee was ensuring Mabel left the ring, Jacques came in and attacked Mo while the official was not watching. The Quebecers were able to keep Mo isolated from his corner, and obtained several two counts, but they couldn't quite finish off the challengers. Mo tagged in his partner, but the Quebecers were able to get Mabel up and suplex the enormous superstar. The Quebecers still couldn't keep Men on a Mission down for a three-count. Men on a Mission, however, did hit Jacques with their stacked Big Splash, and should have won the match, but Johnny Polo occupied the referee long enough for Jacques to recover. Pierre and Jacques were outside of the ring long enough for the referee to award Men on a Mission a countout victory, which unfortunately was not enough to win them the World Tag Team Championship.

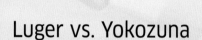

Luger vs. Yokozuna

The first WWE Championship match kept the Madison Square Garden crowd clutching their seats. Yokozuna was the dominant champion set to eliminate the challenge of "Made in the USA" Lex Luger. Despite the rumors blazing through the sports-entertainment business that Lex Luger was going to leave *WrestleMania* the WWE Champion, his loss to Yokozuna meant "The Lex Express" had come to a halt.

Earthquake vs. Adam Bomb

Harvey Wippleman was ready to introduce to the Madison Square Garden crowd the latest giant in his managerial stable, Adam Bomb. But first, Wippleman had some choice insults for the ring announcer, Howard Finkel. He insulted the future Hall of Famer and mocked Howard's new hair. Wippleman then ripped the Fink's tuxedo, which was a step too far and Howard responded by shoving the mouthy manager to the ground. While it probably felt great for Howard to stand up to Wippleman, it led to Adam Bomb coming to the ring, ready to assault Finkel. Luckily for Howard, Bomb's *WrestleMania X* opponent, Earthquake, came to the ring and stopped Adam Bomb before he could do anything. Earthquake suplexed Bomb to the mat, delivered his Earthquake Splash, and collected the pinfall victory in less than a minute. While it wasn't a *WrestleMania* record, it was an impressive feat for the massive Earthquake.

A Double Header

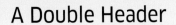

The main event truly embodied the term "Double Header" for both Bret Hart and Yokozuna. This was the second consecutive year the two Superstars met in the main event of *WrestleMania*. This match would also be the second time both Superstars performed on the *WrestleMania X* card, and for Yokozuna, it was the second consecutive *WrestleMania* that required him to compete twice. In celebration of the tenth *WrestleMania*, the match began with a thunderous ovation as the surprise Special Guest Referee, "Rowdy" Roddy Piper, once again made his way to the ring for a main event at *WrestleMania*.

The two Superstars clashed until Yokozuna climbed the turnbuckle for his infamous Banzai Drop. The reigning champion fell backwards onto the mat, giving Hart the opportunity to pin the large Superstar and win the title.

In the end, the "Hit Man" proved he was a survivor and displayed incredible strength, perseverance, and fortitude. In victory and as the new WWE Champion, Bret Hart's performance defined this new era of WWE Superstar. In a symbol of respect, WWE Superstars came to the ring and carried Hart on their shoulders in celebration.

This gesture signified that the Superstar whose WWE career began in 1985 as part of the Hart Foundation was now their guy. Bret Hart reflects, "I think I was looked at as an interim champion, like, 'Let him hold it until we find the right guy, the next super draw.' Like I was the hard-working, trustworthy guy that could hold it. But when I realized that the company went with me over Lex, it went into a different chapter. The guys coming out after the match felt very genuine. It was a magical night for me." By the response from the Madison Square Garden crowd, they could not have agreed more.

WRESTLEMANIA XI

HARTFORD CIVIC CENTER – HARTFORD, CT

April 2
1995

Attendance
16,305

ANNOUNCERS
Jerry "The King" Lawler
Vince McMahon

RING ANNOUNCERS
Howard Finkel

SPECIAL FIELD CORRESPONDENTS
Jim Ross, Todd Pettengill, Nicholas Turturro

SPECIAL CELEBRITY GUESTS
Jenny McCarthy, Pamela Anderson

SPECIAL MUSICAL GUESTS
Salt-n-Pepa

SPECIAL GUEST RING ANNOUNCER
Nicholas Turturro

SPECIAL GUEST TIME KEEPER
Jonathan Taylor Thomas

Event Card

MAIN EVENT – SPECIAL GRUDGE MATCH
- Lawrence Taylor w/ Carl Banks, Chris Spielman, Ken Norton, Reggie White, Rickey Jackson, Steve McMichael def. Bam Bam Bigelow w/ The All-Million Dollar Team (Kama, King Kong Bundy, Irwin R. Schyster, Nikolai Volkoff, Tatanka)

WWE CHAMPIONSHIP MATCH
- Diesel (Champion) w/ Pamela Anderson def. Shawn Michaels w/ Jenny McCarthy

"I QUIT" SUBMISSION MATCH
- Bret "Hit Man" Hart def. Bob Backlund*
  *Special Guest Referee "Rowdy" Roddy Piper

TAG TEAM CHAMPIONSHIP MATCH
- Owen Hart & Yokozuna w/ Jim Cornette and Mr. Fuji def. The Smoking Gunns (Bart Gunn & Billy Gunn) to become new Champions

INTERCONTINENTAL CHAMPIONSHIP MATCH
- Razor Ramon w/ 1-2-3- Kid def. "Double J" Jeff Jarrett (Champion) w/ The Roadie by disqualification

OTHER MATCHES
- Undertaker w/ Paul Bearer def. King Kong Bundy w/ "Million Dollar Man" Ted DiBiase
- The Allied Powers (British Bulldog & Lex Luger) def. Eli & Jacob Blu w/ Uncle Zebekiah

"Times were changing and I think Vince and the company were beginning to grasp that ..."

—Shawn Michaels

Adding Star Power

Though a Diesel-Shawn Michaels match for the WWE Championship was strong enough to headline *WrestleMania*, Vince McMahon felt it was important to add celebrity star power to *WrestleMania XI* to maximize mainstream exposure. WWE signed Pamela Anderson, Jenny McCarthy, Salt-n-Pepa, Nicholas Turturro, and Jonathan Taylor Thomas to appear. But McMahon still wanted more...

Vince McMahon wanted to recruit a celebrity sports figure. Someone who could come into WWE's environment and bring a certain cachet with them, much like Mr. T did for the first two *WrestleMania*s. McMahon wanted NFL star Lawrence Taylor.

While no one questioned L.T.'s athleticism and charisma, not everyone was sure he should have a singles match at *WrestleMania*. Being a great athlete didn't always guarantee a fluid performance in the ring. It was unanimously agreed that Bam Bam Bigelow was the WWE Superstar who had the talent to work with Taylor. Kevin Nash remembers, "Bam Bam was the guy to have the match with L.T., no doubt about it. He was so talented and he could do so much for a guy his size. Bam Bam would be able to lead that match, and we all knew it." Things got off to a heated start at the 1995 *Royal Rumble* when Bigelow crossed paths with the NFL great and attacked Lawrence Taylor.

Preparing a Super Bowl Champion for *WrestleMania*

The Bam Bam Bigelow-Lawrence Taylor storyline became national news. Taylor's star power coupled with WWE's innate talent at promotion garnered the mainstream media attention that *WrestleMania* had not received in many years. Media outlets like *Sports Illustrated*, the New York *Daily News*, *USA Today*, and ESPN's *SportsCenter*, covered the story's progression to *WrestleMania*. Fans were interested. How would L.T., a football deity, fare in the match itself?

On February 28, 1995, WWE held a press conference in Manhattan at the Harley Davidson Cafe where Lawrence Taylor confirmed that he would be competing at *WrestleMania XI* against "The Beast from the East." This led to a phenomenal outdoor Public Workout in the Times Square Canyon of Heroes. The event featured a fusion of matches, in-ring segments, and a stare-down between Bigelow and L.T. that ended in a pure melee right in the heart of New York City!

That same evening, Vince McMahon arranged for Diesel and L.T. to be at Madison Square Garden for a non-WWE event. Kevin Nash remembers, "Somehow Vince got L.T. and I tickets to go to the Garden to watch Michael Jordan's return game against the Knicks. That was the night Jordan wore number 45 and he scored 55 points against the Knicks. They showed us on the Jumbotron and the crowd went absolutely crazy. L.T. was so loved in New York. It was so great for us to have that association with him."

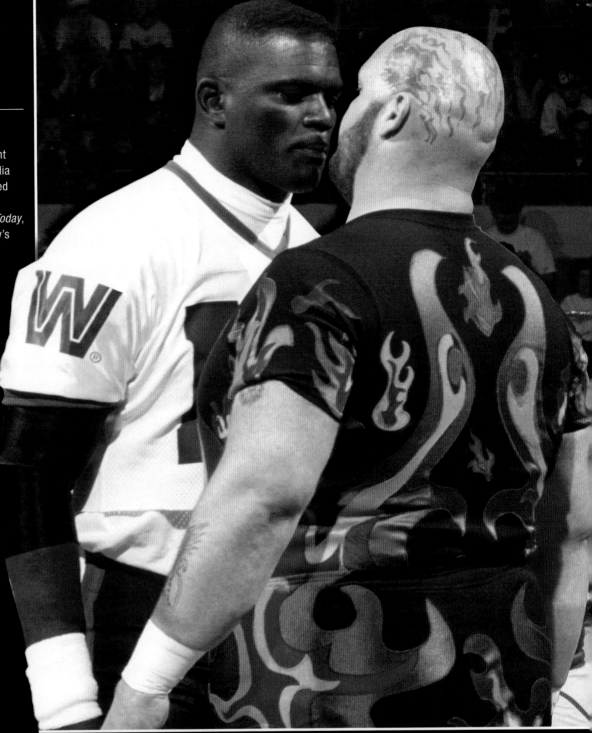

Which is the Main Event?

There was disagreement among some members of the WWE locker room as to which should be the final match of *WrestleMania XI*, the WWE Championship Match pitting Diesel against Shawn Michaels or the Bam Bam Bigelow-L.T. Grudge Match.

Kevin Nash remembers, "Shawn wanted to go on last, and I feel the WWE Championship should always go on last because it's the title. But at the same time, I got the title that November and I hadn't even had 300 matches for my career at that point. I was excited to be there and be in there having a match at *WrestleMania* with my friend."

Vince McMahon remembers, "Oh, it was very risky, putting a non-WWE star in the main event of *WrestleMania*. At the same time, Lawrence Taylor's athleticism is world class. Competing with Bam Bam Bigelow, who at the time as well, his athleticism is world class. It was weighed in terms of design in which you could use the athleticism of Lawrence Taylor and what he could do well, and stay away from what he could not do well as a newcomer to this genre."

"It was very risky, putting a non-WWE star in the main event of *WrestleMania*."

—Vince McMahon

A Different Kind of Superstar

Kevin Nash's basketball background gave him a physical in-ring style that differentiated his Diesel character from most of the giants that preceded him in sports-entertainment. Diesel did not resemble the traditional WWE hero. His mannerisms and persona represented a new direction in WWE character development and storylines. Diesel defeated Bob Backlund in eight seconds to become WWE Champion. "Big Daddy Cool" was in the midst of a break-speed ascent.

According to Shawn Michaels, "Times were changing and I think Vince and the company were beginning to grasp that, but only to a point. Just because villains were getting cheered it didn't mean it was time to switch them to good guys. There was a cool factor to it and that should be ok."

▶ *Diesel defeats Shawn Michaels to retain the WWE Championship*

The Allied Powers vs. Eli & Jacob Blu

Individually, Lex Luger and the British Bulldog were two of the most powerful Superstars in WWE. Together, they were an almost unbeatable team, a multinational pairing whose name harkened back to the days of World War II. They would need all their strength when facing the Blu Brothers, identical twin mountain men who had the added advantage of the ringside assistance of Uncle Zebekiah.

Both teams traded power moves throughout the bout, and the Bulldog and Luger thought they'd won the match repeatedly, only to be frustrated when the brothers used their identical appearance to illegally switch places in the match. Finally, the teamwork of Luger and Bulldog prevailed and they pinned one of the brothers.

▶ *The Allied Superpowers defeat Eli and Jacob Blu at WrestleMania XI*

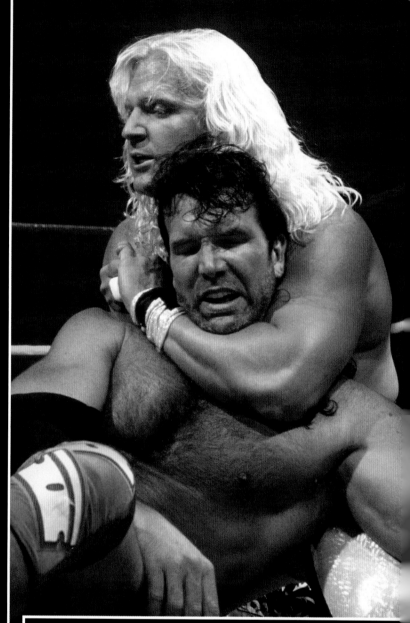

Intercontinental Championship Battle

Self-proclaimed country-music sensation Jeff Jarrett had taken the Intercontinental Championship from Razor Ramon at the 1995 *Royal Rumble*. Jarrett had help—The Roadie had damaged Ramon's knee outside the ring and the injury directly led to his loss. For their *WrestleMania* rematch, Ramon looked to even the odds by adding the 1-2-3 Kid to his corner to watch his back.

The hope was that both sides having a corner man would lead to an equal and fair match, and for the most part, the action was contained within the ring between the two men. Both men came close to pinning their opponent. Jarrett tried to take advantage of Ramon's knee injury by applying a painful Figure Four Leglock. Ramon was able to reverse the move and set Jarrett up for his patented Razor's Edge. The Roadie jumped in the ring and caused a disqualification, and chaos erupted with all four men battling in the ring.

Ramon and Jarrett would continue their bitter rivalry, with each winning the title from the other as the year went on.

Thou Shalt Not Steal

Ted DiBiase and his Million Dollar Corporation had been a thorn in The Deadman's side since that year's *Royal Rumble*. After Undertaker had defeated the Corporation's Irwin R. Schyster, King Kong Bundy confronted Undertaker, but it was just a distraction so that Schyster could steal (or "repossess") the urn that was thought to serve as the basis of Undertaker's power. Undertaker was ready to gain a measure of revenge by facing Bundy at *WrestleMania*.

Despite it being only the fourth match of Undertaker's *WrestleMania* career, the announcers may have been a bit prescient, as they mentioned early in the match that The Deadman had yet to lose at *WrestleMania*. Ted DiBiase, in Bundy's corner, looked to get under the skin of Undertaker by carrying the urn to the ring. Early in the match, Bundy was able to knock Undertaker out of the ring, but that backfired, as The Deadman landed near DiBiase and seized the urn back, giving it to Paul Bearer. The reunion was short-lived, as another member of the corporation, Kama, stole the urn back, promising that he was going to melt it down and wear it on a chain around his neck.

The distraction of losing the urn a second time allowed Bundy to gain the upper hand for a bit, but King Kong's luck did not last. The Deadman was able to pin Bundy after a big boot and a slam. It would be several months before Undertaker could gain revenge against Kama, as the two would settle their score in a Casket Match at *SummerSlam 1995*.

A Big Mystery

While reigning champions the Smoking Gunns had granted Owen Hart a shot at the World Tag Team Championship at *WrestleMania XI*, Owen decided to keep everyone in the dark about the identity of his partner, keeping it a big secret until the match itself. Big was the operative word, as Owen was able to pair with the massive two-time WWE Champion Yokozuna that night. No one had seen the Sumo warrior since the previous year's *Survivor Series*. The Gunns appeared to take it all in stride, but it had to have been a worrisome development.

Despite being unprepared for such a massive opponent, the Gunns took control of the match early. Quick tags and double-team maneuvers, including an impressive double drop kick that knocked Yokozuna out of the ring, made it seem like the champions would keep their titles. But the team of Hart and Yokozuna displayed excellent chemistry, despite it being their first time together in the ring. Yokozuna's devastating Banzai splash allowed Owen to pin Billy Gunn, winning the championship, Hart's first taste of gold in WWE. The champions kept their titles for much of 1995, until the Gunns finally reclaimed the championship in late September.

▶ *Owen Hart pairs with Yokozuna to win the Championship*

I Quit

Any match featuring a pair of two-time WWE Champions squaring off would already be a marquee attraction. Making the bout one in which the loser would have to utter the humiliating phrase "I Quit" upped the ante significantly. Hart and Backlund had fought for Hart's WWE Championship at *Survivor Series*, and Backlund won the title when Hart's mother, Helen Hart, threw in the towel for her son when he was locked in Backlund's devastating Crossface Chickenwing. Hart tried to recapture the championship from Diesel at the *Royal Rumble*, but Backlund attacked Hart, part of the chaos that led to that match being declared a draw.

Hart had numerous reasons to seek revenge, and both men put enough faith in their patented submission moves to lead to the unusual stipulation. To deal with this intensely personal grudge, the WWE named "Rowdy" Roddy Piper special guest referee. Throughout the match, each man looked to soften up his opponent enough to apply his signature move—Backlund attacking Hart's shoulder and arm to make the Crossface Chickenwing more effective and Hart targeting Backlund's legs and knees for his Sharpshooter. Each man came close to applying their favorite move, but Hart finally was able to reverse Backlund's attempt and slap the Crossface Chickenwing onto Backlund himself. Piper determined that Backlund had uttered "I Quit," a final indignity that saw Backlund submitting to his own finishing move.

Friends or Foes

Shawn Michaels earned this Championship Match against his former bodyguard by going wire to wire at the *Royal Rumble*, winning the *Rumble* from the #1 spot. In addition to the title opportunity, he was supposed to be escorted to the ring by Pamela Anderson, but she had other ideas, so Shawn found a substitute. When the time came for the Championship Match, Jenny McCarthy seconded "The Heartbreak Kid." Moments later, to the crowd's delight, Pamela Anderson appeared and escorted Diesel to the ring.

Michaels shares, "That was at the point in my career where I said, 'I'll show them. I'll go out there and I'll make a statement.' Although the match went very well and the upside is you are out there with your buddy, I think *WrestleMania XI* is more known as the *WrestleMania* that L.T. was on."

> ## "Shawn was so ahead of his time in terms of style."
> —Kevin Nash

Nash recalls, "Shawn was so ahead of his time in terms of style. We were the best of friends. We spent so many hours and miles traveling together. Shawn wanted to do this from the time he was a kid."

The match was an entertaining clash of styles, pitting the champion's power against the challenger's technical skills. Michaels grew increasingly frustrated as he continually came tantalizingly close to capturing the title. His Sweet Chin Music put the champion down, but with the referee also down, no one could count the pin. By the time the official recovered, Diesel was able to kick out. With new wind, the champion eventually managed to nail Michaels with a Jackknife Powerbomb, leaving *WrestleMania* with the WWE Championship.

▶ *Pamela Anderson and Jenny McCarthy sit ringside*

A Sports Deity Enters the Ring

The Bigelow-L.T. match boasted a perfect entrance. To combat the various members of Bigelow's Million Dollar Corporation, Taylor put together a squad of NFL greats, including Ken Norton, Jr., Chris Spielman, Rickey Jackson, Carl Banks, Steve McMichael, and Reggie White. The Million Dollar Corporation and Taylor's All Pro Team paraded into the arena like it was Super Bowl Sunday. Both entourages surrounded the ring and provided a great visual backdrop for the match.

From the opening bell, Lawrence Taylor surprised the audience with his footwork and range of motion. WWE Hall of Famer Pat Patterson recalls, "I worked out with L.T. in the ring three weeks prior to *WrestleMania*. I was amazed at what he could do. I tried to tell him, 'Be careful, you don't know how to use the ropes yet.' He was doing all these things like it as normal to him. He couldn't wait to get to *WrestleMania*."

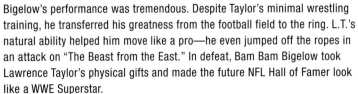

Bigelow's performance was tremendous. Despite Taylor's minimal wrestling training, he transferred his greatness from the football field to the ring. L.T.'s natural ability helped him move like a pro—he even jumped off the ropes in an attack on "The Beast from the East." In defeat, Bam Bam Bigelow took Lawrence Taylor's physical gifts and made the future NFL Hall of Famer look like a WWE Superstar.

Vince McMahon adds, "Again, I have to give credit really to Bam Bam Bigelow, as well as to Lawrence Taylor, but especially to Bam Bam for helping to make that match live up to its expectation and for pulling all that off. It was a great main event."

WRESTLEMANIA XII

ARROWHEAD POND – ANAHEIM, CA

March 31
1996

Attendance
18,853

ANNOUNCERS
Jerry "The King" Lawler, Vince McMahon

SPANISH ANNOUNCERS
Carlos Cabrera, Hugo Savinovich

RING ANNOUNCER
Howard Finkel

SPECIAL FIELD CORRESPONDENTS
Dok Hendricks, Mr. Perfect, Todd Pettengill

Event Card

IRON MAN MATCH FOR THE WWE CHAMPIONSHIP
- Shawn Michaels w/ Jose Lothario def. Bret "Hit Man" Hart (Champion) to become new Champion

HOLLYWOOD BACKLOT BRAWL
- "Rowdy" Roddy Piper def. Goldust w/ Marlena

SIX MAN TAG TEAM MATCH*
- Vader, British Bulldog & Owen Hart w/ Jim Cornette def. Yokozuna, Ahmed Johnson & Jake "The Snake" Roberts w/ Mr. Fuji

TAG TEAM CHAMPIONSHIP MATCH
- The Body Donnas (Skip & Zip) w/ Sunny def. The Godwinns (Henry & Phineas) w/ Hillbilly Jim to become new Champions

GERIATRIC MATCH
- Huckster def. Nacho Man*
*Part of Free-For-All pre-show

OTHER MATCHES
- Undertaker w/ Paul Bearer def. Diesel
- Ultimate Warrior def. Hunter Hearst-Helmsley w/ Sable
- Stone Cold Steve Austin w/ "Million Dollar Man" Ted DiBiase def. Savio Vega

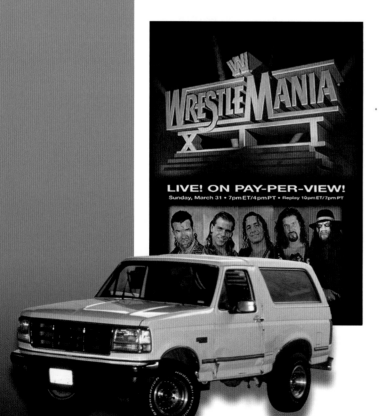

It was a dream match I always wanted to see go an hour. The only two guys in that era that could do a 60-minute Iron Man Match were Bret and Shawn."

—Pat Patterson

Breaking Traditions

Every *WrestleMania* brings some unique traditions to the history of the storied event, and *WrestleMania XII* was no different. For one, the celebrity figures that so often made the event such a spectacle were absent from the twelfth installment of *WrestleMania*. In addition, the show featured the *WrestleMania* debut of two of the greatest Superstars in the history of WWE, Stone Cold Steve Austin and Triple H. It would also be the last *WrestleMania* match of two WWE Champions, Diesel and the Ultimate Warrior. But most of all, this *WrestleMania* would be built around a grueling, one-hour match between two of the greatest in-ring technicians of all time, WWE Champion Bret "Hit Man" Hart and Shawn Michaels.

Six Man Tag Team Match

Managers always pull for their charges to win matches, but Jim Cornette desperately needed his trio (Vader, the British Bulldog, and Owen Hart) to come out on top or there would be dire consequences for him. Yokozuna, who joined with Jake "the Snake" Roberts and Ahmed Johnson, had been a longtime member of Camp Cornette until he tired of the mealy mouthpiece and the two parted ways earlier in the year.

Cornette constantly sent his new team members after Yokozuna, so the Sumo Warrior was looking for revenge against his former advisor. If Yokozuna's team won this match, he would get five minutes alone in the ring with his former manager, although one minute would probably be enough to pulverize Cornette with Yokozuna's devastating Banzai Drop.

With six Superstars in the ring, it's extremely difficult for a single referee to keep control of the action, and the battling in and out of the ring made this match even more challenging. The official was unable to count several near pinfalls because he was dealing with action between members of the two teams that had spilled to outside the ring. Most frustrating of all was when Jake "The Snake" Roberts had put down Owen Hart with his devastating DDT. The Snake was looking to do the same to Cornette, but Vader saved his manager, crushed Roberts with his Vader Bomb move, and recorded the pin for his team. Yokozuna never got his hands on Cornette, luckily for his former manager.

Hollywood Backlot Brawl

With his 1995 WWE debut, Goldust obliterated sports-entertainment barriers and was a harbinger of a revolutionary era that awaited WWE audiences. Dustin Rhodes, who portrayed Goldust, looks back, "It took me about seven months to really get comfortable as the character. It was tough trying to learn the persona and learn to be a villain. I wanted to do something outside of my family's realm, different from my dad, and do something on my own."

Recognized for admiring his opponents in a manner that crossed the lines of friendship and good taste, Goldust took a liking to "Rowdy" Roddy Piper. As the new on-air Interim WWE President, this was not something Piper appreciated. In vintage WWE fashion, the only way to settle this was at *WrestleMania*, in the first-ever Hollywood Backlot Brawl. Rhodes adds, "There was talk originally of my match being a Miami Street Fight with Razor [Ramon], which would've been via satellite from Miami, but that changed. It was a great honor working with a legend like Roddy Piper."

The Hollywood Backlot Brawl, broadcast on a giant screen inside the arena, saw Piper grab an early advantage by using a baseball bat on his bizarre opponent. Goldust decided to get in his car and drive away, but not before hitting Piper with his gold Cadillac. "Rowdy" Roddy gave chase in a white Ford Bronco. Other *WrestleMania* matches continued, but throughout the evening, fans would be updated via car chase scenes, "breaking news" footage, and Roddy Piper calling into the broadcast booth from his cell phone. The car chase made its way to the arena, and Rhodes remembers, "It was awesome. We did a lot of the fighting at Universal Studios in Hollywood. Our cars are beat up, we're beat up, and then we pull up to the arena, stumble through the tunnel, and pop up in the building—it was so cool. When the fans saw me, they just kept booing. And when they saw Piper come through the tunnel, the place just erupted. It was amazing."

▶ *Piper attacks Goldust with a bat*

"It was a great honor working with a legend like Roddy Piper."

—Dustin Rhodes

This wild ride culminated in the ring, where Piper stripped down the provocative one, showing Goldust's ensemble of women's underwear. The physically grueling Hollywood Backlot Brawl helped define Goldust's early days, adding another amazing battle to "Rowdy" Roddy Piper's already unmatched *WrestleMania* resume.

A Rivalry Continues

Fans of the "Texas Rattlesnake" Stone Cold Steve Austin might find it hard to believe, but when he first arrived in WWE, he let advisor Ted DiBiase serve as his mouthpiece. Of course, Stone Cold certainly let his in-ring abilities and moves speak volumes for him, even though he was never one to mind breaking a rule or two in order to win a match. His rivalry with Savio Vega was just heating up heading into *WrestleMania XII*. The two had been paired in a tournament for the vacant World Tag Team Championship, but Austin refused to help Vega in the match and attacked Vega after he was pinned by the Bodydonnas.

The two men had a physical encounter at *WrestleMania XII*, and Austin took advantage of an incapacitated official to hit Vega with Austin's Million Dollar Championship. Austin then used the Million Dollar Dream submission maneuver to put Savio out.

Vega gained a measure of revenge a few months later, defeating Austin in a Caribbean Strap Match, a victory that resulted in Austin losing the services of his manager DiBiase. The severed partnership allowed Stone Cold to become one of the most popular Superstars of all time, so one could argue that the match defeat was the best thing that could have happened.

The Deadman vs. Diesel

The Undertaker-Diesel storyline revolved around both men preventing one another from becoming WWE Champion. Their stalemate began with mind games from "The Phenom" and Diesel's refusal to fear the dark side's powers. This match had additional significance to Diesel, portrayed by Kevin Nash, because, unknown to the general public, he had given notice to WWE. Soon after *WrestleMania XII*, he would become a member of WCW.

Nash recalls, "What people don't understand is I got the title in November '94. A month later, my mom died. That entire run as Champion, I was also dealing with the fact that the year before she died of cancer. I knew she was sick but I wasn't told how sick. I was on the road so much, I didn't get home. I got home right before Christmas to see her, then went back on the road. She passed away, I went back home and buried my mom, was off three or four days, and then I was back on the road. That's the way it was, and that was fine; it's what was expected. So, fast forward to 1996; my WWE deal ended on June 6. My wife was pregnant, and her due date was June 18. I'm going to have a child. There's no way in hell, for the money I made that year in WWE, that I was going to go back on the road and miss seeing my child walk for the first time."

The Ultimate Warrior vs. Hunter Hearst-Helmsley

Fans were ecstatic. After a five-year absence (not counting a quick appearance at the end of *WrestleMania VIII*), the Ultimate Warrior was returning to a *WrestleMania* ring. The fact that he would be clashing with the hated Greenwich snob Hunter Hearst-Helmsley excited fans even more. Helmsley, making his *WrestleMania* debut, wanted to make a spectacular debut by delivering a Pedigree on the former WWE Champion. The Pedigree happened, but it couldn't keep the Warrior down. He popped back up, and proceeded to deliver a flying shoulder block, a gorilla press, and the Warrior Splash to win the match, the Ultimate Warrior's final *WrestleMania*.

This athletic clash between two monsters differed from "Giant vs. Giant" matches of the past. Diesel represented one of the gravest early threats to The Deadman's burgeoning *WrestleMania* Streak. Diesel delivered a pair of jackknife powerbombs, but he could not keep Undertaker down for a three-count. Undertaker was able to give Big Daddy Cool a devastating Chokeslam followed by the Tombstone Piledriver to get the win in the match. Undertaker's victory over Diesel brought the "The Phenom's" *WrestleMania* record to five wins and zero losses.

Iron Man

Bret Hart and Shawn Michaels had parallel careers. Both joined WWE as part of popular tag teams before embarking on singles careers, where each held the Intercontinental Championship on multiple occasions. One difference separated the two—Hart had won the WWE Championship several times, while Michaels had yet to achieve his boyhood dream. Michaels won a second straight *Royal Rumble* match in order to earn another shot at the WWE Championship at *WrestleMania XII*.

Pat Patterson looks back, "It was a dream match of mine that I always wanted to see go an hour. The only two guys in that era that could do a 60-minute Iron Man were Bret and Shawn. I'll tell you something else; Vince didn't want to do it. He was concerned that people would get bored because of the match's length, which happens if you don't have the right two guys. We had the right two guys."

In an Iron Man contest, whoever scores the most decisions by pinfall, count-out, submission, or disqualification in the allotted time is the winner. Bret Hart remembers, "It was Pat Patterson's idea to do the Iron Man Match. I was comfortable wrestling Shawn and putting him over in a straight match. When I won the title from Nash at *Survivor Series*, it was my understanding that Shawn would get his chance to be champ at *WrestleMania*. When I was asked to drop the title to Shawn, I said I would be happy to. I knew that Shawn had worked really hard to get to that level. I always had a lot of respect for Shawn and I looked forward to passing the torch to him."

Vignettes aired of both men training for the match. Shawn Michaels was shown with Jose Lothario, running stadium stairs, performing handstand push-ups, and looking like a well-oiled machine in the ring with sparring partners. Bret Hart was portrayed as the rugged veteran champion who trained as he always trained, running through Calgary, swimming, and returning to the dungeon with his father.

Hart recalls, "I was training on my own, really hard, when the WWE camera crew came up to film my vignettes. I just got home from India and was pretty banged up. I see Shawn doing the Rocky thing and he's looking really fit, and of course he had three months to do this. The first thing they did was film me on the icy bike paths of Calgary so they could get the city skyline. I could run back then but it was all ice, like a hockey rink. Then they went to my house to film me swimming laps in my pool. And I thought it was a good idea until I remembered that I could barely swim. So then the final segment: they take me out to my dad's house and they want my dad to train me like they had Jose with Shawn. I can only imagine how this is going to look to the fans. They show Shawn so fit and so primed, and I don't look like I'm going to beat anybody, but it was still a fun experience."

At the start of the match, the challenger's music played and his mentor Jose Lothario walked to the ring alone. As Lothario entered the ring and pointed to the rafters of the arena, a luminous spotlight turned on "The Heartbreak Kid." In one of *WrestleMania*'s most memorable moments, Michaels took a zip line into the crowd amidst a cascade of flashing lights.

The capacity crowd in Anaheim anxiously awaited the clash between two of the most prolific storytellers sports-entertainment had ever seen. To add to the "heavyweight title fight" feel, a scoreboard and clock were added to the arena's video screen, and onscreen for the pay-per-view audience.

▶ *Vince McMahon never asks a Superstar to do anything he wouldn't do*

As the time ticked away, the two Superstars matched each other move-for-move, Michaels going hold-for-hold on the mat with the "Hit Man," or Hart diving through the ropes onto the floor at "The Heartbreak Kid." For both of these men, this encounter was the ultimate physical and emotional test. The capacity crowd in Anaheim remained emotionally charged as, even after 45 minutes, neither man had recorded a single decision. Bret Hart recounts, "I remember looking at the clock, seeing 4:59, and thinking, 'I can't believe it. We did it. The match was so perfect.'"

Time and again, it looked like one of the men would score a decision. As the clock counted down, Shawn Michaels was locked in Hart's submission Sharpshooter move. Just when it seemed that "The Heartbreak Kid" would give up and see his boyhood dream shattered, time expired. At the end of one hour, both Superstars were beyond the point of physical exhaustion, and no decision had been scored. The match was ruled a draw. Bret Hart started to walk back to the locker room. However, in-ring discussions confirming the original announcement that "there must be a winner," brought the combatants back for "Sudden Death."

"I can't believe it. We did it. The match was so perfect."
—Bret Hart

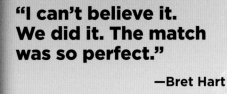

Hart returned to the ring and, after an attack on Shawn Michaels' back, a reversal into the corner enabled "The Heartbreak Kid" to connect with two Superkicks. The referee's hand made contact with the canvas for the final three-count. After an 18-year sojourn, Shawn Michaels boyhood dream came true. Patterson adds, "I enjoyed it so much. More importantly, the fans loved it. I was there, sitting in the audience, and I actually cried after the match. I was so happy that they got to do the match. They really accomplished something special that day."

Bret Hart reflects, "You can take all the wrestlers from previous generations—the Jack Briscoes, the Harley Races, and the Dory Funks—and I don't know of any two wrestlers that ever cut a pace the way Shawn and I did that day. It was a real testimony to both of us as athletes to pour it on the way we did. And I will say one thing about Shawn: he was amazing. He took a lot of punishment in that match. It will always stand out as the hardest match I ever had."

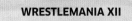

WRESTLEMANIA 13

ROSEMONT HORIZON – CHICAGO, IL

March 23 1997

Attendance 18,211

ANNOUNCERS
Jerry "The King" Lawler
Jim Ross
Vince McMahon

SPANISH ANNOUNCERS
Carlos Cabrera
Hugo Savinovich

FRENCH ANNOUNCERS
Jean Brassard, Ray Rougeau

RING ANNOUNCER
Howard Finkel

SPECIAL FIELD CORRESPONDENTS
Dok Hendricks
Todd Pettengill
Jim Ross

Event Card

WWE CHAMPIONSHIP MATCH
- Undertaker def. Sycho Sid (Champion) to become new Champion

SUBMISSION MATCH
- Bret "Hit Man" Hart def. Stone Cold Steve Austin*
  *Special Guest Referee Ken Shamrock

CHICAGO STREET FIGHT
- Ahmed Johnson & Legion of Doom (Animal & Hawk) def. The Nation of Domination (Farooq, Crush, & Savio Vega) w/ Wolfie D, J.C. Ice, D'Lo Brown & Clarence Mason

WORLD TAG TEAM CHAMPIONSHIP MATCH
- British Bulldog & Owen Hart (Champions) fought Mankind & Vader w/ Paul Bearer to a double countout

INTERCONTINENTAL CHAMPIONSHIP MATCH
- Rocky Maivia (Champion) def. The Sultan w/ Mr. Backlund & Iron Sheik

FOUR-TEAM ELIMINATION TAG TEAM MATCH
- The Godwinns (Henry & Phineas) w/ Hillbilly Jim, The Headbangers (Mosh & Thrasher) vs. Doug Furnas & Philip Lafon, The New Blackjacks (Windham & Bradshaw)

OTHER MATCH
- Hunter Hearst-Helmsley w/Chyna def. Goldust w/Marlena

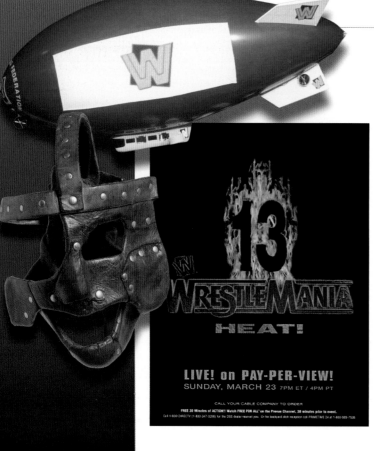

LIVE! on PAY-PER-VIEW!
SUNDAY, MARCH 23 7PM ET / 4PM PT

CALL YOUR CABLE COMPANY TO ORDER

"I saw Steve Austin coming before he did."
—Bret "Hit Man" Hart

Four-Way Tag Team Elimination Match

There was certainly a long line of pairs looking to challenge for the World Tag Team Championship. In addition to the match on the show for the titles, four teams were involved in an elimination match that would see the last remaining team receive a championship shot the next night on *Raw*.

The rules were unique, as while only two men were in the ring at a given time, anyone could tag in another competitor—it didn't have to be a partner. This led to an awkward situation when Blackjack Bradshaw chose to tag in one Headbanger to face his own teammate. Bradshaw was not done creating chaos either. He and his partner Blackjack Windham were brawling outside the ring with Doug Furnas and Phil Lefon when the official tried to break things up. Bradshaw shoved the official down, resulting in his team's disqualification, as well the removal of the team of Furnas and LeFon. The eliminations led to back-and-forth action between the Godwinns and the Headbangers, with each team scoring near pinfalls, until the Headbangers were able to grab the win thanks to their high-flying offense. While Mosh and Thrasher were not successful in their title match the next night, they were able to become tag-team champions later that year.

Four-Team Elimination Tag Team Match

The Headbangers defeat The Godwinns

An Auspicious Debut

The world now knows him as The Rock, but for his *WrestleMania* debut, he went by the name Rocky Maivia, a tribute to his father, Rocky Johnson, and his grandfather, High Chief Peter Maivia. As the WWE's first third-generation Superstar, Rocky had seen success right out of the gate, capturing the Intercontinental Championship early in his career.

However, heading into *WrestleMania 13*, he had to be considered the underdog—he was facing the veteran Sultan, who was also being advised by two former WWE Champions, Bob Backlund and the Iron Sheik. Rocky not only had to deal with the powerful moves of the Sultan, he had to be leery of the two maniacal advisors at ringside. Sultan kept delivering devastating slams, but Rocky was able to kick out of pinning attempts. Rocky used his athleticism to deliver a flying crossbody to pin the Sultan and retain his title, but that's when Backlund and the Sheik struck. The two men attacked Maivia, creating a three-on-one situation. Luckily for Rocky, his father Rocky Johnson was at the event, and he leapt to his son's defense, evening the odds a bit and helping Rocky attain the win.

Pedigree vs. Perversion

Hunter Hearst-Helmsley had already proven his skills and abilities by winning the Intercontinental Championship, but he became even more dangerous with the addition of a bodyguard, Chyna. Emboldened by his new successes, Helmsley made inappropriate overtures to Marlena, Goldust's director. The bizarre Superstar took exception to Hunter's actions, and the two decided to settle things at *WrestleMania 13*.

The two Superstars traded signature moves, with Helmsley continually trying to nail Goldust with the Pedigree, and Goldust using his patented Bulldog, as well as clotheslines. Goldust seemed to have Helmsley set up for the Curtain Call, but he noticed Chyna menacing Marlena outside the ring. The distraction allowed Helmsley to nail the Prince of Perversion with a Pedigree, earning Helmsley the first *WrestleMania* victory of his storied career.

World Tag Team Championship

The team of Owen Hart and the British Bulldog was a well-matched pair. Hart's craftiness and technical abilities meshed perfectly with the power of the Bulldog. They entered *WrestleMania 13* in the midst of a 245-day reign as World Tag Team Champions, the longest-such reign for almost a decade. Paul Bearer's deranged pair of Mankind and Vader represented a significant threat to take the championship.

The strategy of Mankind and Vader was sound—isolate the smaller Hart and keep Bulldog out of the match. Both men used their significant size advantage to punish Hart, but just when it seemed like they would defeat him, he would manage to stave off a pinfall by hitting one of his moves and tagging in the Bulldog. Finally, the Bulldog had Mankind up on his shoulder, ready to hit his running Powerslam, but Mankind was able to slap his Mandible Claw on Smith. Attempted interference by Vader and Hart sent Mankind and the Bulldog crashing to the outside, where the two were counted out. The double countout kept the championship with Hart and Smith, until they eventually lost the titles to the mismatched pair of Shawn Michaels and Stone Cold Steve Austin.

A Brutal Double Switch

For six months, Bret "Hit Man" Hart and Stone Cold Steve Austin were involved in a bitter rivalry. Hart felt Austin had cost him both the *Royal Rumble* match and the WWE Championship, and Austin wanted to prove that he, not, Hart, was the most talented Superstar in WWE. Heading into this match with Steve Austin, Bret Hart still enjoyed a loyal fan following, although pockets of fans were growing tired of the Hit Man's complaints.

The violence that ignited from the opening bell set the stage for the entire match. Former UFC Champion Ken Shamrock's presence as guest referee added to the audience's anticipation of how brutally these men would beat one another. The struggle took both Superstars beyond the barricade and into the Rosemont Horizon crowd.

Finally making it back to the ring, both men set aside wrestling moves to instead brawl with each other. Austin weakened Hart considerably using a Boston Crab, and then looked to embarrass the Hit Man by putting Hart into the Sharpshooter, but the plan backfired, and Hart took control of the match again. While battling outside the ring once more, Austin's forehead was cut open and blood began to pour down his face. Hart then demonstrated how the Sharpshooter should be properly applied. While trapped in the Sharpshooter, a blood-splattered Stone Cold Steve Austin tried to push out of the submission hold. In his effort to escape, Austin created one of the most iconic images in the history of sports-entertainment. Austin did not submit; he passed out. While it meant he lost the match, whether he wanted it or not, he won the loyalty of the fans.

Rather than soak in the victory, Hart pushed the envelope and attacked Austin's injured knee. A rabid Hart continued his onslaught on his battered opponent until Ken Shamrock pulled Hart off Austin by executing a take down. During the postmatch melee, a rare double switch occurred: a blood-soaked Steve Austin was the hero; Bret "Hit Man" Hart was now the villain. Hart was not surprised, remarking "You could feel the change happening. The business was changing, like it always does. Steve was becoming such a great villain that the people started to like him. It became more cool to like him than to boo him."

Speaking about the match itself, Bret Hart remembers, "Artistically, it's maybe the greatest match I ever had. It's a beautiful story. I said it in my interviews at the time and I meant it, I felt that Steve was the best wrestler in the company. I'm sure if I would've stayed with WWE we would have had more great matches down the road."

> ## "Artistically, it's maybe the greatest match I ever had.
>
> —Bret "Hit Man" Hart

AN UNLIKELY TEAM

Mankind is one of the many personas of Mick Foley, who also competed as Cactus Jack and Dude Love. *WrestleMania 13* was Foley's *WrestleMania* debut, but his teaming with Vader had to be considered unbelievable to longtime fans. Sports-entertainment can make for strange bedfellows, but the shared history of these two Superstars made teaming up seem impossible.

When the two competed in WCW years earlier, a brutal encounter in Germany led to Mick Foley losing his right ear in the ring ropes. The idea of teaming up with a man that caused a permanent physical injury like that is something most people would never understand. But as became clear over the years, there aren't many people like Mick Foley.

AUSTIN 3:16

After stints in USWA, WCW, and ECW, Stone Cold Steve Austin finally found a home in WWE. Bret Hart reminisces, "I've always said, I saw Steve Austin coming before he did. I saw him in WCW and I remember telling Vince then that Steve is one of the guys he should get."

Austin's tenure with WWE began as "The Ringmaster," but after becoming extremely dissatisfied with his character, he demanded a change. Steve Austin recalls, "The Ringmaster sucked. I was home one day and my wife at the time was from England and she made me some tea. She said, 'Go ahead and drink that before it gets stone cold.' And that was it. I had my new name."

▶ *Austin wearing his trademark "3:16" on his shirt*

At the 1996 *King of the Ring*, after his victory over Jake "The Snake" Roberts, Austin gave a seething interview that incorporated a new phrase into American pop-culture, "Austin 3:16." "You sit there and you thump your Bible, and you say your prayers, and it didn't get you anywhere! Talk about your Psalms, talk about *John 3:16* … Austin 3:16 says I just whipped your ass!" The remark, a dig at Roberts' quoting of Bible passages, became a phenomenon when fans started showing up at events with signs proclaiming "Austin 3:16." WWE created a T-Shirt with the saying on it, and the shirt became the single greatest-selling item in sports-entertainment history. It served to publicly energize Austin's momentum, and marked his first step towards revolutionizing WWE.

The Legion of Doom vs. The Nation of Domination

There were no rules for this brutal six-man battle that had its seeds planted almost a year before, when Faarooq made his WWE debut by attacking Ahmed Johnson. Faarooq put Johnson on the shelf for months, and when he finally was healthy enough to return, Faarooq had formed the Nation of Domination, and this new group constantly attacked Johnson.

To try and even the odds, Johnson teamed with Hawk and Animal, better known as the Legion of Doom. The trio decided to deal with the entire Nation of Domination. The Chicago Street Fight would have rules and weapons would be legal and encouraged. In fact, the match would see the use of trash cans, a night stick, a wrench, a fire extinguisher, and more. Every time Hawk, Animal, and Ahmed would get the upper hand, the overwhelming number of the Nation would turn the tide. Eventually Hawk and Animal set up Crush for their Doomsday Device and Johnson was able to get the pin. The action continued however, until the Legion of Doom and Johnson set up two of the Nation's lackeys up for an impressive double Doomsday Device, causing the rest of the Nation to hightail their way out of the arena.

Sycho Sid vs. Undertaker for the WWE Championship

There was a great deal of confusion and uncertainty around the WWE Championship in early 1997. After winning the title from Sid at the 1997 *Royal Rumble*, Shawn Michaels should have been on top of the world. But an injury forced him to vacate the title, leading to a four-way match to crown a new champion. Bret Hart won the match, becoming a four-time WWE Champion. His reign lasted a mere 24 hours though, as during a match with Sycho Sid on *Raw*, Stone Cold Steve Austin interfered, costing Hart the title, and making Undertaker's scheduled bout with Sid at *WrestleMania 13* a WWE Championship Match.

Before the title match began, Shawn Michaels and Bret Hart decided to grace Chicago with their presence. Michaels joined the broadcast team for the main event. The Hit Man, still believing that Michaels had faked his injury, stormed the ring to call Michaels a "phony little faker," and Sycho Sid a "fraud." A Powerbomb from Sid sent the Hit Man back to the locker room and the main event was underway.

At the Undertaker's entrance, the Rosemont Horizon was submerged in darkness. "The Phenom" emerged from clouds of smoke and made his way to the ring. Undertaker's first WWE Championship reign in 1991 lasted just six days. Now without Paul Bearer, The Deadman sought to reign once again and rule WWE as its champion.

From the onset, the two behemoths engaged in one of *WrestleMania*'s most physically rigorous encounters. The match included both men's powerful displays of agility and strength. Sid showed some surprising aerial moves, and even tried to beat Undertaker with The Deadman's signature Tombstone Piledriver. But like many men that have clashed with Undertaker, Sid found out that keeping The Deadman down for a three count is a near impossibility. Bret Hart returned to the ring and distracted the champion, which resulted in Sid being planted into the canvas via the Tombstone Piledriver. The Prince of Darkness crossed Sid's arms on his chest and became champion for the second time.

As Undertaker seized the WWE Championship, a conflagration of shadow, thunder, and lightning consumed the Rosemont Horizon. In its closing darkened seconds, *WrestleMania 13* proved to be Undertaker's shining moment.

WRESTLEMANIA XIV

FLEET CENTER – BOSTON, MA

March 29
1998

Attendance
19,028

ANNOUNCERS
Jerry "The King" Lawler
Jim Ross

SPANISH ANNOUNCERS
Carlos Cabrera
Hugo Savinovich
Tito Santana

RING ANNOUNCER
Howard Finkel

Event Card

MAIN EVENT – WWE CHAMPIONSHIP MATCH
- Stone Cold Steve Austin def. Shawn Michaels (Champion) w/ Hunter-Hearst Helmsley & Chyna to become new Champion*
*Special Guest Enforcer "Iron" Mike Tyson

WORLD TAG TEAM CHAMPIONSHIP MATCH
- Cactus Jack & Chainsaw Charlie def. New Age Outlaws (Road Dogg Jesse James & Billy Gunn) (Champions) to become new Champions

INTERCONTINENTAL CHAMPIONSHIP MATCH
- The Rock (Champion) w/ Nation of Domination (D'Lo Brown, Kama, Mark Henry) to def. Ken Shamrock

MIXED TAG TEAM MATCH
- Marc Mero & Sable def. The Artist Formerly Known as Goldust & Luna

EUROPEAN CHAMPIONSHIP MATCH
- Triple H (Champion) w/ Chyna def. Owen Hart

LIGHT HEAVYWEIGHT CHAMPIONSHIP
- Taka Michinoku (Champion) def. Aguila

TAG TEAM BATTLE ROYAL
- Legion of Doom w/ Sunny def. Savio Vega & Miquel Perez, Truth Commission, Bradshaw & Chainz, Mark Henry & D-Lo Brown, Quebecers, Rock N' Roll Express, Farooq & Kama, Jose Estrada & Jesus Castillo, Headbangers, Steve Blackman & Flash Funk, Scott Taylor & Brian Christopher, The D.O.A., The Godwinns, and the New Midnight Express*
*Winner Receives Match for World Tag Team Championship

OTHER MATCH:
- Undertaker def. Kane w/ Paul Bearer

> ## "I'd rather lose money on eight hundred thousand buys than make money on four hundred thousand."
>
> —Vince McMahon

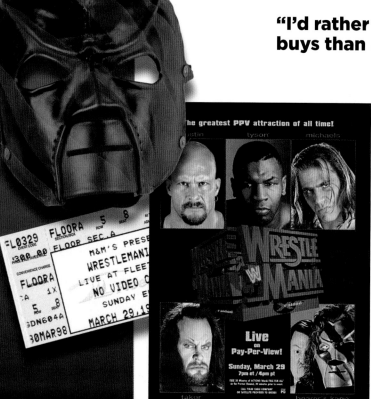

Hosting a Revolution

The world of sports entertainment was in the midst of a revolution. WWE was in an ongoing battle for fans with WCW. In the year since *WrestleMania 13*, WWE had seen the formation and dissolution of the new Hart Foundation, the rise of Stone Cold Steve Austin, the emergence of the cocky bad guy The Rock, the birth of D-Generation X, and the most infamous moment in the history of WWE, the Montreal Screwjob. WWE was looking to launch a new period in their history, and to do so, they wanted to bring in former heavyweight boxing champion and "Baddest Man on the Planet" Mike Tyson. At the time, Tyson had his share of legal problems. He was serving a Nevada State Athletic Commission suspension for biting off a portion of Evander Holyfield's right ear during a boxing match.

Some within the company were concerned that the cost to sign Mike Tyson would preclude *WrestleMania* from becoming a financial success. Advisors told Vince that without Tyson, WWE could do four to five hundred thousand pay-per-view buys and make money. With Tyson, the company would get seven hundred thousand buys and lose money. Vince told them, "Don't you understand? I'd rather lose money on eight hundred thousand buys than make money on four hundred thousand. That's how we grow the business."

Tyson appeared on camera with Shane McMahon as a spectator at the 1998 *Royal Rumble*. The next night on *Raw*, "Iron" Mike Tyson and Stone Cold Steve Austin went nose to nose in the ring. When a fierce brawl ensued, the crowd went wild.

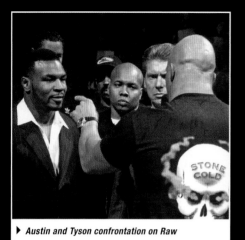

▶ *Austin and Tyson confrontation on Raw*

Angry that the Rattlesnake had ruined his moment with Tyson, Vince McMahon did everything he could to prevent Steve Austin from becoming WWE Champion. To make the odds even longer for Austin, "Iron" Mike would eventually join D-Generation X. Tyson's star power lured the mainstream media to *WrestleMania*, extended its appeal to sports, entertainment, and business outlets, and focused the eyes of millions back on WWE. The stage was set for Boston.

An Epic Battle Royal

WrestleMania XIV opened with 14 tag teams in the ring, including two squads representing the Nation of Domination, two pairings from Los Boricuas, as well as D.O.A., The Rock 'n' Roll Express, the New Midnight Express, the Godwinns, and many more. Going into *WrestleMania*, all the participating teams save one were known by the fans, so there was a great deal of anticipation about the identity of the last team. The crowd exploded when the final pair was revealed to be the Legion of Doom, sporting a new look and a new manager, original Diva Sunny.

The chaotic action was hard to follow until several eliminations started to thin the herd. The Battle Royal had unique rules—once one member of a team was eliminated, the other member of the team had to leave the ring as well. The final four teams came down to DOA, the Godwinns, the new Midnight Express, and the Legion of Doom. After DOA and the Godwinns were knocked out, the Legion of Doom was able to eliminate Jim Cornette's charges and earn the title shot.

The Light Heavyweight Championship

The second bout of the night had an international feel, as WWE's first-ever Light Heavyweight Champion, Taka Michinoku, defended his title against Mexican Superstar Aguila. The two amazed the crowd with aerial moves in and out of the ring. From flying crossbodies to moonsaults, the two men matched each other move for move. Eventually, the Champion was able to hit Aguila with his Michinoku Driver and collect the pin, continuing his reign as WWE Light Heavyweight Champion.

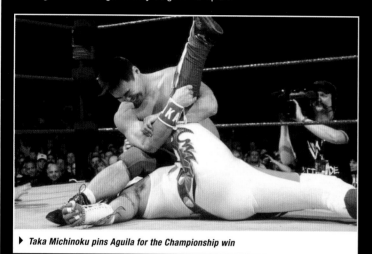

▶ *Taka Michinoku pins Aguila for the Championship win*

Triple H vs. Owen Hart

As half of D-Generation X, Triple H, with WWE Champion Shawn Michaels, taunted and mocked both the WWE Universe and all of their fellow Superstars. The two degenerates clearly had played some role in the Montreal Screwjob, when Michaels "beat" Bret Hart for the WWE Championship.

Triple H remembers the early days of DX, "Shawn and I discussed it before Hall and Nash left. We kept begging Vince to let us do it. We felt the business needed to change to more reality-based concepts. Business was really down. It felt like we were giving people a product that was passé. Everybody hated DX at first; the talent, the agents, Vince, USA Network sent us letters all the time telling us to stop doing what we were doing. The one group that loved it was the fans. The more we did it, the bigger reactions we got. We knew we were on to something."

"The more we did it, the bigger reactions we got. We knew we were on to something."

—Triple H

While Bret Hart left for WCW, his brother Owen stayed behind and continued to battle with D-Generation X, particularly with Triple H over the European Championship. Often though, Hart had to contend with both Helmsley and DX's outside enforcer, Chyna. WWE's Commissioner Sgt. Slaughter decided to take action, ruling that he would be handcuffed to Chyna during the Triple H-Owen Hart *WrestleMania* match for the European Championship.

The unusual move seemed to have the desired effect. On several occasions, Chyna tried to interfere on Triple H's behalf, but Slaughter was there to stop her. Free to focus only on his in-ring opponent, Hart was able to unleash a flurry of moves on Helmsley, and was closing in on a victory when Chyna took the drastic step of throwing a handful of powder in Slaughter's face, blinding him. She was then able to deliver a painful low blow to Hart, setting him up for Triple H's Pedigree move, and a victory for one half of D-Generation X.

Dueling Divas

Today, longtime fans of WWE remember the exploding popularity of Stone Cold, The Rock, and D-Generation X around the time of *WrestleMania XIV*. What they might not remember was another explosive star from that time period, the Diva Sable. Originally serving as the valet to "Marvelous" Marc Mero, the WWE Universe loved everything Sable did, making her the star Mero wanted to be. The more Mero tried to push Sable down, the more fans loved her.

Mero had temporarily partnered with the Artist Formerly Known as Goldust to bring the spotlight back to himself, but the plan backfired as Goldust and his equally bizarre partner, Luna Vachon, turned on Mero and Sable necessitating a mixed tag match at *WrestleMania XIV*. The audience was excited to see Sable's first-ever in-ring action, but Luna kept her distance, either running away or tagging in her partner. The separation did not last, and Sable finally got her hands on Luna, showing a preternatural wrestling ability by executing a variety of moves, including a Powerbomb and finishing Luna off with Marc Mero's signature TKO move. Sable finally broke away from Mero a few months later, and never looked back.

Shamrock Snaps

When one considers the overwhelming popularity enjoyed by The Rock, it's hard to imagine that he was once one of the most reviled Superstars in WWE. The Great One used to be showered with "Rocky Sucks" chants, and his decision to join the Nation of Domination didn't help matters. At *WrestleMania XIV*, he needed to have Nation members Mark Henry, D-Lo Brown, and Kama Mustafa watching his back as he defended his Intercontinental Championship against "The World's Most Dangerous Man" Ken Shamrock.

Shamrock had been trying to get his hands on The Rock for months, and he now had his chance. The match was short and brutal. Rock attacked Shamrock on the outside before the bell even rang, and tried to press his advantage, delivering a People's Elbow, but only managed a two count. Shamrock delivered bruising blows and eventually managed to trap The Rock in his painful Ankle Lock submission maneuver. The Rock tapped and Shamrock won the title. However Shamrock snapped and kept Rock in the Ankle lock, even tossing aside officials that tried to break things up. This blatant disregard for the rules gave the referee no choice but to reverse the decision and give Rock a victory by disqualification, allowing Rock to keep his title and fans to serenade the Great One with their favorite chant once again.

Taking Out the Trash

In one of the strangest stipulations for a *WrestleMania* match to date, the New Age Outlaws had to defend their championship in a match where both members of the opposing team had to be thrown in a dumpster and have the lid closed in order to win. The stipulation meant that anything would go during the match. This brawling style of fight was old hat to Cactus Jack and his partner Charlie, better known as Terry Funk. The Outlaws quickly proved their aptitude for brawling as well and early in the match came close to ending it by getting both of their opponents into the dumpster. However, they failed to close the lid, and the match continued.

Eventually, the wild fight made its way backstage. Cactus slammed both of the Outlaws onto a pallet, and Charlie used a forklift to drop both into a dumpster, trapping them in the receptacle and claiming the World Tag Team Championship. The celebration only lasted a day, as the Outlaws got the decision reversed on *Raw*, pointing out that they were not placed in the designated ringside dumpster, and that the decision was therefore invalid.

▶ *Charlie preparing to drop The Outlaws into the dumpster with a forklift*

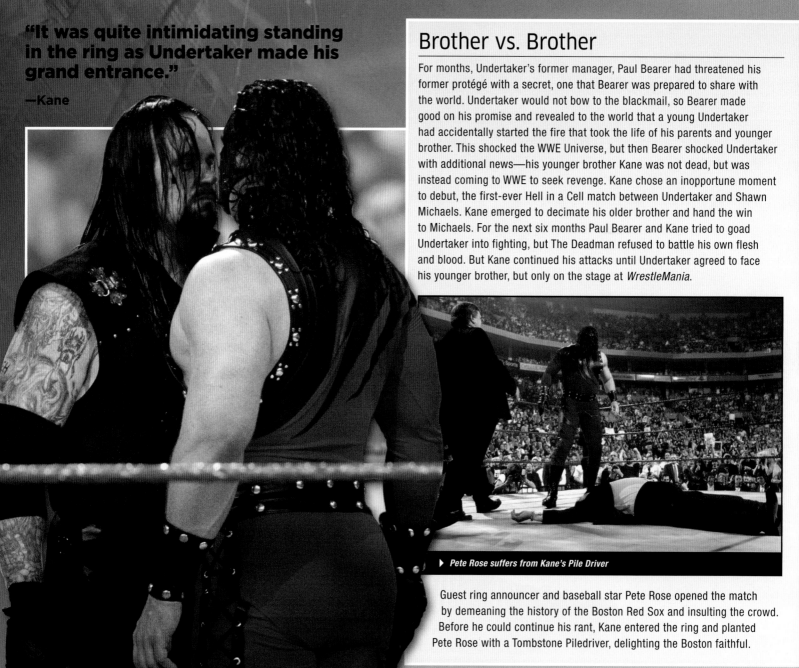

"It was quite intimidating standing in the ring as Undertaker made his grand entrance."
—Kane

Brother vs. Brother

For months, Undertaker's former manager, Paul Bearer had threatened his former protégé with a secret, one that Bearer was prepared to share with the world. Undertaker would not bow to the blackmail, so Bearer made good on his promise and revealed to the world that a young Undertaker had accidentally started the fire that took the life of his parents and younger brother. This shocked the WWE Universe, but then Bearer shocked Undertaker with additional news—his younger brother Kane was not dead, but was instead coming to WWE to seek revenge. Kane chose an inopportune moment to debut, the first-ever Hell in a Cell match between Undertaker and Shawn Michaels. Kane emerged to decimate his older brother and hand the win to Michaels. For the next six months Paul Bearer and Kane tried to goad Undertaker into fighting, but The Deadman refused to battle his own flesh and blood. But Kane continued his attacks until Undertaker agreed to face his younger brother, but only on the stage at *WrestleMania*.

▶ *Pete Rose suffers from Kane's Pile Driver*

Guest ring announcer and baseball star Pete Rose opened the match by demeaning the history of the Boston Red Sox and insulting the crowd. Before he could continue his rant, Kane entered the ring and planted Pete Rose with a Tombstone Piledriver, delighting the Boston faithful.

With Rose dispatched, it was time for Kane to face his brother. Kane recalls, "Having the mask on, waiting to go out at *WrestleMania XIV* was one of the biggest moments of my life. The company had invested a lot into my storyline with Undertaker. It was quite intimidating standing in the ring as Undertaker made his grand entrance."

Undertaker's seventh *WrestleMania* appearance was his most awesome to date. Kane unleashed unprecedented powers similar to his brother's. Just as past *WrestleMania* opponents found it almost impossible to keep Undertaker down, Kane continually kicked out of pinning attempts. Kane also scored a near win with a powerful Tombstone Piledriver of his own on The Deadman. In the end, Undertaker defeated his brother after three Tombstone Piledrivers. Kane looks back, "There was a lot of pressure to deliver that night, and I think we did. Even though I lost, I did so in spectacular fashion, and it made a statement."

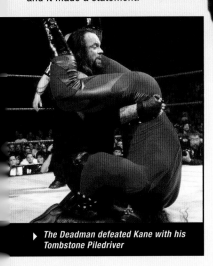
▶ *The Deadman defeated Kane with his Tombstone Piledriver*

Tyson Decides the Match

Heading into *WrestleMania*, Shawn Michaels was in excruciating pain. Landing on a casket at the 1998 *Royal Rumble* crushed one of his spinal discs and herniated two others. In the months leading into *WrestleMania*, Michaels appeared only on *Raw* and at promotional events and there was some concern over whether or not he would perform at *WrestleMania*. Steve Austin remembers, "Things were heating up heading into *WrestleMania*. At the time, Shawn was pretty temperamental; it was hot or cold. His back was bothering him, and I don't think he was in a good place mentally. We didn't even know if he was going to get into the ring."

Despite his best efforts to conceal the injury, agonizing pain was written all over Shawn Michaels' face. Controversial and brash, Michaels was a proud WWE Superstar. His insistence on going through the match was a tribute to his courage as a performer. Michaels looks back, "I was just bitter and angry and wanted to go home. It's always sort of bittersweet. My performance is everything. I didn't care about my reputation here, or if this or that guy liked me. I didn't care how much money I made and if someone made more. I cared about, when I got in there, was my match the best? That night, I just couldn't do what I knew I was capable of doing. Steve didn't miss a step, and he went on to bigger and better things, and that's fantastic."

Austin remembers, "We're in the ring now; we have to have the match. It was what it was. It wasn't the greatest match in the world. Shawn was in a lot of pain that night. Having Mike Tyson as the special enforcer was another big element. You knew something was going to happen—you just wondered when it was going to happen."

Mike Tyson remembers, "When I walked to the ring, the *WrestleMania* crowd in Boston was amazing. I never experienced anything like that. You have to understand at that time I was suspended from boxing. That was a real life-saving experience for me financially, as well. After I did it I wanted to do it again. It's just something I'll never forget. There's nothing like *WrestleMania*."

Tyson was not needed for the majority of the match, as Michaels and Stone Cold battled back and forth. Early on, Triple H and Chyna insinuated themselves into the match, until the official ordered them to leave ringside and go back to the dressing room. Now it was one-on-one, as long as Tyson remained impartial. Stone Cold countered Michaels' famous Sweet Chin Music kick and hit "The Heartbreak Kid" with his patented Stone Cold Stunner. Tyson, who entered the ring when WWE referee Mike Chioda was knocked unconscious, counted the one, two, three. As a perfect beginning to the celebration, Mike Tyson held up an Austin 3:16 shirt and then knocked out a belligerent Shawn Michaels.

▶ *Stone Cold wins the match*

▶ *DX's post match embrace, never shown on the broadcast*

WRESTLEMANIA XV

FIRST UNION CENTER – PHILADELPHIA, PA

March 28
1999

Attendance
19,514

ANNOUNCERS
Jerry "The King" Lawler
Michael Cole
Jim Ross

SPANISH ANNOUNCERS
Carlos Cabrera
Hugo Savinovich

RING ANNOUNCER
Howard Finkel

SPECIAL FIELD CORRESPONDENT
Kevin Kelly

SPECIAL MUSICAL GUEST
Boyz II Men

Event Card

MAIN EVENT – NO DISQUALIFICATION MATCH FOR WWE CHAMPIONSHIP
▨ Stone Cold Steve Austin def. The Rock (Champion) to become new Champion

HELL IN A CELL
▨ Undertaker w/ Paul Bearer def. Big Boss Man

EUROPEAN CHAMPIONSHIP MATCH
▨ Shane McMahon (Champion) w/ Test def. X-Pac

WOMEN'S CHAMPIONSHIP MATCH
▨ Sable (Champion) def. Tori

FOUR CORNERS ELIMINATION MATCH FOR THE INTERCONTINENTAL CHAMPIONSHIP
▨ Road Dogg (Champion) def. Ken Shamrock, Goldust w/ Blue Meanie, Ryan Shamrock, & Val Venis

BRAWL FOR ALL MATCH
▨ Butterbean def. Bart Gunn

WORLD TAG TEAM CHAMPIONSHIP MATCH
▨ Owen Hart & Jeff Jarrett (Champions) w/ Debra def. D'Lo Brown & Test w/ Ivory

TRIPLE THREAT MATCH FOR THE HARDCORE CHAMPIONSHIP
▨ Hardcore Holly def. Billy Gunn (Champion) & Al Snow to become new Champion

OTHER MATCHES
▨ Kane def. Triple H by Disqualification
▨ Mankind def. Big Show by Disqualification*
*Winner Referees Main Event

"There was always a concern from our partners, 'Who could ever replace Hulk Hogan? Who could mean as much in this industry as Hulk Hogan?' Stone Cold did. I'm not saying Stone Cold was bigger or better than Hulk, but it was a different time."

—Linda McMahon

The City of Brotherly Love

Philadelphia has long been one of WWE's greatest cities. WWE events at the Philadelphia Spectrum were legendary since the 1960s. It was only fitting that WWE brought *WrestleMania* to the City of Brotherly Love for the first main event meeting between Stone Cold Steve Austin and The Rock.

▶ *Boyz II Men perform in Philadelphia*

▶ *Owen Hart and Jeff Jarrett battle D-Lo Brown (with Test) in the World Tag Team Championship*

The Hardcore Championship

In late 1998, WWE introduced the Hardcore Championship, a title for matches that not only allowed the use of weapons and outside objects, it practically demanded them. The No Holds Barred style of fighting appealed to a number of WWE Superstars and the fast action resulted in numerous title changes. Both Hardcore Holly and Al Snow felt they had a legitimate claim to the Championship, so the reigning champion, "Bad Ass" Billy Gunn, was forced to defend the title against both men.

Under Triple Threat rules, all men are fighting each other at the same time. It's exciting action, but can also make scoring a pinfall nearly impossible, as the third man will break up any attempts to get the win. Action spilled in and out of the ring as Gunn, Holly, and Snow all looked for items around and under the ring. The Philadelphia crowd loved the use of a hockey stick, as well as Al Snow adding a table to the mix. Snow should have left well enough alone, as Gunn put Snow through the table. Before Gunn could record the pin, Holly knocked him out and stole the win, beginning his second reign as Hardcore Champion.

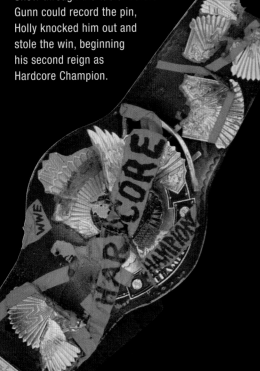

The World Tag Team Championship

The World Tag Team Champions, Jeff Jarrett and Owen Hart, had no way to prepare for their *WrestleMania* opponents because their identities were not revealed until the pre-show. A Battle Royal was held where the last two men remaining in the ring would become a tag team and challenge for the title. When the dust settled on the match, D-Lo Brown and Test were the two remaining.

Even though the two did not get along, let alone have experience teaming together, they kept pushing the champions to the edge, working together better than anyone could have expected. Brown was able to nail Hart with a Sky High move, but Jarrett broke up the pinning attempt. An incident outside the ring involving Ivory and the Pretty Mean Sisters (PMS) distracted both the referee and Test, allowing Hart and Jarrett to double-team Brown and collect the win.

Brawl for All

In the summer of 1998, WWE experimented with a new style of shoot fighting named Brawl for All. The 16-man tournament featured three-round matches that awarded points for takedowns, knockdowns, and punches landed. Everyone had their favorites, including "Dr. Death" Steve Williams, Marc Mero, and Bradshaw, but it's safe to say that few would have predicted Bart Gunn to win it all, or the dominating way he'd run through the bracket.

Gunn faced his biggest challenge at *WrestleMania* when he clashed with pro boxer Butterbean in the Brawl for All match. Vinny Pazienza served as the guest referee, and Boxers Chuck Wepner and Kevin Cooney, along with WWE Hall of Famer, Gorilla Monsoon, were brought in to score the bout. Monsoon, who was in poor health, received an emotional ovation from the crowd honoring his long and storied career.

The extra scoring help was not needed. Butterbean unleashed a flurry of punches that put Gunn down. Gunn managed to get up to resume the bout, but Butterbean knocked him out just two punches later with a savage, cringe-inducing shot that left the audience stunned by its brutality. The bout was a first-round knockout, and Gunn was knocked out of WWE.

"Nobody Owns Me"

That the Mr. McMahon character hated Stone Cold Steve Austin is probably the understatement of the year. From the day after *WrestleMania XIV*, when it became apparent that the Texas Rattlesnake was not going to conform to Mr. McMahon's concept of the ideal champion, McMahon did everything he could to keep Austin from the WWE Championship, aligning with Undertaker, Kane, Mick Foley, and more. He finally found his perfect Superstar when The Rock evolved from the People's Champ to the Corporate Champ at *Survivor Series* 1998. Austin was able to earn a shot at the title at *WrestleMania XIV*, so McMahon needed to stack the deck with a hand-picked referee. He wanted Big Show, but Mankind had other ideas, leading to a match to settle the matter.

During the match, Big Show ruined Mr. McMahon's plan by getting himself disqualified because he repeatedly attacked Mankind with chair shots. Mankind was badly beaten and left the arena on a stretcher, but he'd also earned the position of special guest referee. Mr. McMahon was livid, racing to the ring to give Big Show a verbal lashing. Show almost Chokeslammed the boss, but he was able to calm down. That is, until Mr. McMahon's tirade continued and the owner slapped Big Show in the face. Big Show knocked Mr. McMahon out and left the ring saying, "Nobody owns me."

Every Dogg Has His Day

Just like his fellow New Age Outlaw, Intercontinental Champion Road Dogg had to defend his title against multiple contenders, but he was forced to face three former champions. Road Dogg and Ken Shamrock started the match and traded power moves. Shamrock and Val Venis battled outside the ring and up the rampway, leading the referee to start counting the two men out. When Shamrock realized what was going on, he sprinted back to the ring, but was too late; he'd been counted out and eliminated from the match. The decision did not sit well with the World's Most Dangerous man, and he snapped, delivering powerful belly-to-belly suplexes to both Road Dogg and Goldust before departing to the locker room.

Some confusion with his entourage distracted Goldust long enough for Road Dogg to slam Goldust and pin him, allowing Road Dogg to leave *WrestleMania XV* as Intercontinental Champion.

▶ *Val Venis battles Road Dogg*

Triple H vs. Kane

Triple H and Kane saw a betrayal kick start their rivalry. Triple H's longtime bodyguard and fellow D-Generation X member, Chyna, betrayed Triple H and joined Mr. McMahon's Corporation faction. Kane and Chyna started working together, sabotaging Triple H's efforts toward the WWE Championship. Kane even tried to burn Triple H with a fireball, but he accidentally burned Chyna instead.

▶ *Kane deals with the Super Chicken*

Kane came to the ring awaiting his match, but before he faced Triple H, the Super Chicken mascot jumped him from behind. Kane ripped off the mascot's head, revealing Pete Rose, who was clearly looking for revenge from Kane's Tombstone Piledriver of the previous *WrestleMania*. Rose's plan did not work, and instead he found himself on the receiving end of yet another Piledriver.

Like Rose, Triple H decided to sneak attack the Big Red Monster, delivering a low blow to start the match. Kane quickly regained control, tossing Triple H onto the ring barrier and into the stands. The match went back and forth, until Chyna made her way to ringside, distracting Triple H from delivering a Pedigree. From there, the intensity increased. Kane was close to victory, until Chyna surprised him by hitting him with a chair and Triple H delivered a Pedigree on the same chair. Kane won the match by disqualification due to Chyna's outside interference, but the fans were ecstatic that the DX stablemates had reunited.

▶ *Nicole Bass interferes and gorilla pressed Tori*

▶ *Sable retains the Women's Championship*

The WWE Women's Championship

Since winning the WWE Women's Championship, a change in attitude had come over Sable. She seemed to care less and less for the adoration of her fans and more about feeding her own ego. Tori, a longtime fan, had been helping Sable win her matches, but Sable would berate and mock her admirer to the point where Tori finally demanded a championship match.

Both women showed off some impressive moves, but one exchange resulted in the referee being knocked out. Tori had Sable down, but no one was there to count the pin. So Tori looked to further punish Sable with a Powerbomb, but the massive Nicole Bass came to the ring and gorilla pressed the challenger. Sable then put Tori out with a Sable Bomb and kept her Women's Championship.

The Corporation Claims a Victory

As a member of his father's Corporation faction, Shane McMahon had been a thorn in the side of D-Generation X, particularly X-Pac. Shane O'Mac was able to steal X-Pac's European Championship with the help of Chyna and thought he'd have no trouble defending the title at *WrestleMania* with the help of the Corporation and the Mean Street Posse.

As Shane became the first member of the McMahon family to compete at a *WrestleMania*, the first part of his plan failed when Pat Patterson and Gerald Brisco were unsuccessful in their pre-match attack of X-Pac. X-Pac was able to land offense on Shane, but Corporation hired gun Test attacked X-Pac every time the official's back was turned. X-Pac eventually knocked down Test and was able to focus on Shane. Triple H and Chyna came to the ring, apparently to stop Test's interference and even the odds. It was not to be. Triple H delivered a Pedigree on X-Pac and draped Shane over his fallen DX compatriot. The betrayal was finally clear—Chyna had not rejoined D-Generation X, Triple H had aligned himself with the Corporation. The New Age Outlaws and Kane each came out to gain revenge, but the damage was done, and Mr. McMahon's Corporation had a powerful new ally.

▶ **Edge, then of The Brood, descends to assist Undertaker**

▶ **Triple H aligns himself with The Corporation**

Hell in a Cell

Undertaker's Ministry of Darkness battled Mr. McMahon's Corporation for control of WWE. For months Undertaker waged psychological warfare with the owner of the company, showing up at Mr. McMahon's home and stating he was coming for "her." An enraged Mr. McMahon sent his chief of security, Big Boss Man, after The Deadman and the two were set to meet in the most demonic structure in all of sports-entertainment, Hell in a Cell.

While Hell in a Cell was Undertaker's favorite place to battle, Big Boss Man, being a former prison guard, was also comfortable in a cell. He was able to effectively beat down and bloody Undertaker, even handcuffing The Deadman to the cell at one point. Undertaker's 7-0 *WrestleMania* streak seemed in jeopardy, particularly once Big Boss Man started using his night stick to work over the Ministry of Darkness's leader. However, as so many before have found out, keeping Undertaker down was a tall order. Eventually Undertaker was able to deliver a Tombstone Piledriver and pin the Corporation's head of security.

Undertaker continued his war with Mr. McMahon's forces, eventually revealing that the "her" he sought was the youngest McMahon, Stephanie, who was going to become his dark bride until she was saved by Mr. McMahon's nemesis, Stone Cold Steve Austin.

The Rock vs. Stone Cold Steve Austin

Mr. McMahon wanted his Corporate Champion, The Rock, to leave *WrestleMania* as the champion. When his plan to have Big Show serve as the special guest referee failed, the boss came up with an inspired plan B—Mr. McMahon appointed himself referee of the match. But Shawn Michaels, the WWE Commissioner, came to the ring and informed Mr. McMahon that he, "The Heartbreak Kid," was the only one who could appoint a referee. HBK assigned WWE Referee Mike Chioda to preside over the main event, and banned the entire Corporation from ringside. It was HBK's only role in *WrestleMania* after being such an important part of nine of the previous ten events. It would be understandable if he missed the action, but Shawn Michaels reflects, "It's funny because people have always said, 'You missed the Attitude Era. Does that ever bother you?' It's one of those things … my life turned around, I found the Lord, and I started a family. My priorities, everything in my life, started to change for the better."

With the "No Disqualification" stipulation, Austin and Rock brought a new level of physicality to *WrestleMania*—wildly brawling in the raucous Philadelphia crowd, brutalizing one another with steel chairs, and crashing through the announcers' table. Jim Ross described the bout as "indescribable carnage." The brawl was so uncontrollable three separate referees had to be summoned to the ring before the fourth, Mankind, finally made the three-count.

After reversing a second Rock Bottom, Stone Cold nailed The Rock with his famous Stunner. For the second consecutive year, Austin stood victorious as the newly crowned WWE Champion at *WrestleMania*.

The final moments brought the crowd of more than 20,000 to the breaking point when Austin flattened Mr. McMahon with a Stone Cold Stunner. The Texas Rattlesnake doused the boss with beer and stood over him holding the WWE Championship.

A MAJOR ATTITUDE ADJUSTMENT

Hulk Hogan and the WWE of the 1980s left an indelible mark on sports-entertainment. The iconic hero's message of "saying your prayers and taking your vitamins" encapsulated the hope of America at that time.

Stone Cold Steve Austin represented a different era. Stone Cold embodied the frustrations of the common man and America's rebellious youth. No other individual defined an era of defiance and solidified his legend like he did.

When Austin entered an arena, audiences eagerly anticipated living vicariously through the Texas Rattlesnake. Austin's popularity was such an impactful, cultural force he created his own Smokin' Skull Championship. All of this from someone who was fired from WCW and told he was not marketable. Linda McMahon remembers, "There was always a concern from our partners, 'Who could ever replace Hulk Hogan? Who could mean as much in this industry as Hulk Hogan?' Stone Cold did. He outsold everyone in merchandise, live event attendance, and pay-per-view buys. I'm not saying Stone Cold was bigger or better than Hulk, but it was a different time."

"Axxess provides the opportunity to reflect on the history of the WWE and to give the Universe a look at some of the items that define and represent Superstars and moments in time. Memorabilia exhibits at Axxess display everything from the original WWE title, to André the Giant's boots, from Shawn Michaels show stopping ring gear to "well loved" Money in the Bank briefcases."

—Ben Brown, WWE Archivist
@WWEArchivist

WRESTLEMANIA AXXESS

"Fan Axxess is such a special event because our fans have the opportunity to meet us in person and spend time with us; and we, as Superstars, get to enjoy the same opportunity with them. There are no Superstars without the fans so it's a humbling experience. Axxess is an awesome event on all levels."

—Alicia Fox

John Cena (top), The Usos (bottom), and Lana (right) get involved with the exciting events at Axxess.

"Axxess is one of the greatest events that WWE hosts, year in and year out. It's an awesome interactive fan experience. Personally speaking, I take great joy in meeting the fans who have traveled from around the world to be there. As much as they want to meet me, I in turn want to meet them and say thank you for their support and acceptance of me through the years. At *WrestleMania 30*, I was part of the 'Legends House Open House'. And as we put smiles on people's faces, those that came by to say hello genuinely put a smile on my face at every session that I participated in!"

—Howard Finkel

"Every year WWE raises the bar for what the Fan Axxess event will offer our fans. The way we are able to get so close with our audience is symbolic of how WWE is as a family and an organization. There's no other annual event in entertainment that offers such a high level of interaction. We get to really know our fans and it's wonderful."

—Natalya

WWE's history with fan events at *WrestleMania* traces back to *WrestleMania IV*. What began as a weekend festival for *WrestleMania's IV, V, X, XI,* and *XII*, became an annual event called "Axxess" at *WrestleMania X-Seven*.

Axxess enables WWE's fans to live their dream. They can enjoy a full week of festivities, meet their favorite WWE personalities, watch live matches, participate in Q&A discussions with WWE Superstars and Legends, and even attend autograph sessions.

Aficionados can re-enact their favorite Superstar and Diva entrances while a WWE ring announcer narrates. They can climb the Money in the Bank Ladder and grab the briefcase, experience walking through Death Valley, and explore the 21 tombstones from Undertaker's Graveyard.

History buffs can walk through decades of authentic WWE memorabilia and a *WrestleMania* timeline, and visit a special area dedicated to the WWE Hall of Fame.

Fans can see the latest in WWE action figures from Mattel, enter the WWE 2K Video Game Zone, enjoy photo displays, participate in the WWE Universe Open Casting Call to audition for a role in an upcoming WWE Studios film, and more!

"Axxess is a unique and wonderful way to meet the people who have supported us all these years."

—Shawn Michaels

WRESTLEMANIA 2000

ARROWHEAD POND – ANAHEIM, CA

April 2
2000

Attendance
18,742

ANNOUNCERS
Jerry "The King" Lawler, Jim Ross

SPANISH ANNOUNCERS
Carlos Cabrera, Hugo Savinovich

RING ANNOUNCER
Howard Finkel

SPECIAL FIELD CORRESPONDENTS
Kevin Kelly

Event Card

**FATAL FOUR WAY ELIMINATION MATCH
FOR THE WWE CHAMPIONSHIP**
- Triple H (Champion) w/ Stephanie McMahon def. Big Show w/ Shane McMahon, The Rock w/ Vince McMahon, & Mick Foley w/ Linda McMahon

TRIANGLE LADDER MATCH FOR THE WORLD TAG TEAM CHAMPIONSHIP
- Edge & Christian def. The Hardy Boyz (Matt & Jeff) & The Dudleys (Bubba Ray & D-Von) (Champions) to become new Champions

TRIPLE THREAT MATCH FOR THE INTERCONTINENTAL AND EUROPEAN CHAMPIONSHIPS
- Kurt Angle (Intercontinental Champion & European Champion), Chris Benoit, and Chris Jericho*
  *Chris Benoit won the first fall to become Intercontinental Champion; Chris Jericho won the second fall to become European Champion

SIX PERSON TAG TEAM MATCH
- Too Cool (Grand Master Sexay & Scotty 2 Hotty) & Chyna def. The Radicalz (Dean Malenko, Eddie Guerrero, Perry Saturn)

CAT FIGHT MATCH
- Terri Runnels w/ Fabulous Moolah def. The Kat w/ Mae Young*
  *Val Venis served as Special Guest Referee

THIRTEEN-MAN BATTLE ROYAL FOR HARDCORE CHAMPIONSHIP
- Hardcore Holly def. Crash Holly, Tazz, Gangrel, Pete Gas, Joey Abs, Rodney, Viscera, Thrasher, Mosh, Take Michinoku, Funaki, Farooq

OTHER MATCHES
- Kane w/ Paul Bearer & Rikishi def. D-Generation X (X-Pac & Road Dogg) w/ Tori
- T & A (Test & Albert) w/ Trish Stratus def. Al Snow & Steve Blackman
- Godfather & D-Lo Brown def. Big Boss Man & Bull Buchanan

"We all grew up fans and loved tag team wrestling. We just wanted to put on the kind of match that people would always remember."

—Edge

The First WrestleMania of the New Millennium

Leading into *WrestleMania 2000*, two of WWE's top Superstars were unable to compete. Stone Cold Steve Austin underwent spinal surgery. Not only would he not be in a match at *WrestleMania 2000*, his future as a performer was unknown. Undertaker was recovering from an injury and, like Austin, he would not be appearing at *WrestleMania 2000*. The absence of these two iconic figures would create a void at the event, but that void would be an opportunity for the next generation of Superstars to step up and make their mark.

Godfather & D-Lo Brown vs. Big Boss Man & Bull Buchanan

WrestleMania 2000 got off to an exciting start with rapper and actor Ice-T performing The Godfather's entrance theme as the three men walked to the ring. Dressed in full pimp regalia, they were also accompanied to the ring by the lovely ladies of Godfather's "Ho Train." Their opponents for the evening, Big Boss Man and Bull Buchanan, had no interest in partying and pimpin'.

Spurred on by the crowd, Godfather and D-Lo grabbed an early advantage, but the team of Big Boss Man and Buchanan could not be kept down. The powerful tandem was able to secure the pin and claim victory.

▶ *Ice-T performs the Godfather's entrance theme as Godfather & D-Lo head to ring*

▶ *Big Boss Man and Buchanan defeat Godfather & D-Lo Brown for the victory*

Hardcore Battle Royal

When Crash Holly won the WWE Hardcore Championship, he made the ill-advised decision to institute a 24/7 rule. The new rule meant the Hardcore Champion had to defend his (or her) title at any and all times. If someone appeared with a referee and could pin the Champ, the title could change hands. The idea was entertaining, yet chaotic, and WWE officials decided to suspend the rule leading into *WrestleMania 2000*, when 13 men competed in a 15-minute Battle Royal that could feature as many title changes as possible, but whoever was champion at the end of the match would walk away as champion.

The combatants started in the ring, but the action quickly poured out to ringside. Less than 30 seconds into the match, Tazz suplexed Crash and became the new champion. Tazz's reign was even shorter, as Viscera pinned him 30 seconds later. As the combatants used cookie sheets, fire extinguishers, and numerous other items as weapons, there were six additional title changes until Tazz regained the title with less than a minute to go. The Houdini of Hardcore attacked Tazz with a cookie sheet and secured a pin as time counted down. Just when it seemed that Crash was going to make it to the deadline, his cousin Hardcore Holly hit Crash and Tazz with a glass candy jar and pinned his cousin as time expired, leaving *WrestleMania* as the new WWE Hardcore Champion.

▶ *Hardcore Holly smashes a jar over Crash Holly's head*

Head Cheese vs. T & A

Al Snow continued to look for ways to make his partnership with Steve Blackman more marketable and popular with fans, while Blackman just wanted to focus on their in-ring results. Blackman's approach was probably more sound, particularly with them having to face Trish Stratus' team of Test & Albert. Snow instead introduced to Blackman and the world Chester McCheeserton, a little person mascot dressed as a hunk of cheese.

The best thing that can be said about Chester is that he kept Trish occupied at ringside. Unfortunately, the cheesy mascot could do nothing to counteract the raw power of Test and Albert. Albert delivered a Baldo Bomb on Snow, while Test pinned Blackman. Snow apologized to Blackman for the ill-conceived mascot plan and the two partners beat up the pint-sized hunk of cheese to the delight of the crowd and the horror of the announce team.

▶ *Snow & Blackman attack Chester McCheeserton after the loss to Test & Albert*

A High Flying Spectacle

Tag team wrestling was experiencing a renaissance during the Attitude Era. A number of tandems were lighting it up in arenas all over the world, but three of the most innovative and entertaining were the Dudleys, the Hardys, and Edge and Christian. The three teams had been having thrilling matches with each other over the past year, and now all three teams shared the stage at *WrestleMania 2000* in a Triangle Ladder Match for the World Tag Team Championship.

▶ *Christian and Bubba Ray battle it out*

Going into the match, many felt The Dudleys, thanks to their innovative use of weaponry, were the favorites to retain their championship. While they could handle ladders, Bubba Ray and D-Von Dudley were famous for a different kind of weapon: putting anyone who crossed them through a table. The Hardy Boyz were all about high-flying moves, and ladders would allow them to reach stupendous heights. Edge and Christian were known to use any and all tricks to put their opponents down. Fans wanted to see all that and more at *WrestleMania*, and the three teams would over-deliver.

▶ *The Hardy Boys team up against Bubba Ray*

From the opening bell, the three duos assaulted each other with an aggression that set a new standard for tag team competition. Each Superstar performed a montage of death-defying aerial attacks, brutal ground assaults, and sensational slams. This surreal story unfolded among ten-foot-tall ladders that served as weapons, perches, and the path to the Tag Team Championship title suspended 20 feet in the air. Jeff Hardy sealed his *WrestleMania* legacy when he leaped off the top of a ladder in the aisle and sent Bubba Ray Dudley through a table with his famous Swanton Bomb.

Amid the carnage and trail of broken bodies, Edge and Christian used a table that connected two ladders to reach the World Tag Team Championship and win the match. The crowd gained newfound respect for each team, who left Arrowhead Pond to thunderous applause.

The Wrestling Machine Loses Two Titles

One of the greatest debuts in the history of WWE was that of Kurt Angle. The Olympic Gold medalist made his WWE debut at *Survivor Series 1999*, and within three months had captured both the Intercontinental and European Championships. He constantly bragged to the WWE Universe about his three I's—Intensity, Integrity, and Intelligence. Angle would need all three when he was forced to defend both of the titles in one two-fall match at *WrestleMania 2000*.

▶ *Kurt Angle lost both titles despite never being pinned by Benoit or Jericho*

Under the rules of the unusual match, the first fall was for the Intercontinental Championship and the second fall was for the European Championship. It was bad enough that Angle had to defend both championships against two of the more talented young Superstars in WWE, but he could lose a title in a pinfall decision that didn't even involve him. The match was a display of technical skill from the start. The Superstars traded slams, suplexes, submission maneuvers, and more. The Olympic hero's greatest nightmare came true when Benoit pinned Jericho to win the Intercontinental Championship and Jericho returned the favor, defeating Benoit for the European Championship. No one had defeated Angle, yet he lost both titles. Luckily for Kurt, he would move on to bigger and better things, winning the WWE Championship in October, completing perhaps the greatest debut year in history.

The Kat Fights

Every match at *WrestleMania 2000* involved three or more combatants with the exception of the Catfight between Terri and the Kat. Each of the Divas was coached by a legendary woman from the history of sports entertainment. The Kat was seconded by Mae Young and Terri had the Fabulous Moolah in her corner. Neither Diva was known for her wrestling prowess, so the rule was simple—the first Diva to throw her opponent out of the ring would be declared the winner.

Val Venis had the job of special guest referee. Both Terri and the Kat tried to curry favor with the Big Valbowski by planting lip locks on him, but Venis proved to be an impartial, yet incompetent referee. Twice the Kat had the match won by tossing out Terri, but each time Venis missed the action because he was distracted by Mae Young. To add insult to injury, during the second time, the Fabulous Moolah pulled the Kat out of the ring and rolled Terri back in. Venis turned around and awarded the match victory to Terri.

Intergender Tag Team Match

Since joining WWE, the Radicalz had made quite an early impression, with Dean Malenko already sporting the Light Heavyweight title. Fellow member Eddie Guerrero was eyeing a different prize, as he was smitten with "Ninth Wonder of the World," Chyna, who did not share his interest. Instead she decided to team with the crowd favorites Too Cool to battle three members of the Radicalz team.

The action was fast and furious, except when Chyna tried to get her hands on Guerrero to show him how she really felt. Each time they were supposed to be in the ring together, Latino Heat would scurry back to his corner and tag in one of his partners. Saturn and Malenko nailed some impressive offense, and Scotty 2 Hotty delighted the crowd when he managed to hit his Worm move on both Saturn and Malenko, but the crowd was truly delighted when Chyna finally got a hold of Guerrero. In an amazing show of strength, she executed a Gorilla Press on Guerrero and then a Powerbomb followed by a Slam out of a Sleeper Hold to pin her potential paramour.

A Double Betrayal

Kane thought he had found a friend and partner in X-Pac, and love with Tori. The two Superstars were an effective pair, twice winning the World Tag Team Championship. Eventually though, X-Pac turned his back on his former partner and the two began an intense rivalry. X-Pac was not content with beating the Big Red Monster in the ring, he also stole Kane's girlfriend, Tori. Now Kane wanted revenge on both D-Generation X and his former love. To ensure he'd be in a fair fight, he enlisted Rikishi as his tag-team partner.

Despite the outside interference, Kane and Rikishi were able to gain the win, with Rikishi delivering a brutal Stinkface to Tori, and Kane hitting a Tombstone Piledriver on X-Pac for the win. To complete the night, baseball great Pete Rose again tried to exact revenge on the Big Red Monster, but Charlie Hustle received a Chokeslam and a Stinkface for his trouble.

A NEW FAN EXPERIENCE

WrestleMania 2000 marked the fourth time *WrestleMania* was held in Southern California. To celebrate the Attitude Era's popularity and *WrestleMania*'s heritage, WWE's famous Fan Festival became even larger under its new name, Axxess. The two-day event saw more than 30,000 fans enjoy activities such as autograph sessions, memorabilia exhibits, calling a match with Michael Cole or Howard Finkel, or even getting a keepsake videotape to bring home as a *WrestleMania* memory. Fan Axxess would continue to grow over the years to the must-visit event it has now become during *WrestleMania* weekend.

A McMahon in Every Corner

As Mr. McMahon became more despised, other McMahon family members entered the fray. At this point, the WWE audience knew Vince's son Shane as a trusted confidant to his father; he wasn't afraid to enter the ring to resolve a dispute. Longtime fans remembered him as a referee and WWE official during the late 1980s and early 1990s. Linda McMahon, Vince's wife and WWE CEO, occasionally left the boardroom to appear on television. Linda was often the voice of reason who always strived to do the right thing.

In 1999, fans were introduced to daughter Stephanie during a battle between Mr. McMahon and Undertaker. Originally the innocent apple of her father's eye, Stephanie fell in love with Test. After a trip to Las Vegas went awry, Stephanie married the wrong man. To everyone's shock, including Stephanie's, she married WWE Champion Triple H. Enraging her father, Stephanie decided to stay married to Triple H, and the duo became WWE's most powerful couple. She was the WWE Women's Champion and Helmsley was the WWE Champion. Together, they instituted "The McMahon-Helmsley Era."

The 2000 *Royal Rumble* saw Triple H successfully defend his WWE title against Mick Foley, performing as Cactus Jack. At the same event, The Rock eliminated Big Show to win the *Royal Rumble* match, earning a WWE Championship Match at *WrestleMania 2000*. Big Show claimed the result was incorrect, and that he had won the *Rumble*. When photo evidence was inconclusive, and the two subsequently traded victories, the *WrestleMania* main event became a Triple Threat. Though Foley's loss to Triple H at *No Way Out* meant the Hardcore Legend had to retire, Linda McMahon overturned that ruling during an episode of *RAW*.

By announcing WrestleMania was his final match, Mick Foley was a sentimental favorite with the crowd. To the delight of the WWE Universe, the Hardcore Legend provided exciting moments throughout the clash and kicked out of many pinfall attempts. The wrath of Triple H's signature Pedigree was the one move Foley couldn't escape. After a career filled with emotional moments, Foley's exit in front of the Pond faithful chanting his name was a true hero's sendoff.

For the first time in WrestleMania history, the main event would be a Fatal Four Way Elimination Match for the WWE Championship. Furthermore, a McMahon family member would be in the corner of each of the four participants.

Big Show used his size and power to dominate the early part of the match. Seeing the writing on the wall, the other three Superstars set aside their rivalries and combined efforts to eliminate the seven-foot behemoth, and Big Show was finally eliminated with a Rock Bottom. Earlier in the show, it was revealed that the Main Event was to be "No Disqualification," which gave the combatants far more leeway to use illegal tactics (like low blows) and objects (like a barbed-wire wrapped 2x4) to take out their opponents. The champion looked to be in serious jeopardy of being the next one eliminated when the Rock 'n' Sock Connection joined forces once again, but the alliance proved short-lived as both Foley and The Rock couldn't help themselves and attacked each other.

In the end, it fittingly came down to two of the Attitude Era's biggest Superstars in their physical prime. Triple H and The Rock had battled for WWE gold before, but not when the stakes were this high. The war spilled out to the floor and the tide turned on several occasions.

As expected, physicality was not limited to the Superstars, as members of the McMahon family fought as well. Shane returned to ringside and lacerated his father with a chair shot to the forehead. Mr. McMahon's advisors took him from ringside for medical attention, but Vince returned, clearing Shane from the ring. Vince stunned everyone with an unthinkable double-cross. He leveled his associate, The Rock, with a brutal chair shot to the head. When that didn't put The Rock away, the WWE Chairman repeated the act, ensuring Triple H's victory. This outcome stunned the crowd as it was the first time in WrestleMania history that the show closed with a heel winning the championship. The Rock gained a bit of revenge by leveling Shane, Vince, and Stephanie with Rock Bottoms, but he'd have to wait for another day to retake the WWE Championship.

WRESTLEMANIA X-SEVEN

RELIANT ASTRODOME – HOUSTON, TX

April 1
2001

Attendance
67,925

ANNOUNCERS
Jim Ross
Paul Heyman
"Mean" Gene Okerlund
Bobby "The Brain" Heenan

SPANISH ANNOUNCERS
Carlos Cabrera
Hugo Savinovich

RING ANNOUNCER
Howard Finkel

SPECIAL FIELD CORRESPONDENTS
Jonathan Coachman
Michael Cole

SPECIAL MUSICAL GUEST
Motörhead

Event Card

WWE CHAMPIONSHIP MATCH
- Stone Cold Steve Austin def. The Rock (Champion) to become new Champion

GIMMICK BATTLE ROYAL
- The Iron Sheik def. Brother Love, Bushwhackers, Jim Cornette, Doink, Duke "The Dumpster" Droese, Earthquake, Gobbledy Gooker, Goon, Michael "P.S." Hayes, Hillbilly Jim, Kamala, Kim Chee, One Man Gang, Repo Man, Sergeant Slaughter, Tugboat, and Nikolai Volkoff

TABLES LADDERS & CHAIRS II MATCH FOR THE WORLD TAG TEAM CHAMPIONSHIP
- Edge & Christian def. The Hardy Boyz (Matt & Jeff) & The Dudley Boyz (Bubba Ray & D-Von) (Champions) to become new Champions

STREET FIGHT
- Shane McMahon def. Mr. McMahon w/ Stephanie McMahon-Helmsley*
  *Mick Foley served as Special Guest Referee

WOMEN'S CHAMPIONSHIP MATCH
- Chyna def. Ivory (Champion) to become new Champion

EUROPEAN CHAMPIONSHIP MATCH
- Eddie Guerrero w/ Perry Saturn def. Test (Champion) to become new Champion

HARDCORE CHAMPIONSHIP MATCH
- Kane def. Raven (Champion) & Big Show to become new Champion

SIX MAN TAG MATCH
- The APA (Bradshaw & Farooq) w/ Jacqueline & Tazz def. Right To Censor (Bull Buchanan, The Goodfather, Val Venis) w/ Steven Richards

INTERCONTINENTAL CHAMPIONSHIP MATCH
- Chris Jericho (Champion) def. William Regal

OTHER MATCHES
- Undertaker def. Triple H
- Kurt Angle def. Chris Benoit

> ## "I was feeling a little bit stale. I've always liked being the bad guy. If I could go back in time, I would never have done that."
>
> —Stone Cold Steve Austin

The War is Over

After a span of nearly six years, the conflict known as "The Monday Night War" was over. On March 26, 2001, it was announced that WWE had purchased the WCW's assets. That evening, WWE aired a special simulcast; audiences could watch WWE's *Raw* and the final episode of *WCW Monday Nitro* together. While WCW and ECW were out of business, things were booming at WWE. In fact, for the first time since *WrestleMania VIII*, the Showcase of the Immortals was going to be held in a dome instead of an arena. The second-largest *WrestleMania* crowd to date, trailing only the indoor-event record of *WrestleMania III*, would be taking in the action live in Houston's historic Astrodome.

Failed Revenge

William Regal was excited to throw his newfound power around as the new commissioner of WWE until Chris Jericho interrupted his inauguration and started mocking the snobbish Regal. That may have been a mistake as Regal put Jericho in a series of brutal Handicap Matches. Not learning his lesson, Jericho relieved himself in Regal's tea, which the commissioner unknowingly drank. Enraged that he had been besmirched, Regal decided to further punish Jericho by challenging him to a match for Jericho's championship at *WrestleMania X-Seven*.

Regal's strategy to begin the match was to attack Jericho's injured shoulder, a shoulder Regal himself had injured on a *SmackDown* leading into *WrestleMania*. Regal kept control of the match, executing a double underhook suplex from the middle turnbuckle to score a near win. Spurred on by the fans, Jericho counterattacked, hitting a Bulldog and a Lionsault to put Regal down for the three count to retain his Intercontinental Championship.

Ring Righteousness

Steven Richards was unhappy with some of the programming choices being made by WWE, so he wanted to decide what was best for the WWE Universe. His organization, the Right to Censor (RTC) had converted adult film Superstar Val Venis and former pimp the Godfather (now calling himself the Goodfather) and other Superstars to his cause. Numerous WWE Superstars, including Tazz, had a problem with the RTC's tactics, so he recruited the Acolyte Protection Agency to team with him in a fight with the RTC at *WrestleMania*.

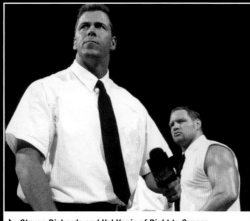

▶ *Steven Richards and Val Venis of Right to Censor*

▶ *Tazz battles Val Venis outside the ring*

All six men immediately went after each other before the bell rang, leading Jim Ross to observe that the only man in the ring was the referee. Things started to settle down as Venis took on Tazz before Buchanan and Goodfather took turns unleashing their power moves. Tazz was eventually able to tag in Bradshaw, who crushed Goodfather with his patented Clothesline from Hell, which secured the win for his three-man team.

Triple Threat for the Hardcore Championship

The Hardcore Championship had brought its own unique brand of competition to the WWE, and the current champion, Raven, brought a whole new level of insanity to title defenses. To drive that point home, Raven wheeled a shopping cart full of weapons to the ring for his Triple Threat Match at *WrestleMania*. Knowing he had to face two veteran giants like Kane and Big Show, Raven needed all the help he could get.

With falls counting anywhere, it wasn't long before the three men were out of the ring and battling throughout the backstage area. Nothing was out of bounds—Raven was thrown through a window, Kane went crashing through a door, and Big Show and Kane crashed through a wall. Kane even used a golf cart to run Raven down. The three eventually battled back to the entrance stage where Kane threw both of his competitors off the stage and slammed onto Big Show, pinning the giant to become the new WWE Hardcore Champion.

▶ *Kane tosses Raven through a window during the Hardcore Championship Match*

Test vs. Eddie Guerrero

Looking to capture the European Championship for himself, Eddie Guerrero had been playing mind games with the current champion, Test. To further mess with the powerful Test, Guerrero came to the ring with fellow Radicalz member Perry Saturn. Psychologically, it sent the message that Test should keep the action in the ring or he might have to deal with a two-on-one situation.

For the most part, Test controlled the match with his power moves. Saturn did take advantage of a distracted referee to sneak into the ring to attack Test and let his partner Guerrero jump on the offensive. Test regained the upper hand until the third member of the Radicalz, Dean Malenko, raced to ringside to argue with the referee. While the official was occupied, Saturn tossed the European Championship to Guerrero, who clocked Test with the title and pinned him to become the new European Champion.

Kurt Angle vs. Chris Benoit

While no championship was at stake, both men were looking to lay claim to the title of best mat technician in WWE. Angle had been made to tap out a few weeks earlier, but he claimed it didn't count because it wasn't during an official match. Both men brought their "A" game, trading moves and countermoves to create near pinfall situations. Benoit kicked out of a pin following Angle's Olympic Slam, and Benoit's Diving Headbutt could not keep Angle down for a count of three. Angle was about to be in a world of hurt, set up for a submission move, but the arrogant Olympian used an illegal groin shot and a handful of tights to record the pin.

Short and Sweet

Ivory knew that Chyna posed a considerable threat to her Women's Championship reign, so she couldn't have been too upset when Chyna was shelved with an injury. Chyna tried to make a comeback at the 2001 *Royal Rumble* in a title match against Ivory, but she returned to the ring too soon and reinjured her neck. Thinking that Chyna's career was over, Ivory proceeded to mock the Ninth Wonder of the World, but Chyna returned to attack her rival and challenge her to a match at *WrestleMania X-Seven*. Ivory would only agree if Chyna would sign a document waiving any liability if Ivory permanently injured Chyna. Chyna agreed and the match was set.

The match was short and (for Chyna) sweet. Chyna used her power moves to devastate Ivory and take the WWE Women's Championship.

McMahon vs. McMahon

The McMahon family narrative continued to settle family scores on live television to the delight of the WWE Universe. Mr. McMahon was flying high— he was about to vanquish his long-time rival WCW, his sports-entertainment company was seeing record revenue and profit, and he was engaged in a public affair with Trish Stratus. Daughter Stephanie didn't think her father was doing anything wrong, but his son Shane was extremely unhappy and let his father know. The two came to blows on several occasions, leading to the son challenging his father to a Street Fight at *WrestleMania*.

> ## "Storylines that included behind-the-scenes elements with our family were very well received by our audience."
>
> **—Linda McMahon**

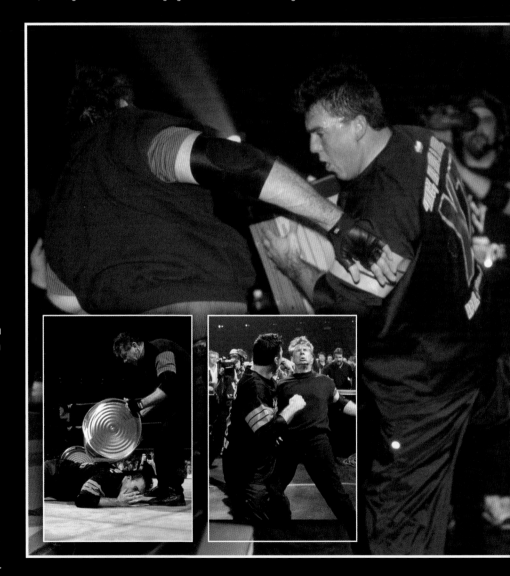

During the final episode of WCW's *Nitro*, Mr. McMahon made an appearance gloating that he held the future of WCW in his hands. But later that night, Shane shocked his father by informing Mr. McMahon that the name on the contract read "McMahon"—Shane McMahon—and that WCW would once again rule over WWE. Audiences became even more intrigued, wondering what would happen in the Street Fight between them at *WrestleMania*. Linda McMahon remembers, "We conducted some consumer research, and it confirmed that storylines that included behind-the-scenes elements with our family were very well received by our audience. For instance, when Vince went on television and said he wanted a divorce, I began to receive letters from fans asking if we were really getting a divorce."

This match involved all four McMahons, Trish Stratus, and special guest referee Mick Foley. To get her out of the way, Vince put Linda into a mental institution and kept her under sedation while he became embroiled in a torrid affair with Trish Stratus. The war of words between father and son became so intense that Mr. McMahon told Shane, "I'll never forgive your mother for giving birth to you."

Once the bell rang, the violent story of "Father versus Son" began to unfold. The two beat one another from pillar to post, using everything from kendo sticks to garbage cans. Mr. McMahon endured an early barrage and then turned on his son, beating him mercilessly. During the match, daughter Stephanie handed out face slaps to Shane, Stratus, and Foley. As he did so many times before, Shane McMahon showed no fear as a performer, effortlessly flying through the air as he launched attacks against his father.

The match's conclusion featured a stunning twist. Linda rose from her chair and kicked Mr. McMahon in his family jewels. After an assist from Foley, the Hardcore Legend, Shane dropkicked his father in the face with a garbage can to score the pinfall. In victory, mother and son embraced as Mr. McMahon lay in the ring, unconscious.

Delivering Some TLC

The three teams that had battled for the World Tag Team Championship in a Triangle Ladder Match at *WrestleMania 2000* had upped the ante with a TLC—Tables, Ladders, and Chairs—match at the 2000 edition of *SummerSlam*. Once again, the World Tag Team Championship hung 20 feet high above the ring, but ladders were not the only allowable weapon—now tables and chairs were part of the destructive equation. Like any blockbuster, the match was so successful that it demanded a sequel, and TLC would be bigger and badder on the grand stage of *WrestleMania X-Seven*.

The six men showed a blatant disregard for their own safety or the wellbeing of their opponents, crashing through tables, leaping high off ladders, and punishing their own bodies. Each of three teams had a third supporter that ran to the ring to increase the carnage, with Spike Dudley helping his brothers, Rhyno assisting Edge & Christian, and Lita joining with Team Extreme. When it seemed that the match couldn't push the limits of punishment any further, Edge administered a Spear off a 20-foot ladder onto Jeff Hardy, who was dangling from the championship title above the ring. Edge remembers, "If I thought about it I probably wouldn't have done it. In no way did I envision that it would be the most replayed moment of my career. We didn't go over it once. We go without a net, without pads, without stunt people. We just do it and it's one of the beautiful things about what we do and one of those things people don't understand. Jeff's a maniac and I'm a maniac. We just went." Moments later, Bubba Ray and Matt Hardy soared off a ladder, over the top rope, and crashed

through four tables. Edge and Christian finally managed to scale the ladder and retrieve the championships. Regardless of who won or lost, each man was brutalized. TLC II showed the price these six Superstars were willing to pay to entertain the audience, and to be considered the best tag team in the world.

The Gimmick Battle Royal

While the WWE Universe enjoys the new and exciting direction the company continues to take, there is a never-ending fondness for the Superstars of the past as well. The WWE paid homage to 19 of these greats (and not-so-greats) during this over-the-top Battle Royal. The live crowd roared with excitement and approval for each

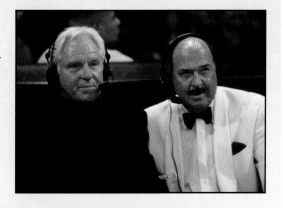

introduction, including a pair of former WWE Champions, the Iron Sheik and Sgt. Slaughter, as well as colorful characters Kamala, Earthquake, Doink the Clown, the Bushwhackers, and more. Even the bizarre Gobbledy Gooker made an appearance. For the fans at home, commentary by Mean Gene Okerlund and Bobby "The Brain" Heenan was an additional blast from the past.

The key to a Battle Royal is to be the last man remaining; the total number of eliminations only pads a Superstar's stats. So although two of the final three in the ring, Sgt. Slaughter and Hillbilly Jim, had recorded multiple eliminations, the only elimination that mattered was the final one, and once Jim took out the Sergeant, the Iron Sheik snuck up and dumped the Hillbilly, winning the match with his only elimination. To the approval of the crowd though, the Sheik's longtime rival, Sgt. Slaughter, returned to the ring to put his former nemesis in the Cobra Clutch.

Undertaker vs. Triple H

In all the years Undertaker and Triple H rose to fame in WWE, they had never crossed paths—until *WrestleMania X-7*. Triple H elaborates, "Going into *WrestleMania* that year, there was all this speculation about my opponent, even me having a 'Boxer vs. Wrestler' match with Mike Tyson. We might have been less than a month out from *WrestleMania*. Taker didn't have an opponent and neither did I. So, Vince said, 'We're going to have you and Taker work together.' In a couple of weeks, we built a huge angle out of me just going to the ring, saying, 'I have beaten everybody there is to beat' and going through this big list. And when I got to the end of the list … 'gong.' Here comes Undertaker, saying, 'You haven't beaten me yet.' That was it. People got really into it; we had a hell of a match."

The wild battle spilled out onto the Astrodome floor and even overflowed into the production station. The crowd went berserk when Undertaker Chokeslammed Triple H off the production scaffold, onto the floor. More than once, "The Game" regained the initiative, thanks to his resilience and trusty sledgehammer." After a heated exchange, a bloodied Undertaker defeated Triple H with The Last Ride powerbomb. The man from the dark side remained undefeated at the Showcase of the Immortals.

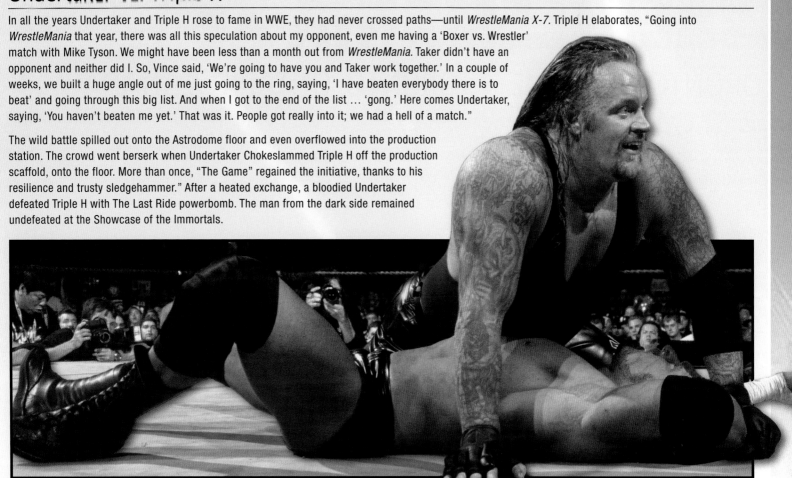

The Rock vs. Stone Cold Steve Austin

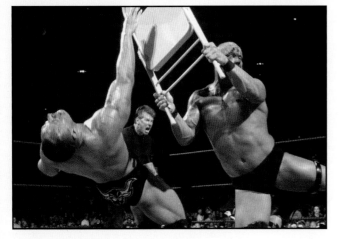

Fans around the world fervently anticipated the main event showdown. While the Texas Rattlesnake recovered from spinal surgery, out of action for almost a year, The Rock became WWE's centerpiece. On his return, Stone Cold Steve Austin intended to reclaim his top position. In contrast, The Rock vowed to demonstrate that things should remain as they were. Austin grew up south of Houston, in Victoria, Texas. Revered in his home state, he entered the Astrodome to a hero's welcome. The Rock approached *WrestleMania X-7* with the confidence of the WWE Champion, but also as a man who was headlining his third consecutive *WrestleMania*.

Early in the match, Stone Cold Steve Austin and The Rock exploded into offensive campaigns. They exchanged failed attempts to perform the other's finishing move. Both Superstars were prepared to exploit the No Disqualification stipulation and do everything necessary to exit Houston as the victor.

Once again, Mr. McMahon's uncontrollable desire to exert his will over a championship match brought him ringside. With both competitors' faces covered in blood, Austin committed an unfathomable act; he began to collaborate with Mr. McMahon. At first, no one in the Astrodome could believe it. But as the match continued, it was apparent that Steve Austin had made a deal with Satan himself.

The Rock utilized the Sharpshooter; Austin employed the Million Dollar Dream. Neither man would be pinned. In an act that disgusted fans, Stone Cold unloaded a savage campaign of chair shots onto The Rock, causing the Astrodome crowd to boo its hometown hero. But in this violent onslaught, Austin revealed a ruthless aspect of his personality. He would do anything to win the WWE Championship, even if it meant shaking the hand of the repugnant Mr. McMahon. This unholy alliance led to Austin's victory over The Rock, making him WWE Champion for the fifth time in his career. The Texas Rattlesnake's fans watched in confusion and horror as the champion and his new ally celebrated the victory.

WRESTLEMANIA X8

TORONTO SKYDOME – TORONTO, ONTARIO, CANADA

March 17
2002

Attendance
68,237

ANNOUNCERS
Jerry "The King" Lawler
Jim Ross

SPANISH ANNOUNCERS
Carlos Cabrera
Hugo Savinovich

RING ANNOUNCER
Howard Finkel

SPECIAL FIELD CORRESPONDENTS
Jonathan Coachman
Lillian Garcia
Michael Cole

SPECIAL MUSICAL GUESTS
Drowning Pool
Saliva

Event Card

UNDISPUTED CHAMPIONSHIP MATCH
■ Triple H def. Chris Jericho (Champion) w/ Stephanie McMahon to become new Champion

TRIPLE THREAT WOMEN'S CHAMPIONSHIP MATCH
■ Jazz (Champion) def. Lita and Trish Stratus to retain the Championship

ICON VS. ICON MATCH
■ The Rock def. Hollywood Hulk Hogan

FATAL FOUR WAY ELIMINATION MATCH FOR THE WORLD TAG TEAM CHAMPIONSHIP
■ Billy & Chuck (Champions) def. The Hardy Boyz (Jeff & Matt), the APA (Bradshaw & Farooq) and the Dudley Boyz (Bubba & D-Von) to retain the Championship

NO DISQUALIFICATION MATCH
■ Undertaker def. "Nature Boy" Ric Flair

HARDCORE CHAMPIONSHIP
■ Maven (Champion) fought Goldust to a no contest*
*Spike Dudley, Hurricane, Mighty Molly, Christian, and lastly Maven all scored pinfalls to become Hardcore Champion during the event

EUROPEAN CHAMPIONSHIP MATCH
■ Diamond Dallas Page (Champion) def. Christian to retain the Championship

INTERCONTINENTAL CHAMPIONSHIP
■ Rob Van Dam def. William Regal (Champion) to become new Champion

OTHER MATCHES
■ Stone Cold Steve Austin def. Scott Hall w/ Kevin Nash
■ Edge def. Booker T.
■ Kurt Angle def. Kane

> ## "To have a match with Hulk Hogan at *WrestleMania* was very special. It was one of the most incredible nights of my career."
>
> —The Rock

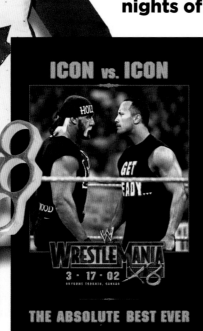

Only One Left Standing

The year following *WrestleMania X-Seven* was tumultuous. Mr. McMahon's son, Shane, had purchased WCW and, in a shocking twist, a number of former ECW Superstars formed an Alliance with the WCW invaders. This new group, led by Shane McMahon, Stephanie McMahon, and Paul Heyman, made life miserable for WWE until *Survivor Series*, when a "Winner Take All" Match left WWE the sole surviving company. However, the disappearance of the Alliance did not end Mr. McMahon's troubles. To bankroll the Alliance, his two children had each sold their shares of WWE to Ric Flair, who now controlled half of WWE, making him an equal partner with Mr. McMahon.

The in-ring action was greater than it had ever been. For the first time ever, the WCW and WWE Champions met to crown an Undisputed WWE Champion, with Chris Jericho being the first to ever hold that title. None of that mattered to Mr. McMahon, who only cared about ridding his company of Ric Flair, and went so far as to bring the nWo in to accomplish the job. The WWE debut of the New World Order would lead to one of the biggest clashes in *WrestleMania* history, one that would see a Legend battle an Icon.

The Power of The Punch

Recently, William Regal had introduced a new, devastating knockout blow he called "The Power of the Punch." While he wanted the world to think it was his strength that levelled opponents, fans knew it was the brass knuckles that Regal secretly wore. Former ECW Superstar Rob Van Dam would have to contend with Regal's rule breaking when he challenged Regal for the Intercontinental Championship in the opening match of *WrestleMania X8*.

Regal wasted no time trying to use his secret weapon to quickly end the match, but Van Dam managed to kick the knuckles out of Regal's hands and out of the ring. The two traded moves and countermoves, but RVD's unique brand of offense slowly gave him the advantage. Regal rolled out of the ring to retrieve his brass knuckles. The referee spotted the object and seized it. Not to be deterred, Regal had a second pair hidden in his trunks. But as Regal attempted to slip them on, Van Dam kicked him, followed it up with a 5-Star Frog Splash, and pinned his opponent to become the new Intercontinental Champion.

DDP vs Christian

Christian had been on a bit of a losing streak since starting his singles career. Rather than take his defeats in stride, he'd been throwing temper tantrums. Eternal optimist Diamond Dallas Page helped Christian get back on the winning path. Rather than thank Page, Christian attacked DDP, claiming he didn't need anyone's help. The two decided to settle things in a match for Page's WWE European Championship.

Making his in-ring *WrestleMania* debut, Page unleashed a flurry of offense, countering Christian's moves into Page's Diamond Cutter for the win.

▶ *Regal's brass knuckles are seized by the referee*

The WWE Hardcore Championship

A former school teacher, Maven made his mark in WWE by winning the *Tough Enough* competition and shockingly eliminating Undertaker from the *Royal Rumble*. Then he won the Hardcore Championship to defend against Goldust at *WrestleMania X8*.

Like past Hardcore Matches, a variety of weapons were used throughout the bout. Goldust brought a new twist by only using gold-painted items. The Superstars were wearing each other down with relentless attacks when the 24/7 rule brought a bizarre ending to the match—with both men down, Crash Holly ran to the ring and pinned Maven to win the title.

It was not the last time fans would see the Hardcore Championship defended that night, as through the rest of the evening, backstage updates would see The Hurricane, Mighty Molly, and Christian each win the title, before Maven pinned Christian to reclaim the title and hopped into a cab to leave the arena.

▶ *RVD wins the Intercontinental Championship*

Kane vs. Kurt Angle

It was certainly a clash of styles to see former Olympian Kurt Angle take on the Big Red Monster Kane. The two had been battling ever since Angle believed Kane had cost Kurt a shot at the Undisputed WWE Championship, and Angle looked to get revenge at *WrestleMania X8*.

Early on in the match, Angle tried to demonstrate his wrestling "superiority" by executing one of Kane's trademark moves, a flying clothesline. This only angered the monster and he hit Angle with one of his own. The two battled back and forth with Kane ready to deliver his powerful Tombstone Piledriver before Angle was able to turn the move into a rollup, securing the win for the former Olympian.

The Nature Boy faces The Deadman

After a decade away from *WrestleMania*, the "Nature Boy" made his return. The on-air co-owner of WWE may have wished he'd stayed away longer, as he had to battle an angry Undertaker looking to take his undefeated record at the Showcase of the Immortals to 10-0.

The match was brutal and violent. Flair came tantalizingly close to ending The Streak when he locked Undertaker in the Figure Four, but the American Badass was able to make it to the ropes, forcing a break of the hold. Flair amazed The Deadman by kicking out of a pin attempt following a Last Ride, but he could not repeat the feat after a Tombstone. Despite the loss, the return to *WrestleMania* meant a great deal to the "Nature Boy," "When I first came back, I wasn't supposed to wrestle. I was sitting in the arena and [Triple H] said, 'Undertaker wants to wrestle you. He asked to wrestle you at *WrestleMania*.' I couldn't wait. We had a good match, well, mine was passable, Undertaker carried me to a good match."

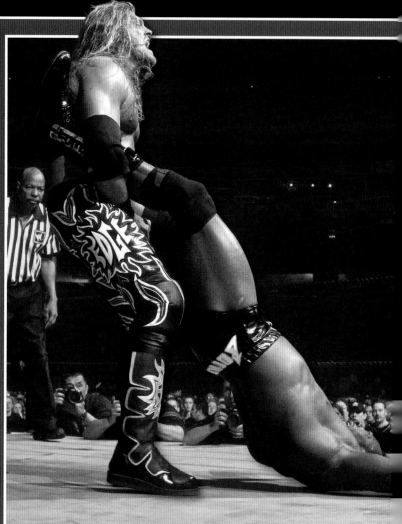

▶ *Undertaker gestures 10-0 as his perfect record starts to become "The Streak"*

Edge vs. Booker T

WWE Superstars have clashed over championships, family feuds, the love of a woman, and many other slights and indignities. It is fair to say that only once in *WrestleMania* history has a match seen its roots develop in a battle over a Japanese endorsement deal. Booker T was sure he'd been chosen as the spokesman for a Japanese shampoo company, but to the five-time WCW Champion's chagrin, Edge got the nod instead.

Early on in the match, it looked like Booker T would gain his measure of revenge, but Edge was able to counter Booker's offense with some high-flying moves of his own. Booker had excited the crowd with his Spinaroonie, but Edge delighted his hometown with his own version of Booker's move. He followed that up with the Edgecution to gain the pin.

Stone Cold Steve Austin vs. Scott Hall

The day before the event, two of the matches changed. Kevin Nash explains, "The original plan was for Scott and I to buck Austin. Hogan would lose to Rock and then we would come down and put the boots to Rock. In 24 hours, it changed to Austin stunning Scott and I, and then us going down to the ring in the Hogan-Rock match and getting pummeled. It was too soon. Enough time had not passed from the Monday Night War. I think WWE had the 'All hail the victor' mindset, and they had every right to. But there was a lot of money that could've been made."

When the bell rang, the Texas Rattlesnake was ready to avenge his missed opportunity to become WWE Champion. The pairing of Hall inside the ring and Nash on the outside created trouble throughout the match. One would entangle the referee while the other assaulted Austin. The future looked bleak for Stone Cold. Twice Austin took control, but both times, Nash would take out the referee.

Finally, several WWE officials ejected Nash from ringside. Once the match was a level playing field, Austin landed consecutive Stone Cold Stunners on Hall to win the match.

Jeff Hardy and Chuck Palumbo battle it out in the Four-Corners Elimination Match

Four-Corners Elimination Match

Chuck and Billy, in the midst of their first reign as World Tag Team Champions, were already facing long odds to leave *WrestleMania* with the titles when they had to defend them against three other teams, but when each of those teams had been World Tag Team Champions previously, the challenge seemed virtually impossible.

Three-time champions the Acolyte Protection Agency (APA) hammered the champions from the start of the match. Billy and Chuck seemed destined to be the first team eliminated until they made a blind tag to bring in six-time champions the Dudleys to face the APA. Bradshaw still attempted to punish the champs, and that lack of focus cost his team when the Dudleys hit him with a 3-D and eliminated the APA from the match.

The champions rested on the ring apron, gathering their strength while old rivals the Dudleys and five-time former champs the Hardys battled away. Matt hit his Twist of Fate on Bubba Ray and his brother Jeff followed up with a Swanton Bomb to pin Bubba Ray and eliminate the Dudleys, leaving just the Hardys and the champions. Jeff's attempt to repeat the Swanton failed, and Chuck and Billy plastered Jeff with the title, allowing them to pin him and retain their championship.

The Passing of the Torch

When the Great One faced the Immortal Hulk Hogan, fans got to see a rare bout featuring two generation-defining Superstars. An epic stare-down stopped the clock, with dueling chants of 'Rocky, Rocky' and 'Hogan, Hogan' filling the SkyDome. Hogan showed he still possessed his famous strength, and the rising energy from the crowd inspired the man who was competing in his first *WrestleMania* in nine years. Vince McMahon adds, "The audience reacted very favorably to Hulk Hogan, which was a surprise to most of us. We thought it was going to be more of a 50/50 reaction from the audience."

The roars reached deafening levels as Hogan "Hulked up" and the crowd waited for Hulkamania to prevail once more. But in the end, this story would conclude after a People's Elbow brought The Rock victory.

> ## "Most guys would've panicked and blew the match. Not Rock."
> —Hulk Hogan

In a show of mutual respect, the two shook hands. After expelling Hall and Nash from the SkyDome, the Hulkster, at The Rock's insistence, gave the fans what they had hoped to see—his famous post-match celebration. Though Hogan's only two *WrestleMania* losses would be at SkyDome, the Legend was gracious in defeat. The two men walked side by side and when Hogan raised The Great One's arm, it symbolized sports-entertainment's time-honored tradition: the passing of the torch.

Hogan adds, "Before we went out there, Rock's dad, Rocky Johnson, said to him, 'Just listen to Hogan.' I listened to him and he listened to me. When we got in the ring and he was booed by 68,000 people, he handled it better than I ever could. Most guys would've panicked and blew the match. Not Rock. He hung in there with me and by the end of that match, when I shook his hand, the torch was passed."

The Rock adds, "Around this time I felt I had accomplished everything I had wanted to in WWE. When I heard Hulk was coming back, I thought there would be great interest in us wrestling. To have a match with Hulk Hogan at *WrestleMania* was very special. It was one of the most incredible nights of my career."

Women's Championship Triple Threat

While Lita and Trish Stratus had each played a supporting role in the previous year's event, *WrestleMania X8* saw the two future Hall of Fame Divas make their in-ring *WrestleMania* debuts. They faced a tall order as each was looking to dethrone the reigning WWE Women's Champion, the powerful Jazz.

Understanding the challenge of beating a champion like Jazz, Lita and Trish often worked together to attack her, which made the match often seem more like a Handicap Match, and made Jazz's offensive displays all the more impressive. The champion knocked Stratus out of the ring, leading to extended one-on-one action between her and Lita, but Stratus eventually made it back to the ring and again the two challengers teamed up to take out Jazz before finally setting their sights on each other. Trish backed Lita into a corner, but missed a flying attack that once again knocked her out of the ring and allowed Jazz to take advantage with a Fisherman's Suplex off the middle ropes to pin Lita and to successfully defend her title.

▶ *Trish Stratus connects with Jazz*

▶ *Jazz celebrates with the title*

THE RETURN OF THE GAME

In May of 2001, Triple H suffered a potentially career-ending injury, "I planted my left leg and it felt like a lightning bolt hit me. I felt my entire left quad muscle roll up my thigh. I knew as soon as I did that I tore something really bad. I got down to Birmingham, Alabama to see Dr. Andrews. After my surgery, he said that he didn't know anybody—he had checked with other doctors—and he couldn't think of anybody that had come back from the surgery that I had. He told me I might not wrestle ever again."

After his surgery, Triple H relocated to Birmingham to undergo a grueling, carefully supervised, physical rehabilitation regimen. Triple H remembers, "I never put it in my head that I wasn't going to wrestle again. I said I'll do whatever I have to. I moved into the Embassy Suites hotel and stayed there for nine months. I rehabbed every single day, two sessions a day, seven days a week. When I got close to being able to wrestle, Vince sent a ring down and they put it up and that became part of my training."

The Undisputed Championship

The main event for the WWE Championship was between a man looking to reestablish his dominance, and an Undisputed Champion who was adept at playing the pompous scoundrel. In the essence of "Good versus Evil," "The Game's" estranged wife, Stephanie McMahon, seconded Chris Jericho to the ring.

Each step Triple H took on his surgically repaired left leg was a step closer toward redemption. A complication created another obstacle. Triple H recalls, "I had some pain going into *WrestleMania* and went to Dr. Andrews for a checkup. He told me I was lucky to be walking. One of my sutures pulled a chunk of bone off the side of my kneecap, and I had a big split up my kneecap. He told me I needed to stay off it. I told him I was going into the biggest match of my career. He told me to do the best I could. I just taped it up and kept going."

Jericho antagonized Triple H by attacking his wounded leg. Meanwhile, Stephanie kept the referee on his toes. Triple H received one of the loudest ovations of the night when he leveled Stephanie with a Pedigree. He had a second one saved for Jericho, and it led to a pinfall victory and the championship.

Chris Jericho reflects, "It was huge for Triple H. It's always a bad thing to get hurt. It takes something away from you. Not only do you have to deal with a physical issue, but a mental one as well. To have him come back and reassume his mantle, his position, meant a lot to him. It meant a lot to me to help him get there."

"To have gone through everything I had gone through, the reception I got at Madison Square Garden, winning the *Rumble*, and to be able to end up at *WrestleMania* and win the championship from Chris Jericho, I couldn't have written it any better," remarked Triple H.

▶ *Chris Jericho drop kicks Triple H*

WRESTLEMANIA XIX

SAFECO FIELD – SEATTLE, WA

March 30
2003

Attendance
54,097

RAW ANNOUNCERS
Jerry "The King" Lawler
Jim Ross

SMACKDOWN ANNOUNCERS
Michael Cole, Tazz

SPANISH ANNOUNCERS
Carlos Cabrera, Hugo Savinovich

RAW RING ANNOUNCER
Howard Finkel

SMACKDOWN RING ANNOUNCER
Tony Chimel

SPECIAL FIELD CORRESPONDENT
Jonathan Coachman

SPECIAL MUSICAL GUESTS
Ashanti, Limp Bizkit

Event Card

WWE CHAMPIONSHIP MATCH
- Brock Lesnar def. Kurt Angle (Champion) to become new Champion*
  *If Kurt Angle was counted out or disqualified he'd lose the Championship

STREET FIGHT
- Hulk Hogan def. Mr. McMahon*
  *If Hulk Hogan lost he would be forced to retire

WORLD HEAVYWEIGHT CHAMPIONSHIP MATCH
- Triple H (Champion) w/ "Nature Boy" Ric Flair def. Booker T to retain the Championship

CAT FIGHT
- Stacy Keibler, Torrie Wilson, and the Miller Light Cat Fight Girls (Kitana Baker & Tanya Ballinger) went to a No Contest

TRIPLE THREAT MATCH FOR THE WWE TAG TEAM CHAMPIONSHIP
- Team Angle (Charlie Haas & Shelton Benjamin) (Champions) def. Los Guerreros (Chavo Guerrero & Eddie Guerrero) and Chris Benoit & Rhyno to retain the Championship

TRIPLE THREAT MATCH FOR THE WOMEN'S CHAMPIONSHIP
- Trish Stratus def. Jazz and Victoria (Champion) w/ Stevie Richards to become new Champion

HANDICAP MATCH
- Undertaker def. Big Show and A-Train

CRUISERWEIGHT CHAMPIONSHIP MATCH
- Matt Hardy (Champion) w/ Shannon Moore def. Rey Mysterio to retain the Championship

OTHER MATCHES
- The Rock def. Stone Cold Steve Austin
- Shawn Michaels def. Chris Jericho

"*WrestleMania* is the night where classic matches are made."

—Chris Jericho

Two Competing Brands

The conflict between co-owners Mr. McMahon and Ric Flair led to WWE's unprecedented decision to split their roster into two distinct brands, *Raw* and *SmackDown*. Each show had its own roster of Superstars and Divas, its own championships, its own general managers, and its own announce teams. *WrestleMania XIX* would be the first time the two brands co-produced the Showcase of the Immortals.

The Cruiserweight Championship

Since breaking off on his own, Matt Hardy (or more accurately Matt Hardy version 1.0) had shown a new "Mattitude" that the WWE Universe did not find appealing. The fans may not have liked Matt's actions, but they couldn't argue with the results. Despite a constant battle to make the weight limit, Hardy was the reigning Cruiserweight Champion heading into *WrestleMania XIX*. He would be defending the title against a longtime WCW Superstar making his *WrestleMania* debut, Rey Mysterio.

Hardy took early control of the match, clearly having studied Mysterio's tendencies and countering several of his moves. Mysterio had difficulty gaining any momentum, as Hardy's devoted follower, Shannon Moore, would make his ringside presence felt any time he thought his mentor was in danger. In one spectacular sequence, Rey reversed a top-rope move by Hardy into an amazing Hurricanrana, but Moore prevented Rey's planned 619 follow-up. Rey then nailed Hardy with a 619 later in the match, but Matt was able to avoid the West Coast Pop and roll Mysterio up for a pinfall victory.

The Streak Continues

For his 11th *WrestleMania* appearance, Undertaker recruited a partner, Nathan Jones, for his match against the formidable duo of Big Show and A-Train. It was supposed to be the first time in his storied *WrestleMania* career that Undertaker would be appearing as part of a team. However, before the show even started, Show and A-Train jumped Jones backstage and left him lying, turning the bout into a 2-on-1 Handicap match, leaving The Deadman on his own once again.

The decision to remove Undertaker's partner paid dividends at first, as any time The Deadman started to ramp up his offense, the numbers game of Show and A-Train derailed Undertaker, slowing him down with power moves of their own. Undertaker delighted the crowd by going Old School with his top-rope walking move. Just when it looked like Big Show and A-Train were going to combine to end Undertaker's undefeated *WrestleMania* streak, Nathan Jones came racing in from the back to attack Show and even the odds, allowing Undertaker to deliver a punishing Tombstone Piledriver to pin A-Train and win the match.

Women's Championship Triple Threat Match

In a partial repeat of their *WrestleMania X8* match, Jazz and Trish Stratus would once again be part of a Triple Threat Match for the WWE Women's title. This year however, both would be challenging Victoria, the maniacal newcomer to WWE who was also the reigning Women's Champion. Accompanied to the ring by Stevie Richards, Victoria had held the title since the previous year's *Survivor Series*.

While it was every woman for herself throughout the match, Victoria and Jazz often worked together to take down the former three-time champion Stratus. The alliance would be short-lived, as after they knocked Stratus down, one would turn on the other. Despite the odds being stacked against her, Stratus was close to winning the title. To save Victoria, Richards tried to incapacitate Trish by hitting her with a steel chair. He missed and the chair bounced off the ring ropes and knocked him out. Stratus took advantage by hitting Victoria with a Chick Kick to win her fourth WWE Women's Championship.

WWE Tag Team Championship

With the brand split, the World Tag Team Championship became sole property of *Raw*. General Manager Stephanie McMahon created the WWE Tag Team Championship for her *SmackDown* program. The fourth-ever champions were Shelton Benjamin and Charlie Haas, also known as Team Angle, a pair of former NCAA champion wrestlers that worked with WWE Champion Kurt Angle.

Team Angle, who'd also be called the World's Greatest Tag Team, would be defending their title against a former championship team, Los Guerreros, as well as a newly formed pairing of Chris Benoit and Rhyno. While only two men were supposed to be in the ring at any given time, all six often battled in and out of the ring, electrifying the crowd with exciting action, high-flying moves, and amazing mat techniques. Rhyno thought he'd won the match for his team when he hit a Gore on Chavo Guerrero, but Benjamin tagged himself in and pinned Guerrero, keeping the Championship with Team Angle.

▶ *At times all of the teams battled in and out of the ring simultaneously*

Shawn Michaels vs. Chris Jericho

Growing up, Chris Jericho idolized Shawn Michaels. When Jericho signed with WWE, it was assumed that "The Heartbreak Kid's" in-ring career was over, and that the two would never cross paths in the ring. But after Michaels' triumphant return at 2002's *SummerSlam*, the two would meet on the Grandest Stage of Them All.

Y2J was out to prove that he was a more captivating performer and a more charismatic individual, and that his skills were now superior to Michaels'. The former Undisputed Champion wanted to end "The Heartbreak Kid's" career once and for all. Michaels prepared for his first *WrestleMania* match since his 1998 WWE Championship Match with Stone Cold Steve Austin.

> **"It's a great story of someone getting to work with their hero, and then in the end sticking it to them."**
>
> **—Chris Jericho**

During their match, Chris Jericho mocked Shawn Michaels, while physically punishing him at the same time. Jericho verbally berated HBK, yelling, "I'm better than you!" He even went so far as to emulate Michaels' signature pose and use his Sweet Chin Music kick against him. Jericho went to great lengths to prove he was better than Michaels. But HBK lived up to his "Mr. WrestleMania" moniker, pinning the arrogant Jericho. After the hard-fought match, Michaels offered Y2J a hug, and Jericho hugged his former idol before turning their embrace into a knee to HBK's groin.

Chris Jericho remembers, "I really love the match with Shawn. It's a great story of someone getting to work with their hero, and then in the end sticking it to them. It's my favorite *WrestleMania* moment."

Pillow Fight!

Things got a little lighthearted as Jonathan Coachman brought out the stars of the Miller Lite Catfight commercial for a special Pillow Fight on a bed set up on the stage. Both Stacy Kiebler and Torrie Wilson decided to get involved as well, much to the delight of announcer Jerry "The King" Lawler. The four women battled until they decided a better tactic would be to pants the Coach, and then pin him, so that all four ladies left *WrestleMania* victorious.

▶ *The women decide to "pants" the Coach and pin him*

The World Heavyweight Championship

When Brock Lesnar won the WWE Championship from The Rock at *SummerSlam 2002*, Stephanie McMahon scored quite the coup for *SmackDown* when she signed the Next Best Thing to defend the title exclusively on her program. Not to be outdone, *Raw* GM Eric Bischoff brought back the World Heavyweight Championship and awarded it to Triple H, who had reverted to his rule-breaking ways. His challenger for the title at *WrestleMania* was Booker T, the five-time WCW World Heavyweight Champion.

From the first tie-up, Triple H knew he was in for one of the most contested title defenses of his championship reign. "The Game" brought his signature precision and resilience to combat Booker T's intensity and drive. While Booker looked to be gaining the upper hand, Triple H's ace in the hole, business advisor Ric Flair, helped turn the tide by working over Booker's knee outside the ring. The Game would further exploit this injury with a variety of moves targeting the injured body part. While Booker did make a brief comeback, the damage to the knee was too great, giving Triple H enough of an opening to nail Booker with a Pedigree and allow him to retain his championship.

Street Fight

Hulk Hogan's return in 2002 launched the renaissance of Hulkamania. A rebirth of the red and yellow led to standing ovations in arenas. The mantra "Hulk Still Rules" was fully realized when, more than 15 years after winning his first WWE Championship, Hogan defeated Triple H and won the WWE title for a sixth time. Mr. McMahon couldn't stand the Hulkster's return; the once close friends were now bitter rivals. Both men wanted to take credit for the creation of Hulkamania and the creation of *WrestleMania*, and decided to settle matters in the ring.

Vince McMahon reflects, "I think it was something that was inevitable. A way I like to think of it is, 'What's real and what's Memorex?' Who created Hulkamania—did Vince McMahon or Terry Bollea? I said then, Hogan had caused me a great deal of frustration in my life from time to time. There were times I wished I could have choked him. So it made for very compelling television." Hulk Hogan adds, "There wouldn't be a Vince McMahon without a Hulk Hogan and vice-versa. During that time we had a lot of things we had to work out."

> **"There wouldn't be a Vince McMahon without a Hulk Hogan and vice-versa."**
>
> **—Hulk Hogan**

The two men responsible for launching WWE's national expansion and *WrestleMania* were now in the center of the ring about to bludgeon one another beyond recognition. Mr. McMahon had a deranged look in his eyes, the look of a man driven to kill Hulkamania. The Street Fight was gruesome. Mr. McMahon jumped from the top of a ladder and crashed through the Spanish announce table onto the Hulkster. McMahon tried everything to win the match, even aligning himself with Hogan's *WrestleMania I* opponent, "Rowdy" Roddy Piper. But Hot Rod's attack on Hulk would not be enough—Hogan dropped his famous leg on Mr. McMahon.

AUSTIN HOSPITALIZED

The day before *WrestleMania*, something didn't feel right to Steve Austin. Austin remembers, "I was at the gym with Kevin Nash and my legs were shaking a lot. I get back to the hotel and my heart starts pounding like it's going to come out of my chest. I thought I was going to die. I see a WWE employee in the hallway and I told her I needed help. She called 9-1-1. I stayed in the hospital overnight. I had an anxiety attack brought on by me just not taking care of myself."

Jim Ross recalls, "Steve was dealing with a lot of things. He was working night after night, and still had a bad neck that could end his career at any time."

Stone Cold decided to compete at *WrestleMania*, but he knew he had to be careful. Austin reflects, "My mind was fine, but my body was telling me it was time to wind this thing down."

Stone Cold Steve Austin vs. The Rock

The Rock was still electrifying audiences, but he chose to perform at a reduced schedule to balance his WWE career with his burgeoning Hollywood film schedule. He thought he'd accomplished everything he could in WWE, with one minor exception. His two *WrestleMania* losses to Stone Cold Steve Austin were unacceptable to the Great One, and he wanted another shot at the Texas Rattlesnake. When Austin accepted, the greatest rivalry in the Attitude Era was set for a third *WrestleMania* chapter.

From the very start of their match, the Texas Rattlesnake and the Brahma Bull kept the Safeco crowd on their feet in a classic, chaos-fueled brawl. Anywhere they could go was considered "fair game"—the aisles, into the crowd, on announce tables, raising the intensity of this rivalry.

Both men used the other's signature moves. The Rock went so far as to put Austin's vest on while continuing to fire away at the Rattlesnake. Austin continued to prove he was WWE's toughest S.O.B. It took three Rock Bottoms for the Great One to keep Stone Cold down for the three count and finally get a victory over Austin. Rock then left the ring first, giving Austin the opportunity to be alone in the ring, for Rock (and Jim Ross) knew something nobody else knew—the world had just seen Stone Cold Steve Austin's last match.

The rigors and pressure of a brilliant career had taken their toll. Steve Austin was no longer able to compete at the level that met his own high standards. Unlike many in the public eye, Austin was not looking for a farewell tour or an emotional send-off. He just wanted to get through the match and return home to Texas.

The Rock remembers, "I'm proud to call him my friend. It was an honor for me to be out there with him. I wanted him to know I couldn't thank him enough for all the years he helped me and everything he did for me. You're only as good as your opponent in this business. I told him I loved him. It was a very special moment."

Steve Austin shares, "It was an incredible moment. We went through so much together, and now it was time for us to go down our separate roads. I told him I loved him, too. It was something I'll always keep with me."

The WWE Championship

When Brock Lesnar debuted in WWE, fans of pure mat wrestling hoped that he would cross paths with the 1996 Olympic Gold Medalist and WWE Superstar Kurt Angle. Angle was in the midst of his third WWE Championship reign and enjoyed one of the fastest ascents to stardom WWE had ever seen.

When Lesnar won the 2003 *Royal Rumble*, he punched his ticket into the main event at *WrestleMania XIX*. Leading into the event, Angle did everything he could to avoid competing against "The Next Big Thing"— even recruiting his brother to take his place in a match. To make things fair, *SmackDown* General Manager Stephanie McMahon set the stipulation for *WrestleMania*: if anyone interfered on Angle's behalf, or if he got himself counted out or disqualified, he would forfeit the title to Lesnar.

What the audience didn't know was that Kurt Angle was dealing with a severe neck injury. As opposed to vacating the WWE Championship, Angle made the decision to risk permanent injury to compete at *WrestleMania*. The Olympian knew that surgery would be required directly following the match. Lesnar remembers, "I was worried about just touching the guy. His neck could have snapped at any second so I was really worried about everything I did with him."

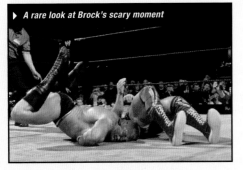

▶ *A rare look at Brock's scary moment*

Angle tried to get under Lesnar's skin initially by keeping his distance from the Next Big Thing. Lesnar was ferocious in his aggression; he displayed a confidence in the ring often reserved for elite, veteran performers. The contest was an unbelievable exchange of holds, counter-holds, and maneuvers highlighting the grappling skills of both men. As Angle lay on the canvas, Lesnar climbed to the top rope. In a frightful moment, Lesnar jumped to perform a Shooting Star Press—a backflip in mid-air that lands on the opponent like a big splash. Lesnar did not successfully finish the move and jammed his head in between the ring mat and Angle's body. Though Lesnar was seriously injured, he was somehow able to finish the match. He defeated Kurt Angle with his F-5 and became WWE Champion in his *WrestleMania* debut.

WRESTLEMANIA XX

MADISON SQUARE GARDEN – NEW YORK, NY

March 14
2004

Attendance
18,500

RAW ANNOUNCERS
Jerry "The King" Lawler
Jim Ross

SMACKDOWN ANNOUNCERS
Michael Cole, Tazz

SPANISH ANNOUNCERS
Carlos Cabrera, Hugo Savinovich

RAW RING ANNOUNCER
Howard Finkel

SMACKDOWN RING ANNOUNCER
Tony Chimel

SPECIAL FIELD CORRESPONDENTS
Jesse "The Body" Ventura, Jonathan Coachman, Lillian Garcia

SPECIAL MUSICAL GUESTS
The Boys Choir of Harlem

Event Card

TRIPLE THREAT MATCH FOR THE WORLD HEAVYWEIGHT CHAMPIONSHIP
- Chris Benoit def. Triple H (Champion) and Shawn Michaels to become new Champion

WWE CHAMPIONSHIP MATCH
- Eddie Guerrero (Champion) def. Kurt Angle to retain the Championship

WOMEN'S CHAMPIONSHIP MATCH*
- Victoria (Champion) def. Molly Holly to retain the Championship
  *Hair vs. Title. If Molly Holly lost her head would be shaved

FATAL FOUR WAY MATCH FOR THE WWE TAG TEAM CHAMPIONSHIP
- Scotty 2 Hotty & Rikishi (Champions) def. Basham Brothers (Danny & Doug), World's Greatest Tag Team (Charlie Haas & Shelton Benjamin) and APA (Bradshaw & Farooq) to retain the Championship

CRUISERWEIGHT OPEN MATCH
- Ultimo Dragon def. Shannon Moore; Jamie Noble def. Ultimo Dragon; Jamie Noble def. Funaki; Jamie Noble def. Nunzio; Billy Kidman def. Jamie Noble; Rey Mysterio def. Billy Kidman; Rey Mysterio def. Tajiri; Chavo Guerrero w/ Chavo Classic def. Rey Mysterio to retain the Championship

PLAYBOY EVENING GOWN MATCH
- Sable & Torrie Wilson def. Stacy Keibler & Miss Jackie

HANDICAP MATCH
- Randy Orton, Batista, & Ric Flair def. The Rock'n'Sock Connection (The Rock & Mick Foley)

FATAL FOUR WAY MATCH FOR THE WORLD TAG TEAM CHAMPIONSHIP
- Booker T & Rob Van Dam (Champions) def. La Resistance (Renee Dupree & Sylvain Grenier), Mark Jindrak & Garrison Cade, and the Dudley Boyz (Bubba Ray & D-Von) to retain the Championship

UNITED STATES CHAMPIONSHIP MATCH
- John Cena def. Big Show (Champion) to become new Champion

OTHER MATCHES
- Undertaker w/ Paul Bearer def. Kane
- Goldberg def. Brock Lesnar*
  *Stone Cold as Special Guest Referee
- Christian def. Chris Jericho w/ Trish Stratus

> ## "To be in that environment and to come out holding the U.S. Title high, that's what you live for. It's why we lace 'em up."
> —John Cena

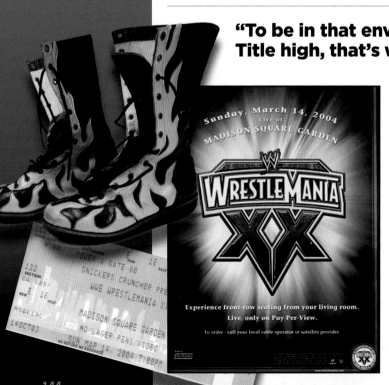

Where it All Begins... Again

For the twentieth annual *WrestleMania*, WWE returned to its home of New York and MSG, the site of the first and tenth *WrestleMania* events. The show would be a unique blend of veterans like Shawn Michaels and Undertaker, and new blood, as future champions John Cena, Randy Orton, and Batista would all make their Showcase of the Immortal debuts at *WrestleMania XX*, making the show's tagline "Where it All Begins … Again" so fitting.

The United States Championship

The third *WrestleMania* to be presented at Madison Square Garden opened with a match that kept the crowd on their feet from the opening bell. John Cena made his *WrestleMania* debut by challenging Big Show for the giant's United States Championship. While in later years Cena would spark a divided crowd reaction, the New York fans were firmly in his corner from the beginning, particularly when the Doctor of Thugonomics delighted the WWE Universe with a freestyle rap before Big Show made his way to the ring.

His rap proved to be prophetic as he boasted that "the main event was on first." Cena went on to be in the main event in the next three *WrestleManias* and several more after that.

Big Show's power moves kept him in control of the match early on, leading the announcers to question whether the newcomer Cena was overmatched. Cena would answer their doubts emphatically when he lifted up the Big Show for Cena's patented Attitude Adjustment. The unprecedented show of strength allowed Cena to leave MSG as the United States Champion. Cena looks back, "I've been fortunate to be put in a lot of big-time matches. I've been fortunate enough that there are a few that have gone my way. To be in that environment and to come out holding the U.S. Title high, that's what you live for. It's why we lace 'em up."

Sudden Death Fatal 4-Way Match

The unlikely tag team pairing of Booker T and Rob Van Dam experienced immediate success, winning the World Tag Team Championship from Evolution. The former WCW and ECW stars would need to take their partnership to another level when they defended their championship against three talented teams.

Both the teams of La Resistance and Cade & Jindrak were making their *WrestleMania* debuts. The champions were at quite a disadvantage, as whatever team scored the first pinfall would win the championship. The four teams all displayed incredible athleticism, with none of the pairings giving an inch. At one point, the Dudleys thought they had the match won, but their attempt at a match-closing 3-D failed. Rob Conway eventually found himself on the receiving end of Booker T's Scissors Kick and Rob Van Dam's 5-Star Frog Splash, and the champions retained their World Tag Team Title.

▶ *Booker T lands a kick on Rob Conway*

Chris Jericho vs. Christian

An insulting bet began the end of a longtime friendship. Christian and Chris Jericho made a bet over which of them could score with a Diva first. But in trying to win the bet, Jericho developed feelings for Trish Stratus, and continued to pursue her. Christian felt that Jericho's interest in Trish was screwing up his priorities, and attacked Trish to drive the point home. An enraged Jericho challenged his former friend to a match at *WrestleMania*.

From the start of the contest, neither man held back, hitting brutal moves and punishing submission attempts on the other. The action spilled out of the ring, where Jericho locked Christian in the Walls of Jericho, but he smartly broke the hold to return to the ring and avoid a double count-out. The battle continued, with Christian breaking rules to gain an advantage. With both men down, Trish raced to the ring, where Christian menaced her until Jericho threw him out. Jericho went to check on Stratus, but thinking it was Christian again, she lashed out with an elbow that struck Y2J in the face, leading Jericho to be pinned by Christian. After the match, Trish turned on Jericho completely, planting a kiss on Christian.

The Rock 'n' Sock Connection Returns

Randy Orton, the Intercontinental Champion, had become known as "The Legend Killer." The Evolution member soon set his sights on Hardcore Legend Mick Foley. With each confrontation, the outcome turned more violent. Though fighting courageously, Foley fell victim to the numbers game and often felt the wrath of Evolution.

> **"I never thought of myself as being on that level of the guys [The Rock would] consider returning for. When he told me it was a big deal to him, it meant a lot to me."**
>
> —Mick Foley

There was only one way for him to even the odds—reform The Rock 'n' Sock Connection. Mick Foley remembers, "I knew Rock had not had a match in a while and was open to coming back for something that was a big deal. I never thought of myself as being on that level of the guys he'd consider returning for. When he told me it was a big deal to him, it meant a lot to me."

WrestleMania XX was special for the Evolution trio as well. Randy Orton remembers, "Being in the ring with The Rock, Mick Foley, and Ric Flair at *WrestleMania* in Madison Square Garden, my first *WrestleMania*, 20 years after my father was part of the main event for the first one in the same building—it was very special."

▶ *Evolution (Randy Orton, Batista, and Ric Flair) defeat Rock 'n' Sock for the win*

The match also marked the first time, with The Rock and Randy Orton, two third-generation Superstars appeared in the same match together. The Rock reflects, "Being back as part of The Rock 'n' Sock Connection at *WrestleMania XX* meant everything to me. To come back for *WrestleMania* and team with someone I admire and respect, who gave his body for me every time we went against each other, was amazing."

Rock and Foley delighted the crowd by hitting their best moves against Evolution, including an elbow off the ring apron by Foley onto Flair, and The Rock working the Flair strut into his People's Elbow routine. But each time Rock 'n' Sock came close to victory, the Evolution trilogy would cheat to stay in the match. Things got more chaotic as the match went on until Randy Orton hit Mick Foley with an RKO to win.

HONORING LEGACIES

In 2004, WWE expanded *WrestleMania* weekend by adding a Hall of Fame induction ceremony to the extravaganza. On the eve of *WrestleMania XX*, the remarkable careers of Big John Studd, Bobby "The Brain" Heenan, Don Muraco, Greg "The Hammer" Valentine, Junkyard Dog, Harley Race, Jesse "The Body" Ventura, Sgt. Slaughter, Superstar Billy Graham, and Tito Santana were celebrated. In addition, WWE honored its first celebrity inductee with the selection of Pete Rose.

Playboy Evening Gown Match

Both Sable and Torrie Wilson had previously appeared on covers of *Playboy*, and were set to appear again, this time together. Miss Jackie and Stacy Keibler took exception to the extra attention their Diva rivals were getting, so they challenged the pair to a Playboy Evening Gown Match at *WrestleMania XX*.

Before the match started, Sable suggested a modification. Rather than tear off each other's gowns, why not strip them off at the start of the match and compete in their lingerie? The crowd roared its approval to the idea, and three of the Divas, Sable, Wilson, and Keibler, removed their dresses. Only Jackie objected, so Sable and Wilson grabbed her and tore her gown off to level the playing field.

The inter-promotional match was short, but the crowd greatly enjoyed it. Keibler used her famously long legs to punish Wilson, but when Jackie tagged in to continue the match, Torrie rolled her up for the pin, claiming the victory for the *Smackdown* Divas.

▶ *Torrie and Sable tear Jackie's gown off to level the playing field*

Goldberg vs. Brock Lesnar

In the second of three inter-promotional matches, Brock Lesnar faced Goldberg. The two had been at odds since the *Royal Rumble*, when Lesnar, the reigning WWE Champion, caused Goldberg to be eliminated from the match, and Goldberg repaid the Next Big Thing the following month by interfering in Lesnar's title defense at *No Way Out*. The only place they could settle the score was at *WrestleMania*.

From the opening bell, the match did not receive its proper attention from the audience. Earlier that weekend, a mainstream media leak reported *WrestleMania XX* would be both Lesnar's and Goldberg's final WWE appearances. This infuriated the audience, who expressed their displeasure with both Superstars rather vocally.

Goldberg hit a devastating Spear, but Lesnar managed to kick out of the pinning attempt. Goldberg, in turn, did not stay down for a three-count after Lesnar's F-5 move. Goldberg finally managed to hit a Spear and Jackhammer to secure the win. Special Guest Referee Steve Austin restored order to the ring, and gave the fans what they wanted when he hit both men with Stone Cold Stunners.

▶ *Lesnar recieves a Stone Cold Stunner*

The Cruiserweight Open

In a fast-moving Gauntlet match for Chavo Guerrero's Cruiserweight Championship, the eight challengers drew numbers and the first two, Shannon Moore and Ultimo Dragon, started in the ring, with a new competitor entering after each pinfall or decision. Dragon took out Moore, but submitted to Jamie Noble, who then took out Funaki in a *WrestleMania*-record eight seconds, followed by a count-out victory over Nunzio. Noble's luck ran out against Billy Kidman, who powerbombed Jamie and pinned him, but Kidman was then taken out by fan favorite Rey Mysterio. Mysterio looked to be in trouble against Tajiri, but Akio's attempt to help Tajiri removed both men from the match, leaving Mysterio with the champion, Guerrero. Mysterio found it difficult to mount sustained offense when he had to deal with a Chavo in the ring and another Chavo outside the ring. Having had enough, Rey launched himself at Chavo Sr. and took the champ's father out of the equation, but the loss of focus allowed Guerrero to steal a pin and retain his title.

▶ *Rey Mysterio launches himself at Chavo Guerrero*

Sudden Death Fatal 4-Way

Just as the World Tag Team Champions had earlier in the show, the WWE Tag Team Champions, Rikishi & Scotty 2 Hotty, faced three other teams looking to wrest the title from its current holders. Once again, the match would be settled with a single pinfall, meaning the champions need not even be involved in the decision.

Too Cool faced three formidable pairings, including two former tag champ teams (the APA and the World's Greatest Tag Team), as well as the Bashams, a pair of brothers that would be future champions. Too Cool was further challenged by the varying styles of their opponents, from the mat skills of Shelton Benjamin and Charlie Hass to the brawling styles of the APA. Benjamin may have placed too much faith in his skills, as he tried o suplex the massive Rikishi, and was butt bumped out of the ring for his trouble. Rikishi followed that up with a Bonzai Drop on a member of the Bashams for a 3-count victory.

▶ *Rikishi's Bonzai Drop gets the 3-count*

Title vs. Hair

For the second straight year, Victoria entered *WrestleMania* as the WWE Women's Champion. This year, however, she had the support of the WWE Universe as she faced Molly Holly, an adversary so sure of herself that she was willing to put up her hair as collateral for the match.

As the two entered the arena, a barber's chair was set up on the stage, serving as an ominous reminder of what was at stake for Holly. It may have been an excellent motivational tool, for Holly quickly took control of the match. The two traded offensive moves and pinning attempts, but the challenger kept the upper hand. Holly's arrogance probably cost her the match however, when she tried to finish Victoria off with the champion's own Widow's Peak finisher. Victoria was able to wriggle her way out of the move and pin Holly. Quickly realizing the ramifications, Holly tried to escape through the crowd, but Victoria stopped her and strapped her into the barber's chair where she shaved Molly's head.

Eddie Guerrero vs. Kurt Angle

For most of the WWE Universe, the story of Eddie Guerrero winning the WWE Championship was an inspiring tale. Kurt Angle did not agree. The Olympic Champion went on a diatribe about how the personal problems that Guerrero overcame made him unfit to be WWE Champion. Angle asserted that he was the future of WWE, not Guerrero.

Kurt Angle was relentless in his attacks. The Olympic Gold Medalist utilized his unmatched grappling attacks with submission holds in hopes that a mat-based offense would ground the legendary champion.

Eddie Guerrero employed all of his knowledge to defend against Angle's assaults. The champion knew that Angle would build to Kurt's devastating Ankle Lock, so Guerrero employed an ingenious bit of strategy—he loosened the laces on his boot on the foot he knew Angle would attack. When Angle eventually did slap the move on, Guerrero was able to slip out of the boot, leaving Angle holding just an abandoned piece of footwear. Guerrero, taking advantage of Angle's shock, wrapped Angle in a small package and put an end to the match. Eddie Guerrero not only survived, but also retained his position as WWE Champion.

Undertaker vs. Kane

The appearance of smoke, flames, druids, and the ever-creepy Paul Bearer meant only one thing—Undertaker's return as the man in black. Leaving behind his American Badass persona, Undertaker returned to the darkness, reclaiming his role as The Deadman and striking fear into everyone foolish enough to face him.

His opponent was his brother Kane, who thought he had rid WWE of The Deadman by burying him alive at 2003's *Survivor Series*. From the *Royal Rumble* on, Kane was haunted by signs that his brother would be back and seeking his revenge at *WrestleMania XX*. Even when Undertaker made his way to the ring, Kane continued to doubt his authenticity, screaming "you're not real!" Undertaker answered Kane's doubts with several right hands. Kane recovered enough to take out his older brother with a Chokeslam, but while Kane taunted Paul Bearer, The Deadman sat up, crushed Kane with a Chokeslam of his own, and delivered a Tombstone Piledriver to extend his *WrestleMania* Streak to 12-0.

For the next decade Undertaker's Streak would be a focal point of *WrestleMania* as The Deadman put down challenger after challenger, ensuring they would all Rest In Peace. Undertaker's continual breathtaking performances amazed fans and solidified his position as an enduring WWE icon.

Triple Threat Match for the World Heavyweight Championship

The main event represented the first time the World Heavyweight Championship would be decided in a Triple Threat Match at *WrestleMania*. Triple H, the reigning champion, had several challengers feeling they should be the number one contender. Chris Benoit had won the *Royal Rumble*, spending a record 62 minutes in the ring and outlasting 29 other men to earn a title shot in the main event. At the same time, Shawn Michaels had battled Triple H to a no contest, and HBK felt he deserved a shot to settle his issues with the Game once and for all.

Shawn Michaels remembers, "*WrestleMania XX* was big. It's the 20th anniversary of the show people associate me with, and I'm in the main event for the World Heavyweight Championship, and it's at Madison Square Garden. You can't really beat that. It also confirmed for me that I made the right decision of coming back."

With all three men competing at the same time, the match was brutal and wildly entertaining. Each came tantalizing close to winning the title, but the third man broke up any pinfall attempt to keep the match going. It seemed like it was going to become a one-on-one match between Triple H and Shawn Michaels when the two former DX partners put their differences aside to cooperate and perform a double-suplex on Chris Benoit, putting him through the Spanish announcer's table. But Benoit came back to prevent Triple H from pinning a bloody Shawn Michaels. Benoit finally locked Triple H into the Crippler Crossface and the fading champ had no choice but to submit. Future events would forever alter the perception of this moment. At the time, however, it was a cathartic celebration of an eighteen year trek through sports-entertainment.

WRESTLEMANIA 21

STAPLES CENTER – LOS ANGELES, CA

April 3
2005

Attendance
20,193

RAW ANNOUNCERS
Jerry "The King" Lawler
Jim Ross

SMACKDOWN ANNOUNCERS
Michael Cole
Tazz

SPANISH ANNOUNCERS
Carlos Cabrera
Hugo Savinovich

RAW RING ANNOUNCER
Howard Finkel

SMACKDOWN RING ANNOUNCER
Tony Chimel

SPECIAL FIELD CORRESPONDENTS
Jonathan Coachman

SPECIAL MUSICAL GUEST
Motörhead

Event Card

WORLD HEAVYWEIGHT CHAMPIONSHIP MATCH
▨ Batista def. Triple H (Champion) w/ "Nature Boy" Ric Flair to become
new Champion

WWE CHAMPIONSHIP MATCH
▨ John Cena def. John Bradshaw Layfield (Champion) to become new Champion

SUMO MATCH
▨ Akebono def. Big Show

INTERPROMOTIONAL MATCH
▨ Kurt Angle def. Shawn Michaels

WOMEN'S CHAMPIONSHIP MATCH
▨ Trish Stratus (Champion) def. Christy Hemme w/ Lita to retain the Championship

LEGEND VS. LEGEND KILLER – INTERPROMOTIONAL MATCH
▨ Undertaker def. Randy Orton

MONEY IN THE BANK LADDER MATCH
▨ Edge def. Chris Benoit, Shelton Benjamin, Chris Jericho, Christian, and Kane

OTHER MATCH
▨ Rey Mysterio def. Eddie Guerrero

> **"I saw John Cena and thought this could be the guy
> that ends up becoming the next WWE Champion."**
>
> —John Bradshaw Layfield

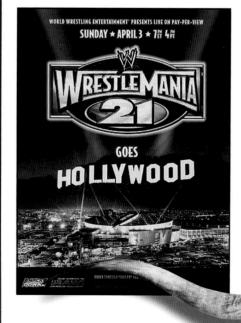

A Return to Tinsel Town

For *WrestleMania 21*, the theme was "*WrestleMania* Goes Hollywood." Parody film trailers featuring WWE Superstars and Divas set the mood, and energized the WWE Universe, who sold out LA's Staples Center in less than one minute.

Friendly Competition?

History was made in the opening contest of *WrestleMania 21*. For the first time at *WrestleMania*, the reigning WWE Tag Team Champions entered the ring to do battle against each other. Much had changed for Eddie Guerrero in the year since *WrestleMania XX*. Just one year earlier, Guerrero had entered *WrestleMania* the WWE Champion, and had successfully defended the title. But Guerrero had hit a bit of a skid in singles competition. It wasn't all bad—he had managed to win the WWE Tag Team Championship with Rey Mysterio, and the two could have defended the titles at *WrestleMania 21*. But Guerrero wanted to prove himself by himself, so he challenged his own partner to a match. Vickie Guerrero remembers, "They had such a genuine love for each other and always had each other's backs. Eddie truly loved Rey."

The two Superstars amazed the Los Angeles crowd throughout their match. Guerrero's skills in the ring and through the air were matched by Mysterio's innovative offense. Despite being tag team partners, neither man held back. Twice in rapid succession, Eddie delivered his Three Amigos, a set of three suplexes, and looked to follow the six suplexes with his Frog Splash to finish off Rey and win the match, but Mysterio had enough ring presence to roll out of the way before the move hit. Guerrero grew increasingly frustrated as Mysterio was able to kick out of pinfall attempts, preventing him from getting the win. Mysterio eventually hit Guerrero with a Hurricanrana and was able to pin Latino Heat. Guerrero showed good sportsmanship, shaking Mysterio's hand at the end of the match, but his frustration was visible. The friendly bout planted the seed for a vicious in-ring rivalry in which Guerrero's inability to beat Mysterio caused him to snap.

Money in the Bank Ladder Match

The brainchild of Chris Jericho, the Money in the Bank concept involved climbing a ladder and retrieving a briefcase suspended 20 feet above the ring. The briefcase contained an open contract for a WWE or World Heavyweight Championship Match. The agreement would be valid for one year and could be cashed in on the date, time, and location of the winning Superstar's choosing. Jericho, Edge, Chris Benoit, Shelton Benjamin, Kane, and Christian all lined up for a shot at the briefcase.

Kane recalls, "I loved the concept. When I heard the roster, I focused on upping my game. I was going in there against opponents who were masters of the Ladder Match. We wanted to have the best match we could. None of us knew what to expect."

The WWE Universe probably thought they knew what to expect from past Ladder Matches, including the *WrestleMania X* classic bout between Shawn Michaels and Razor Ramon, as well as the Triangle Ladder Match for the Tag Team Championship at *WrestleMania 2000*, but Money in the Bank was a whole new level. Like the *WrestleMania 2000* match, there were six competitors in the ring, but there were no teams or alliances. Every man was out for himself, and each was willing to wreak maximum havoc on his five opponents, leaping off ladders and using the steel structures as powerful weapons. Shelton Benjamin in particular demonstrated innovative and athletic ways to incorporate the ladders into his already impressive arsenal of moves. Everyone in the match had a moment in the sun and each left the ring regretting how close they'd come to securing the guaranteed title opportunity— everyone but Edge. The TLC veteran used his expertise in ladder-based combat to enable him to climb the rungs of steel to win the match. Edge reflects, "I didn't fully understand the concept of Money in the Bank at first. To me it was one of those, 'There will be a Championship hanging up there? A contract?' I truly felt like, I'll get to the main event, but I don't think this is the route to do it. And I was really, really wrong. I don't mind admitting it."

Edge held on to his title opportunity for almost 10 months, until he cashed in on John Cena, right after Cena had completed a grueling Elimination Chamber Match to retain his WWE Championship. Cena was barely able to stand when Edge, earning his "Ultimate Opportunist" moniker, came to the ring, pinned Cena, and became the WWE Champion for the first time in his career. Edge's tactics set the blueprint for several future briefcase holders to follow.

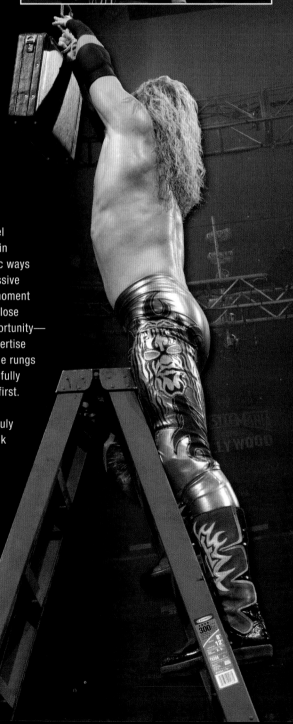

A HERO'S RETURN

When WWE Superstar Eugene went to the ring to greet the *WrestleMania 21* crowd, Muhammad Hassan and manager Daivari interrupted. Hassan ranted about not being included in *WrestleMania*. He decided to have his *WrestleMania* moment, at the expense of Eugene, when he and Daivari attacked.

The crowd's boos quickly changed to rousing applause when the opening notes of "Real American" rang out in the Staples Center. The energy of Hulkamania, like it had done so proudly before, permeated the City of Angels. One night after his WWE Hall of Fame induction, Hulk Hogan quickly disposed of both villains, saving Eugene from imminent injury.

Legend vs. Legend Killer

In the beginning of 2005, Randy Orton decided to further his "Legend Killer" reputation by challenging Undertaker's undefeated *WrestleMania* Streak. Orton remembers, "It was definitely exciting. It was a matter of getting to know Undertaker in a business manner. When you're new like I was at the time, you want to impress him. Luckily, he liked how I worked in the ring. He knew I wasn't going to break his nose by accident, which is an art that is somewhat lost today."

Orton antagonized Undertaker by slapping him on *SmackDown*. Orton also enlisted his father—the infamous "Cowboy" Bob Orton—to help intensify the antagonism. Orton was prepared to do everything he could to take down Undertaker. In every arena, father and son were met with endless jeers from the crowd. Despite the fan's enmity, both were grateful for the opportunity to work together. Randy remembers, "My dad really enjoyed being a part of it. We got to travel together, and I got to learn from him. It was cool to be by his side like that. We became closer than we had ever been because of this business. "

At *WrestleMania*, the Legend Killer came to put an end to Undertaker. The Deadman had never encountered such youthful power and athleticism during his *WrestleMania* Streak, and "Cowboy" Bob's interference brought Orton to within inches of ending it. Orton even managed to reverse a Chokeslam into an RKO. Orton decided to use Undertaker's own Tombstone Piledriver to end the match. The arrogant decision cost the Legend Killer, as Undertaker reversed the move into a Tombstone on Orton, giving Undertaker the win and a 13-0 record at *WrestleMania*.

The WWE Women's Championship

Christy Hemme was in the midst of a meteoric rise in WWE. The 2004 *Raw* Diva Search winner was celebrating her appearance on the cover of *Playboy* and was debuting the cover on *Raw* when Trish Stratus came to the ring to mock Hemme, knocking Christy out with a Chick Kick. The rookie Hemme issued a challenge for Stratus' WWE Women's Championship. Stratus gladly accepted, thinking Hemme had no wrestling ability or training. But Stratus was in for a surprise when she learned that her old foe Lita had been training Christy.

The two clashed in the ring, with Hemme stunning Stratus with surprising wrestling acumen, including getting a two-count with a Twist of Fate. Stratus was finally able to take her challenger out with a Chick Kick, and leave *WrestleMania 21* with her title intact.

Shawn Michaels vs. Kurt Angle

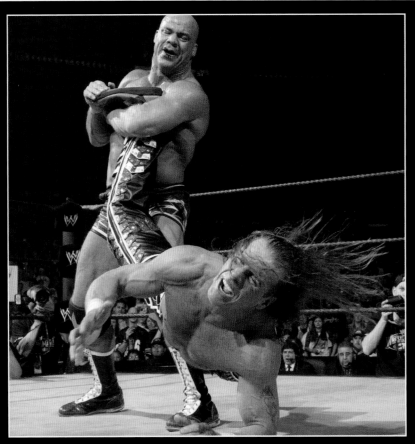

At the 2005 *Royal Rumble*, Shawn Michaels eliminated Kurt Angle from the match. As a result, Angle assaulted Michaels in a rage, beginning a powerful rivalry. Over the next several weeks, Angle promised to prove that anything Shawn Michaels could do, he could do better. Angle won a Ladder Match, beat Michaels' former Rockers partner Marty Jannetty, and arrived accompanied by Michaels' former manager, Sensational Sherri. He even had his own version of HBK's entrance, which he dubbed "Sexy Kurt." To further disrespect Michaels, Angle turned on Sherri and put her in the Ankle Lock.

Shawn Michaels remembers, "The expectations were very high. There's a pressure that comes from living up to those expectations. That was often intimidating, but this was probably one of the most intimidating because Kurt and I both were talented enough to tear the house down and everybody knew that. So that's what they were expecting us to do."

Throughout the epic battle, both men kicked out of several pinfall attempts. But the deciding factor turned out to be Angle's Ankle Lock. Twice, Michaels fought his way out of the punishing submission maneuver, but the third time was the charm. Angle wedged Michaels in the Ankle Lock, and despite furious attempts by "The Heartbreak Kid" to break loose, the match came to an end. Michaels recalls, "I don't think anyone thought in a million years that I'd tap out to the Ankle Lock. It was my suggestion. I thought it was the right thing to do. It was just a matter of doing it and getting the most out of it, making it meaningful. I thought it was a phenomenal story."

Sumo Match

WWE can often be counted on to bring strange and unusual attractions to the Showcase of the Immortals. *WrestleMania 21* was no exception, as the WWE Universe was treated to a Sumo match pitting the Big Show against Sumo champion Akebono. Seeing the Big Show in traditional sumo garb was surprising enough, but seeing Show facing an opponent that outweighed him was even more rare.

The live crowd was able to enjoy all the ceremony and trappings of the world of Sumo, before the two men locked up in the circle. The goal was to push one's opponent out of the circle, and Akebono quickly used his strength to push Show to the edge of the circle, but Big Show was able to push the action back to the center, surprising the Sumo Champion. Once again Akebono got Show close to the line, when Big Show picked up the 500-plus pound behemoth and reversed their positions. Show's advantage was short-lived, as Akebono was able to flip Big Show out of the circle and out of the ring completely to win the exhibition.

The WWE Championship

For the 20th time in *WrestleMania* history, the WWE Championship was going to be defended. But to the anger and dismay of John Bradshaw Layfield, the match would not be the final *WrestleMania 21* contest. JBL recalls, *"This is not to disrespect the guys in the main event, but I thought it was an awful mistake not to let Cena close the show at WrestleMania 21. It was clear that John was going to be "the guy" for the company. I said it then and they disagreed with me. I think they would agree with me now."*

The WWE Champion entered the Staples Center in his own stretch limousine, accompanied by a police escort. As WWE's longest reigning Champion entered the ring, phony $100 bills imprinted with JBL's face fell from the arena's rafters.

As John Cena made his way down the aisle, his childhood dream flashed before him. In only his second appearance at The Showcase of the Immortals, the brash young Superstar was prepared to engage the "Wrestling God" in a battle for the richest prize in sports-entertainment.

JBL displayed the confidence, power, and presence of a champion. His ruthless

trademark moves dominated the number one contender for nearly the first ten minutes of the match. Cena refused to stay down. But whenever it seemed the young lion was going to stem the tide, the veteran brawler remained a step ahead and regained the advantage.

John Cena's defiance and perseverance kept him in the fight and enabled him to avoid a Clothesline from Hell attempt. To the shock of millions around the world, Cena summoned the strength to send the hateful Champion crashing to the canvas with an Attitude Adjustment. The referee's hand touched the mat for the three-count, and JBL's title reign, the longest in ten years, was over. The result symbolized a changing of the guard in WWE, as Cena would indeed become "the guy" for an entire generation of WWE fans. John Cena remembers, "It was bananas. I jumped in the crowd. There's a famous shot of just me leaning on strangers holding up the championship. You'll hear people say they wanted to be champion since they were a kid. That's the absolute truth. To be able to have a moment like Randy "Macho Man" Savage becoming champion at *WrestleMania*, they can't take that away from me."

PIPER'S PIT

"Rowdy" Roddy Piper just had to meet the man that many considered the meanest S.O.B. in the WWE. On a special episode of *Piper's Pit* at *WrestleMania 21*, he did just that when Stone Cold Steve Austin appeared on Piper's show. The two WWE rebels traded insults and slaps, until Carlito appeared, mocking both icons. Stone Cold took out the upstart with a Stone Cold Stunner before he and Piper celebrated with a couple of beers. Despite their momentary camaraderie, Stone Cold ended the segment by dropping Piper with a Stone Cold Stunner. Just what you'd expect from the baddest S.O.B. in WWE history.

The Student Becomes the Teacher

When Batista won the 2005 *Royal Rumble*, the Animal had to choose which title he would attempt to win in the main event of *WrestleMania 21*. World Heavyweight Champion Triple H tried to encourage his Evolution stablemate to jump to *SmackDown* and challenge JBL for the WWE Championship, making a persuasive argument that with both titles in the Evolution fold, they would rule all of WWE. Batista saw through the ruse. Triple H was trying to convince Batista to go to *SmackDown* to protect his own championship. Instead, Batista told Triple H and Ric Flair that he'd be taking the World Heavyweight title from The Game at *WrestleMania*. Triple H explains, "It was time for Dave to step out of Evolution. Leading into *WrestleMania* people were begging for him to turn."

WrestleMania 21 marked Triple H's fourth *WrestleMania* main event, and the second with "Nature Boy" Ric Flair leading him to the ring. Flair's infamous interference to preserve the championship reign of Triple H became known as "The Flair Factor," and it was acknowledged as an obstacle Batista would have to overcome.

As the match started, questions still loomed: Did Batista learn enough from Triple H to defeat him on the Grandest Stage of Them All? Was Batista's sheer power enough to beat one of the most dominating men to ever enter the ring? Would the Flair Factor eventually decide the fate of this contest?

In the early moments of the match, Batista utilized his massive frame and brute strength, while the champion employed his expert ring acumen, along with the tactics of Ric Flair, to neutralize Batista's incredible power. The pendulum continued to swing, but the turning point in the match occurred after Batista reversed a Pedigree attempt on the steel steps and catapulted his mentor into the ring post. The World Heavyweight Champion was severely wounded and began to lose large amounts of blood. Batista's inner Animal sensed it was time to seize the opportunity.

After taking a beating, The Game found an opening for a desperate attempt to defeat his former protégé. The audience witnessed one of the closest near pinfalls of the night when Triple H nailed The Animal with the World Heavyweight Championship. Then, in a last attempt, Triple H positioned Batista for the Pedigree. Batista exerted his will and incredible strength to successfully free himself. This gave The Animal the ability to turn the tide for the final time. Batista hoisted his former mentor into the air and used the Batista Bomb to throw him down with a vengeance.

The match was over. Batista accomplished the impossible—he defeated his mentor and overcame the odds. As a blood-covered Triple H left the ring, Batista closed the show with a celebration befitting a champion.

Batista reflects, "For years, even before I was with the WWE, I had made up my mind this is what I wanted to do, this is what I love, this is what I have a passion for. Being handed that title, I just broke down crying … It still means that much to me where I still break down when I think about it. Because I thought that kind of stuff doesn't happen to guys like me, dreams don't happen to guys that grow up with nothing. But obviously they do."

WRESTLEMANIA 22

ALLSTATE ARENA – CHICAGO, IL

April 2
2006

Attendance
17,159

RAW ANNOUNCERS
Jerry "The King" Lawler, Jim Ross

SMACKDOWN ANNOUNCERS
Michael Cole, Tazz

SPANISH ANNOUNCERS
Carlos Cabrera, Hugo Savinovich

RAW RING ANNOUNCER
Lillian Garcia

SMACKDOWN RING ANNOUNCER
Tony Chimel

SPECIAL FIELD CORRESPONDENTS
Josh Mathews, Todd Grisham

SPECIAL MUSICAL GUEST
Michelle Williams, P.O.D.

Event Card

WWE CHAMPIONSHIP MATCH
- John Cena (Champion) def. Triple H to retain the Championship

PLAYBOY PILLOW FIGHT
- Torrie Wilson def. Candice Michelle

TRIPLE THREAT MATCH FOR THE WORLD HEAVYWEIGHT CHAMPIONSHIP
- Rey Mysterio def. Randy Orton and Kurt Angle (Champion) to become new Champion

NO HOLDS BARRED MATCH
- Shawn Michaels def. Vince McMahon

CASKET MATCH
- Undertaker def. Mark Henry

WOMEN'S CHAMPIONSHIP MATCH
- Mickie James def. Trish Stratus (Champion) to become new Champion

HANDICAP MATCH
- The Boogeyman def. Booker T and Sharmell

HARDCORE MATCH
- Edge w/ Lita def. Mick Foley

UNITED STATES CHAMPIONSHIP MATCH
- John Bradshaw Layfield w/ Jillian Hall def. Chris Benoit (Champion) to become new Champion

MONEY IN THE BANK LADDER MATCH
- Rob Van Dam def. Shelton Benjamin, "Nature Boy" Ric Flair, Finlay, Matt Hardy, and Bobby Lashley

WORLD TAG TEAM CHAMPIONSHIP MATCH
- Big Show and Kane (Champions) def. Carlito and Chris Masters

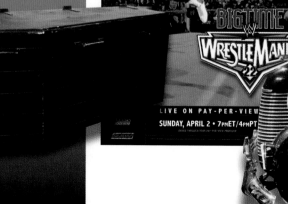

> ## "A true champion is not defined by how much they are admired, but their ability to stand up in the face of adversity."
>
> —John Cena

Big Time

WrestleMania 22 marked the third time WWE's annual spectacular visited Chicago. Since *WrestleMania 13*, the Rosemont Horizon had become the Allstate Arena and WWE had evolved into a formidable global entertainment entity.

The World Tag Team Championship

Carlito and Chris Masters were a pair of young Superstars making their in-ring *WrestleMania* debuts. They were challenging the reigning champs, Kane and Big Show, who had already appeared in a combined 13 *WrestleMania* events. Taking on these two giants of the ring would be a significant challenge on any night, but doing it at their first *WrestleMania* was a tall order.

What the challengers lacked in experience, they more than made up for in confidence. Carlito's Caribbean cool came from his impressive array of moves, and Masters boasted that no Superstar could break his Masterlock, and to date, no one had.

Early in the match, Masters demonstrated his strength by taking Kane to the mat with a shoulderblock, but Kane showed surprising athleticism with a dropkick. After Big Show entered the match, Carlito seemed unhappy that his partner tagged him in, and when Big Show started throwing him around, it was easy to see why. Masters did get Kane in his Masterlock, but Show saved his partner from submitting. Masters tried to help Carlito by attacking Kane, but the move ended up taking out his own partner, who was then Chokeslammed by Kane for the three count.

Money in the Bank Ladder Match

With the first-ever Money in the Bank match being such a rousing success at *WrestleMania 21*, it was no surprise the match returned at *WrestleMania 22*. In a testament to the brutality of the concept, only one Superstar, Shelton Benjamin, returned to compete in the match a second straight year. He was joined by five new participants: "Nature Boy" Ric Flair, Bobby Lashley, Finley, Matt Hardy, and Rob Van Dam.

Benjamin showed the newcomers how things were done early in the match when he ran up a ladder propped against the ring ropes to dive onto several of his competitors outside the ring. Meanwhile, Lashley attempted to use his power to take out his competition before using the ladders, and Matt Hardy suplexed Flair off the top of a ladder, taking him out of the competition. Van Dam tried to take Benjamin out as well by delivering a Rolling Thunder onto a ladder, but Shelton rolled out of the way and RVD connected with the unforgiving steel. With the size and strength of Lashley, it took Finley, Hardy, and Benjamin working together to Power Bomb him off a ladder. The carnage continued until RVD thought he had a clear path to the briefcase, but Benjamin amazingly leapt from the ropes to the top of a ladder to stop RVD. Matt Hardy soon joined the battle by adding a second ladder. Van Dam knocked down the other two competitors, and seized the Money in the Bank opportunity.

The United States Championship

A year after having his lengthy reign as WWE Champion end at *WrestleMania 21*, John Bradshaw Layfield was pursuing the United States Championship. He boasted that, after beating Benoit for the United States Title like he beat the late Eddie Guerrero for the WWE Title, he would be the greatest technical wrestler in WWE.

During the match, JBL relied more on this brawling style than the technical expertise he allegedly possessed, although he did rile the crowd by imitating Guerrero's mannerisms and attempting to hit Guerrero's Three Amigos Suplex move. Benoit also used the Three Amigos, but it was clearly a tribute, and not a mockery. Benoit seemed bound to retain the title when he locked JBL in the Crippler Crossface, but the self-proclaimed Wrestling God was able to flip Benoit over and, using the ropes for leverage, pin the champ's shoulders to the mat for a three count, becoming the new United States Champion.

The Hardcore Legend vs the Rated-R Superstar

When Edge lost a WWE Championship Match to John Cena on *Raw*, he held Mick Foley's officiating responsible for the loss. Enraged, Edge taunted Foley, describing him as a teddy bear whose best days were behind him. The more Edge publicly shamed Mick Foley, the more he awakened the aggression sleeping within the Hardcore Legend. Their *WrestleMania* clash wouldn't be a standard mano-a-mano contest, but a thrilling Hardcore Match. WWE even brought in Joey Styles, the former hardcore voice of ECW, to call the action.

Edge came to the ring carrying a baseball bat and unleashed an early assault. He looked to wrap up the match early by hitting Foley with a Spear, but Edge seemed to be hurt more by the move than the Hardcore Legend. Foley prepared for such a possibility by wrapping his midsection in barbed wire. Edge's shoulder lacerations from the ill-timed Spear were soon joined by head wounds thanks to "Barbie," Foley's barbed-wire encased bat, as well as numerous puncture wounds on Edge's back thanks to hundreds of thumbtacks. Mick was also the worse for wear, as Edge raked Barbie over his midsection and face. The brutality even extended to Mr. Socko, whom Foley wrapped in barbed wire before shoving him into the mouths of Edge and his fiendish valet, Lita.

Edge committed an act of unprecedented cruelty, dousing Foley with lighter fluid. In one of sports-entertainment's most extreme acts, Edge speared the Hardcore Legend through a flaming table, eliciting Styles's trademark line, "Oh my god!". As both men lie on the arena floor, suffering singed body tissue, Edge gathered the strength to pin Mick Foley. The capacity crowd marveled at a match they'd never forget. Even in defeat, the Hardcore Legend left *WrestleMania* amid chants of "Foley, Foley, Foley."

Edge looks back, "That's just one thing like 'Man I would not do that again.' I burned a bunch of hair off my head and all the hair off my arms. I burned my knuckles and my triceps. As I crawled over I looked at my arm because it was smoking and I could smell my skin. People thought I cut my eyeball because blood went down through my eye. The match was a graphic, disturbing visual, but it worked.

Fear the Boogeyman

Booker T had been dodging the undefeated newcomer Boogeyman every chance he could, feigning injuries in order to get out of signed matches. It was somewhat understandable, as in addition to in-ring talent, Boogeyman had shown bizarre behavior, including his herky-jerky movements and his penchant for devouring live worms and spitting said worms onto his opponents. But *SmackDown* General Manager Teddy Long had enough and ordered not only Booker, but also his wife Sharmell, to face Boogeyman in a Handicap Match at *WrestleMania 22*.

Sharmell was clearly petrified as she walked to the ring with her husband, and even more frightened when Booker T had her start out in the match. But that was a ruse, as when Boogeyman turned his back on Booker to confront Sharmell, Booker jumped the odd Superstar from behind and attacked him. The advantage was short-lived, and Boogeyman had Booker down and cornered. The strange Superstar then snacked on a handful of worms, and was advancing on Booker, when Sharmell overcame her fear and looked to save Booker by trying to hit Boogeyman with his own staff. Sadly, he turned around and kissed Sharmell, transferring some of his live worms to her mouth. She fled the ring in disgusted horror and Boogeyman pinned Booker to win his *WrestleMania* debut.

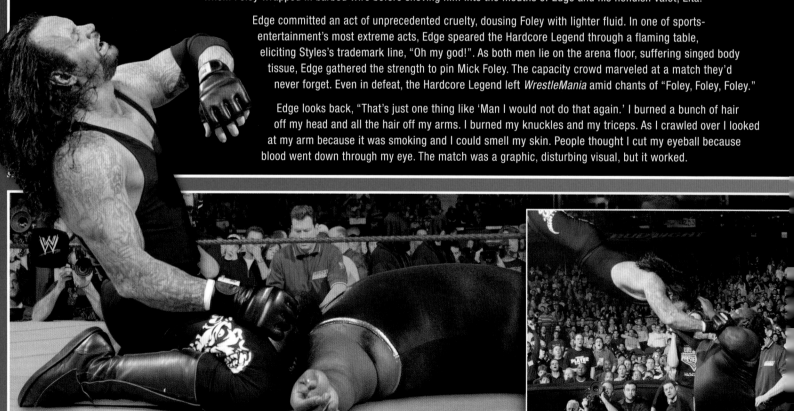

Shawn Michaels vs. Mr. McMahon

When Mr. McMahon continued to revel in the actions of 1997's Montreal Screwjob, Shawn Michaels suggested that McMahon move on. That's where the conflict began. No one tells Mr. McMahon what to do, so he decided to make Michaels' life a living hell, sending both his son and the Spirit Squad against Michaels, and making the Heartbreak Kid another member of the "Kiss My Ass" Club. Things had to be settled at *WrestleMania 22*, in a No Holds Barred Match.

Some were surprised that Mr. McMahon was Shawn Michaels' next *WrestleMania* opponent, given Michaels' history of career-defining performances. Shawn Michaels remembers, "Everybody sort of chuckles that I went from Kurt Angle at *WrestleMania 21* to Vince McMahon the following year because Vince, as he admits, is limited from an athletic standpoint. I looked at it as having a *WrestleMania* off, and going out there and having a fun match."

Mr. McMahon opened the match by unveiling his picture on a framed cover of *Muscle & Fitness* Magazine. HBK had enough of the Chairman's grandstanding, and smashed the picture. Any time the odds were even, the Heartbreak Kid outclassed Mr. McMahon, but twice outside forces interfered to wear down Michaels—first the Spirit Squad and then Shane McMahon. But Michaels was not to be denied, first dispatching the cheerleaders, and then cuffing Shane to the ring.

Several times HBK had the Chairman set up for Sweet Chin Music, but he rejected the opportunity, choosing instead to further punish Mr. McMahon, finally leaping off an enormous ladder to put a trashcan-encased McMahon through a table. HBK recalls, "I previously got up on that ladder and said, 'Not doing it, it's too high. I'd like a smaller one put underneath the ring.' I mean, they were told not to have that size ladder under the ring. I pulled it out at the show and, man, that thing kept coming, and it just kept coming. Of course, you get up there in front of over 17,000 people and realize, 'Oh, my goodness, this is that same one I said no to,' but at that point you have to go for it." Before he went for it, HBK gave the crowd a subtle tease of things to come, unleashing a signature DX chop gesture.

Vince McMahon reflects, "It meant so much for me personally to be in the ring with Shawn Michaels … Whenever there's a situation like that, I'm really concerned that, after the match is over, my opponent isn't going to be as well off as they were coming into the match. The pressure is on me. Shawn Michaels could be in the ring with anyone, quite frankly, and everyone comes out better as a result of it. And that was a true test of Shawn Michaels to be in the ring with me and to come out looking better than he did walking in."

Casket Match

As Undertaker's *WrestleMania* Streak grew in length and prominence, WWE Superstars knew that whoever beat The Deadman and ended the Streak would gain immortality. Mark Henry, The World's Strongest Man, wanted his shot at Undertaker, and was even willing to endure a Casket Match to make it happen.

In a Casket Match, pinfalls and submissions do not matter; the only way to win is to put your opponent in the casket and shut the lid on him. Henry used his legendary strength to soften up Undertaker, even rolling The Deadman into the casket, but Undertaker pulled him in as well and the men traded attacks. The two competitors made it back into the ring, battling to a point where Henry stood outside the ring, trying to collect himself. In one of the most memorable moments in *WrestleMania* history, Undertaker dove over the top rope, over the casket, and onto Henry. The spectacular move dazed Henry, allowing The Deadman to bring him back to the ring where he gave the World's Strongest Man a Tombstone and rolled him into the casket to win the match.

Henry remembers, "It's difficult to explain what it's like to be in the ring with Undertaker because one, you're standing there and you have to watch what's coming to you. Then his presence, the lights are turned on, and then the mind games, and then you have all of the talent that he possesses and the respect he commands. *WrestleMania* is his playground."

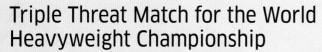
The WWE Women's Championship

When new Diva Mickie James joined WWE she was most excited to be working with her idol, Trish Stratus. Mickie enjoyed tag teaming with Trish, and was willing to stand up for the champion whenever she needed assistance. Over time, Mickie's interest in Trish became more obsessive, making Stratus more uncomfortable. Stratus eventually asked for some distance between the two, and Mickie snapped, attacking Trish, and vowing to win her championship at *WrestleMania 22*.

Throughout the match, Mickie showed she was willing to do anything necessary, repeatedly targeting Trish's injured leg. While in obvious pain, Trish was able to counter several of Mickie's moves. Both came very close to winning the match, but Mickie finally surprised Trish with her version of the Chick Kick (which she called the Mick Kick) to knock Trish down and obtain the three-count, winning the WWE Women's Championship.

Triple Threat Match for the World Heavyweight Championship

A smaller competitor in a sport of giants, Rey Mysterio dreamed of becoming World Champion. His road to the main event at *WrestleMania* started at the 2006 *Royal Rumble* match, where Mysterio outlasted 29 other men to earn a shot at the World Heavyweight Championship. Randy Orton, who Rey eliminated to win the *Rumble*, said horrible things about Mysterio's recently passed friend Eddie Guerrero to goad Rey into putting up his title shot in a match. Orton stole a victory, putting the Viper in the main event. Orton recalls, "I remember when I was asked to say those negative things about Eddie, and the first thing I did was talk to Rey and talk to Vickie. She said it's what Eddie would've wanted, to help the story between Rey and I, because he loved the business and would still want to be a part of it."

With Mysterio and Orton both challenging for the title, Kurt Angle, the Champion, seemed like the forgotten man in the match. But leading into *WrestleMania*, he made both men tap to his Ankle Lock and swore that no one could beat him.

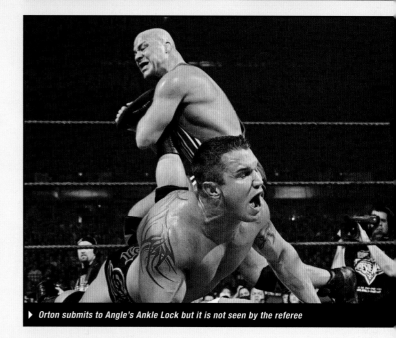
▶ *Orton submits to Angle's Ankle Lock but it is not seen by the referee*

▶ *Mysterio receives a double-German Suplex*

The three combatants prepared to face off in a Triple Threat Match for the World Heavyweight Championship. Before the starting bell rang, a seething Randy Orton took the Championship from referee Charles Robinson and used it to drill Kurt Angle. Early action saw Orton and Mysterio vie for control, crucial because the contest ended after the first pinfall, whether or not the champion was involved.

At two different points, Angle appeared to retain his title, when both opponents tapped out to the Ankle Lock submission. But because the referee's attention was diverted both times, the match continued. Mysterio displayed the same fortitude that won the *Royal Rumble*. He reversed the champion's attempt at an Angle Slam and sent him out of the ring. Mysterio connected a 619 to Randy Orton, using that momentum to pin the Legend Killer after hitting a West Coast Pop to claim the title.

Rey Mysterio looks back, "I was never alone in that ring; I felt Eddie was by my side the entire time, looking over me. It was something we had talked about for a long time. That one day, it would be nice to have that gold and to be the one carrying it. Then, all the years of sacrifice, damage to my body, and being away from my family … to one day be the World Heavyweight Champion. It was awesome. I felt that I had broken barriers because, not only did I become champion, there had not been a wrestler my size, Hispanic, and masked that carried the World Championship. So, it opened doors for Superstars that resemble me."

Playboy Pillow Fight

In a change of pace between the World Heavyweight Championship and the WWE Championship Matches, two Divas that had graced the cover of *Playboy* magazine, Candice Michelle and Torrie Wilson, battled in *WrestleMania's* first-ever Playboy Pillow Fight.

Although there was a bed and pillows in the ring, the pillows were not much in play, though the Divas did toss each other on the bed. While both women started the match in long, elegant gowns, those dresses were torn or cut off and the two continued to battle in their underwear. Candice thought she'd won the match when she threw Torrie into the corner and planned to finish her off with a running splash. But Torrie ducked out of the way and cradled Candice for a three-count to win the match.

John Cena vs. Triple H

When the *Royal Rumble* winner chose to challenge for the World Heavyweight Championship, a Road to WrestleMania tournament was held to choose the challenger to John Cena's WWE Championship. 10-time World Champion Triple H claimed the prize, and looked to win his 11th World Title in his 11th *WrestleMania* match. Even though John Cena was the defending champion, the years of experience the challenger had on Cena caused most to consider Cena the underdog heading into the match. The combatants arrived in style, with the King of Kings rising from the floor on his throne in his barbaric regalia. Cena's entrance was heralded by an entourage of tommy gun-wielding gangsters, including CM Punk.

From the opening bell, the crowd was squarely in the corner of the challenger Triple H. The more The Game pummeled the champion, the louder the audience roared with excitement—even when Triple H brandished his infamous sledgehammer from beneath the ring. Cena continued to fight back, even hitting Triple H with a backdrop onto the unforgiving steel of the entrance ramp. Triple H showed his mettle and determination by kicking out of Cena's pinfall attempt, and regained momentum by tossing the champion into the ring steps.

Finally, after stringing together some of his famous power moves, Cena gained control and even locked Triple H in the STF submission—but his advantage would be temporary. Triple H stayed one step ahead and devastated the Champion with a variety of moves. After seconding HBK's DX chop from earlier in the night, it seemed like Triple H was ready to finish the champion off. However, Cena reversed an attempted Pedigree. He slapped Triple H in the STF for the second time, and now there was no escape. The stunned crowd watched as John Cena overcame tremendous obstacles to defend the Championship and defeat the "King of Kings."

WestleMania XII vs. Ultimate Warrior

WrestleMania 13 vs. Goldust

WrestleMania XIV vs. Owen Hart for the European Championship

WrestleMania XV vs. Kane

WrestleMania 2000 vs. Big Show, Mick Foley, The Rock in a Fatal Four Way Elimination Match for the WWE Championship

TRIPLE H – THE EVOLUTION OF A KING

WrestleMania XXIV vs. John Cena and Randy Orton in a Triple Threat Match with for the WWE Championship

WrestleMania XXVI vs. Sheamus

WrestleMania XXVII vs. Undertaker in a No Holds Barred Match

WrestleMania 25 vs. Randy Orton for the WWE Championship

WrestleMania XXVIII vs. Undertaker in an "End of an Era" Hell in a Cell Match

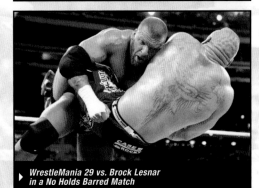

WrestleMania 29 vs. Brock Lesnar in a No Holds Barred Match

▶ *WrestleMania X-Seven vs. Undertaker*

▶ *WrestleMania XIX vs. Booker T. for the World Heavyweight Championship*

▶ *WrestleMania 21 vs. Batista for the World Heavyweight Championship*

▶ *WrestleMania X8 vs. Chris Jericho for the Undisputed Championship*

▶ *WrestleMania XX vs. Chris Benoit and Shawn Michaels in a Triple Threat Match for the World Heavyweight Championship*

▶ *WrestleMania 22 vs. John Cena for the WWE Championship*

In *WrestleMania*'s illustrious 35-year history, Triple H has gone to war 23 times at the "Showcase of the Immortals."

Audiences first saw him at *WrestleMania XII* in 1996 as the posh Hunter Hearst Helmsley. Over the next several years the affluent Greenwich, Connecticut, blue blood morphed into the leader of the rebel faction D-Generation X. By dismantling his opponents and amassing a vast collection of accolades, Triple H emerged as his own man and earned the monikers The Game, The Cerebral Assassin, and even The King of Kings.

With an arsenal of battle gear and an array of entrances, all evoking a carnival of emotions, Triple H's dramatic *WrestleMania* performances changed the very landscape of sports entertainment.

For nearly two decades, he has represented an unmatched standard of excellence at the Showcase of the Immortals. A 14-time World Champion, each ounce of his being is consumed with being the best. Triple H's style is one of precision, and features an economy of movement making him one of the most time-honored performers WWE's grand stage has ever witnessed. Behold the King of Kings, for there is only one.

▶ *WrestleMania 30 vs. Daniel Bryan*

▶ *WrestleMania 32 vs. Roman Reigns for the WWE Championship*

▶ *WrestleMania 34 with Stephanie McMahon vs. Kurt Angle and Ronda Rousey in a Mixed Tag Team Match*

▶ *WrestleMania 31 vs. Sting*

▶ *WrestleMania 33 vs. Seth Rollins in an Unsanctioned Match*

▶ *WrestleMania 35 vs. Batista in a No Holds Barred Match*

WRESTLEMANIA 23

FORD FIELD – DETROIT, MI

April 1
2007

Attendance
80,103

RAW ANNOUNCERS
Jerry "The King" Lawler, Jim Ross

SMACKDOWN ANNOUNCERS
John Bradshaw Layfield,
Michael Cole

ECW ANNOUNCERS
Joey Styles, Tazz

SPANISH ANNOUNCERS
Carlos Cabrera, Hugo Savinovich

RAW RING ANNOUNCER
Lillian Garcia

SMACKDOWN RING ANNOUNCER
Tony Chimel, Theodore R. Long

ECW RING ANNOUNCER
Justin Roberts

HALL OF FAME RING ANNOUNCER
Howard Finkel

SPECIAL FIELD CORRESPONDENTS
Josh Mathews, Todd Grisham

SPECIAL MUSICAL GUEST
Aretha Franklin

Event Card

WWE CHAMPIONSHIP MATCH
- John Cena (Champion) def. Shawn Michaels to retain the Championship

LUMBERJILL MATCH WWE WOMEN'S CHAMPIONSHIP
- Melina (Champion) def. Ashley to retain the Championship

BATTLE OF THE BILLIONAIRES – HAIR VS. HAIR MATCH
- Bobby Lashley (w/ Donald Trump and former Miss USA Tara Conner) def. Umaga (w/ Vince McMahon and Armando Alejandro Estrada)

WORLD HEAVYWEIGHT CHAMPIONSHIP MATCH
- The Undertaker def. Batista (Champion) to become new Champion

UNITED STATES CHAMPIONSHIP MATCH
- Chris Benoit (Champion) def. Montel Vontavious Porter to retain the Championship

MONEY IN THE BANK LADDER MATCH
- Mr. Kennedy def. Edge, CM Punk, King Booker (with Queen Sharmell), Jeff Hardy, Matt Hardy, Finlay, and Randy Orton

OTHER MATCHES
- The Great Khali def. Kane
- The ECW Originals (Rob Van Dam, Sabu, The Sandman, Tommy Dreamer) def. The New Breed (Elijah Burke, Kevin Thorne w/ Ariel, Marcus Cor Von, Matt Striker)

> ## "I was out to prove that I could hang with Shawn Michaels. I hope he enjoyed it as much as I did."
> —John Cena

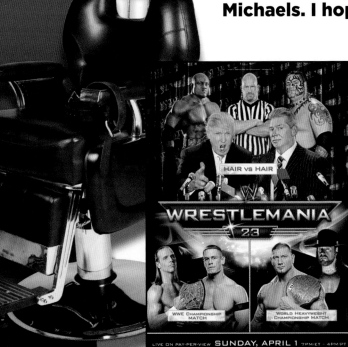

LIVE ON PAY-PER-VIEW **SUNDAY, APRIL 1** 7PM/ET - 4PM/PT

A Return to the Motor City

The success of *WrestleMania III* at the Silverdome in Pontiac, Michigan, cemented WWE as a national sports-entertainment powerhouse. Two decades later, *WrestleMania* returned to Detroit as a global entertainment entity. WWE's annual spectacular had become a destination event for fans from all over the world.

▶ *Aretha Franklin reprises her role from WrestleMania III*

Money in the Bank

For the previous two years, the six-man Money in the Bank match was a highlight of *WrestleMania*. Always looking to make things bigger, badder, and better, WWE added two more competitors to the match, featuring Superstars from all three brands: *Raw*, *SmackDown*, and *ECW*.

CM Punk was the first Superstar to suffer from the brutality of the match, when Edge nailed the Straight-Edge Superstar with a ladder, before coming within inches of securing the briefcase.

> ## "It's a mess, a mess of metal and flesh. I think the ladder matches are more dangerous than Hell in a Cell."
> —Randy Orton

▶ *Matt Hardy threatens to harm Queen Sharmell*

▶ *Jeff Hardy leaps onto the Rated-R Superstar*

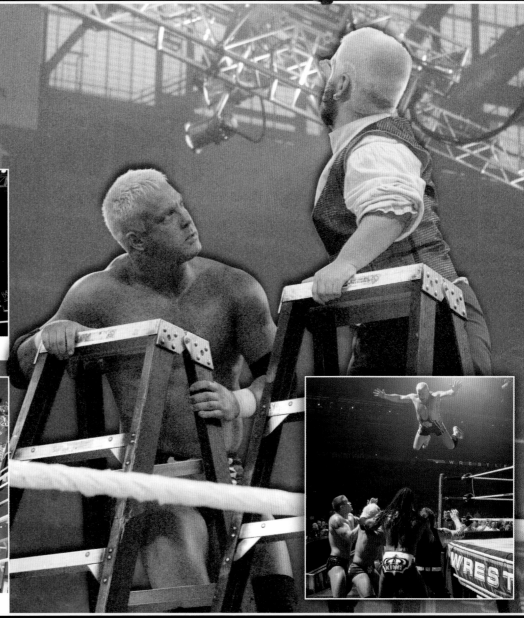

Fans wondered whether the two Hardy brothers would work together to eliminate the competition. Matt and Jeff quickly answered that question when they started trading blows in the ring. They were not the only tag team to refuse to work together. Former Rated RKO partners Randy Orton and Edge knocked each other off ladders, and the match got worse for Edge. The "Rated R Superstar," who had never lost at *WrestleMania*, saw his Money in the Bank dreams end when he was put through a ladder draped from the ring to the ring barricade by a flying Jeff Hardy, who effectively eliminated himself from the match with the daring maneuver.

Orton says, "Money in the Bank should definitely be considered one of the most dangerous types of matches. It's a mess, a mess of metal and flesh. I think the ladder matches are more dangerous than Hell in a Cell."

King Booker and Matt Hardy battled at the top of two ladders, inches away from the briefcase. Queen Sharmell interfered until Hardy threatened to give her a Twist of Fate unless Booker came back down to the ring. Booker descended to save his wife, receiving the Twist instead. A bloodied Finlay then gave Matt Hardy the Celtic Cross on a ladder and was greeted by a surprise from underneath the ring—the Leprechaun Hornswoggle. It looked like Finlay's sidekick was going to make it to the briefcase until Mr. Kennedy lifted him onto his shoulders and performed his famous Plunge from the top of the ladder.

CM Punk saw his fingertips graze the dangling briefcase, but his comeback came to an abrupt halt when Mr. Kennedy battered Punk with a ladder before capturing the briefcase.

Batista vs. Undertaker

Heading into the 2007 *Royal Rumble* match, no one had won the Rumble from the #30 spot, and Undertaker had never won the *Royal Rumble*. Both of these facts became history when Undertaker took care of business, and The Deadman could then look to extend his unprecedented *WrestleMania* winning streak with a championship victory at *WrestleMania 23*. He had his pick of championships, but he decided to face World Heavyweight Champion Batista at the Showcase of the Immortals.

Batista remembers, "Facing Undertaker at *WrestleMania* was one of my dream matches. The way the match was built was so important. No one had stood up to Undertaker the way I did. … That made for a more competitive feel so people were wondering, 'Will Undertaker's Streak be broken?' I knew otherwise but what was really important was I wanted to steal the show. I think Undertaker did as well."

"No one had stood up to Undertaker the way I did."

—Batista

In the battle's opening moments, both competitors exchanged furious blows. Batista's power gave him the early advantage and The Animal became the aggressor. Pushed by his opponent, the champion took an unusual risk, as Batista climbed to the top rope and hit a flying shoulder block on Undertaker. Whether it was keeping his championship or the allure of ending The Streak, the Animal was prepared to do anything.

Undertaker's prowess in *WrestleMania* was clearly established throughout his amazing Streak. The Deadman grabbed the match's momentum, and hit Batista with signature maneuvers like Snake Eyes, Old School, and the Leg Drop on the ring apron.

Batista withstood Undertaker's fury, and came close to ending the match by slamming The Deadman through the ECW announcer's table and hitting Undertaker with a Batista Bomb. Undertaker was able to kick out, so a frustrated Batista went to hit a second Batista Bomb, but the resourceful Undertaker turned the move into a Tombstone Piledriver. The Deadman pinned the Animal, winning the World Heavyweight Championship and continuing the greatest streak in sports-entertainment.

Though no longer World Heavyweight Champion, Batista understood how well the match had been received by the audience, "I felt like we should have been main event. I still feel like we should have been main event but after the match, I knew that we were the main event. I knew we stole the show and I came back and said at the top of my lungs, 'Follow that' because I knew we tore the house down. Everyone was on their feet at the end of that match. Maybe I should have kept my mouth shut but I was so proud to have gone through that. I felt like I had finally earned Undertaker's respect. I got a little grief from doing that but I didn't care. Still don't."

The United States Championship

Ever since he signed the most lucrative free-agent contract in *SmackDown* history, fans wanted to see MVP challenge the best and challenge for championships, to see if his boasts could be backed up. Fans got that chance at *WrestleMania 23*, when MVP was set to face Chris Benoit for the United States Championship.

Never one to shy away from grand entrances, MVP made his way past two rows of cheerleaders to reach the ring for his *WrestleMania* debut. The champion was more about the match to come, and made his way to the ring with little fanfare. While the two men exchanged early lockups, Benoit started his wrestling clinic, putting MVP's head in a leg lock, and then looked to execute a German Suplex. But the brash newcomer showed that he could back up his bravado and threw Benoit out of the ring. The match continued at this pace with Benoit hitting some trademark moves, with MVP showing surprising blocks and counters for some of the others, including his ability to halt a Benoit superplex. Experience eventually did win out as Benoit was able to hit a succession of German Suplexes and a diving headbutt to pin MVP and retain his United States Championship.

Hair vs. Hair Battle of the Billionaires

Donald Trump had been connected to *WrestleMania*, hosting *WrestleMania IV* and *V*, and appearing at *WrestleMania XX* as well, but he'd never been involved in a match. Ever since Donald Trump had upstaged Mr. McMahon at "Fan Appreciation Night," the two titans of industry had been clashing. Rather than settle things in the ring directly, each man chose an in-ring proxy, with Mr. McMahon picking the Intercontinental Champion, Umaga. Donald Trump's delegate was ECW World Champion, Bobby Lashley. The egotistical Mr. McMahon and Trump decided that whoever's Superstar lost would have his head shaved bald.

Both Umaga and Lashley showed their amazing power throughout the match. While the Chairman of WWE was sure about his choice of the Samoan Bulldozer, he tried to further tilt the contest in his favor when Umaga attacked the special guest referee Stone Cold Steve Austin. With Austin down, Shane McMahon and Umaga attacked Bobby Lashley. The younger McMahon climbed to the top rope, and blasted a battered Lashley with his Coast-to-Coast leap across the ring. Shane-O-Mac then donned a referee shirt and began acting as an official in place of Austin. Shane McMahon did not serve as the referee long as Stone Cold returned and took care of Shane, while Trump took down Mr. McMahon, with "The Billionaire Clothesline." Umaga received a Stone Cold Stunner and a spear from Lashley. The Dominator pinned Umaga, and Mr. McMahon's fate was sealed. He tried to escape, but Stone Cold caught his long-time rival, and Austin, Lashley, and Trump shaved McMahon bald.

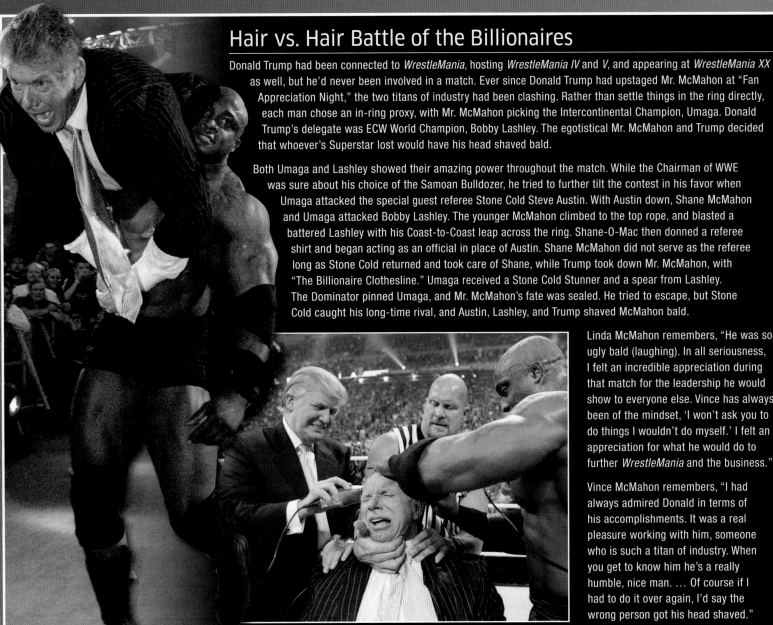

Linda McMahon remembers, "He was so ugly bald (laughing). In all seriousness, I felt an incredible appreciation during that match for the leadership he would show to everyone else. Vince has always been of the mindset, 'I won't ask you to do things I wouldn't do myself.' I felt an appreciation for what he would do to further *WrestleMania* and the business."

Vince McMahon remembers, "I had always admired Donald in terms of his accomplishments. It was a real pleasure working with him, someone who is such a titan of industry. When you get to know him he's a really humble, nice man. ... Of course if I had to do it over again, I'd say the wrong person got his head shaved."

Kane vs. The Great Khali

Sports-entertainment is a land of giants, but few men were as towering as the Great Khali. At more than seven feet tall, Khali had blazed a trail of destruction through the WWE, and few could stand up to his size and power. One Superstar, Kane, felt he was up to the challenge, and they met in a *Raw* vs. *SmackDown* interpromotional match.

Khali set an early tone for the match by tossing Kane out of the ring, and then slamming him to the mat several times. No one had been successful getting the massive Khali off his feet and Kane was having no luck either. The Big Red Monster was eventually able to turn the tide and became the first WWE Superstar to scoop up Khali and slam him to the mat, but Kane was only able to keep Khali down for a two-count. Khali however put Kane on the mat with a crushing choke bomb and pinned the Great Red Monster for his first *WrestleMania* victory.

8-Man Tag Team Match

The WWE Universe had shown such a strong interest in all things ECW that WWE re-launched the land of extreme the summer before *WrestleMania 23*. The new ECW was a mix of the competitors that had built the original show, as well as young upstarts that were looking to make their own history. A clash between these ECW Originals and the New Breed was inevitable and set for the grand stage of *WrestleMania 23*. Tommy Dreamer remembers, "I was at the first *WrestleMania* as a fan and remember it like it was yesterday. I was very excited when I was told the ECW Originals were going to be in a tag match at *WrestleMania*."

After making their way to the ring through the packed Ford Field crowd, the four originals took early control by hitting Matt Striker and Elijah Burke with double-team attacks from Sabu, The Sandman, and Tommy Dreamer. Marcus Cor Von changed the momentum of the match, and the New Breed isolated Tommy Dreamer and obtained several near falls.

Dreamer was finally able to reach his corner and tag in reinforcements. Rob Van Dam thrilled Ford Field with his unique offense. After a classic ECW-style brawl broke-out, RVD soared high above the ring and crushed Matt Striker with a Five-Star Frog Splash. The hardcore icons that were so instrumental in creating the original ECW stood victorious.

Lumberjill Match

Ashley, the 2005 Divas Search champion, was receiving significant media coverage thanks to her victory in the Divas competition and her cover appearance on *Playboy* magazine. Melina, who thought the spotlight should always be on her, wanted to shut down Ashley and was even willing to risk her WWE Women's Championship. The two were set to clash at *WrestleMania 23* in a Lumberjill match, in which the other WWE Divas would surround the ring.

Melina was confident that her in-ring experience would make this an easy match, but Ashley surprised the Women's Champion with an opening barrage of attacks. Melina rolled out of the ring to catch a breather, forgetting that the Lumberjills would put her right back in the ring. The two battled back and forth, with Ashley coming close to winning after flipping Melina out of a corner of the ring. Ashley even rolled Melina up, but the veteran champion was able to roll through the move and pin her upstart challenger with a roll-up and a bridge.

John Cena vs. Shawn Michaels

For John Cena's WWE Championship defense at *WrestleMania*, he would be facing Mr. WrestleMania, Shawn Michaels. Michaels recalls, "When I came back I just wanted to help. Being in the main event at [*WrestleMania*] *XX* was cool and it was like 'who'd thunk it.' I was excited to go out there with John. He's such a hard worker. He's a good kid. He's not a kid anymore but certainly at the time that's how I looked at him. He's incredibly respectful. He looked at it as an opportunity. That's what made coming back so fun."

To start the match, The Heartbreak Kid came out swinging. HBK remained in control, wearing Cena down. The Champion avoided an attack in the corner, which cut open Michaels' forehead. Cena capitalized on the opening and began to build momentum against a bloodied HBK. Michaels attempted a desperation move, but his superkick missed the Champ, instead hitting the referee and knocking the official out of the ring.

Without an official scrutinizing the match, the rules were bent, broken, and crushed into a fine dust. Michaels delivered a devastating Piledriver to the Champ, planting Cena's skull into the steel steps. Michaels rolled the now-bleeding Cena back into the ring, and a second referee sprinted to the ring to make the count. His late arrival gave Cena just enough time to recover and kick out after a count of two. Michaels had come so close, but the match continued. The battle continued until Cena's upper body strength locked "The Heartbreak Kid" in his STF submission hold. The crowd's clamor provided the soundtrack as Shawn Michaels fought with all his heart. In the end, Cena's power subdued the icon, and the Champ retained his title.

John Cena reflects, "That's one *WrestleMania* that I really enjoyed. ... I got to a level in my career where I felt even more confident in my abilities and I think when anyone is in there with somebody like Shawn Michaels he's the best. I was at a point where no longer am I going to be carried; I was out to prove that I could hang with Shawn Michaels. I hope he enjoyed it as much as I did. I know he has tons of *WrestleMania* moments. I certainly know I'm not number one but I certainly hope he doesn't forget that night because I certainly never will."

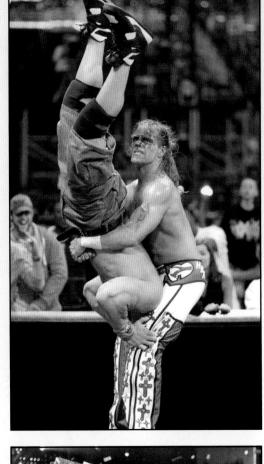

WRESTLEMANIA XXIV

CITRUS BOWL—ORLANDO, FL

March 30
2008

Attendance
74,635

RAW ANNOUNCERS
Jerry "The King" Lawler, Jim Ross

SMACKDOWN ANNOUNCERS
Jonathan Coachman, Michael Cole

ECW ANNOUNCERS
Joey Styles, Tazz

SPANISH ANNOUNCERS
Carlos Cabrera, Hugo Savinovich

RAW RING ANNOUNCER
Lillian Garcia, William Regal

SMACKDOWN RING ANNOUNCER
Justin Roberts, Theodore R. Long

ECW RING ANNOUNCER
Tony Chimel, Armando Estrada

HALL OF FAME RING ANNOUNCER
Howard Finkel

SPECIAL FIELD CORRESPONDENTS
Mike Adamle, Todd Grisham

SPECIAL MUSICAL GUESTS
John Legend, Jones High School Marching Band

SPECIAL GUEST HOSTESS
Kim Kardashian

SPECIAL GUEST RING ANNOUNCER
Snoop Dogg

Event Card

WORLD HEAVYWEIGHT CHAMPIONSHIP MATCH
- Undertaker def. Edge (Champion) to become new Champion

NO DISQUALIFICATION MATCH
- Floyd "Money" Mayweather def. Big Show by knockout

WWE CHAMPIONSHIP TRIPLE THREAT MATCH
- Randy Orton (Champion) def. John Cena and Triple H to retain the Championship

PLAYBOY BUNNYMANIA LUMBERJILL MATCH
- Beth Phoenix and Melina w/ Santino Marella def. Maria and Ashley

CAREER THREATENING MATCH
- Shawn Michaels def. "Nature Boy" Ric Flair

ECW CHAMPIONSHIP MATCH
- Kane def. Chavo Guerrero (Champion) to become new Champion

BATTLE FOR BRAND SUPREMACY
- Batista (SmackDown) def. Umaga (Raw)

MONEY IN THE BANK LADDER MATCH
- CM Punk def. Shelton Benjamin, Chris Jericho, Carlito, Montel Vontavious Porter (MVP), Mr. Kennedy, and John Morrison

BELFAST BRAWL
- John Bradshaw Layfield def. Finlay w/ Hornswoggle

> ## "Everything I am today, everything I have today, everything I will be is because of sports-entertainment."
>
> —"Nature Boy" Ric Flair

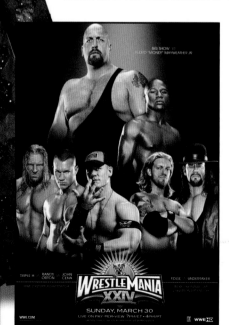

A Change in Scenery

The original site for *WrestleMania XXIV* was Orlando's Amway Arena, a venue that accommodated an estimated 18,000 people for a ring event. Vince McMahon believed *WrestleMania* needed to be located in Orlando, Florida, but felt that it had to be hosted in a larger venue—the more than 74,000-seat Citrus Bowl. Over the next year, WWE invested millions of dollars transforming the aging Citrus Bowl into a spectacular vision of imagination and innovation.

▶ *Citrus Bowl - before*

▶ *Citrus Bowl - after*

Belfast Brawl

For months there had been a rumor circulating that Mr. McMahon had an illegitimate son, and that that he was a WWE Superstar. To the great shock of the Chairman, this son was revealed to be Hornswoggle, Finlay's leprechaun sidekick. Mr. McMahon wanted to show the newest member of his family a bit of tough love, so he forced Hornswoggle to face him in a Steel Cage Match. Mr. McMahon was tough on the leprechaun, but it was nothing compared to the brutality served up by John "Bradshaw" Layfield. JBL came to the ring, cuffed Finlay to the cage, and devastated Hornswoggle. When Mr. McMahon demanded an explanation for JBL's actions, he explained that Hornswoggle was not, in fact, a McMahon, but rather, the child of Finlay, who'd come up with the ruse to give his son a better life. Finlay was furious at the attack on his boy, so he sought revenge at *WrestleMania XXIV*.

With a Belfast Brawl having no disqualifications and no count outs, the two bruisers pummeled one another in and out of the ring with Singapore Canes, garbage cans, cookie sheets, and steel steps. Finlay's shillelagh was used by both men as well, but it was a traditional move that scored the victory, as JBL hit his Clothesline from Hell to put down Finlay and win the match.

Money in the Bank Ladder Match

For the fourth installment of Money in the Bank at *WrestleMania*, four competitors with previous MITB experience squared off against three men new to that match. Seeing that all three previous Money in the Bank opportunities had been successfully cashed in for World Championships, all seven knew this was an opportunity to become part of the main-event mix.

MVP demonstrated he was a quick study when he leveled many other competitors with a ladder. He was on top of the world until Jericho out-jousted him with a ladder of his own. New competitors often bring new ideas to this match, as John Morrison demonstrated by performing a moonsault on four other participants while holding a ladder. The veterans had some impressive moves as well. Shelton Benjamin leaped on Mr. Kennedy as Kennedy was looking to suplex Morrison from the top of a ladder, and ended up powerbombing both men.

Carlito and Kennedy worked together to toss Benjamin out of the ring. Jericho, Carlito, Kennedy, and CM Punk all battled at the top of two ladders under the briefcase, but all four men ended up falling to the mat. With six men down, it looked like MVP was destined to win, until a previously injured Matt Hardy made his first WWE appearance in more than five months to take out MVP.

CM Punk used the ladder as a battering ram to prevent Kennedy from becoming the first two-time Money in the Bank winner. CM Punk would not be denied in a furious fight with Chris Jericho. Both men had their hands on the briefcase. The resourceful CM Punk hooked Jericho in a Tree of Woe from the ladder and secured the briefcase, and in the process, took his career to another level.

Battle for Brand Supremacy

With Superstars still competing exclusively on either *Raw* or *SmackDown*, both WWE programs were always looking to prove who had the superior product. This competitive spirit led to matches like the Battle for Brand Supremacy at *WrestleMania XXIV*. *Raw* General Manager William Regal

challenged *SmackDown* to choose a Superstar to face *Raw*'s Umaga in a one-on-one match at *WrestleMania XXIV*. *Smackdown*'s Teddy Long offered the perfect opponent—three-time World Champion Batista.

One of the more agile big men in sports-entertainment, Umaga kept Batista off balance with a variety of punches and kicks. One impressive kick knocked The Animal out of the ring. Batista was able to regain momentum, and finish off the Samoan Bulldozer with a Batista Bomb. For that night at least, *SmackDown* gained the upper hand.

ECW Championship

Before the *WrestleMania XXIV* pay-per-view began, the Citrus Bowl crowd enjoyed a 24-man Battle Royal. The last man standing would enjoy an additional prize—a spot on the *WrestleMania* card, challenging Chavo Guerrero for his ECW Championship. Kane outlasted the other 23 competitors to earn the opportunity.

Chavo Guerrero came to the ring and then defiantly gestured to the entrance. He was ready to face Kane. Unfortunately for Guerrero, he underestimated the mind games the Big Red Monster was willing to play. Kane appeared from the opposite side of the ring. Chavo finally turned around and walked right into a Chokeslam. Kane became the new ECW Champion in a matter of seconds.

Ric Flair vs. Shawn Michaels

In November 2007, Mr. McMahon told Ric Flair that his career would be over upon his next loss. Knowing he couldn't remain undefeated forever, Flair decided to challenge Shawn Michaels for a match at *WrestleMania*. Ric Flair reflects, "Being in the ring with Shawn was great. He just said to me, and no one said this to me in my life, he said, 'Just shut up and listen to me tonight and don't say a word.' I said, 'Okay.' We walked out the door and he said, 'Let's do it.' It was very emotional. I cry when I think about it."

Shawn Michaels laughs and adds, "The one demand I had made on him before the match was, 'You don't say anything!' I know you've been a ring general your whole life but not tonight. You do not speak (motions zipping his mouth).' That was a big pill for him to swallow and he did it for me."

With the families of both men sitting at ringside, the match began with a Shawn Michael's slap across the Nature Boy's face. Both men traded holds, body blows, and reverse knife-edge chops. Michaels almost suffered permanent injury after an Asai Moonsault missed the mark and sent him crashing through the *Raw* announcers' table. The impact stilled the crowd to an eerie silence; no one knew if Shawn Michaels would be able to continue. The consummate opportunist, Flair focused his attacks on HBK's right knee. Shawn Michaels endured Flair's assault until Mr. WrestleMania backdropped his idol out of the ring and onto the floor.

When it appeared that Michaels was set to seal Ric Flair's fate with Sweet Chin Music, his admiration for Flair brought him to a stop in mid-motion. Even in the midst of battle, Shawn Michaels was riddled with conflict. Flair came back and locked Michaels in the Figure Four in the center of the ring. Mustering all his strength, Shawn Michaels made it to the ropes to force a break in the hold.

After being hit with two Superkicks, the Nature Boy, battered and beaten, returned to his feet. With his fists clenched, like so many times before, Flair was ready to continue the fight. Overcome with emotion, Shawn Michaels said, "I'm sorry, I love you," and administered a third Sweet Chin Music. Ric Flair's majestic in-ring WWE career came to an end.

BunnyMania Lumberjill Match

This Divas tag team match pitted two Divas featured in *Playboy*, Ashley and Maria, against WWE Women's Champion Beth Phoenix and Melina. Phoenix was a force of nature, but Ashley took the fight right to her, hitting her with a flip. Both women tagged out, and Maria threw Melina out of the ring, where the Divas surrounding the ring punished the unpopular Melina before putting her back in. Ashley and Maria kept attacking Melina, until she was able to reverse the momentum and toss Ashley out of the ring.

For more than two decades the WWE Universe learned that anything could happen at *WrestleMania*, and this match proved the adage with a temporary blackout at the Citrus Bowl. In the resulting chaos, Maria hit a top-rope move on the Glamazon and almost pinned Phoenix until Santino Marella got involved. His actions angered Jerry "The King" Lawler, who punched Santino out. The ringside confrontation allowed Beth Phoenix to nail Maria with her patented Fisherman's Suplex, scoring the pinfall victory.

Triple Threat Match for the WWE Championship

Randy Orton entered the WWE Championship Match at *WrestleMania XXIV* facing two motivated challengers. After appearing in 11 consecutive *WrestleMania*s, Triple H had to miss *WrestleMania 23* due to a catastrophic quad injury suffered in a match against Randy Orton. John Cena, also injured in a match with Randy Orton, was forced to surrender the WWE Championship, and most thought he'd be out for close to a year. However, Cena shocked the WWE Universe as a surprise entrant who went on to win the 2008 *Royal Rumble*. So the champion, Orton, was facing two men who had both championship aspirations and personal scores to settle with him.

Randy Orton, never one to miss a chance at a cheap shot, drilled Triple H with the Championship title but soon found himself on the receiving end of a John Cena onslaught. Rather than work together, Cena and Triple H battled for who was going to attack the champion. This allowed Orton to find an opening and begin beating on both challengers.

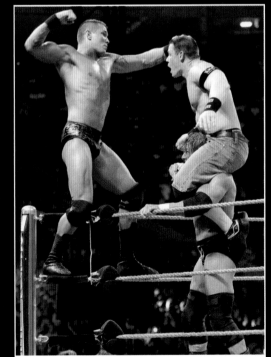

▶ *Orton prepares to land the cross body on Cena*

Alliances shifted as two longtime foes worked together to take out the third member of the Triple Threat match. Triple H had Cena on his shoulders and Randy Orton landed the cross body on Cena off the top rope. No one man kept the upper hand for long. Orton hit both challengers with a double DDT, but could only secure two counts. Cena slapped his STF submission on Orton, but Triple H helped the Champion break the hold. A Pedigree from Triple H to Cena appeared to have sealed the victory and a 12th WWE Championship reign, but Orton punted Triple H in the skull and pinned Cena himself.

Orton remembers, "No one thought I would successfully defend the title that night. ... In general, the feeling was I was going to the Citrus Bowl to lose. Retaining the championship at *WrestleMania XXIV* in a match against John Cena and Triple H was a big moment."

Anything Goes

Big Show had been away from WWE rings for more than a year when he returned at *No Way Out 2008*. Rather than soak in the adulation returning Superstars receive, Big Show angered the WWE Universe by threatening to injure Rey Mysterio. Mysterio's friend, undefeated boxer Floyd "Money" Mayweather, jumped out of the crowd to defend Rey and broke Show's nose in the melee. Show challenged the boxing star to a match at *WrestleMania XXIV*, and Money accepted. Big Show remembers, "I was very excited when I heard about this angle. Originally, this was supposed to be a tag. It was supposed to be Batista and Rey against Floyd and myself. Rey got hurt. Batista got hurt. Then it manifested into, again, Vince's brilliance, Giant vs. Boxer."

Both participants appeared on *Larry King Live* to promote the match. King recalls, "The Boxer-Wrestler match with Mayweather and Big Show was a great idea, and an example of great promoters working together. Vince McMahon is a tremendous promoter and marketer. Floyd Mayweather is the greatest personal marketer since Muhammad Ali. The Big Show is a tremendous athlete and physical sight. The David versus Goliath aspect to the match was brilliant. ... Of course Mayweather didn't have a slingshot."

This was a Street Fight; anything goes and there had to be a winner. Mayweather kept his distance and used his speed to hit Big Show with several body shots. The cocky Mayweather called for a water break, drinking his water from a chalice. An infuriated Big Show pulverized a member of Mayweather's entourage, knocking him from the ring apron to the floor. Big Show hoisted him up and slammed him into the ring. Mayweather's self-confidence quickly turned to concern.

Big Show began to manhandle his opponent, but Mayweather leaped on Show's massive back and administered a sleeper hold. Big Show broke the hold and began mauling Mayweather. The World's Largest Athlete stepped on his left arm, chopped him, stepped on his back, and flattened him with a side slam, bringing gasps from the crowd. Mayweather's handlers tried to remove their prizefighter from the match, but Show dragged the boxer back to the ring.

> **"[Mayweather] was a better pro in the ring than some guys that I have been in the ring with that have done this for years."**
>
> —Big Show

Members of the Mayweather entourage entered the ring and attacked Big Show with a chair; Mayweather then used the chair to level Big Show with several chair shots. The boxer then used brass knuckles to deliver a knockout punch for the win. Big Show recalls, "The match was excellent. Better than I thought it was going to be. I didn't know how Floyd was going to work in front of 70,000 people. ... He was a better pro in the ring than some guys that I have been in the ring with that have done this for years. He understood the showmanship. He understood what his role was. He understood the David versus Goliath story. His natural ability as an entertainer just blossomed. He gave one hell of a performance. It was one of the best things that I have been a part of in my career."

The World Heavyweight Championship

Undertaker won an Elimination Chamber match at *No Way Out* to earn a shot at Edge's World Heavyweight Championship. Edge vowed to be the man to end Undertaker's undefeated Streak at *WrestleMania*. Edge recalls, "It's still my crowning moment, even more so than winning the World Title for the first time or the Tag Team Title or the Intercontinental Title, those are all amazing and I will never forget them. But walking out there and seeing the spectacle of it and the setup over the ring and just how everything looked... Then I'm going down there against Undertaker. I remember walking down to the ring and I lost feeling in my arms because I was so amped up. If you watch it back you might see me trying to shake my hands out because I am walking to the ring and I am looking at him and he's giving me the Undertaker stare and I couldn't feel my hands. Thankfully they came back. It was an amazing experience."

Edge launched an early attack on The Deadman, stunning the WWE Universe by withstanding an early barrage by Undertaker, and taking control of the match. The Ultimate Opportunist looked to sap Undertaker of his power by targeting The Phenom's back with repeated attacks. Edge looked to press his advantage with a high-risk top-rope maneuver, but The Deadman recovered and tossed Edge off the top rope onto the floor. Undertaker amazed the crowd and crushed Edge by diving over the top rope and out of the ring onto the Rated-R Superstar.

Edge's prior attack on Undertaker's back allowed him to regain the upper hand. The Rated-R Superstar dropped Undertaker on the ring barricade, further assaulting The Deadman's lower back. Rolling Undertaker back into the ring, he could only score a two-count against The Phenom.

The evenly-matched foes continued to push each other's limits. Undertaker hit Snake Eyes, but Edge countered with a drop kick. Edge's Spear was stopped by Undertaker and turned into a Chokeslam.

Edge managed to kick out, stunning Undertaker. Both men came close to winning the match on several occasions, but when the official was knocked out inadvertently, Edge looked to finish Undertaker with some illegal moves. When Undertaker delivered a Tombstone, a replacement official raced to the ring to make the count, but Edge kicked out.

After Edge drilled him with another Spear, The Phenom locked Edge in his Hell's Gate submission hold. The pain was too great and the champion tapped out. The Deadman won the World Heavyweight Championship yet again, and advanced his amazing Streak to 16-0.

WRESTLEMANIA 25

RELIANT STADIUM – HOUSTON, TX

April 5
2009

Attendance
72,744

ANNOUNCERS
Jerry "The King" Lawler, Jim Ross, Michael Cole

SPANISH ANNOUNCERS
Carlos Cabrera, Hugo Savinovich

RAW RING ANNOUNCER
Lillian Garcia

SMACKDOWN RING ANNOUNCER
Justin Roberts

HALL OF FAME RING ANNOUNCER
Justin Roberts

SPECIAL FIELD CORRESPONDENT
Todd Grisham

SPECIAL MUSICAL GUESTS
Kid Rock, Nicole Scherzinger

SPECIAL GUEST TIMEKEEPER
Mae Young

Event Card

WWE CHAMPIONSHIP MATCH
- Triple H (Champion) def. Randy Orton to retain the Championship

TRIPLE THREAT MATCH FOR THE WORLD HEAVYWEIGHT CHAMPIONSHIP
- John Cena def. Edge (Champion) & Big Show to become new Champion

INTERCONTINENTAL CHAMPIONSHIP MATCH
- Rey Mysterio def. John Bradshaw Layfield to become new Champion

EXTREME RULES MATCH – BROTHER VS. BROTHER
- Matt Hardy def. Jeff Hardy

HANDICAP ELIMINATION MATCH
- Chris Jericho def. "Rowdy" Roddy Piper, Jimmy "Superfly" Snuka, and Ricky "The Dragon" Steamboat w/ "Nature Boy" Ric Flair

25-DIVA BATTLE ROYAL TO CROWN MISS WRESTLEMANIA
- Santina eliminated Beth Phoenix and Melina to be crowned Miss WrestleMania. Other participants included Alicia Fox, Layla, Maria, Joy Giovanni, Rosa Mendes, Sunny, Torrie Wilson, Miss Jackie, Gail Kim, Jillian Hall, Eve Torres, Tiffany, Kelly Kelly, Molly Holly, Maryse, Katie Lea Burchill, Natalya, Victoria, Brie Bella, Nikki Bella, Mickie James, and Michelle McCool

MONEY IN THE BANK LADDER MATCH
- CM Punk def. Shelton Benjamin, Mark Henry w/ Tony Atlas, Kane, Montel Vontavious Porter (MVP), Finlay w/ Hornswoggle, Kofi Kingston, and Christian

OTHER MATCH
- Undertaker def. Shawn Michaels

> **"When you work with individuals like Shawn and Undertaker, there is an extraordinary amount of emotion and pride that goes into the art they are creating."**
>
> —Vince McMahon

WrestleMania's Silver Celebration

A record-breaking crowd traveled to Houston to celebrate a quarter century of *WrestleMania* history. After *WrestleMania X-Seven* at the Astrodome, many at WWE hoped the Showcase of the Immortals would return to Houston, and for the *25th Anniversary of WrestleMania*, Reliant Stadium served as the venue.

Money in the Bank Ladder Match

Once again, eight men looked to win the Money in the Bank Ladder Match and its guaranteed World Championship opportunity. Six of the eight competitors had previously competed in Money in the Bank, including the previous year's winner, CM Punk. Only Mark Henry and Kofi Kingston were new to the concept.

To start the match, some competitors chose to battle in the ring, while others dove out of the ring looking for a ladder. Five Superstars scrambled up two ladders, battling each other to try and reach the briefcase, but Kane and Mark Henry toppled the two ladders, sending the men crashing to the ring and floor. Money in the Bank newcomer Kofi Kingston seemed born to perform in these matches when he leapt over a ladder attack by Christian and Shelton Benjamin and later raced up a ladder being held by Mark Henry in an unsuccessful attempt to steal the briefcase.

Some high-risk maneuvers proved just as hazardous for the initiator of the action as the victims, such as Shelton Benjamin's flip off a ladder on the entrance ramp and Christian's Unprettier on CM Punk off a ladder straddling another ladder and the ring ropes. The match came down to Kane and CM Punk, and although the Big Red Monster had Punk in a chokehold, the Straight Edge Superstar unleashed a barrage of kicks to Kane's head until he fell off the ladder and Punk claimed the briefcase, becoming the first two-time Money in the Bank champion.

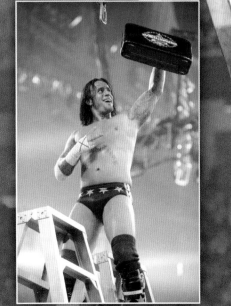

Battle Royal to Crown Miss WrestleMania

As part of the celebration of the *25th Anniversary of WrestleMania*, WWE decided to crown its first-ever Miss WrestleMania. To earn the honor, a Diva only had to outlast 24 other Divas and win the 25-Diva *Miss WrestleMania* Battle Royal. The competition featured most of the current Divas, as well as past faces, including original Diva Sunny, Torrie Wilson, Molly Holly, Victoria, Miss Jackie, Divas Champion Maryse, Women's Champion Melina, plus Beth Phoenix, Mickie James, Natalya, Maria, Alicia Fox, the Bella Twins, and more.

Every woman wanted to win the Miss WrestleMania crown, leading to a furious exchange between Michelle McCool and Mickie James. The two Divas eliminated each other during a power struggle that took them from the top rope, twirling and crashing down to the floor. Beth Phoenix sent 10 Divas out of the ring, while Brie and Nikki Bella combined to eliminate another six.

When Beth Phoenix and Melina were suddenly dumped over the top rope by a new Diva which fans didn't recognize, the crowd was stunned. During the coronation ceremony this new Diva claimed to be Santina, Santino Marella's twin sister from Italy. Natalya recalls, "That Battle Royal in particular was a whirlwind. To have 25 Divas from the past and present, along with Santina who loved to stick her nose where it didn't belong, was so much fun. I wish it could've been a little longer because there was more of a story to tell between myself and Beth Phoenix, but we were able to give a fun glimpse of what was to come."

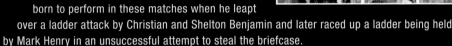

Jericho vs. Three Legends

One of the surprise films of 2008 was *The Wrestler*, featuring Mickey Rourke's heart-rending portrayal of an aging, down-and-out professional wrestler. Chris Jericho used the film to express his disdain for the WWE Legends he once idolized, but that he felt hung on to the spotlight for too long. To prove his point, Jericho agreed to face three Hall of Famers, "Rowdy" Roddy Piper, "Superfly" Jimmy Snuka, and Ricky "The Dragon" Steamboat, in a Handicap Gauntlet Match at the *25th Anniversary of WrestleMania*. Chris Jericho remembers, "Originally, I was supposed to work with Mickey Rourke at that show and then it just didn't work out. I was kind of stranded with nothing and then we came up with this idea to do a series of matches against the Legends."

Jericho had to defeat all three Legends. But, if he was pinned, forced to submit, or counted out once, he would lose the match. Jericho was confident he could handle the Legends, but Piper surprised Y2J with an early attack, including a drop kick. Snuka managed to get his licks in, and then tagged Steamboat, who entered a *WrestleMania* ring for the first time since *WrestleMania IV*.

▶ *Rourke knocks out Jericho*

Ricky Steamboat recalls, "I was worried about being the performer people remembered. I was 56 years old and hadn't had a match in 15 years. But I got the adrenaline rush when I walked out like I did at the Silverdome. I don't know if it's like riding a bike where you just get back on and ride, but I was able to perform the way I needed to for the match, the fans, and myself."

The former Undisputed Champion endured the Legends' offense and began to turn the tide after he forced Superfly to surrender to his Walls of Jericho. Wasting little time, Y2J threw Steamboat out of the ring, and pinned Piper with a Running Enzuigiri.

Jeff Hardy vs. Matt Hardy

The Hardy Boys will be remembered as one of the greatest tag teams in sports-entertainment history, but when they pursued individual glory, Matt Hardy became jealous of his brother Jeff's success. Matt began to sabotage Jeff's World Championship opportunities, and when Jeff learned the extent of his brother's betrayal, he decided to get his revenge at the *25th Anniversary of WrestleMania*.

Having enjoyed so many *WrestleMania* moments together, the Hardys were now set to battle each other in an Extreme Rules Match. The match resembled a human demolition derby. Jeff, always known to take crazy chances, first put his brother through a double stack of tables before his daredevil campaign backfired when he missed a leg drop attempt off a 30-foot ladder. The battle came to an end when Matt regrouped from the assault and dropped his younger brother with a Twist of Fate inside a steel chair.

The Intercontinental Championship Match

While JBL had relocated to New York, he still bragged to the Houston crowd that he would gladly serve as their hero and inspiration, particularly given how meaningless their lives were. The Wrestling God was clearly confident that he would be successfully defending his Intercontinental Championship against Rey Mysterio.

Layfield tried to make his job even easier by hitting Mysterio with a boot to the face before the match started. But when the bell rang, Mysterio would have the last laugh.

As soon as the match started, Mysterio stunned JBL with an Enziguiri, a 619, and a Splash from the top rope. In 21 seconds, a new Intercontinental Champion was crowned. An embarrassed JBL took the microphone and quit.

From the moment he entered the ring, Steamboat looked like he had turned back the hands of time. The Dragon flipped Jericho out of the ring and then dove out onto the former Undisputed Champion. The men battled back and forth until Jericho ended the match by hitting the Codebreaker.

In the wake of the match, Jericho lashed out and leveled Ric Flair, but that wasn't enough for him. In victory, Jericho demanded an apology from Mickey Rourke. The actor answered Jericho's challenge and entered the ring. Jericho probably regretted his action, as Rourke knocked Jericho out with a left hook.

Undertaker vs. Shawn Michaels

The two names most associated with *WrestleMania* are Undertaker, with his incomparable Streak, and Shawn Michaels, "Mr. WrestleMania." Shawn Michaels decided that he, more than anyone, deserved to try and end The Streak at the 25th Anniversary of *WrestleMania*. Undertaker accepted the challenge, warning Michaels that he might regret making it.

Shawn Michaels used his quickness to dodge early attacks from The Phenom and land strikes of his own. The more Shawn Michaels hit Undertaker with glancing blows, the more The Deadman stalked his audacious challenger, waiting to unleash his demonic offense. Undertaker started tossing the Heartbreak Kid around like a rag doll, but Michaels responded with chops and attacks on The Phenom's leg, setting him up for a figure-four leg lock.

Undertaker was able to work his way out of the submission hold and he blasted HBK with Snake Eyes. Undertaker wanted to end the match with a Chokeslam, but Shawn turned the move into a second submission move, the Crossface. Undertaker was able to deliver a side slam in order to get out of the Crossface, and then locked Mr. WrestleMania in the Hell's Gate submission.

HBK leapt from the top rope with a Moonsault, but Undertaker had the move well scouted and drove Michaels into the arena floor. Driven by a similar element of risk, Undertaker went for his remarkable running dive over the top rope when Shawn Michaels pulled a cameraman into Undertaker's path of destruction. The cameraman was expected to bear the brunt of the offensive but Undertaker landed on his head instead.

This produced yet another intense moment in *WrestleMania* lore as the referee began his count. While no one imagined that The Streak would end on a count out, Undertaker remained on the floor. The referee's count continued and as of "9" Undertaker was still on the ground. Somehow, in under a second, The Deadman made it back into the ring. Shawn Michaels recalls, "When you spend enough time with somebody even if you're not the closest of friends, you know them. I know Mark Calloway and the fact of the matter is if he's not dead, I already know we're finishing that match. It's *WrestleMania* and it's just that simple."

Both men fought proudly, continuing to pummel the other in toe-to-toe rounds of haymakers, reversals, and heart-stopping near pinfalls. The Streak was never in greater jeopardy than when, after crushing The Phenom with an elbow from the top rope, HBK was able to hit Sweet Chin Music. Despite that powerful kick, Undertaker kicked out at two.

When Michaels leapt off the top rope in an attempt to hit The Deadman with a Moonsault, Undertaker caught him in midair and administered a final Tombstone. The victory ran Undertaker's Streak to 17-0 and Shawn Michaels, even in defeat, lived up to his Mr. WrestleMania moniker.

Vince McMahon remembers, "When you work with individuals like Shawn and Undertaker, there is an extraordinary amount of emotion and pride that goes into the art that they are creating. By the way, they didn't like each other, which means that the performance is all the more extraordinary. If you like someone or you have similar interests, it makes it an easier dance, so to speak. They did not like each other going into that, yet they put on this unbelievable performance. Coming out of that performance, they had unbelievable respect for each other. That's the thrill of the big payoff, the respect that you earn by performing at that level. That's what our business in performance is generally all about— it's the giving, not the taking. You had two individuals who wanted to have the best match ever. That was their goal and they accomplished it."

Triple Threat Match

For the second consecutive year, Edge entered *WrestleMania* as World Heavyweight Champion. He thought he'd be defending the title against Big Show, but his wife, *SmackDown* General Manager Vickie Guerrero, instead put him in the difficult position of having to defend the title against both Big Show and Triple H in a Triple Threat Match. John Cena blackmailed Guerrero into adding Cena to the match in place of Triple H, or he'd reveal that Vickie had been cheating on her husband, having an affair with Big Show. After being added to the match, Cena spilled the beans anyway, increasing the tension and animosity in the three-way confrontation.

John Cena came out firing on all cylinders, attacking both Edge and Big Show. But when you have Big Show, the World's Largest Athlete, in the match, momentum can change with a single giant-sized punch, and Show rocked Cena to take control. Edge's attempt to align with Big Show backfired, and the World's Largest Athlete began to dole out massive amounts of punishment. The almost 500-pound Superstar annihilated his opposition with bone-shattering right hands, and crushing corner attacks. The crowd let out a collective gasp when Show stepped on Cena, but John was able to recover and toss the massive Giant out of the ring.

Later, Big Show became tangled in the ropes and rendered immobile, so Edge and John Cena tried to finish each other off. Vickie Guerrero climbed on the ring apron to shout instructions and encouragement, but that turned out to be a bad idea, when Edge's spear missed John Cena and nailed her instead. This distraction allowed Big Show, freed from the ropes by the referee, to take control again, beating both men and blasting John Cena with a Knockout Punch.

Each man came so close to winning the match, only to have the third participant break up a pinning combination or submission attempt. Thinking Cena was down, Edge tried to level Big Show by leaping on Show's back and locking on a Sleeper hold. But John Cena then performed one of the most incredible moves in WWE history, lifting both Big Show and Edge (a combined 735 pounds) on to his back for an Attitude Adjustment. Edge slipped off, but Cena sent Big Show crashing to the mat. He then picked up Edge, giving the Rated-R Superstar an Attitude Adjustment as well, dropping Edge onto Show. Cena then pinned the massive Big Show to become the World Heavyweight Champion.

Triple H vs. Randy Orton for the WWE Championship

Recent fans of WWE that watch the Authority do "what's best for business" may find it hard it believe, but for years Triple H and Stephanie McMahon kept their marriage under wraps from the WWE Universe, choosing to separate their professional and private lives. That all changed when Randy Orton, the winner of the 2009 *Royal Rumble* match decided to get into the head of the WWE Champion Triple H by targeting The Game's father-in-law Vince McMahon, brother-in-law Shane McMahon, and wife Stephanie McMahon. The Viper wanted the WWE Championship and was willing to cross any line to get it. Orton elaborates, "I slapped the hell out of Vince and kicked him as hard as I could. Same with Shane. It was extremely intense. I RKO'd and DDT'd Stephanie and kissed her on the mouth. It was full of drama and suspense. I feel that was the best work I've ever done. I wish we could do more work like that."

Triple H didn't want to just defend the championship, he wanted to hurt Orton for all the heinous actions Orton and his Legacy minions had performed. But an additional match stipulation would keep The Game in check—if he were disqualified or counted out, he would lose the Championship.

Triple H began the battle with a flurry of strikes to Randy Orton's body but Orton soon stunned the champion with an early RKO. Rather than go for the pinning attempt, Orton looked to punt Triple H in the head, the move he'd used on the Champ's father-in-law and brother-in-law. Triple H avoided the attack and hit Orton with a Pedigree, but The Viper rolled out of the ring before he could be pinned.

On several occasions, Triple H considered brutal attacks, such as striking Orton with a television monitor or delivering a Pedigree onto the announce table, but the moves would have caused a disqualification and the loss of his Championship. Even worse, the hesitation in both cases gave Orton time to recover and take control of the match, including using his DDT move on The Game out on the floor outside the ring.

Orton crept under the ring and brandished Triple H's sledgehammer. Triple H regained his composure and punted Randy Orton's skull as The Viper slithered into the ring. Triple H was then able to hit Orton with another Pedigree and gain the pinfall victory, retaining his title.

Despite the stunning performance by both Superstars, the match fell a bit flat with the audience. Orton remembers, "We followed Taker and Shawn. When you're kicking out of Tombstone Piledrivers, Chokeslams, and Superkicks that's a pretty big deal. Me and Triple H had the best story going into *'Mania* by far. But I think the people had just seen one of the best matches ever prior to ours and they were spent. They were just spent. I remember Hunter and myself being a little disappointed with how the reaction was but we knew why. Shawn and Taker put on a hell of a match."

WRESTLEMANIA XXVI

UNIVERSITY OF PHOENIX STADIUM – GLENDALE, AZ

March 28
2010

Attendance
72,219

ANNOUNCERS
Jerry "The King" Lawler, Matt Striker, Michael Cole

SPANISH ANNOUNCERS
Carlos Cabrera, Hugo Savinovich

RAW RING ANNOUNCERS
Justin Roberts, Savannah

SMACKDOWN RING ANNOUNCER
Tony Chimel

HALL OF FAME RING ANNOUNCER
Howard Finkel

SPECIAL FIELD CORRESPONDENT
Josh Mathews

SPECIAL MUSICAL GUESTS
Fantasia, United States Air Force Armed Guard Drill Team

Event Card

STREAK VS. CAREER
- Undertaker def. Shawn Michaels

WWE CHAMPIONSHIP MATCH
- John Cena def. Batista (Champion) to become new Champion

10-DIVAS TAG TEAM MATCH
- Michelle McCool, Vickie Guerrero, Alicia Fox, Layla, & Maryse def. Beth Phoenix, Kelly Kelly, Mickie James, Gail Kim, & Eve Torres

WORLD HEAVYWEIGHT CHAMPIONSHIP MATCH
- Chris Jericho (Champion) def. Edge to retain the Championship

NO HOLDS BARRED LUMBERJACK MATCH
- Bret "Hit Man" Hart def. Mr. McMahon*
  *Bruce Hart served as Special Guest Referee

MONEY IN THE BANK LADDER MATCH
- Jack Swagger def. Christian, Dolph Ziggler, Drew McIntyre, Evan Bourne, Kane, Kofi Kingston, Matt Hardy, MVP, and Shelton Benjamin

TRIPLE THREAT MATCH
- Randy Orton def. Ted DiBiase and Cody Rhodes

UNIFIED WWE TAG TEAM CHAMPIONSHIP MATCH
- Show Miz (The Miz & Big Show) (Champions) def. John Morrison & R-Truth

OTHER MATCHES
- Rey Mysterio def. CM Punk w/ Luke Gallows & Serena*
  *If Mysterio Loses, He Must Join the Straight Edge Society
- Triple H def. Sheamus

> **"I came out of *WrestleMania 25* feeling such peace...I questioned if that should've been my last one. I don't know if you can wrestle a perfect match but if you can't, my match with Taker is as close as you can get."**
>
> —Shawn Michaels

For the first time ever, *WrestleMania* came to the Southwest, as *WrestleMania XXVI* became the University of Phoenix Stadium's highest attended live entertainment event drawing fans from all 50 United States and 26 countries. The event was also broadcast around the world on pay-per-view in more than 100 countries and 20 languages.

The Unified WWE Tag Team Championship

The Miz and John Morrison were a successful tag team, winning both the WWE Tag Team Championship and World Tag Team Championship. The duo eventually split and The Miz found additional tag team gold by partnering with the World's Largest Athlete, Big Show. John Morrison and R-Truth looked to claim the tag championship for themselves. They'd had some non-title success against ShowMiz leading in to *WrestleMania XXVI*, so they felt confident that they could strike gold at the Showcase of the Immortals.

The former partners started the match against each other. Morrison and R-Truth isolated The Miz from his partner, punishing the Awesome One with quick tags and aerial maneuvers. Morrison was set to end the match by delivering Starship Pain to a prone Miz, but Show pulled his partner out of the ring. The champions took control of the match when Big Show tagged in and used his massive size and strength against the challengers, including slamming R-Truth against the ring post. With Morrison and Miz battling inside the ring, Show made a blind tag of his partner that Morrison did not see. Morrison went to spring off the ropes, but instead received a Knockout Punch from the World's Largest Athlete. Show pinned Morrison, allowing ShoMiz to retain their championship.

Randy Orton vs. Cody Rhodes vs. Ted DiBiase

For over a year, the Legacy was a feared faction in WWE, featuring second- and third-generation Superstars Randy Orton, Cody Rhodes, and Ted DiBiase. Even though the group was highly successful with Orton winning the WWE Championship, the other two members tired of doing Orton's bidding and turned on The Viper. Looking to get revenge, Orton agreed to face the other two members of the Legacy in a Triple Threat Match at *WrestleMania XXVI*.

While a Triple Threat Match features every man for himself, with the first competitor to score a pinfall or submission winning the bout, Rhodes and DiBiase claimed they would work together to ensure that Orton did not win the match. Orton used his experience to initially separate his two foes, but the numbers game soon reared its ugly head. DiBiase and Rhodes used their tag team experience to work together and attack Orton, and it seemed like Orton would soon be the victim of a pinfall. Cody Rhodes climbed to the top rope to hit another move, but DiBiase jumped on Orton to pin The Viper. Rhodes pulled DiBiase off their former Legacy leader and the two argued. For all their talk about each not caring who pinned Orton, it became quickly apparent that both wanted to record a *WrestleMania* victory, and this led to the former tag team partners attacking each other in and out of the ring.

Orton caught both Rhodes and DiBiase in his famous DDT off the ring ropes. Orton then punted Cody Rhodes in the skull, and countered Ted DiBiase's Million Dollar Dream with an RKO for the pinfall victory.

Money in the Bank Ladder Match

The 6th Annual *WrestleMania* Money in the Bank Match featured 10 Superstars competing for the coveted championship contract. Christian, Kofi Kingston, Matt Hardy, Shelton Benjamin, Kane, and MVP had all participated in previous matches, while Dolph Ziggler, Drew McIntyre, Jack Swagger, and Evan Bourne were making their *WrestleMania* debuts.

To open the match, Shelton Benjamin, MVP, and Kofi Kingston united and used the ladder as a battering ram to neutralize Kane. Jack Swagger used a ladder as a spear to clear the ring of his opponents. But, the "All-American American" experienced the flip side of the coin when he became trapped under that very ladder. Evan Bourne had the briefcase in his reach, but then performed his Air Bourne shooting star press off the ladder onto Christian. Things turned for Bourne seconds later when Matt Hardy tossed him off the ladder, sending him plunging to the canvas.

Kofi Kingston demonstrated ingenuity and athleticism by using two sections of destroyed ladders as stilts to walk across the ring, only to be hit by Drew McIntyre.

Matt Hardy was inches away from capturing his dream when Christian and Kane climbed ladders to battle him above the ring. The Big Red Monster crashed to the floor, while a Twist of Fate off the ladder resulted in serious damage to both Hardy and Christian. Christian returned to scale the ladder and began a furious fight with Jack Swagger, who slammed him in the face with the briefcase, claiming the win.

Triple H vs. Sheamus

Sheamus amassed one of the most incredible debut years that WWE had ever seen, including dominating ECW, becoming the first-ever Irish-born WWE Champion, and scoring victories over John Cena and Randy Orton. Sheamus believed the last item on his agenda of domination would be to defeat Triple H on the Grand Stage of *WrestleMania*.

The Game found himself in an unusual position at the beginning of the match. Triple H was generally the aggressor, but Sheamus took early control of the match with his strength and brutality.

Rey Mysterio vs. CM Punk

CM Punk used his charisma and leadership to form the Straight Edge Society, a group of Superstars that knew they were better than you, or at least that's what they'd always say. Railing against the WWE Universe and what he saw as their weaknesses and failings, CM Punk was also fixated on Rey Mysterio after Mysterio cost him a spot in the Money in the Bank match. The Straight-Edge Superstar had the audacity to interrupt Mysterio's daughter, Aalyah's, birthday celebration on *SmackDown* and challenge Mysterio to a match at *WrestleMania*. But Punk set a unique stipulation to the match—if Mysterio lost, he would be forced to join the Straight Edge Society.

Mysterio had no interest in working for his rival, so Rey took early full control of the match with his high-flying offense. Punk turned the tide of the match by countering Mysterio's flying body press into a belly-to-belly suplex and pinning combination. After nailing Rey with a roundhouse kick to the cranium, Punk came within inches of defeating him. The two battled in and out of the ring, with Punk slamming Mysterio into the ring steps outside the ring.

Back in the ring, Rey started building amazing momentum, and had Punk set up for a 619. Straight Edge convert Serena blocked Rey from hitting the move on her leader, and Luke Gallows jumped to the ring apron on the other side. Rey looked trapped and Punk recovered to set Mysterio up for a Go To Sleep. Rey countered the move with a Hurricanrana, sending Punk barreling into Luke Gallows. Mysterio connected with the 619 and his famed Springboard Splash to pin Punk.

Triple H planted Sheamus on the mat for a DDT. Twice, The Game tried to finish the match with his signature move, the Pedigree, but in both cases, Sheamus was able to counter the move and regain control of the match. Sheamus finally had Triple H up on his back, ready to deliver a Celtic Cross attempt when The Game broke free and leveled the newcomer with a Pedigree. Though Triple H was the victor, Sheamus proved his mettle as a main event Superstar.

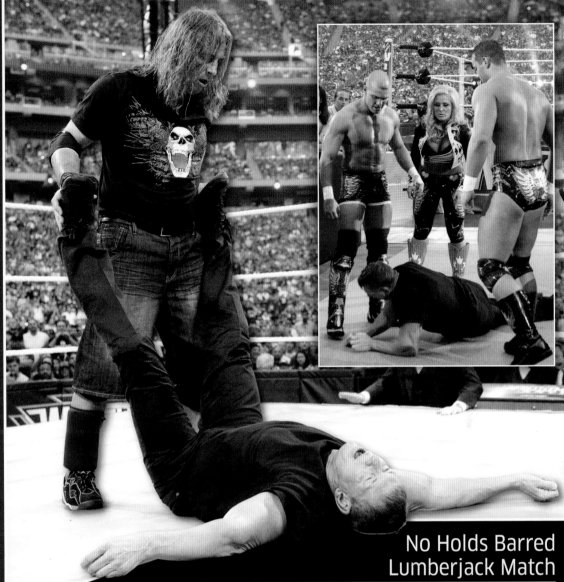

No Holds Barred Lumberjack Match

In 2010, WWE audiences witnessed a moment they never thought they would see: Bret "Hit Man" Hart as the Guest Host on *Monday Night Raw*. After Hart buried the hatchet with longtime rival Shawn Michaels, he called out Mr. McMahon, looking to get closure on 1997's infamous Montreal Screwjob. Mr. McMahon seemed just as willing to make amends, and the two shook hands and raised each other's arm as a sign of friendship. It was a ruse, as Mr. McMahon kicked an unsuspecting Hart in the groin. Mr. McMahon agreed to face Hart at *WrestleMania XXVI* in a No Holds Barred Match.

During the match introductions, Mr. McMahon informed Bret that he was going to be screwed once again, this time on the grand stage of *WrestleMania*. The Chairman announced that Hart's brothers, sisters, nephews, and nieces would serve as the Lumberjacks for the match and Bret's brother Bruce would be the guest referee. McMahon's plan of paying off the Hart family to support him over Bret backfired. Rather than Vince screwing Bret, the Hart family screwed Vince, taking the Chairman's money, but still standing by Bret. Bret then began to work out more than a decade of frustration, systematically dismantling Mr. McMahon. Bret tossed Vince out of the ring, and the family got their licks in as well, highlighted by a spectacular Hart Attack clothesline courtesy of David Hart Smith and Tyson Kidd.

Mr. McMahon attempted to escape under the ring, to no avail. Hart punished McMahon, whipping him with a belt and crushing him with repeated chair strikes. After unleashing 13 years of personal anguish, the "Hit Man" decided it was time to end things in proper fashion. Bret Hart locked Mr. McMahon in the Sharpshooter where the Chairman immediately tapped out in submission. Like so many times during his distinguished career, Bret Hart and his family stood in the ring united, rejoicing in Bret's victory. Bret Hart remembers, "When I walked to the ring I remembered back to when I had my stroke and I was sitting in a wheelchair. Vince was the first person who called me, during my darkest hours. I never thought I'd ever see a moment like *WrestleMania XXVI*. It was very special."

Chris Jericho vs. Edge

Their match at *WrestleMania* saw Chris Jericho and Edge raise the bar for World Heavyweight Championship competition. These former tag team partners were so familiar with each other's attacks and strategies that it was impossible to predict who would emerge as the victor.

Jericho gained the upper hand and began to wear Edge down. The Rated-R Superstar turned the tables with a shoulder block, sending the champion crashing into the announce table. Edge floored Jericho with a flying clothesline off the ring apron, followed by a top-rope, sit-out Facebuster. Edge continued to display strength and endurance while countering Jericho's defense, including turning Y2J's Walls of Jericho into a pin attempt.

Chris Jericho regained the advantage, including a near fall when he turned Edge's Spear attempt into a Codebreaker. Despite Edge's determination, Jericho eventually defeated him with a second Codebreaker to retain the championship.

10-Diva Tag Team Match

Vickie Guerrero was looking to have her own *WrestleMania* moment, so the *SmackDown* consultant would be making her in-ring *WrestleMania* debut. Leaving nothing to chance, Guerrero stacked her team with WWE Women's Champion Michelle McCool, Divas Champion Maryse, the other half of LayCool, Layla, and Alicia Fox. Her competition was just as strong, with five past or future champions on the team, including Beth Phoenix, Gail Kim, Mickie James, Kelly Kelly, and Eve Torres.

The inexperienced Guerrero may have made an error when she started off the match for her team. Each of the Divas on the opposing team had past issues with Vickie, so they isolated her in their corner and all took turns beating her. The referee lost complete control of the match and Divas from both sides began entering and leaving the match with no official tags. Guerrero's side took over, clearing the ring of every Diva except Kelly Kelly, who Michelle McCool nailed with a Faith Breaker. LayCool then helped Guerrero to the top rope, where she hit her version of the Frog Splash on an already down Kelly Kelly to score an easy victory for her team, giving Guerrero her moment in the spotlight.

The WWE Championship

Batista and John Cena had followed parallel paths to the top of the WWE, with each winning their first World Championship at *WrestleMania 21*. In the time since though, Batista felt that WWE put all its marketing and support behind John Cena instead of him. Batista believed this was a mistake and that he should have been the face of WWE. With Mr. McMahon's blessing, The

▶ *Cena shows his haters some love*

Animal had defeated Cena for the WWE Championship a month earlier, and now he wanted to destroy the face of WWE at *WrestleMania XXVI*.

As expected, the two powerhouse Superstars opened the match with early moves highlighting their strength. By targeting Cena's surgically repaired neck, Batista was in early control of the bout, and seemed to be on his way to delivering on his promise to crush Cena. Even when Cena seemed to regain momentum, Batista would counter moves, turning an Attitude Adjustment into a crushing DDT. Cena displayed his grappling proficiency when he locked Batista in the STF. Batista escaped and again managed to block an Attitude Adjustment.

Cena attempted to nail Batista with a high-risk aerial maneuver, but The Animal caught Cena in midair and turned the attack into a Batista Bomb. Both men showed amazing will and determination, kicking out of each other's signatures moves and blocking additional attempts as well. Cena reversed another Batista Bomb attempt, and used the momentum to lock The Animal in the STF submission. Batista tapped out, ending his championship reign. Once again, John Cena was WWE Champion. The two would battle at the next two pay-per-view events, with Cena retaining his championship both times. Batista became so frustrated that he quit WWE, and was not seen in the ring for years until his 2014 return.

Career vs. Streak

The match between Shawn Michaels and Undertaker at the *25th Anniversary of WrestleMania* was considered one of the greatest matches in *WrestleMania* history, even winning the previous year's Slammy Award for Match of the Year. Most competitors would take pride in the great match and how close they came to ending Undertaker's Streak. Shawn Michaels was not most competitors—Mr. WrestleMania wanted one more shot at The Streak and challenged Undertaker to another *WrestleMania* encounter. Undertaker refused, feeling he'd already proven he could beat the Heartbreak Kid, so Michaels went about changing Undertaker's mind, including costing The Deadman his World Heavyweight Championship at the 2010 *Elimination Chamber*. Undertaker finally agreed to the rematch, with a caveat. Shawn would have to put his career on the line. If Michaels lost, he was finished in the ring.

Undertaker opened the match by striking Michaels with his dreaded Snake Eyes and Old School attacks. The Heartbreak Kid realized his only chance of blunting the severity of these assaults was to counter them with grapples and holds. Michaels' defense turned into offense, and Undertaker began favoring his left knee.

Michaels seized the opportunity, and his focused attack altered the match's tone as HBK kept Undertaker grounded, diminishing The Phenom's size and strength advantages. Undertaker retaliated by focusing on Michaels' surgically corrected back. When a Leg Drop on the apron caused more harm to The Deadman than Michaels, the Heartbreak Kid locked the Lord of Darkness in the Figure Four. Undertaker escaped, delivered a devastating Chokeslam on Mr. WrestleMania, and went to finish off the match with a Tombstone. But Michaels wasn't through; he escaped and rolled The Deadman into an Ankle Lock submission. The two continued their ferocious fight outside the ring, where Michaels attempted a high-flying maneuver and instead was hit with a Tombstone. In and out of the ring, both men emptied their tanks, hitting impressive move after move. Undertaker locked Michaels in the Hell's Gate submission move, but HBK turned it into a pin attempt.

Michaels then scored a near pinfall when he hit Undertaker with Sweet Chin Music. Michaels kicked out of a Last Ride, and nailed The Phenom with another Sweet Chin Music, as well as a moonsault that put both Undertaker and Michaels through the announce table.

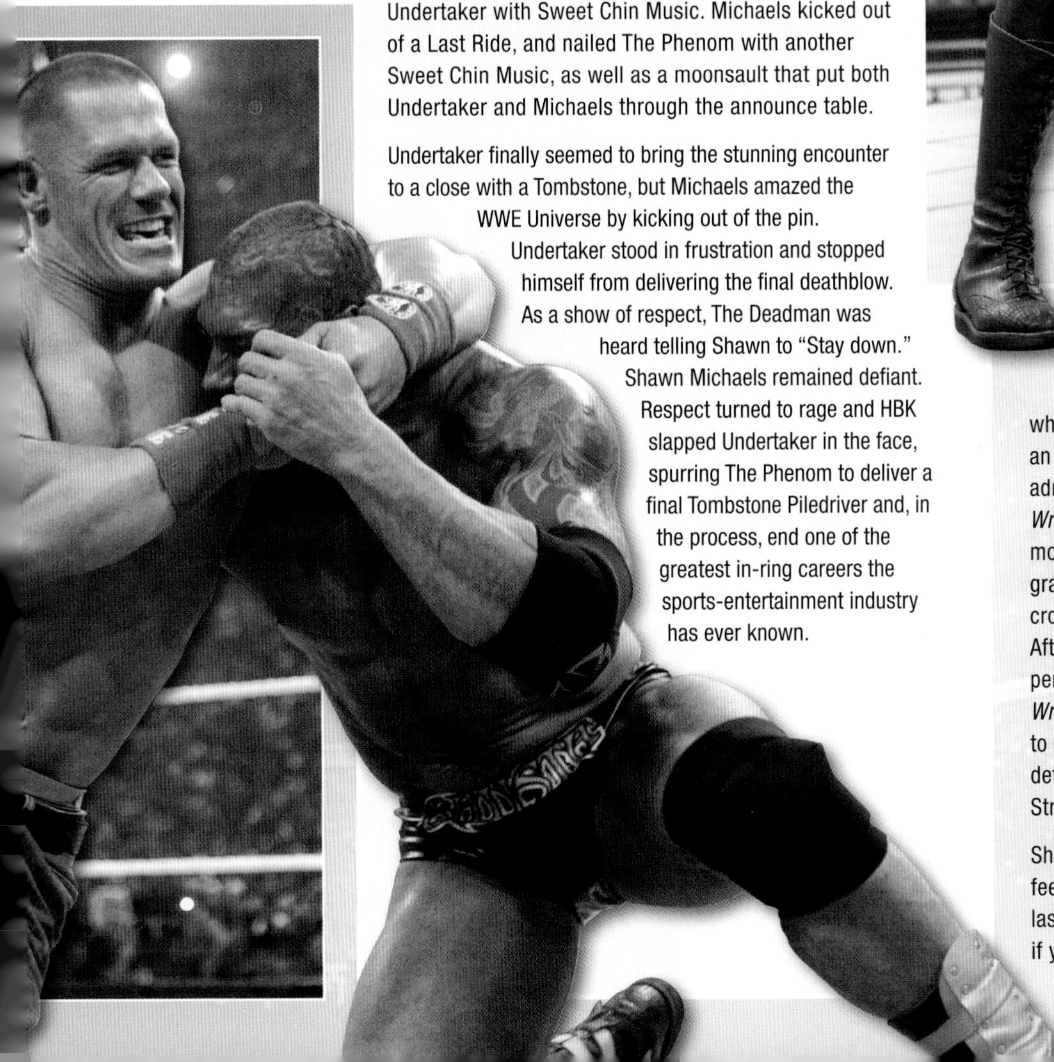

Undertaker finally seemed to bring the stunning encounter to a close with a Tombstone, but Michaels amazed the WWE Universe by kicking out of the pin. Undertaker stood in frustration and stopped himself from delivering the final deathblow. As a show of respect, The Deadman was heard telling Shawn to "Stay down." Shawn Michaels remained defiant. Respect turned to rage and HBK slapped Undertaker in the face, spurring The Phenom to deliver a final Tombstone Piledriver and, in the process, end one of the greatest in-ring careers the sports-entertainment industry has ever known.

Undertaker helped the fallen Michaels back to his feet where the two embraced in an ultimate show of admiration and respect. In *WrestleMania XXVI's* final moments, Michaels gratefully bowed to the crowd's standing ovation. After his repeat performance at *WrestleMania XXVI*, it was clear HBK made the right decision to give The Streak one more run for his money. Even in defeat, Shawn Michaels was victorious. He did not break The Streak, but he rode off into the sunset as Mr. WrestleMania.

Shawn Michaels remembers, "I came out of *WrestleMania 25* feeling such peace...I questioned if that should've been my last one. I don't know if you can wrestle a perfect match but if you can't, my match with Taker is as close as you can get."

WRESTLEMANIA XXVII

GEORGIA DOME – ATLANTA, GA

April 3
2011

Attendance
71,617

ANNOUNCERS
Booker T, Jerry "The King" Lawler, Jim Ross, Josh Mathews, Michael Cole

SPANISH ANNOUNCERS
Carlos Cabrera, Hugo Savinovich

RING ANNOUNCER
Justin Roberts, Ricardo Rodriguez

HALL OF FAME RING ANNOUNCER
Howard Finkel

SPECIAL MUSICAL GUEST
Keri Hilson

SPECIAL GUEST HOST
The Rock

Event Card

WWE CHAMPIONSHIP MATCH
- The Miz (Champion) w/ Alex Riley def. John Cena to retain the Championship

SIX-PERSON MIXED TAG MATCH
- John Morrison, Trish Stratus, & Snooki def. Dolph Ziggler & LayCool (Layla & Michelle McCool) w/ Vickie Guerrero

NO HOLDS BARRED MATCH
- Undertaker def. Triple H

EIGHT-MAN TAG MATCH
- Kane, Big Show, Santino Marella, & Kofi Kingston def. The Corre (Wade Barrett, Ezekiel Jackson, Justin Gabriel, & Heath Slater)

WORLD HEAVYWEIGHT CHAMPIONSHIP MATCH
- Edge (Champion) w/ Christian def. Alberto Del Rio w/ Ricardo Rodriguez & Brodus Clay to retain the Championship

OTHER MATCHES
- Michael Cole w/ Jack Swagger def. Jerry "The King" Lawler*
  *Stone Cold Steve Austin as Special Guest Referee
- Randy Orton def. CM Punk
- Cody Rhodes def. Rey Mysterio

"The only true challenge I have left is ending The Streak."

—Triple H

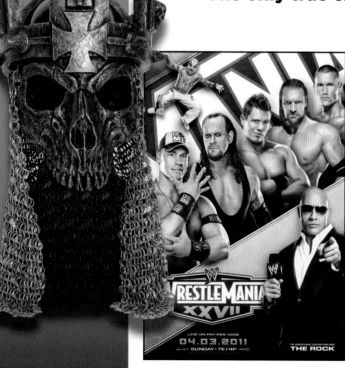

WrestleMania Comes to Atlanta

Atlanta, Georgia has long been renowned as a sports-entertainment metropolis. A former backyard for the NWA and WCW promotions, Atlanta's Omni was one of the world's most recognized venues. *WrestleMania XXVII* marked the first Showcase of the Immortals hosted in the state of Georgia. Tickets went on sale in November of 2010 and sold out in just minutes.

In February 2011, for the first time in seven years, The Rock appeared in the ring on WWE's flagship program, *Raw*, for a special announcement—he would be the Special Guest Host of *WrestleMania XXVII*. The Rock promised to "Layeth the Smacketh Down" in Atlanta, Georgia.

The World Heavyweight Championship

Alberto Del Rio burst onto the WWE scene in the summer of 2010. The Mexican aristocrat dominated in the ring, putting countryman Rey Mysterio and others on the shelf with injuries thanks to his Cross Armbreaker submission move. After winning the biggest Royal Rumble Match in history (with 40 competitors), Del Rio got to choose which title he would challenge for at *WrestleMania XXVII*. He decided to face Edge for the World Heavyweight Championship, perhaps considering that the Rated-R Superstar had twice been unsuccessful in defending the title at *WrestleMania*. Del Rio was already confident, but he looked to further stack the deck by bringing his personal ring announcer Ricardo Rodriguez and bodyguard Brodus Clay. Edge decided to blunt the numbers advantage by having former tag team partner Christian in his corner.

As soon as the bell rang, Del Rio attacked Edge, intending to further exacerbate an injury to the champion's left elbow. Despite Del Rio's furious assault, Edge refused to be intimidated. Del Rio miscalculated a dive, and crashed to the Georgia Dome floor. Known for being the Ultimate Opportunist, Edge seized the opening and connected with his own air attack on Del Rio. The champion began to string some offense together and win a battle of reversals, until a second unsuccessful trip to the top rope put Del Rio back in the driver's seat.

Del Rio's bodyguard Brodus Clay tried to interfere, and Christian prevented the unfair advantage. In the midst of the chaos, Edge was locked in Del Rio's lethal Cross Armbreaker submission. Battling through the pain, Edge managed to break the hold, and put Del Rio in a submission of his own.

The Mexican Aristocrat broke free of the hold, but couldn't escape a Spear. Edge successfully defended his World Heavyweight Championship. The WWE Universe rejoiced, not knowing they had just witnessed the last match in Edge's career. A neck injury forced Edge to vacate the championship the following week.

Edge remembers, "As much as my retirement was forced it was also the right time. I'd been competing for eight years after getting spinal fusion surgery, longer than anybody else that got one. Did I expect to have my last match at *WrestleMania XXVII*? No. I would've liked to been able to do right by Alberto, I would have liked to wrestle Christian at *WrestleMania XXVIII* but things happen. You can't dwell on them. And now it's how do you live life and be a good human being. As cliché as that sounds that's where I'm at now…it's a good place to be."

Rey Mysterio vs. Cody Rhodes

During a match between Cody Rhodes and Rey Mysterio, Mysterio's knee brace caught Rhodes on the face, causing permanent damage to the self-proclaimed "Dashing One"'s looks. Rhodes, now wearing a protective clear mask, would hide his flawed face when coming to the ring, although most of the WWE Universe felt he was making too big a deal about nothing. Rhodes did not agree and was seeking revenge for the injury at *WrestleMania*.

Rhodes knew he'd need every advantage he could get, "I had changed my whole gym routine from Olympic Lifts to a HIT [High Intensity Training] regimen because I needed every element to be able to bring oxygen into my muscles for more speed. If there is a Justice League of professional wrestling and John Cena is Superman, then Rey Mysterio is the Flash. He's fast."

Mysterio opened with rapid-fire offense until Rhodes used his protective mask as a weapon. Rhodes then countered Rey's Hurricanrana into an Alabama Slam. Rhodes stayed on the attack and refused to give Mysterio any breathing room, even impressing the crowd with his hanging vertical superplex from the top rope.

Mysterio was able to counter Rhodes' Cross Rhodes finisher and build some momentum of his own. Rey gained some revenge on Rhodes by pulling the Dashing One's mask off and using it as a weapon. Rhodes took things to another level by clocking Rey on the face with Mysterio's own knee brace when the official's back was turned. Rhodes was able to hit his Cross Rhodes signature move and pin Mysterio and pick up a career-defining *WrestleMania* victory.

8-Man Tag Team Match

After the Nexus fractured under the split leadership of CM Punk and Wade Barrett, Barrett formed a new group, the Corre, in which all members were equals. To make their name, the new group was running roughshod over WWE. Big Show was a constant target, so he recruited Kane and the tag team of Santino Marella and Vladimir Kozlov to face the Corre in an 8-man tag team match at *WrestleMania*. The Corre tried to cut their opponents down a man by taking Kozlov out the day before *WrestleMania*, but Kofi Kingston stepped up and joined the team.

Santino got off to a quick start against Heath Slater. When the Milan Miracle tagged in Big Show, the World's Largest Athlete steamrolled over Slater. Ezekiel Jackson's interference unleashed chaos. Kane and Kofi Kingston cleaned house, and Kofi flew off the ring apron taking down Justin Gabriel and Ezekiel Jackson. The Corre's *WrestleMania* debut ended quickly after Santino hit Heath Slater with the Cobra, and Big Show annihilated the future One-Man Band with the Knockout Punch for the win.

Seeking Vengeance

CM Punk doesn't forgive and he doesn't forget. Two years earlier, Orton punted Punk in the head, forcing Punk to forfeit the World Heavyweight Championship. Punk returned the favor at the 2011 *Royal Rumble*, preventing Randy Orton from winning the WWE Championship. Afterward, CM Punk told Orton, "As long as you and I breathe the same air you will never be WWE Champion again." Each man was eager to devastate his opponent at *WrestleMania XXVII*.

Punk wasn't just angry at Randy Orton; he was becoming increasingly frustrated at WWE. Instead of rewarding talent, Punk felt WWE got behind Superstars that were good for the corporate brand or willing to kiss Mr. McMahon's ass. He seethed at the thought that The Miz was in the main event of the night, when he believed Miz wasn't half the competitor that Punk was.

"I could detail so many different things, so many straws that broke the proverbial camel's back, but a big one was Miz being in the main event of *WrestleMania*. There wasn't a better bad guy in the business than me. To watch somebody literally just get handed this ... I just didn't get it."

Jerry "The King" Lawler vs. Michael Cole

When Jerry "The King" Lawler looked back on his remarkable 40-year career in sports entertainment, there was one thing the Hall of Famer had not yet accomplished—a match at *WrestleMania*. He almost entered *WrestleMania XXVII* as the WWE Champion, but his broadcast partner, Michael Cole, cost him the match. It wasn't surprising—Cole had been insulting The King, his career, and even his family for months. Cole took so much joy in costing The King his *WrestleMania* moment that Lawler decided to challenge Cole to a match at *WrestleMania XXVII*.

Cole underwent special training from Jack Swagger and planned to have his trainer with him at ringside. Promising to be the new Mr. WrestleMania, Michael Cole entered the Showcase of the Immortals exuding confidence and wearing an orange singlet to honor his alma mater, Syracuse University. But when Special Guest Referee Stone Cold Steve Austin rang the bell, and Lawler attacked and took out Swagger, Michael Cole realized what he had gotten himself into.

The Jersey Shore Comes to WWE

Vickie Guerrero was not a happy woman. When Snooki Polizzi made a special appearance on *Raw*, Vickie expected the *Jersey Shore* star to be impressed by Vickie. Instead, Snooki insulted the loud-mouth Guerrero and inserted herself into a LayCool match later in the show. A furious Guerrero challenged Snooki to compete in the ring in a match against the team of LayCool and her business associate Dolph Ziggler. Snooki, teaming with Trish Stratus and John Morrison, accepted.

The match got off to an awkward start when Dolph Ziggler got into Polizzi's face, telling her she didn't belong in the ring, and Snooki expressed her disagreement by slapping him. Trish Stratus began the match for her team, but she found McCool a tough opponent. When Stratus used her Matrix move, McCool, having scouted Stratus' tendencies, delivered an elbow to Trish's midsection. McCool then took Stratus to the corner of the ring, looking to finish the former seven-time champion off with a Faithbreaker. But Trish countered the move and hit her own Facebuster.

The battle spilled out of the ring and Stratus took out both members of LayCool with a double clothesline off the apron. Ziggler tried to get involved, but John Morrison took the Showoff out with Starship Pain. Trish then tagged Snooki in, and it was the *Jersey Shore* star's time to shine by hitting a double springboard elbow on Michelle McCool, and following that move up with a cartwheel splash to secure the win for her team.

It was a monumental slap in the face to somebody who has as much pride as I do." This frustration would build up to a series of spectacular "pipe bomb" promos throughout the following summer, but for now, CM Punk had to deal with Randy Orton.

Randy Orton launched a swift attack in the opening moments of the match. CM Punk seized control when he kicked the steel steps into Orton's injured leg. The two competitors traded blows until the Straight Edge Superstar jumped from the top rope and drilled Orton's head with a knee drop.

When it looked like Randy Orton got a second wind and would regain the advantage, CM Punk returned fire on Orton's injured knee. Orton looked to once again punt a downed CM Punk in the skull, but The Viper collapsed. Punk was delighted, thinking the match was in the bag. Punk dodged an RKO attempt and climbed to the top turnbuckle to launch an aerial attack, but as he flew through the air, The Viper caught the Straight Edge Superstar in midair and delivered a spectacular RKO for the victory.

When Swagger recovered and jumped "The King" from behind, the plan became clear. Cole would distract referee Steve Austin inside the ring, and outside, Jack Swagger would beat on Jerry Lawler. Cole picked up where Swagger left off, punishing Lawler's left ankle. The King fought back to his feet and started gaining his retribution on Cole. Jack Swagger attempted to save Cole by throwing in the towel, but referee Steve Austin used it to wipe his brow, and threw it back. Cole, infuriated, started shouting at Austin, who shoved the mouthy broadcaster right into Lawler, who inflicted more and more punishment until he forced Cole to submit to the ankle lock.

During the Austin Beer Bash, the match's outcome was changed. Read by Announcer Josh Mathews, an email from the Anonymous *Raw* General Manager informed everyone that Stone Cold Steve Austin overstepped his bounds by becoming physically involved in the match. As a result, "The King" was disqualified and Michael Cole was the winner. After the bad news, the messenger, Josh Mathews received a Stunner for his troubles.

A Legendary Battle

February 21, 2011, saw Undertaker return to WWE on *Raw*, but before he could address the audience, Triple H interrupted The Deadman. After an intense stare down, both men looked at the *WrestleMania XXVII* logo.

Not a single word was spoken. At that moment neither a handshake nor a contract signing nor a press conference was necessary. It was understood that the two remaining Legends from WWE's fabled Attitude Era were going to face each other at the 27th Showcase of the Immortals. Triple H later explained that he'd done everything in his career except end The Streak.

Triple H opened the match with a barrage of punches, but Undertaker recovered and dumped Triple H out of the ring and onto the floor. Triple H speared Undertaker through Michael Cole's announcing pod and returned to the ring. The Phenom reversed a Pedigree attempt and back dropped Triple H off the announce table. Looking to finish off The Game, Undertaker launched himself over the top rope onto his adversary.

Moving on pure instinct, The Game reversed an attack from The Deadman and put Undertaker through the Spanish announce table with a Spinebuster. The match would see a number of near pinfalls, with the first coming after Undertaker Chokeslammed Triple H. Undertaker came close to winning again, but Triple H kicked out of the Last Ride powerbomb. The Cerebral Assassin came tantalizingly close to ending The Streak, but Undertaker managed to kick out of three pinfall attempts that followed Pedigrees. A frustrated Triple H obtained a steel chair and repeatedly pounded Undertaker with it, denting the chair. Triple H could be heard screaming "Stay down, stay down!" but Undertaker refused. The Phenom summoned all of his power to return to his feet. Triple H employed one final tactic, hitting Undertaker with a Tombstone Piledriver. The crowd roared, assuming that the match was over. However, Undertaker dug deep and kicked out once again.

Feeling like he had no other option, Triple H went under the ring to get his weapon of choice, the sledgehammer. Returning to the ring with the sledgehammer, The Game looked to clock The Deadman, but instead Undertaker locked Triple H in the Hell's Gate submission. Unable to reach the ropes or break the hold, The Game fought with every ounce of strength he had. The struggle continued, with Triple H even holding up the sledgehammer. But in the final moments, Undertaker showed that even for the King of Kings, there is no escape from Hell's Gate. Triple H tapped out, and Undertaker's Streak extended to 19-0. Though Undertaker prevailed, the victory was hard won. Triple H left the ring under his own power while the battered Undertaker did not. Though The Streak had been preserved, this *WrestleMania* score had yet to be settled.

The Miz vs. John Cena

When The Miz won the WWE Championship, he fulfilled a lifelong dream. The former *Real World* star looked to make another dream come true when he defended the title in the main event of *WrestleMania XXVII*. His opponent was an all-time great, John Cena, competing in his eighth consecutive *WrestleMania*.

Since becoming the special guest host of *WrestleMania XXVII*, The Rock had engaged in a war of words with Cena. Much of the WWE Universe was buzzing about a potential clash between the two. Even though he was the WWE Champion heading into the match, fans seemed focused on everyone but The Miz. The Awesome One showed what a mistake that was when he got the better of John Cena several times heading into *WrestleMania*.

The Miz surprised the crowd with a strong collection of moves that gave him early control, and a two-count on Cena. However, Miz made the mistake of trying a high-risk top-rope maneuver that Cena avoided. As if to show the champion how it was done, John nailed the Awesome One with a leg drop off the top rope that got him his first two-count of the match. Looking for any advantage, The Miz had his protégé Alex Riley distract the referee while he removed the pad from a turnbuckle. Cena blocked Miz's attempt to ram his head into the corner, and then started building momentum with a Five Knuckle Shuffle and STF. The champion barely reached the rope to force a break.

Cena dropped Miz with the Attitude Adjustment but the referee was nowhere to be found, having been knocked out as the two competitors collided with him. Riley took advantage of the situation and drilled Cena with his titanium briefcase. Just when it seemed Miz would be victorious in his title defense, Cena kicked out of the pin attempt.

The crowd was disappointed when both men were counted out and the match was ruled a draw. It seemed like an anticlimactic ending to *WrestleMania*. The Guest Host of *WrestleMania XXVII* agreed. The Rock's music played, and the Brahma Bull hit the ring. He ordered that the match be restarted with no count out and no disqualification. Suddenly, The Great One used his ruling as an opportunity to drop Cena with a Rock Bottom and guarantee that he would not win the WWE Championship. The Rock was not done.

Before leaving, he decided there was still someone who deserved a whipping: The Miz. The Brahma Bull showed no ring rust as he destroyed the WWE Champion with a People's Elbow. Miz may have won the match, but he came out on the losing end of his encounter with the Great One. The Miz recalls, "There was a point in the match where I got tackled over the barricade and my head hit the concrete floor. I was concussed and don't remember any of the match. But it was huge to be a villain and successfully defend the WWE Championship at *WrestleMania*. It's even bigger that it was against John Cena and that The Rock, who is why I wanted to be a WWE Superstar, was part of it."

Frustration setting in, The Miz tried to hit Cena a second time with the briefcase. Cena ducked the attack and Miz instead nailed Riley. While Cena's Attitude Adjustment brought the champion down for the second time, it could not keep the Awesome One down for the three count. Miz rolled out of the ring, but Cena followed and launched a clothesline that sent Miz over the barricade. When Miz tried to leave the match, a crazed Cena dove over the barricade and slammed both men to the floor.

WRESTLEMANIA XXVIII

SUN LIFE STADIUM – MIAMI, FL

April 1
2012

Attendance
78,363

ANNOUNCERS
Jerry "The King" Lawler
Jim Ross
Michael Cole

SPANISH ANNOUNCERS
Carlos Cabrera
Marcelo Rodriguez

RING ANNOUNCER
Justin Roberts

SPECIAL FIELD CORRESPONDENT
Josh Mathews
Matt Striker

HALL OF FAME RING ANNOUNCER
Howard Finkel

SPECIAL MUSICAL GUESTS
Flo Rida
MGK

Event Card

ONCE IN A LIFETIME
- The Rock def. John Cena

WWE CHAMPIONSHIP MATCH
- CM Punk (Champion) def. Chris Jericho to retain the Championship

TEAM JOHNNY VS. TEAM TEDDY
- Dolph Ziggler, The Miz, Jack Swagger, Mark Henry, David Otunga & Drew McIntyre w/ John Laurinaitis, Vickie Guerrero & Brie Bella def. Zack Ryder, Kofi Kingston, R-Truth, Santino Marella, Booker T & The Great Khali w/ Theodore Long, Eve Torres, Nikki Bella, Hornswoggle & Aksana

END OF AN ERA HELL IN A CELL MATCH
- Undertaker def. Triple H*
  *Shawn Michaels as Special Guest Referee

INTERCONTINENTAL CHAMPIONSHIP MATCH
- Big Show def. Cody Rhodes (Champion) to become new ChampionWorld Heavyweight Championship Match
- Sheamus def. Daniel Bryan (Champion) w/ AJ Lee to become new Champion

OTHER MATCHES
- Maria Menounos & Kelly Kelly def. Beth Phoenix & Eve
- Kane def. Randy Orton

> **"Rock versus Cena. *WrestleMania*. Once in a lifetime. Epic."**
>
> —Shawn Michaels

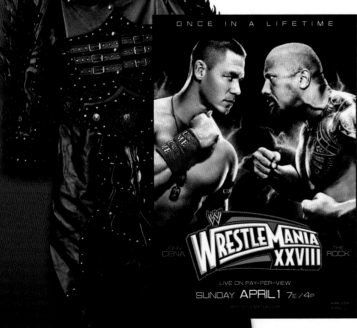

Once in a Lifetime

Every year, the WWE Universe eagerly anticipates a new edition of *WrestleMania*, but the excitement reached a fever pitch leading into *WrestleMania XXVIII*. For the first time, everyone knew what the main event would be for an entire year, and what a match it was. Two generational icons were squaring off, as after more than a year of insults and animosity, John Cena and The Rock would battle each other in the outdoor venue of Sun Life Stadium in Miami, Florida.

World Heavyweight Championship Match

After he won the Money in the Bank match guaranteeing him a shot at the World Heavyweight Championship at any time, Daniel Bryan bided his time. Unlike previous winners that used moments of weakness to ensure a victory, Bryan pledged to save his shot for *WrestleMania*. However, Bryan went back on his word and defeated a downed Big Show for the championship in December. Sheamus, after winning the 2012 Royal Rumble match, chose to challenge Bryan for the World Heavyweight Championship, promising that he was going to kick champion Daniel Bryan's teeth down his throat.

Coming to the ring, Bryan danced down the ramp, shooting a single finger on each hand in the air, exclaiming "Yes!" as they reached for the sky. Although the WWE Universe was not as fully behind Bryan as they would be when he formed "Team Hell No" tag team and began his pursuit of the WWE Championship, they did love to chant "Yes!" along with him. In some respects, it was the beginning of a movement, one that would become one of the most powerful fan-generated movements in WWE history.

When the bell for the match rang, Daniel Bryan insisted on receiving a good luck kiss from his girlfriend, AJ Lee. As Bryan turned around, he walked right into a Brogue Kick to his face. Sheamus went for the cover and in 18 seconds was crowned the new World Heavyweight Champion.

The Intercontinental Championship

Cody Rhodes was feeling pretty good about his past year. He'd picked up an impressive victory over Rey Mysterio at *WrestleMania XXVII* and was in the midst of a long reign as Intercontinental Champion, more than 230 days. When it was clear Rhodes would have to defend his championship against Big Show, Cody decided to get into the head of the World's Largest Athlete. Rhodes harassed Big Show and aired videos that centered on Big Show's less than flattering moments at *WrestleMania*.

The World's Largest Athlete stepped over the top rope at Sun Life Stadium seeking redemption. Big Show's determination resulted in his manhandling the Intercontinental Champion. Show quieted the crowd so they could all hear his massive chop to Cody Rhodes' chest. His colossal hand left a crimson red splotch on the Dashing One.

Rhodes did not allow the onslaught to continue; he turned the tables on his giant opponent in an impressive fashion. The champion used his speed and ring presence to stun Big Show long enough to attack Show's knee. Rhodes' offensive assault ended when a Spear from Big Show virtually split the champion in half. Feeling re-energized, Show cocked back his right arm and crushed the champion with the Knockout Punch. After years of embarrassment and disappointment, the World's Largest Athlete finally had created his *WrestleMania* moment, winning the Intercontinental Championship.

The Demon Returns

Heading into *WrestleMania XXVIII*, the Big Red Monster, Kane, was suffering from an identity crisis. Feeling he'd become too soft, Kane returned to wearing his fearsome mask, and believed that facing Randy Orton at *WrestleMania* would help unleash his inner demon. After Kane cost Orton a match for the World Heavyweight Championship, Orton was only too happy to face Kane in the ring in order to gain some revenge.

Knowing that Kane had a significant advantage in the power department, Orton quickly adapted his strategy and focused on keeping Kane on the canvas. But Kane was able to use his strength to punish The Viper. The Big Red Monster hit Orton with a vicious Chokeslam, but Orton kicked out of the pinfall and then regained control of the match. Orton hit Kane with a powerslam and a DDT from the ropes, but he couldn't keep Kane down for a count of three. Orton tried to finish off Kane with an RKO off the middle rope, but Kane was able to reverse the move into a second Chokeslam, also from the middle rope. This was enough to keep Orton down for a three-count. The monster was back, and he'd made a statement to the rest of the WWE Superstars about his evil intentions.

Kelly Kelly & Maria Menounos vs. Beth Phoenix & Eve

Maria Menounos, in addition to being an actress and journalist, is an avid member of the WWE Universe. She has guest hosted *Raw*, inducted Bob Backlund into the WWE Hall of Fame, and appeared on many WWE broadcasts. While many were happy to see her, WWE Women's Champion Beth Phoenix did not share the enthusiasm. The two had butted heads over the years, and when Menounos was interviewing Kelly Kelly—and not Phoenix—on *Extra* to promote *WrestleMania XXVIII*, an enraged Phoenix and cohort Eve raided the set. The war of words escalated and in the heat of the stand-off, Menounos accepted a challenge from the Glamazon for a match at the 28th Show of Shows.

Despite an injury suffered in training for *Dancing with the Stars*, Menounos bravely entered the ring. When the bell rang, former friends Kelly Kelly and Eve Torres slugged it out. Kelly wowed the crowd with her high-flying maneuvers. Kelly tagged in her partner, but Maria found herself isolated by Eve and Beth Phoenix. The two took turns targeting Maria's injured ribs, and Beth Phoenix pummeled the actress in the middle of the ring. Maria was finally able to tag in her partner, and Kelly Kelly began to dominate the match. The former Divas Champion was unstoppable, even reversing Beth Phoenix's Glam Slam, turning into a Bulldog and dropping the Glamazon. Menounos re-entered the match and rolled up Phoenix for the pinfall victory for her team.

Brand Warfare

WWE's two flagship programs, *Raw* and *SmackDown,* each had their own General Manager that ruled their respective shows, making matches and serving as final arbiters. The interim GM of *Raw*, John Laurinaitis thought one person should be the final authority on both shows, and that one person should be him. *SmackDown* GM Theodore Long wanted to keep his position running *SmackDown*, but was interested in taking over *Raw* as well. Each man had their supporters and detractors, so a 12-Man tag match was set to see which General Manager would take the reins of both WWE programs.

End of an Era

Undertaker had added to his Streak at *WrestleMania XXVII* by forcing Triple H to submit, but the match took even more out of The Deadman, as he needed help leaving the ring after the match. Undertaker was haunted by the match, deciding he wanted another bout with The Game to prove himself and his Streak. Undertaker came to *Raw* in 2012 to challenge Triple H to a rematch, but The Cerebral Assassin declined, knowing what he would have to do to Undertaker to ensure the end of The Streak. It took the combined efforts of Undertaker and Shawn Michaels to convince Triple H to take the match. The Game eventually accepted, but only on the condition that it was a Hell in a Cell Match. To add even more intrigue, the Heartbreak Kid was named the Special Guest Referee.

Once the three men were sealed in the demonic structure, Undertaker immediately unleashed his pent-up rage. A flurry of blows staggered The Game, and The Phenom also used the steel ring steps to further his assault of Triple H. Not to be taken down so easily, Triple H mounted a comeback, but made the tactical error of attempting a Pedigree too early in the match, which Undertaker countered, giving him control once again. It was soon clear that the two were in for a long battle, as neither could keep his opponent down for long, not even a count of three. Triple H assaulted The Deadman with a steel chair, but Undertaker kept kicking out of pinfall attempts.

Shawn Michaels did his best trying to keep control of the match and stop it before it got out of hand, but Triple H and Undertaker were both driven to continue the match regardless of the long-term damage they were doing to themselves as well as their opponent. Triple H even introduced his weapon of choice—a sledgehammer that he used on Undertaker. In another pin attempt, The Phenom kicked out before the count of three.

The team captains, David Otunga for *Raw* and Santino Marella for *SmackDown*, managed an impressive roster of former champions. *Raw* made headlines with its last minute addition—the sole former WWE Champion in the match, The Miz.

The match kicked off with Kofi Kingston for *SmackDown* and Dolph Ziggler for *Raw*. The contest featured fast tags from both teams and strong double-team maneuvers. Mark Henry gave Booker T the World's Strongest Slam and the Great Khali chopped Henry, followed by a double team attack from Kofi Kingston and R-Truth.

The Long Island Iced-Z, Zack Ryder, entered the match and cleaned house with his high-powered offense. Ryder was dominating The Miz and seemed to be on his way to scoring a victory for Team Teddy. That all changed when Eve prematurely entered the ring to celebrate, distracting Ryder. Before he realized what was happening, Miz dropped Zack with the Skull Crushing Finale and scored the victory for Team Johnny.

After the match, Ryder tried to make sense of what had transpired. He thought Eve was going to apologize. Instead she punted him below the belt and left him in the ring, twisted in pain.

The two men even attacked Michaels to prevent him from ending the match prematurely. The near pinfalls continued to pile up as both men came within inches of achieving their goal of either ending or sustaining The Streak.

Undertaker tattooed The Game repeatedly with chair shots to his spine. Struggling to get up, Triple H again reached for his sledgehammer, but The Deadman ripped the weapon from his hands and used it on Triple H. The Phenom followed that up with a Tombstone Piledriver, finally ending the match with a pinfall victory.

As the crowd roared its approval of both men, Shawn Michaels and Undertaker helped Triple H to his feet and carried him out of the ring. The three men walked to the top of the ramp, and in a stirring moment of mutual admiration, they gazed out on the sea of fans one final time, embraced, and exited *WrestleMania*, together.

The WWE Championship

In 2012, CM Punk was in the midst of a historic reign as WWE Champion. Chris Jericho returned to WWE looking to regain the WWE Championship, as well as prove to the world that CM Punk was a Chris Jericho "wannabe." Jericho wanted the WWE Universe to know that he, not CM Punk was "the best in the world." Jericho won a Battle Royal to earn a shot at Punk's WWE Championship at *WrestleMania XXVIII*.

CM Punk took control of the match early, but Jericho, knowing that CM Punk would lose the title if he were disqualified, slapped the champion repeatedly, hoping to provoke Punk into crossing the line. Jericho kept pushing the champ's buttons, yelling at Punk about his father, looking to drive the Straight Edge Superstar to the breaking point.

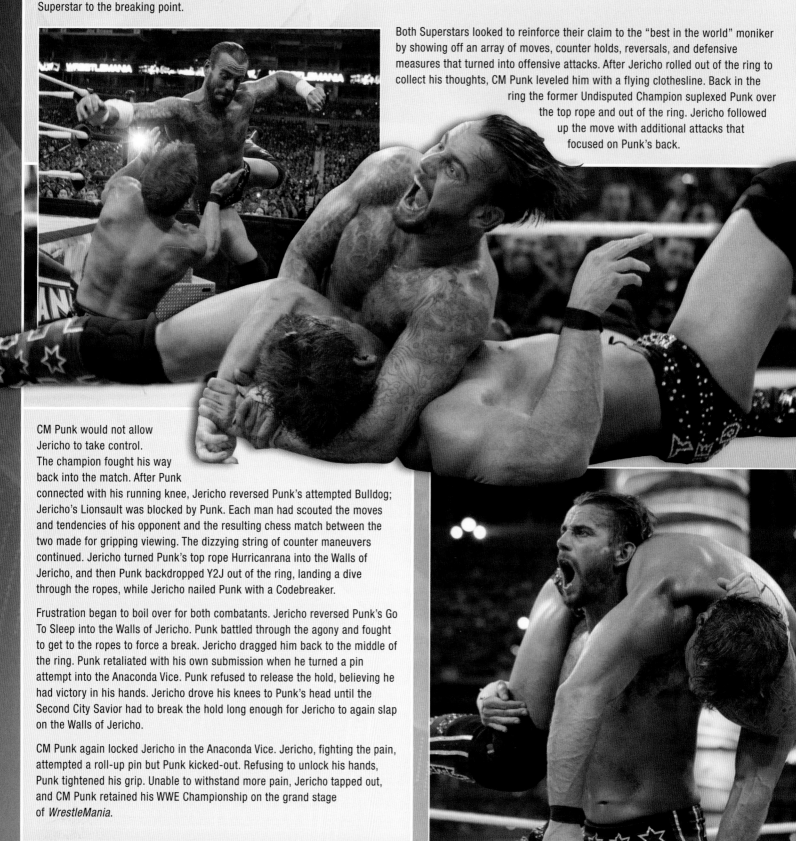

Both Superstars looked to reinforce their claim to the "best in the world" moniker by showing off an array of moves, counter holds, reversals, and defensive measures that turned into offensive attacks. After Jericho rolled out of the ring to collect his thoughts, CM Punk leveled him with a flying clothesline. Back in the ring the former Undisputed Champion suplexed Punk over the top rope and out of the ring. Jericho followed up the move with additional attacks that focused on Punk's back.

CM Punk would not allow Jericho to take control. The champion fought his way back into the match. After Punk connected with his running knee, Jericho reversed Punk's attempted Bulldog; Jericho's Lionsault was blocked by Punk. Each man had scouted the moves and tendencies of his opponent and the resulting chess match between the two made for gripping viewing. The dizzying string of counter maneuvers continued. Jericho turned Punk's top rope Hurricanrana into the Walls of Jericho, and then Punk backdropped Y2J out of the ring, landing a dive through the ropes, while Jericho nailed Punk with a Codebreaker.

Frustration began to boil over for both combatants. Jericho reversed Punk's Go To Sleep into the Walls of Jericho. Punk battled through the agony and fought to get to the ropes to force a break. Jericho dragged him back to the middle of the ring. Punk retaliated with his own submission when he turned a pin attempt into the Anaconda Vice. Punk refused to release the hold, believing he had victory in his hands. Jericho drove his knees to Punk's head until the Second City Savior had to break the hold long enough for Jericho to again slap on the Walls of Jericho.

CM Punk again locked Jericho in the Anaconda Vice. Jericho, fighting the pain, attempted a roll-up pin but Punk kicked-out. Refusing to unlock his hands, Punk tightened his grip. Unable to withstand more pain, Jericho tapped out, and CM Punk retained his WWE Championship on the grand stage of *WrestleMania*.

Generations Collide

The night after *WrestleMania XXVII*, John Cena confronted The Rock. The Great One, the host of the event, nailed Cena with a Rock Bottom, costing Cena his match for the WWE Championship. The two men agreed to settle their animosity in the ring at the following year's *WrestleMania*. For one year, the WWE Universe would debate the possibilities of what would happen when these two larger-than-life icons faced each other, in a "Once in a Lifetime" match. Jerry "The King" Lawler recalls, "I've been in this business over 40 years and there have not been too many matches that we never thought we would see. This was one of them. It was like if you had "Iron" Mike Tyson in his prime going against Muhammad Ali in his prime, though this was possible. It was really going to happen."

The two men locked up a few times to start the bout, but they were equally matched, with neither gaining an early advantage. Rock finally started to gain control, surprising Cena with a few arm drags and a cradle for an early near pinfall. Cena reversed the momentum with shoulder blocks and a powerful headlock. He further punished The Great One with a thunderous belly-to-belly suplex and a grueling bear hug.

"My beef with The Rock was that he said he loves the company, then leaves the company and I don't understand it."

—John Cena

The Brahma Bull fought back and sought to regain the upper hand with a DDT. The Rock looked to electrify the crowd with the People's Elbow, but Cena grabbed the Great One's ankle and went for an STF. Cena then hit Rock with a Five Knuckle Shuffle.

It seemed the war would come to a quick end when Cena drove The Great One to the canvas with an Attitude Adjustment, but The Rock was able to kick out after two. The record-breaking crowd erupted with chants in support of both heroes. It was then The People's Champion's turn to almost end the battle, but Cena would not stay down after a Rock Bottom.

For one of these men to emerge victorious, he would have to push his body beyond human limits. Cena went for it all when he climbed to the top rope and hit a flying leg drop on The Great One, but The Rock rebounded and locked in the Sharpshooter. It took almost an inhuman will for Cena to drag himself to the ropes and force The Rock to break the hold.

After escaping The Great One's Sharpshooter a second time, John Cena found the strength to retaliate and locked The Rock in his submission move of choice, the STF. Cena used his weight as leverage to wear down The Brahma Bull. Victimized by a damaging hold, The Rock began to fade as his eyes rolled to the back of his head. Now, The Great One was searching for the will to make it to the ropes.

With both men physically battered, the war became one of attrition. Feeding off the kinetic energy from his hometown brethren, The Rock landed the move he used to defeat the likes of Austin, Hogan, and Triple H—his fabled People's Elbow. Even that strike could not keep John Cena's shoulders pinned to the mat. The Rock climbed to the top rope to use a move from his early repertoire, the flying cross body. John Cena rolled through the move, still holding onto The Rock, and returned to a standing position. With The Great One on his shoulders, Cena drove him down with an Attitude Adjustment. But rather than pin The Rock, Cena decided to finish off The Great One with a Cena-style People's Elbow. Rock popped up and intercepted Cena, nailing him with a Rock Bottom and securing a three-count. The year-long battle was finally over, and The Rock had made a triumphant in-ring return to *WrestleMania*. The Rock looks back, "I always knew I was going to return to WWE, I just didn't know when. This is a business I grew up in through my grandfather and my dad. I've always kept in close contact with Vince and we've become incredibly close and I so appreciate that relationship."

WRESTLEMANIA 29

METLIFE STADIUM – EAST RUTHERFORD, NJ

April 7
2013

Attendance
80,676

ANNOUNCERS
Jerry "The King" Lawler,
John Bradshaw Layfield,
Michael Cole

SPANISH ANNOUNCERS
Carlos Cabrera, Marcelo Rodriguez

RING ANNOUNCER
Justin Roberts, Lillian Garcia,
Ricardo Rodriguez

SPECIAL FIELD CORRESPONDENT
Josh Mathews, Matt Striker

HALL OF FAME RING ANNOUNCER
Howard Finkel

SPECIAL MUSICAL GUEST
Sean "Diddy" Combs

Event Card

WWE CHAMPIONSHIP MATCH
- John Cena def. The Rock (Champion) to become new Champion

NO HOLDS BARRED MATCH
- Triple H w/ Shawn Michaels def. Brock Lesnar w/ Paul Heyman

WORLD HEAVYWEIGHT CHAMPIONSHIP MATCH
- Alberto Del Rio (Champion) w/ Ricardo Rodriguez def. Jack Swagger w/ Zeb Coulter to retain the Championship

WWE TAG TEAM CHAMPIONSHIP MATCH
- Team Hell No (Daniel Bryan & Kane) def. Dolph Ziggler & Big E. Langston w/ AJ Lee

OTHER MATCHES
- Undertaker def. CM Punk w/ Paul Heyman
- Fandango def. Chris Jericho
- Mark Henry def. Ryback
- The Shield (Dean Ambrose, Roman Reigns, & Seth Rollins) def. Big Show, Randy Orton, & Sheamus

> **"You think you can beat me.
> I know I can beat you."**
>
> —The Rock

WrestleMania Comes Home

The 29th Showcase of the Immortals was a special homecoming for WWE. *WrestleMania 29* was the fifth time the event was to be held in the New York City metropolitan area and the third in the State of New Jersey: New York was home for *WrestleMania*'s *I*, *II*, *X*, and *XX*; *WrestleMania*'s *IV* and *V* took place in New Jersey.

The Shield Takes on Three Champions

During the WWE Championship Match at the 2012 Survivor Series, three men broke through the crowd and attacked John Cena and Ryback. These self-proclaimed Hounds of Justice called themselves The Shield, and they launched an immediate assault on WWE's most beloved heroes. Big Show, Sheamus, and Ryback decided to settle things against The Shield at *WrestleMania 29*. When Ryback started running into problems with Mark Henry, he was pulled from the six-man match for a singles confrontation with the World's Strongest Man. Big Show and Sheamus had an impressive substitution added to their squad—The Viper, Randy Orton. The trio of former World Champions was intimidating, but could they work together to accomplish their goals against a well-oiled machine like The Shield?

Seth Rollins remembers, "From the moment we walked in [to WWE] we had a different kind of confidence. We respected our opponents but didn't feel pressure to live up to their or anyone else's expectations. The pressure was on us to do what we do."

Sheamus and Roman Reigns locked up to open the match, with the Celtic Warrior gaining the early upper hand. Sheamus and Randy Orton demonstrated excellent teamwork, but when it seemed that their side had the advantage, The Shield's smothering attacks tilted the pendulum back to their side.

Growing impatient, Big Show tagged himself into the match. The World's Largest Athlete ripped off Dean Ambrose's Kevlar vest and chopped his chest until it was crimson red. The two teams battled back and forth until Sheamus clubbed Seth Rollins on the ring apron. Eventually The Shield did take control and set Sheamus up for their devastating Triple Powerbomb, but Big Show saved the Celtic Warrior by taking everyone down with one Spear.

The trio of champions seemed to be ending the match, but their massive egos got in the way. Orton tagged himself in, forcing Big Show out of the ring. The Apex Predator fought off Ambrose and delivered an RKO on Seth Rollins, but he ultimately succumbed to a Roman Reigns Spear. After the match, an irate Big Show turned his back on his teammates and blasted them both with his Knockout Punch.

Randy Orton shares, "Those guys were getting their big push and were undefeated. It was a little weird going in because I felt on mine and Show's experience alone we should've beat them. But they wanted to do this storyline where Show punched me. I didn't like it. I wanted to become a villain and pitched some ideas but it wasn't the right time. I felt we could've done more but it was still a fun experience."

Strength and Power

The match-up between The World's Strongest Man, Mark Henry, and Ryback was the classic battle of strength and power. There would be few technical wrestling moves, as each man would look to impose his will on his foe. After both men collided like two freight trains, Henry scored the first takedown with a massive clothesline. Mark Henry's power continued to rock the ring and Ryback along with it. The World's Strongest Man dominated Ryback and wore him down with his powerful bear hug.

As chants of "Feed me more" began to echo, Ryback fought back and finally knocked Mark Henry down with his Meat Hook Clothesline. Feeling the tide turn, Ryback showed his Herculean power and hoisted his 400-pound opponent into the air for the Shell Shock. Henry used his experience and grabbed the top rope, crushing Ryback's spine and pinning him.

Henry's attempt to induct Ryback into the Hall of Pain backfired. The Human Wrecking Ball fought back and leveled Henry with a Shell Shock.

The WWE Tag Team Championship

An unlikely pair, Team Hell No was one of the most dominant tag teams in WWE. Their incessant bickering led to anger management sessions, but when they were on the same page against a common enemy, Kane and Daniel Bryan were a dominant force. Dolph Ziggler believed he and his enforcer, Big E Langston, could unseat the WWE Tag Team Champions at *WrestleMania 29*.

Before the battle began, Ziggler mocked Daniel Bryan's kiss with AJ Lee at *WrestleMania 28*, and the match almost ended as quickly as that infamous match when Bryan tagged Ziggler with a kick to the head. Bryan dazzled the WWE Universe and kept Ziggler back on his heels with an array of moves and holds. The match changed tone when each man tagged in their partners, with Big E lifting the Big Red Monster for three consecutive backbreakers before sending Kane to the canvas.

Langston, in his WWE debut, continued to impose his will on Kane in a way that had never been seen before. He launched an incredible display of strength when he powered out of Kane's Chokeslam. Ziggler and Langston kept Kane down. Ziggler almost captured the tag titles for his team after hitting Kane with his Famouser and Zig Zag. But the Big Red Monster could not be kept down.

Kane remembers, "Daniel Bryan is a great performer. I had the most fun doing the Team Hell No stuff that I've ever had in my entire career because I was able to do something completely different and be the comedic element on the show."

Though he cashed it in the next night to become World Champion, when an attack with his Money in the Bank briefcase was foiled, Ziggler paid the price. Kane planted Dolph with a thunderous Chokeslam and Daniel Bryan followed that with a headbutt off the top rope. Team Hell No successfully defended their crown and left *WrestleMania 29* to the ovation of "YES! YES! YES!"

The World Heavyweight Championship

In early 2013, Alberto Del Rio captured both the support of the WWE Universe as well as his first World Heavyweight Championship. While Del Rio had the support of many, he could not count Jack Swagger or his manager Zeb Colter among them. Colter felt Del Rio had just come to America to steal an American title. Jack Swagger wanted to reclaim the World Heavyweight Championship and show Alberto Del Rio what his America was all about.

Del Rio took early control, but Colter was able to distract Del Rio, allowing Swagger to claim control of the match. The first near fall of the bout occurred when Swagger hit the champion with his Swagger Bomb.

This was a hard fought match with a number of reversals and counter attacks. Each Superstar was looking to soften up his opponent for his signature submission move—Swagger with the Patriot Lock and Del Rio with his Cross Armbreaker.

Chris Jericho vs. Fandango

For months the WWE Universe was teased with the debut of Fandango, a ballroom dancer as well as in-ring competitor. However, the flamboyant Superstar kept cancelling his debut match because he felt that no one was properly pronouncing his name. Chris Jericho took this as an opportunity to butcher the dancer's name and humiliate him at all WWE events. Enraged, Fandango attacked Jericho on WWE television and set his first match in WWE at *WrestleMania*.

Fandango recalls, "There was a male dance team in developmental that dissolved but Vince still wanted a dancer character. I embraced the ballroom dancing world. I'd train three days a week up to four hours a day and collaborate with stylists on wardrobe. It was surreal. I knew for it to be successful I'd have to dive right in."

Once the bell rang, Chris Jericho started out quickly giving Fandango a furious welcome to *WrestleMania*. Y2J hit high-impact moves like his Codebreaker and a flying cross body from the top rope out to the floor. Jericho dominated the contest until Fandango countered a Y2J move and kicked him in the face.

Fandango briefly took control of the match, but the six-time World Champion remained one step ahead. Jericho's dominance continued but the elusive Fandango countered every move. The ballroom master threw Jericho into the ring post, and then nailed Y2J with a top-rope leg drop from halfway across the ring.

Jericho kicked out and avoided two additional leg drop attempts from the top rope. After Jericho missed his patented Lionsault, Fandango reversed the Walls of Jericho and rolled Y2J up for the victory, becoming the first Superstar to have his WWE debut match at *WrestleMania* and win.

Each was willing to pin his foe as well, and Del Rio thought he had the match won after an Enziguiri kick to Swagger. However, Zeb Coulter's influence impacted the match once again when he put Swagger's leg on the rope to stop the referee's count.

After Swagger attacked the champion outside the ring, he took longer than usual to re-enter. This gave Del Rio an opening and he took Swagger down with the Cross Armbreaker. Within 10 seconds of being locked in the dreaded submission, Swagger tapped out. In the shadows of Lady Liberty, Alberto Del Rio was victorious defending his World Heavyweight Championship.

The Streak Advances

On the heels of his historic 434-day reign as WWE Champion, CM Punk set his sights on another WWE milestone—Undertaker's undefeated Streak at *WrestleMania*. CM Punk wanted to further cement his own immortality by being the one to end The Deadman's reign of dominance.

In the buildup to *WrestleMania 29*, Undertaker's longtime manager, Paul Bearer, passed away. Rather than show the future Hall of Fame manager respect, Punk mocked Bearer as well as Undertaker. Punk even stole Undertaker's urn and used it as a weapon against The Phenom in the weeks leading into their *WrestleMania* encounter.

The Phenom attacked Punk to kick off the match, and Punk replied with a slap across The Deadman's face. The Straight Edge Superstar was trying to provoke Undertaker into getting himself disqualified, which would end The Streak. Undertaker refused to take the bait and also kept a watchful eye on the evil genius Paul Heyman, who lurked ringside with the urn. The Deadman paid tribute to his friend with the message "R.I.P. PB" on his tights.

Undertaker looked to hit Old School, but Punk was able to counter the move with a painful arm drag off the top rope. CM Punk then nailed his own version of Old School on The Deadman. Punk had several near falls, and Paul Heyman could be heard shrieking, "You're one second away from ending The Streak, you're one second away from ending The Streak."

The Streak seemed over when Punk landed a crushing top-rope elbow into The Phenom's heart. Once again, The Deadman dug deep and kicked out of a pinfall, and then hit Punk with a Chokeslam. When it seemed that Undertaker had rebounded and would send Punk straight to Hell, Punk escaped a Last Ride through the Spanish announce table and blasted The Deadman with a Roundhouse Kick. Punk then took to the air and landed a second flying elbow drop, this time while Undertaker lay on the Spanish Announce Table. When all seemed lost, Undertaker made it back into the ring just before the referee's 10-count.

CM Punk preyed on a weakened Deadman, but Undertaker regained control and locked Punk in Hell's Gate. Punk battled through the pain, first turning into a pinning predicament, then putting the Phenom in his Anaconda Vice submission.

As a forlorn Paul Heyman looked on, Undertaker reversed CM Punk's Go To Sleep and crushed Punk with a Tombstone Piledriver. The most time-honored performer in *WrestleMania* history extended The Streak to 21-0 and defended the memory of his friend, Paul Bearer.

Triple H vs. Brock Lesnar

Since returning to WWE, Brock Lesnar had targeted Triple H, twice breaking The Game's arm and putting Triple H out of action. Lesnar made things even more personal by breaking the arm of Triple H's best friend, Shawn Michaels and putting Mr. McMahon in the hospital. Triple H finally returned and he challenged Lesnar to a match at *WrestleMania*. Paul Heyman, representing Lesnar, agreed to the match on two conditions. The bout would be No Holds Barred and if The Game lost, his career as an in-ring competitor would be over.

The Beast Incarnate was obsessed with ending the storied career of Triple H. Knowing that Paul Heyman might try to involve himself in the bout, Shawn Michaels decided to second Triple H.

From the opening bell, it was clear that each man was interested in more than winning the match—each wanted to hurt his opponent. Triple H and Brock Lesnar exchanged vicious strikes, punches, clotheslines, and kneelifts. When it seemed that The Game was taking early control, Lesnar landed a belly-to-belly suplex. Lesnar continued the attack with a suplex through the Spanish announcers' table, and a second belly-to-belly suplex. The Beast then unleashed a primal scream as he continued to dominate with a third belly-to-belly suplex, a near pinfall, and devastating German Suplexes.

Lesnar threw Triple H out of the ring, and then turned his sights on Shawn Michaels. The preoccupation with the Heartbreak Kid cost Lesnar, as Triple H recovered and started to dominate the match outside the ring and back in. But Lesnar reversed a potential Pedigree and set Triple H up for an F-5. Shawn Michaels came in to save his friend, but Lesnar put Shawn Michaels down with an F-5. Triple H tried to use his trusty sledgehammer, but Lesnar turned the assault into an F-5, and a near pinfall.

No matter what attack Lesnar launched, Triple H refused to be defeated. With blood running down his mouth, Brock used the steel steps as a battering ram to beat down The Game. Lesnar could be heard yelling, "It's over. Retire!" In that moment, Triple H responded with a slap across The Beast's face. Lesnar put Triple H in the abominable Kimura Lock. Fending off the pain, Triple H found a way to break the hold.

In what became a test of will, Lesnar locked the hold another three times, sitting on the top rope to apply additional pressure. The Game fought through the agony to hit a Spinebuster on Lesnar and break free of the move. The Game then attacked Lesnar's left shoulder. Triple H turned the tables and gripped Brock Lesnar in his version of the Kimura Lock. When the meddlesome Paul Heyman attempted to interfere, he was greeted by Shawn Michaels' Sweet Chin Music Superkick.

Still locked in the hold, Lesnar displayed his incredible strength when he lifted Triple H's 255-pound frame and drove him onto the steel steps. The break from the hold would be temporary as The Cerebral Assassin slapped the hold on The Beast again. The rising Beast broke the hold in this battle of sheer will. Triple H drove Lesnar's skull into the steel steps with a DDT, while still having the Kimura locked. Triple H crawled to his sledgehammer and nailed the Beast with a strike to the head. The Cerebral Assassin delivered a Pedigree on the steel steps, and pinned Lesnar, winning the match and saving his career.

The Rock vs. John Cena

The drama of *WrestleMania's* main event once again made mainstream entertainment headlines. After their battle at *WrestleMania XXVIII*, The Rock and John Cena knew one another's attacks, tactics, and tendencies. The two had an epic encounter for pride the year before, and now they were fighting for the richest prize in sports-entertainment, the WWE Championship.

In the year since his historic clash with The Great One, John Cena had suffered a series of professional setbacks. For Cena, he couldn't help but trace the decline to a mistake he made in the closing moments of his first *WrestleMania* encounter with The Rock that he felt cost him the match. *WrestleMania 29* represented a golden opportunity for redemption.

Once again, the two Superstars immediately tested one another. The Brahma Bull took the early advantage, but Cena bounced back and began to wear The Rock down with a calculated offense. As John Cena began to unload, both men engaged in a heated exchange of counters and reversals. Rock dodged a second flying shoulder block from the challenger; Cena turned The Rock's Spinebuster into an STF but the Great One kicked out. The Rock countered Cena's suplex attempt and locked him in the Sharpshooter.

Both icons refused to budge as Cena turned a People's Elbow into an STF. As Cena missed his flying leg drop off the top rope, the Great One connected with the People's Elbow. Neither man could keep the other down for the three-count. The crowd remained on the edge of its seat. Cena was so close to redemption, and The Rock was so close to successfully defending the WWE Championship.

The intensity grew. The Rock countered an Attitude Adjustment, and Cena countered The Rock Bottom. The Rock broke the battle of counters with a thundering DDT.

Though The Rock was poised to end the match with his Rock Bottom, Cena landed the ultimate reversal when he drove The Rock down with the Attitude Adjustment. John Cena pinned the Great One and reclaimed the WWE Championship.

John Cena paid his opponent the ultimate tribute, pointing to The Rock and exiting the ring for the Brahma Bull to take center stage. When The Rock walked up the ramp, Cena was waiting for him. The two raised one another's hand to the crowd. John Cena remembers, "*WrestleMania 29* was without a doubt the biggest night of my career. There could not have been a brighter stage to have a moment like that. It was more than a match to me. It truly was redemption. The Rock and I shared a personal moment in the ring and I feel we do have a mutual respect for one another. I am a dedicated WWE Superstar. It's what I love to do."

"The Undertaker's Streak means perfection. Being in the Casket Match with Undertaker at *WrestleMania 22* was one of the most exciting moments in my career. Twenty-one men had done it, and twenty-one men failed."

—Mark Henry

THE STREAK 21-0

Ask Not For Whom The Bell Tolls...

▶ *WrestleMania VIII* vs. Jake "The Snake" Roberts

▶ *WrestleMania VII* vs. Jimmy "Superfly" Snuka

▶ *WrestleMania IX* vs. Giant Gonzales

▶ *WrestleMania XI* vs. King Kong Bundy

WrestleMania XII vs. Diesel

WrestleMania 13 vs. Sycho Sid to become WWE Champion

"Undertaker is the last outlaw of WWE. In my mind, just because of what he's done, Undertaker is Mr. WrestleMania."

—John Cena

All streaks must begin with a single win. Undertaker's brilliance at the Showcase of the Immortals commenced in 1991 when a Tombstone Piledriver defeated the legendary Jimmy "Superfly" Snuka at WrestleMania VII.

After that fateful day, The Deadman prevailed at the Show of Shows in various forms of battle twenty more times. As his list of fallen opponents grew, the butcher's bill tallied sports-entertainment's most prolific entities—all driven by the irresistible allure of ending WWE's most heralded record.

For over two decades, eighteen men sought to end The Deadman's legacy. These victims paid for their sins at the hands of the dreaded Deadman.

No other experience could compare to standing across the ring from Undertaker at WrestleMania.

Though Undertaker's legendary Streak finally came to an end at the hands of Brock Lesnar at *WrestleMania 30*, it stands as a daunting monument to all who would dare cross The Deadman.

Ask not for whom the bell tolls. When the Reaper finds you, your time has come. As the Undertaker said to each tortured soul in defeat, "Rest… In… Peace."

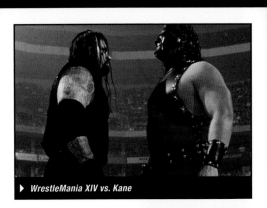

WrestleMania XIV vs. Kane

WrestleMania X-Seven vs. Triple H

"The Streak is the ultimate record that will never be topped."

—Jerry "The King" Lawler

WrestleMania XV vs. Big Boss Man in a Hell in a Cell Match

WrestleMania X8 vs. "Nature Boy" Ric Flair in a No Disqualification Match

▶ WrestleMania XIX vs. A-Train and Big Show in a Handicap Match

▶ WrestleMania XX vs. Kane

"The Streak is the be-all end-all. It is what has defined Undertaker's career; it is what has defined Undertaker's legacy."

—Michael Cole

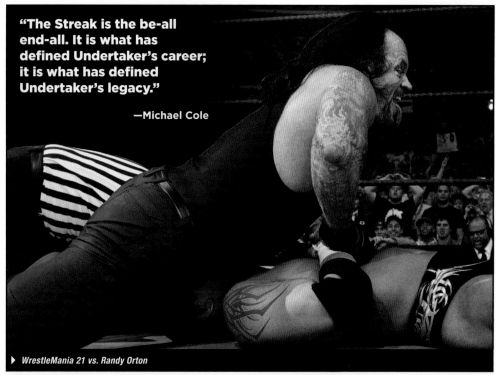
▶ WrestleMania 21 vs. Randy Orton

▶ WrestleMania 22 vs. Mark Henry in a Casket Match

▶ WrestleMania 23 vs. Batista to become World Heavyweight Champion

WrestleMania XXIV vs. Edge to become World Heavyweight Champion

WrestleMania XXVII vs. Triple H in a No Holds Barred Match

WrestleMania 25 vs. Shawn Michaels

WrestleMania XXVI vs. Shawn Michaels in a Streak vs. Career Match

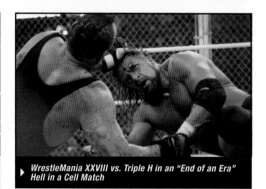

WrestleMania XXVIII vs. Triple H in an "End of an Era" Hell in a Cell Match

"Undertaker transcends the generations of our business and he is a sight to behold. The Streak is something that has become lore. It's a testament to who he is and a benchmark that I believe will never be duplicated in our business. It just can't be done."

—Triple H

WrestleMania 29 vs. CM Punk

WRESTLEMANIA 30

MERCEDES-BENZ SUPERDOME – NEW ORLEANS, LA

April 6

2014

Attendance

75,167

ANNOUNCERS
Jerry "The King" Lawler, John Bradshaw Layfield, Michael Cole

FRENCH ANNOUNCERS
Christophe Agius, Philippe Chéreau

SPANISH ANNOUNCERS
Carlos Cabrera, Marcelo Rodriguez, Ricardo Rodriguez

RING ANNOUNCERS
Justin Roberts, Lillian Garcia, Stephanie McMahon

SPECIAL FIELD CORRESPONDENT
"Mean" Gene Okerlund

HALL OF FAME RING ANNOUNCER
Howard Finkel

SPECIAL GUEST HOST
Hulk Hogan

Event Card

TRIPLE THREAT MATCH FOR THE WWE CHAMPIONSHIP
■ Daniel Bryan def. Randy Orton (Champion) and Batista to become new Champion

THE VICKIE GUERRERO DIVAS CHAMPIONSHIP INVITATIONAL
■ AJ Lee (Champion) def. Aksana, Alicia Fox, Brie Bella, Cameron, Emma, Eva Marie, Layla, Naomi, Natalya, Nikki Bella, Rosa Mendes, Summer Rae, and Tamina Snuka to retain the Championship

THE ANDRE THE GIANT MEMORIAL BATTLE ROYAL
■ Cesaro def. Alberto Del Rio, Big Show, Big E, Brad Maddox, Brodus Clay, Cody Rhodes, Darren Young, Damien Sandow, David Otunga, Dolph Ziggler, Drew McIntyre, Fandango, Goldust, The Great Khali, Heath Slater, Jinder Mahal, Justin Gabriel, Kofi Kingston, Mark Henry, The Miz, R-Truth, Rey Mysterio, Santino Marella, Sheamus, Sin Cara, Titus O'Neil, Tyson Kidd, Xavier Woods, and Yoshi Tatsu

SIX MAN TAG TEAM MATCH
■ The Shield (Dean Ambrose, Roman Reigns, & Seth Rollins) def. Kane & The New Age Outlaws (Road Dogg Jessie James & Billy Gunn)

OTHER MATCHES
■ Brock Lesnar w/ Paul Heyman def. Undertaker
■ John Cena def. Bray Wyatt w/ Erick Rowan and Luke Harper
■ Daniel Bryan def. Triple H w/ Stephanie McMahon*
*Winner is placed in main event for WWE Championship

"With these people, I'm stronger than ever."

— Daniel Bryan

Three Legends, One Ring

After several years away, the Immortal Hulk Hogan was coming home to WWE, preparing to serve as the host of *WrestleMania 30*. The Hulkster kicked off the event by coming to the ring to welcome the live crowd, as well as the more than one million viewers watching live worldwide. The audience received an incredible treat when Hogan was joined in the ring by Stone Cold Steve Austin. While conventional wisdom would have predicted a Stone Cold Stunner to the Hulkster, Austin thanked Hogan for his contributions in making the Showcase of the Immortals what it is today. But the surprise didn't end there.

The Superdome was electrified when The People's Champion, The Rock, made his way to the ring. As three of sports-entertainment's greatest luminaries convened, a generation of fans' lifelong dreams came to life. The Rock paid tribute to the two men who were once his *WrestleMania* adversaries. The once-in-a-lifetime gathering appropriately concluded with an Austin Beer Bash.

NETWORKING WITH THE WWE

In early 2014, WWE made history with the launch of the WWE Network. The treasure trove of new and historical footage allowed fans to access the rich history of WWE, WCW, ECW, WCCW, and more. In addition, the network would serve as the new home for WWE's pay-per-view events, starting with *WrestleMania 30*.

Daniel Bryan vs. Triple H

At *SummerSlam 2013*, Triple H conspired to destroy Daniel Bryan's dream of being WWE Champion. For eight months, Triple H and Stephanie McMahon—known as the Authority—along with their hand-selected champion Randy Orton, seized every opportunity to demoralize Daniel Bryan.

The more they attempted to crush Bryan's spirit, the more people stood up to defend him, culminating in an Occupy *Raw* sit-in that demanded Triple H face Bryan at *WrestleMania 30*. Triple H accepted, with the stipulation that the winner of the match would be added to the WWE World Heavyweight Championship Match later in the show.

Bryan controlled the match's early stages, matching the King of Kings hold-for-hold. Bryan brought the crowd to its feet when he planted WWE's Chief Operating Officer with a tornado DDT off the ring apron. Feeding on the Yes! Movement's energy, Bryan laid out The Game with a high-risk aerial attack, but Triple H was able to counter the move and throw Bryan out of the ring. The Cerebral Assassin then focused his punishment on Bryan's already injured left shoulder.

Bryan nailed Triple H in the corner with several running dropkicks. Triple H crushed the resurgence, reversing an air attack and locking in the Crossface. Bryan appeared to be fading and risked losing use of his left arm if he remained locked in the hold much longer. Bryan's impenetrable will to fight gave him the strength to power out of the hold and turn the tables.

Courageously fighting with one arm, Bryan launched an aerial assault with an awesome missile dropkick from the top rope. However, Triple H reminded Bryan and the WWE Universe why he was one of the all-time greats, as he surprised Bryan with a powerful Spinebuster. It looked like Bryan was finished for good when The Game flattened him with a Pedigree, but Daniel would not be kept down.

Summoning the strength to reverse two Pedigree attempts, Daniel Bryan struck down The Cerebral Assassin with a vicious kick. Then Bryan thwarted Triple H's belly-to-back suplex, taking down Triple H with his running knee attack. Bryan was able to hold Triple H down for a three-count. Daniel Bryan had won the match and would be competing for the WWE World Heavyweight Championship.

Just when he thought the fight was finished, Bryan was attacked by an incensed Stephanie McMahon and blindsided by Triple H. The ruthless attack on Bryan's arm continued, with Triple H battering it around the ring post and with a steel chair. Bryan had to be taken to the locker room with assistance from WWE's medical staff, making the WWE Universe wonder if he'd be able to compete in the main event.

The Shield Reigns Supreme

After serving as mercenaries for The Authority for months, The Shield broke off on their own, evolving into fan favorites and earning the wrath of the Director of Operations, Kane. The Big Red Monster, with the aid of the New Age Outlaws, ambushed The Shield on several occasions, and looked to put The Hounds of Justice in their place at *WrestleMania 30*.

Dean Ambrose and Kane, starting off for their two teams, traded early attacks, with Ambrose gaining the initial advantage. He tagged in Roman Reigns, who downed Kane and was battering the Outlaws until Kane grabbed him by the throat. Kane's grip wouldn't last, as the tenacious Seth Rollins launched an aerial attack on WWE's Director of Operations. Rollins wowed the crowd by then diving over the top rope to hit Kane on the floor with a spectacular dive.

The Shield was not to be denied. Reigns Speared all three of his opponents at the same time, and then The Hounds of Justice broke out a special version of their infamous triple Powerbomb. The move usually crushed a single competitor, but they used it to devastate two men, as both Road Dogg and Billy Gunn were sent crashing to the mat. Not only had The Shield emerged victorious in their second straight *WrestleMania*, they had never looked more dominant.

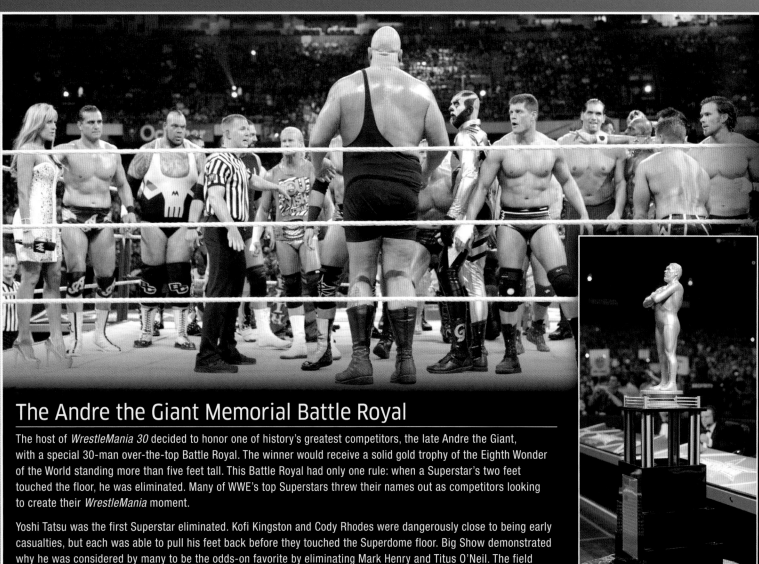

The Andre the Giant Memorial Battle Royal

The host of *WrestleMania 30* decided to honor one of history's greatest competitors, the late Andre the Giant, with a special 30-man over-the-top Battle Royal. The winner would receive a solid gold trophy of the Eighth Wonder of the World standing more than five feet tall. This Battle Royal had only one rule: when a Superstar's two feet touched the floor, he was eliminated. Many of WWE's top Superstars threw their names out as competitors looking to create their *WrestleMania* moment.

Yoshi Tatsu was the first Superstar eliminated. Kofi Kingston and Cody Rhodes were dangerously close to being early casualties, but each was able to pull his feet back before they touched the Superdome floor. Big Show demonstrated why he was considered by many to be the odds-on favorite by eliminating Mark Henry and Titus O'Neil. The field thinned as Cody Rhodes ousted his former tag team partner Damien Sandow and Big E tossed Justin Gabriel high over the top rope.

Big Show press-slammed R-Truth to the floor, and Cesaro eliminated Rey Mysterio. Numerous exciting exchanges later, just four Superstars remained: Alberto Del Rio, Big Show, Cesaro, and Sheamus. Del Rio and Sheamus wasted no time in attacking each other. Del Rio locked Sheamus in his Cross Armbreaker, but Sheamus's amazing strength saw him lift Del Rio off the mat while still locked in the hold. In the ensuing struggle, their combined momentum carried them both to elimination. It came down to Big Show and Cesaro. Cesaro, making his *WrestleMania* debut, displayed astonishing strength. He picked up the 450-pound Big Show, stepped to the ropes, and slammed him out of the ring. The scene bore an eerie resemblance to a cherished *WrestleMania* memory involving the trophy's namesake. Twenty-seven years after the Slam Heard 'Round the World, Cesaro and this generation's giant created a new *WrestleMania* moment. The Swiss Superman won the inaugural André the Giant Memorial Battle Royal, and Big Show acknowledged his feat with a respectful handshake.

Rest in Peace

It was one of sports-entertainment's most passionate debates: Should Undertaker's Streak ever end, and if so, who should be the one to end it? Virtually no two opinions on the topic were alike. However, the question of *will* The Streak end always drew the same answer: Never. Undertaker echoed this sentiment in the storyline leading up to *WrestleMania 30*, promising there are three guarantees in life, "death, taxes and The Streak."

Since Brock Lesnar's return to WWE in 2013, he had dominated in the ring. His manager, Paul Heyman, felt the Beast should have been competing in the WWE World Heavyweight Championship Match at *WrestleMania*. Instead, The Authority gave Lesnar an open contract to face anyone at *WrestleMania 30*, and Undertaker stepped up as the man to accept that challenge. Undertaker and Brock Lesnar had a WWE history dating back to the early 2000s when they had a number of epic battles for the WWE Championship. Their mutual hostility emerged when the two crossed paths after one of Lesnar's UFC fights. But nothing compared to the rage evident as they entered the ring on this day.

Undertaker took early control when he blasted Lesnar with his Snake Eyes move. Lesnar used his mixed martial arts background to target The Deadman's massive legs. The Beast then took down Undertaker with an F-5, generating the match's first close pinfall. But Undertaker escaped just before the referee's three-count, and then locked Lesnar in the Hell's Gate submission. It looked like the Beast was going to tap out, but instead he lifted Undertaker into the air and slammed him down to the canvas. Undertaker locked Lesnar in the move a second time, but again Lesnar freed himself by slamming The Phenom a second time.

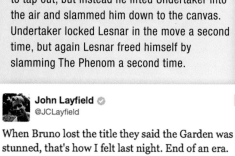

John Layfield ✔
@JCLayfield
☑ Follow

When Bruno lost the title they said the Garden was stunned, that's how I felt last night. End of an era. #thankYouTaker #LoveThatGuy

9:24 AM - 7 Apr 2014

568 RETWEETS 531 FAVORITES

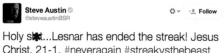

Steve Austin ✔
@steveaustinBSR
☼ˇ ☑ Follow

Holy s✱✱...Lesnar has ended the streak! Jesus Christ. 21-1. #neveragain #streakvsthebeast #WWE

↩ Reply ⇄ Retweet ★ Favorite ••• More

The Miz ✔
@mikethemiz
☼ˇ ☑ Follow

I am speechless...The Deadman never dies but the streak does. @WWE

↩ Reply ⇄ Retweet ★ Favorite ••• More

"I feel now like how I did when that b*stard Bruce Dern killed John Wayne in *The Cowboys*. The Streak is over."

—Jim Ross

21-1

Lesnar took control of the match again, and nailed Undertaker with a second F-5. Sensing he could terminate sports-entertainment's greatest legacy, Lesnar went for the pin. Undertaker got up before the three-count, proving he would push himself past normal physical limits to preserve his *WrestleMania* dominance.

Undertaker set Lesnar up for a second Tombstone Piledriver, but Lesnar suddenly countered the move, and hit The Deadman with a third F-5. The Beast went for the cover. The referee counted one, two—the world hung in the balance. Undertaker, unlike so many times before, did not kick out of a pinning attempt—the referee's hand slapped the mat a third time, making the pinfall official.

An eerie silence came over the Superdome; the WWE Universe was thunderstruck. All that could be heard was Paul Heyman exclaiming, "Oh my God … Oh my God!" Heyman's verbal reaction was plastered on the faces in the crowd, who just sat with mouths agape. The silence hung for a solid five minutes, with many thinking a mistake was made, or a swerve was planned that would reverse the outcome. But it was not to be. In a shocker of epic proportions, debaters of The Streak's fate got their answer—the Beast was the final one in a record that now read 21-1.

As the dust settled, social media exploded and a new debate raged on, one that will never reach a conclusion…

Unbelieving stares filled the Superdome

The Usos ✓
@WWEUsos

The streak.....is broken. Man....#WrestleMania30

11:02 PM - 6 Apr 2014

1,167 RETWEETS 1,509 FAVORITES

Diamond Dallas Page ✓
@RealDDP

Follow

That was an awesome match between @theundertaker and @BrockLesnar. It took a UFC badass to take down the dead guy. Great job guys. #Wwe

10:46 PM - 6 Apr 2014

112 RETWEETS 146 FAVORITES

Sean Waltman ✓
@TheRealXPac

Follow

With all due respect, that should have been saved for a Roman Reigns or someone else to build towards the future.

Reply   Retweet   Favorite   ••• More

"WHAAAAAAATTT?!?!?!?!?
The Streak is over???

—Hornswoggle

John Cena vs. Bray Wyatt

Leading into *WrestleMania 30*, the demented Bray Wyatt and his followers decided to target John Cena and expose the monster that he claimed was living inside Cena. Wyatt interfered in Cena's championship match at the 2014 *Royal Rumble*, costing him the chance to become the WWE World Heavyweight Champion. Cena challenged Wyatt to a match at *WrestleMania 30*. Other demonic Superstars, not to mention a strong contingent of fans, have tried to break the infallible spirit of Hustle, Loyalty, and Respect. Would the New Face of Fear be the one to cause Cena to crack, or would his heroic legacy remain unblemished?

At the beginning of the match, Bray Wyatt fell to his knees, imploring John Cena to finish him. The strange psychological ploy proved effective, as Wyatt's early domination of John Cena silenced the Superdome crowd. Even when Cena took control of the match, it seemed to favor the demented Wyatt, as the harder Cena hit Bray Wyatt, the harder Wyatt would laugh. John Cena was battling Bray Wyatt, the two family members outside the ring, as well as Wyatt's lurid fixation on the darkness he insisted lived within Cena.

After mounting a brief comeback, Cena went for his Five Knuckle Shuffle. Wyatt shocked Cena by rising from the mat and using his chilling spider walk. Cena tried to regain control with a leg drop from the top rope, but Wyatt caught him and nearly crushed Cena's spine with a Powerbomb. John Cena fought back, using all his strength to slam Bray Wyatt with the Attitude Adjustment. Luke Harper interfered, kicking Cena in the face, but Cena would get retribution when he speared the Wyatt disciple through the barricade.

Wyatt's demented behavior continued when he handed Cena a chair, dropped to his knees, and invited Cena to strike him down. Instead, Cena used it to knock Erick Rowan off the ring apron. Cena fought his way out of an attempted Sister Abigail and finished Wyatt with an Attitude Adjustment.

Cena reflects on the match, "I wanted to see what he was made out of. I've said it openly since the beginning of 2014 that the future of this business will go through me. I mean that. We have so many young Superstars with the Eye of the Tiger, not just wanting to be here but wanting to own it. Competition breeds motivation. I like that. I want their best. Bring me everything you got. Bray did that."

The Vickie Guerrero Championship Invitational

Entering *WrestleMania 30*, AJ Lee was the longest reigning Divas Champion in history. It helped to have an enforcer like Tamina Snuka on her side, running interference when any strong challenger emerged. Vickie Guerrero had enough, and forced AJ to defend her championship in a match against 13 other Divas, including AJ's ally Tamina. The first Diva to score a pinfall or submission would be the Divas Champion. AJ did not have to be involved in the decision to lose her championship. Clearly the odds were against the champion retaining her title.

Five former Divas Champions participated: Alicia Fox, Brie Bella, Layla, Natalya, and Nikki Bella. Meanwhile, nine women—AJ Lee, Aksana, Cameron, Emma, Eva Marie, Naomi, Rosa Mendez, Summer Rae, and Tamina Snuka—made their in-ring *WrestleMania* debuts.

Things began badly for the champion and her bodyguard Tamina, when the Divas got them into the center of the ring and tossed them to the floor. The chaos continued with Divas flying in and out of the ring. After Alicia Fox took out Emma with the Scissors Kick, the match's pace quickened.

▶ *Nikki and Brie Bella take out the competition*

Meanwhile, the Bellas' tandem offense took out Tamina, followed by double-dropkicking AJ Lee off the ring apron. For a moment it seemed that the twins would fight, but instead they both dove out of the ring, taking out the rest of the competition. However, when the twins returned to the ring, they got into a shoving match, as each believed she should be the next champion.

Amid the bedlam, the resourceful champion carefully selected her moment to strike. AJ Lee crept behind Naomi and locked her in the lethal Black Widow submission move. Naomi tried to battle through the pain, but the agony was too great and she had to tap out. AJ Lee defied the odds and outlasted all the Divas to retain her championship.

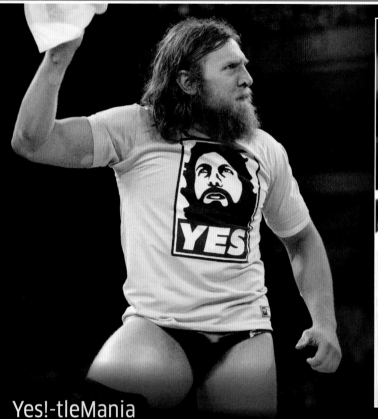

Yes!-tleMania

WrestleMania 30's closing act turned into something that neither Randy Orton nor Batista wanted: a Triple Threat Match that now included Daniel Bryan. Two years after the groundswell of "Yes" chants began at *WrestleMania XXVIII* and countless setbacks later, The Bearded Warrior had been catapulted by the WWE Universe's voice all the way to the grandest stage. Whether the former Evolution stablemates liked it or not, they had company in the main event of *WrestleMania 30*. Daniel Bryan had vaulted one last hurdle by beating Triple H in the night's opening match, earning a shot at WWE's richest prize.

Despite having his shoulder compromised in the evening's first match, Daniel Bryan started off strong, hitting Orton with a drop kick, and reversing a Batista Bomb into a flip of Batista out of the ring. Orton targeted Bryan's injured arm and threw him out of the ring as well. With Bryan incapacitated, Orton and Batista began to battle both in and out of the ring. Batista tried to deliver a Batista Bomb onto the ring steps, but Orton backflipped The Animal onto the steel instead.

Randy Orton and Batista continued to trade blows until Daniel Bryan suddenly dropped both men with a missile dropkick. Bryan continued to punish both men with kicks to the head until Orton caught Bryan's leg and delivered a T-Bone Suplex.

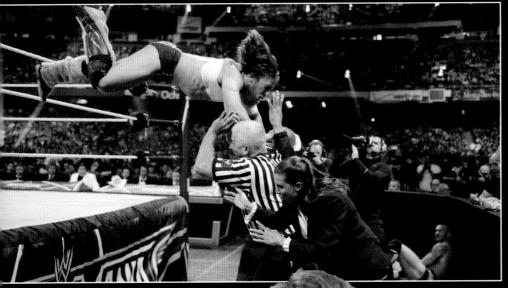

Triple H and Stephanie McMahon abruptly appeared at ringside, and The Game dragged the official out of the ring, replacing him with their own hand-picked referee. Batista planted Daniel Bryan with a brutal Spinebuster and a Batista Bomb, but Bryan kicked out of the pin. Bryan recovered long enough to take out the crooked referee, Triple H, and Stephanie.

Realizing that Bryan was still a significant threat to win the match, Orton and Batista decided to work together to take out the interloper. The Viper slammed Daniel Bryan's face, while Batista hit Daniel with a television monitor. The double-team culminated in a Batista Bomb into an RKO that broke the announcers' table. As medical personnel attended to Bryan, it seemed like Orton and Batista would finally get their one-on-one match. But Bryan would not be denied, refusing medical attention and returning to the ring.

Fighting on instinct, Bryan reversed an RKO and wrapped the champion in the Yes! Lock. Batista broke the hold, but soon found himself in the same unenviable position. When Randy Orton went to punt Batista in the skull, Bryan leveled the champion with a running knee attack. Batista then delivered a thunderous Batista Bomb on The Viper. Once again, Bryan appeared seemingly out of nowhere and nailed The Animal with another running knee strike. With Randy Orton battered on the Superdome floor, Daniel Bryan applied one last Yes! Lock, and Batista had no choice but to tap out.

In that moment, Daniel Bryan's lifelong journey had reached its apex. Daniel Bryan had become the WWE World Heavyweight Champion, and he had done it feeding off the power of one word, "YES!" Later that evening, reflecting on his titanic struggle to reach the mountaintop, an emotional Bryan managed to muster two powerful words to his faithful supporters via Twitter—"Thank you."

WRESTLEMANIA 31

LEVI'S STADIUM – SANTA CLARA, CALIFORNIA

March 29
2015

Attendance
76,976

ANNOUNCERS
Michael Cole, Jerry "The King" Lawler, John Bradshaw Layfield

RING ANNOUNCERS
Lilian Garcia, Eden Stiles

HALL OF FAME RING ANNOUNCER
Howard Finkel

SPECIAL MUSICAL GUEST
Aloe Blacc, Kid Ink, Skylar Grey, Travis Barker

Event Card

MAIN EVENT—WWE CHAMPIONSHIP MATCH
- Seth Rollins defeated Brock Lesnar (Champion) w/ Paul Heyman and Roman Reigns to become new Champion
- Triple H defeated Sting
- Undertaker defeated Bray Wyatt

UNITED STATES CHAMPIONSHIP MATCH
- John Cena defeated Rusev (Champion) w/ Lana to become the new Champion

LADDER MATCH FOR THE INTERCONTINENTAL CHAMPIONSHIP
- Daniel Bryan defeated Bad News Barrett (Champion), Dean Ambrose, Dolph Ziggler, R-Truth, Luke Harper, and Stardust to become the new Champion

FATAL 4-WAY MATCH FOR THE WWE TAG TEAM CHAMPIONSHIP
- Tyson Kidd & Cesaro (Champions) w/ Natalya defeated The Usos (Jimmy & Jey) w/ Naomi, Los Matadores (Diego and Fernando) w/ El Torito, and Big E & Kofi Kingston from the New Day w/ Xavier Woods
- AJ Lee & Paige defeated the Bella Twins
- Randy Orton defeated Seth Rollins (with J&J Security)

2ND ANNUAL ANDRÉ THE GIANT MEMORIAL BATTLE ROYAL
- Big Show defeated Adam Rose, Alex Riley, Big E, Bo Dallas, Cesaro, Curtis Axel, Damien Mizdow, Darren Young, Epico, Erick Rowan, Fandango, Goldust, Heath Slater, Hideo Itami, Jack Swagger, Jimmy Uso, Kane, Kofi Kingston, Konnor, Mark Henry, The Miz, Primo, Ryback, Sin Cara, Titus O'Neil, Tyson Kidd, Viktor, Xavier Woods, and Zack Ryder

> ## "Even after 30 years, I never experienced anything like this."
> —Sting

A Year of Firsts

In its first 30 years, *WrestleMania* was located in California five times, always in southern California. For *WrestleMania 31*, the event finally moved to the Bay Area, selling out Levi's Stadium, home to the NFL's San Francisco 49ers. There were plenty of in-ring firsts as well—starting with the WWE in-ring debut of Sting, a long-time franchise player in WCW, who faced Triple H in a one-on-one competition. The WWE Universe also got their first glimpse of UFC Champion Ronda Rousey, and witnessed a shocking end to the show, featuring the first Money in the Bank cash-in to ever occur at *WrestleMania*.

Living up to Big Expectations

The World's Largest Athlete, Big Show, came to *WrestleMania 31* with unfinished business. The year before, most had expected him to win the inaugural André the Giant Memorial Battle Royal. He'd come tantalizingly close, being the last competitor eliminated by the winner, Cesaro. He was once again a favorite for *WrestleMania 31*, but as JBL pointed out in commentary, Big Show had never actually won a Battle Royal in WWE despite his massive proportions. Show decided to leave little to chance, eliminating ten other competitors, including the previous year's winner, to become the 2015 André the Giant Battle Royal victor.

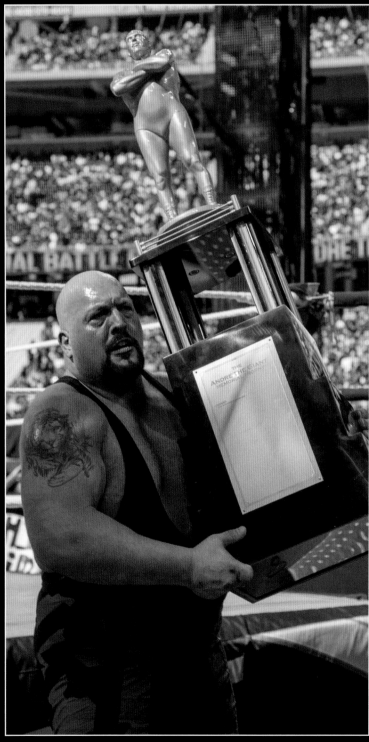

▶ The *"World's Largest Athlete"* carries the André the Giant Memorial Battle Royal trophy, an award worthy of his stature.

▶ *Chaos reigns in a Fatal 4-Way match as two triple top-rope suplexes occur simultaneously.*

Taking Out Three Other Teams

The odds are never in the champions' favor in a Fatal 4-Way Tag Team Championship match. Not only do they have to deal with three other teams, but they don't even have to be involved in the decision to lose their titles, since the first team to record a decision would claim the titles. With WWE Tag Team Champions Cesaro and Tyson Kidd facing this situation, they decided to take steps to make their title defense a little easier at *WrestleMania 31*. First, Cesaro targeted Jey Uso's ailing shoulder, tossing him into the announcer's desk in the opening moments of the match. Jey Uso was taken out of the stadium by medical personal, leaving his brother Jimmy on his own. Even down to seven men, the match was pure chaos; no one could get a three count with numerous other competitors breaking up pinning attempts. With almost everyone down, Jimmy Uso splashed Big E off the top rope, but Cesaro tagged himself in and stole the pin, allowing his team to retain their titles.

Climbing the Ladder? Yes! Winning a Title? Yes!

Daniel Bryan's *WrestleMania 30* was a storybook ending. A capacity crowd in the Superdome chanted "Yes!" along with him after he bested Randy Orton and Batista to capture the WWE World Heavyweight Championship. But the year following was anything but a happy ending as a neck injury forced Bryan to relinquish the title and spend most of the year on the sidelines. He was ready to return to action at *WrestleMania 31*, and was looking to capture the Intercontinental Championship. To do so, Bryan would have to outlast six other men and climb the ladder to grab the title. It seemed that some of the competitors, most notably Luke Harper and Bad News Barrett, were more interested in using the ladders as weapons to incapacitate their opponents. Harper tossed Dean Ambrose out of the ring onto a ladder set up across the barrier. It seemed Barrett would retain his title when he took out Dolph Ziggler, Stardust, and R-Truth with brutal Bull Hammer moves, but Bryan clocked Barrett with a running knee and outbattled Ziggler at the top of the ladder to grab the title and win his first Intercontinental Championship.

▶ *For the second straight year, Daniel Bryan left WrestleMania with a title (top right), but it wasn't easy. He battled six other men in a brutal ladder match. Bryan's kicks on competitors like Luke Harper (bottom left) were even rougher when ladders were involved.*

The Viper Strikes the Future

Throughout most of 2014, The Authority ruled WWE, using both Randy Orton and Seth Rollins to impose their will on the WWE locker room. Eventually the two figureheads of The Authority came to blows and The Authority kicked Orton out with Seth injuring Orton with a vicious Stomp move on the ring steps. When Orton returned to action, it seemed like he was back in the good graces of The Authority, but it was just a ploy to get revenge on Rollins. He finally got a one-on-one encounter with Rollins at *WrestleMania 31*. Orton wailed on Rollins in a corner early, but J&J Security looked to interfere on Rollins' behalf. They may have regretted the decision when Orton gave the pair a devastating double DDT on the floor. Their distraction did allow Rollins to gain the upper hand in the match, until Orton reversed a Curb Stomp into a nasty beating. The two traded moves with both men kicking out of his opponent's finishing maneuvers. Rollins thought he had the contest won, but Orton reversed a second curb stomp into an elevated RKO on Rollins for the three count.

▶ *Seth Rollins leaps from the top-rope attack before Randy Orton reverses it into an RKO.*

"Seth Rollins may be the future, and I certainly believe he is, but that future is not today."

—JBL

WWE vs. WCW, the Final Chapter

In the years since WWE had won the Monday Night War and purchased its rival WCW, almost every major WCW Superstar had competed in WWE, with one exception—the man known as Sting. The WWE Universe speculated endlessly about dream matchups between Sting and the WWE's biggest Superstars, but the enigmatic icon, known as WCW's Franchise, stayed away until he'd finally had enough of Triple H and The Authority running roughshod over WWE and challenged Triple H to a match at *WrestleMania 31*.

After a pair of spectacular entrances, the two standard bearers for their respective companies paced the ring, staring each other down. The two began the match tentatively, trading chops, headlocks, and a Sting dropkick that leveled a surprised Triple H. Sting kept control until Triple H dodged a Stinger Splash on the outside and Sting rammed into the wall. The Game increased the punishment by tossing Stinger into the ring steps and continued hammering him until Sting reversed a move into his patented Scorpion Deathlock. Before Triple H had to consider tapping out to the painful submission hold, D-Generation X (Road Dogg, Billy Gunn, and X-Pac) ran to the ring to interfere. The distraction allowed Triple H to nail Sting with a Pedigree, but Sting kicked out. Triple H decided to fetch his trusty sledgehammer, but this led to the New World Order coming out to take on D-Generation X and assist Sting. The two factions battled outside the ring while Sting kept the Game locked in a second Scorpion Deathlock. Sting thought he had the match won until Shawn Michaels hit Sting with Sweet Chin Music.

Again Triple H went for his sledgehammer, but the nWo handed Sting his signature baseball bat to even the score. The "Franchise" used his bat to snap Triple H's sledgehammer in two. Sting went to hit one last Stinger splash, but Triple H used the broken sledgehammer to hit Sting and cover him for the decisive three count. In a surprising show of sportsmanship, Triple H offered his hand to Sting and the two shook hands to close the match.

▶ *What started off as a one-on-one confrontation between Triple H (top left) and Sting (top right) quickly devolved into warfare when D-Generation X and the New World Order factions, emerged to support their former members.*

Battling the Bellas

Nikki Bella was the WWE Divas Champion and her twin sister Brie was more than happy to help keep the title on Nikki by attacking her #1 rival, Paige. To even the playing field, AJ Lee started teaming with Paige to create a two-on-two scenario at *WrestleMania 31*. Paige started the match aggressively, hammering at the Divas Champion Nikki. But before Paige could tag in AJ, Nikki dropped Paige with an Alabama Slam, knocked AJ off the ring, and started driving Paige's head into the mat. With AJ incapacitated outside the ring, the twins methodically worked over Paige, tagging in and out of the ring. Paige tossed the Bellas out of the ring, giving AJ enough time to recover and tag into the match. While Paige dealt with Brie outside the ring, AJ wrapped Nikki in her Black Widow submission move, and Nikki was forced to tap out, giving the duo of AJ Lee and Paige the victory.

◀ *Nikki Bella floors Paige by draping her over her shoulders and dropping Paige to the mat.*

▶ *United States Champion Rusev rolls to the ring in a Russian tank.*

Battles for the United States Championship

John Cena's first *WrestleMania* moment was capturing the United States Championship from Big Show in the opening match of *WrestleMania XX*. While he had gone on to win multiple World Championships, eleven years later he was ready to recapture the United States Championship in order to take it from Rusev, the arrogant Bulgarian Superstar who claimed the title for his adopted homeland, Russia.

The champion entered *WrestleMania 31* undefeated and had no plans to suffer his first WWE loss under the bright lights. Rusev tried to play mind games with Cena by entering the ring area on a Russian tank, but Cena would not take the bait. Instead, the Superstar entered the ring after an inspirational video amped up the WWE Universe.

Early in the match, Rusev delivered a headbutt and an overhead suplex to secure a two count. The "Bulgarian Brute" decided to humiliate Cena further by parading around the ring waving the Russian flag, but when he leaned over Cena to mock him with Cena's own "you can't see me" gesture, Cena kicked Rusev and launched a comeback. Cena tried to finish Rusev off with an Attitude Adjustment, but Rusev fought out and hit Cena with a kick. Rusev continued to punish Cena with power moves, but Cena managed to kick out of each pin attempt. Lana's attempt to insert herself in the match backfired spectacularly when Rusev accidently ran into her and Cena turned that accident into an Attitude Adjustment and a three count. Finally, Cena had the victory and the United States Championship.

▶ *The Rock and Ronda Rousey celebrate in the ring after dispatching The Authority.*

The Rock and Rousey

Triple H and Stephanie McMahon were proud to announce that the WWE Universe had set an attendance record at Levi's Stadium, with 76,976 fans in attendance. However, they were even more happy to take credit for all of WWE's growth and success since the first *WrestleMania*. When the WWE Universe started booing the egotistical leaders of The Authority, Triple H poured it on even more, bragging that he beat Sting and that they effectively owned all the Superstars of WWE and all the members of the WWE Universe. This was a bridge too far for "The People's Champion" The Rock who made his way to the ring to set Triple H and Stephanie straight.

In addition to exclaiming that The Authority did not own the people or The People's Champion, The Rock went on to challenge Triple H to create a *WrestleMania* moment then and there, mocking Triple H's manhood when he initially refused. Before the two could come to blows, Stephanie came between them. The verbal sparring between The Rock and Stephanie continued until Stephanie slapped The Rock and mocked him for not being able to strike back.

The Rock, of course, maintained his cool, but he found someone at ringside who would challenge Stephanie: UFC Bantamweight Champion Ronda Rousey. The Rock invited Rousey to join him in the ring. Stephanie tried to talk Rousey out of doing anything, first with flattery and then with threats. Things did not end the way Stephanie hoped, as Rousey, in a display of might, first tossed Triple H out of the ring and then sent Stephanie packing as well.

▶ *Undertaker uses the ring ropes to slam Bray Wyatt with a leg drop.*

A Post-Streak Victory

Despite it being a year later, much of the WWE Universe had still not recovered from the shocking end to Undertaker's undefeated *WrestleMania* streak. In fact, the WWE Universe had not seen Undertaker since Brock Lesnar had defeated him at *WrestleMania 30*. Sensing a weakened Undertaker, Bray Wyatt challenged Undertaker to a match at *WrestleMania 31*, hoping to hand him another *WrestleMania* loss and establish himself as WWE's new "Face of Fear". Undertaker accepted the challenge.

Wyatt charged at the "Dead Man" and received a big kick for his troubles. Undertaker then dropped Wyatt with a pair of shoulder blocks followed by his Old School maneuver. Wyatt was able to retaliate with a clothesline move before driving Undertaker out of the ring. Undertaker quickly recovered and nailed Wyatt with a leg drop on the ring apron. Wyatt proved to be a resilient foe, peppering Undertaker with lefts and rights to regain the upper hand in the match. Undertaker did manage to briefly lock Wyatt in a Hell's Gate submission hold, but Bray fought his way out and managed a two count on Undertaker after a Fallaway Slam. Undertaker reversed a Sister Abigail into a chokeslam and a Tombstone Piledriver maneuver, but Wyatt kicked out of the pin. Wyatt did manage to surprise Undertaker with a Sister Abigail, but the "Dead Man" kicked out of the pin. After the two traded blows, Wyatt attempted another Sister Abigail, but Undertaker delivered another Tombstone Piledriver instead to record the pinfall and the victory.

Reigns' Reign Delayed

After making his initial mark on WWE as one third of The Shield, "The Big Dog" Roman Reigns stepped up to singles competition. He was ready to reach the top of the WWE mountain, winning the 2015 *Royal Rumble*, which guaranteed him a title shot in the main event of *WrestleMania 31*. His opponent, reigning WWE Champion "The Beast" Brock Lesnar. If Reigns was going to become the WWE Champion, he was going to have to earn it at *WrestleMania* against one of the most dominant champions in WWE history.

Lesnar, accompanied by his advocate Paul Heyman, circled the ring, glaring up at his opponent Reigns like a big cat stalking its prey. Reigns launched himself at the champion, hammering Lesnar with blows that temporarily caused Lesnar to stagger, but he then countered with a powerful German suplex and an F5 move. Rather than go for a pin attempt, Lesnar dished out more punishment, landing three additional German suplexes. Reigns fought back with a few punches, but Lesnar decked the challenger once again. Every time Reigns would gain some momentum, Lesnar would regain control of the match with his sheer power and devastating suplexes. After a few more suplexes and an F5, Lesnar finally decided to go for the pin but to the shock of the champion, Reigns kicked out before the three count. Reigns further enraged Lesnar by kicking out after a third F5 move. As Lesnar tried to inflict more damage on the challenger, Reigns finally turned the tide by driving Lesnar into a ring post, then hitting him with multiple Superman Punches and Spears. Out of desperation, Lesnar hit Reigns with another F5 which left both men down in the ring. Then came an unexpected interruption.

"The Architect", Seth Rollins, sprinted to the ring with his Money in the Bank briefcase, and cashed it in, turning the main event of *WrestleMania 31* into a Triple Threat Match. Rollins hit Lesnar with a Stomp move, but "The Beast" had Rollins up for an F5 until Reigns hit Lesnar with a Spear, saving his former Shield partner. Rollins then delivered a Stomp to Reigns, pinning The Big Dog and stealing the WWE Championship from both the title holder and his #1 challenger.

▶ *The bout between Brock Lesnar and Roman Reigns (left) was crashed by Money in the Bank winner Seth Rollins, who stole a victory and claimed the WWE Championship (right).*

WRESTLEMANIA 32

AT&T STADIUM – ARLINGTON, TEXAS

April 3
2016

Attendance
101,763

ANNOUNCERS
Michael Cole, John Bradshaw
Layfield, and Byron Saxton

RING ANNOUNCERS
Lilian Garcia, Eden Stiles

SPECIAL MUSICAL GUESTS
Fifth Harmony, Snoop Dogg

Event Card

MAIN EVENT—WWE CHAMPIONSHIP MATCH
- Roman Reigns defeated Triple H (Champion) w/ Stephanie McMahon to become new Champion

HELL IN A CELL MATCH
- Undertaker defeated Shane McMahon

TRIPLE THREAT MATCH TO CROWN THE INAUGURAL WWE WOMEN'S CHAMPION
- Charlotte Flair w/ Ric Flair defeated Becky Lynch and Sasha Banks to become new Champion

  LADDER MATCH FOR THE INTERCONTINENTAL CHAMPIONSHIP
  - Zack Ryder defeated Kevin Owens (Champion), Sami Zayn, Dolph Ziggler, The Miz, Sin Cara, and Stardust to become new Champion
    - Team Total Divas (Alicia Fox, Brie Bella, Eva Marie, Natalya, and Paige) defeated Team B.A.D. & Blonde (Emma, Lana, Naomi, Summer Rae, and Tamina)

- Chris Jericho defeated AJ Styles
- The Rock defeated Erick Rowan w/ Bray Wyatt and Braun Strowman

NO HOLDS BARRED STREET FIGHT
- Brock Lesnar w/ Paul Heyman defeated Dean Ambrose

3RD ANNUAL ANDRÉ THE GIANT MEMORIAL BATTLE ROYAL
- Baron Corbin defeated Adam Rose, Bo Dallas, Curtis Axel, Damien Sandow, Darren Young, Fandango, Diamond Dallas Page, R-Truth, Tatanka, Tyler Breeze, Goldust, Heath Slater, Jack Swagger, Kane, Konnor, Mark Henry, Viktor, Big Show, and Shaquille O'Neal

SIX-MAN TAG MATCH
- The League of Nations (Alberto Del Rio, Rusev, and Sheamus) w/ King Barrett defeated The New Day (Kofi Kingston, Big E, and Xavier Woods)

UNITED STATES CHAMPIONSHIP MATCH
- Kalisto (Champion) defeated Ryback
- The Usos (Jimmy & Jey) defeated The Dudley Boyz (Bubba Ray & D-Von)

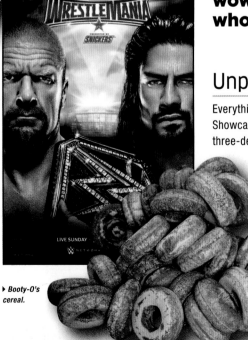

▶ *Booty-O's cereal.*

> **"I had this stupid grin on my face, like wow... a guy from Gainesville, Georgia, who finally made it to *WrestleMania*."**
>
> —AJ Styles

Unprecedented Struggles for Power

Everything is bigger in Texas, and that saying applies to *WrestleMania* as well. "The Showcase of the Immortals" came to Dallas for *WrestleMania 32*, and an almost three-decade-old attendance record fell by the wayside, as more than 101,000 fans filled AT&T Stadium. The McMahon family suffered two serious defeats: Shane McMahon's attempt to take control of WWE fell in a hellacious battle with Undertaker; and Shane's sister, Stephanie, and her husband, Triple H, collectively known as The Authority, lost a significant portion of their power when Roman Reigns defeated Triple H and won the WWE World Heavyweight Championship.

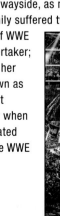

The Bigger They Come...

Some of the most entertaining WWE matches feature competitors with vastly different styles and sizes. United States Champion Kalisto faced such a challenge at *WrestleMania 32*, defending his title against Ryback, a man 9in (23cm) taller and 120lbs (54kg) heavier than the champion. This size disparity made Ryback confident he would win easily, and the early portions of the match seemed to bear out his confidence as he tossed the smaller champion around "like a ragdoll," according to announcer Jerry "The King" Lawler. Kalisto, however, demonstrated he had his own high-flying offense,

hitting Ryback with a Top-rope Bulldog and two knees into the challenger's chest. Ryback reclaimed control of the match with a modified Michinoku Driver and a potent Spinebuster. But his luck changed when Kalisto hit a drop toehold that drove Ryback's skull into an exposed turnbuckle. The champion then hit the stunned challenger with his spectacular Salida del Sol for the three-count victory.

◀ *Kalisto shows off his United States Championship to the WWE Universe.*

10-Women Tag Action

Perhaps tiring of the positive press received by the cast of TV reality show *Total Divas*, Team B.A.D. (Naomi & Tamina) aligned themselves with Summer Rae, Lana, and Emma to take on Natalya, Brie Bella, Paige, Alicia Fox, and Eva Marie in a five-on-five battle. Alicia Fox and Summer Rae started the action for their respective teams, but the official soon lost control of the match when members from both teams got involved without waiting for official tags. When the match settled down, Team B.A.D. & Blonde isolated Paige and punished her with power moves from Tamina and rapid tags to her partners. Paige was finally able to tag in Brie Bella, who got Naomi into her trademark Yes Lock!, forcing Naomi to tap out.

▶ *Team Total Divas lifts Brie Bella to celebrate her clinching the win for their team.*

Past and Present Collide

The Usos thought that they had valuable allies and mentors in The Dudley Boyz, but D-Von and Bubba Ray turned on the Uso brothers after an eight-man tag match and sent Jimmy and Jey through tables. Looking for revenge, The Usos challenged The Dudleys to a tag match at *WrestleMania 32.*

At first, The Usos may have regretted their decision as, immediately after the bell rang, The Dudleys attacked, dumping Jey out of the ring, so they could focus all their attention on Jimmy. Bubba Ray attempted to further embarrass Jimmy by calling out the damage he was doing to him and how they used to do the same to his Superstar father, Rikishi. This showboating allowed Jimmy to recover long enough to nail Bubba Ray with a Superkick and tag in his brother Jey. The fresher Uso managed to unleash a series of kicks and pin D-Von for the win. However, The Usos weren't finished—they got revenge by putting both of the Dudley Boyz through tables with splashes, creating their own memorable *WrestleMania* moment.

Ryder Captures Gold

For the second consecutive year, the Intercontinental Champion was forced to defend the title against six other opponents in a Ladder Match. Kevin Owens had to feel that the odds of keeping his title weren't great, seeing that Bad News Barrett had lost the title in the same type of match the year before. As soon as the match started, all the competitors rushed out of the ring searching for ladders, leaving Owens alone in the center. Each time his opponents attempted to re-enter the ring, Owens knocked them out again, until his former best friend Sami Zayn started brawling with him, the duo unleashing furious blows on each other. Dolph Ziggler impressed the WWE Universe with a flurry of Superkicks, until Kevin Owens took him out with a kick of his own. Owens also nailed Zayn with a frog splash onto a ladder. Sin Cara almost made it to the top, but Owens tipped over the ladder, sending Cara crashing down and through another ladder, which had Stardust on it. With everyone down, the cocky Miz thought he had the title won, but Zack Ryder sprinted up the ladder, pushed The Miz off, and grabbed the title to claim his first-ever Intercontinental Championship.

▶ *Zack Ryder drops an elbow off the ladder onto The Miz.*

> ## "Zack Ryder, for over a decade of futility in WWE, has the ultimate answer for those who doubted... Zack Ryder is the Intercontinental Champion!"
>
> —Michael Cole

▶ *Chris Jericho tries to force AJ Styles to submit to the Walls of Jericho.*

Spoiling AJ's WrestleMania Debut

The 2016 *Royal Rumble* featured one of the most exciting debuts in WWE history—that of international phenomenon AJ Styles. While the WWE Universe loved seeing Styles compete in the ring, one man, Chris Jericho, was jealous of the praise the fans showered Styles with, believing they should only cheer him, "Y2J." So he ambushed Styles after the pair competed as a tag team and the rivalry between the two escalated until only a match at *WrestleMania 32* would settle their issues.

Styles gained an early advantage by clotheslining Jericho out of the ring. He then tried to launch himself onto Jericho, but Y2J was able to dropkick him, following up with a Neckbreaker and a Flying Elbow. Styles recaptured the momentum by raining a series of blows and kicks on Jericho, beginning a dizzying back and forth between these two evenly matched competitors. Jericho thought he had the match won with his trademark Walls of Jericho maneuver, but Styles fought out. Styles then locked Jericho in his Calf Crusher but Jericho managed to battle his way out of this painful submission hold. The two matched each other hold for hold, counter for counter, until both were exhausted.

Styles looked to end the match once and for all with one last Phenomenal Forearm, but Jericho leaped in the air just in time and reversed the move into a Code Breaker that allowed him to secure the three count and win this tight contest.

A Legendary Beatdown

Generally, The New Day—Xavier Woods, Kofi Kingston, and Big E— have a numbers advantage in their tag team matches. Even though the matches are two on two, the third member of The New Day is usually ringside and often inserts himself into the flow of the match. The League of Nations was able to turn the tables on The New Day, when the four men challenged The New Day at *WrestleMania*. Only Alberto Del Rio, Sheamus, and Rusev were competing, but King Barratt accompanied his stablemates to the ring, giving the League a one-man advantage. At first, the team didn't need any help. They isolated Xavier Woods from his corner and, by tagging in and out quickly, punished him with a variety of moves. Xavier finally made it back to his corner and the match became more even, thanks to Big E's power and Kingston's high-flying moves. But the League's extra man advantage eventually counted. Woods had tagged back into the match, and the official was distracted by members of both teams fighting at ringside. Sheamus sent Woods into the ropes and King Barrett struck him with his Bull Hammer maneuver, allowing Sheamus to record the three count for the victorious League of Nations.

The real highlight came at the end of the match. The League celebrated their victory in the ring, and King Barrett got on the mic to proclaim that no three men could ever beat the League of Nations. To the wild approval of the live audience, three legendary Hall of Famers came to the ring—Shawn Michaels, Mick Foley, and Stone Cold Steve Austin. The League mocked these former champions, pointing out that they still had a four-on-three advantage; however, things evened up when The New Day pulled King Barrett out of the ring, allowing Michaels to hit Sweet Chin Music on Del Rio, Foley to use his Socko Claw on Sheamus, and Stone Cold to deliver a Stunner on Rusev. The New Day then tossed Barrett back into the ring, and the boastful King got all three moves performed on him. The New Day tried to celebrate in the ring with the legends, but Stone Cold gave Woods a Stunner for their impertinence.

▶ *The New Day mock Hall of Famers Shawn Michaels, Stone Cold Steve Austin, and Mick Foley.*

▶ *Dean Ambrose stuns Brock Lesnar by blasting him with a fire extinguisher.*

"The Lunatic" and "The Beast"

If you ask most of Brock Lesnar's opponents, they would admit that Suplex City is a place they'd rather never visit again. But Dean Ambrose is not like most competitors. In the months leading up to *WrestleMania 32*, every time Brock beat down "The Lunatic Fringe," he would get up, ready for more. Lesnar even sent Ambrose to the hospital, but Ambrose drove an ambulance back to the arena and dragged himself to the ring, saying that Lesnar could not keep him down. He challenged "The Beast" to a No Holds Barred Street Fight, and Paul Heyman, Lesnar's advocate, gladly accepted.

Lesnar came charging out of the gate at the start of the match, hitting Ambrose with a trio of brutal suplexes. Ambrose grabbed a kendo stick and unleashed a series of blows on Lesnar, but that only seemed to anger "The Beast" and he nailed Ambrose with a few more suplexes. He stomped Ambrose in the corner and followed up with two more suplexes. Lesnar begain taunting Ambrose, but he turned the tide by hitting Lesnar with a low blow, more kendo stick shots and, while Lesnar was out of the ring, a flying dive. Ambrose seemed ready to take things too far when he pulled out a chainsaw, but thankfully it refused to start. Ambrose went to the top rope for a high-flying maneuver, but Lesnar caught him and delivered a top-rope superplex that sent Ambrose hurtling out of the ring. Lesnar tried to pull Ambrose back into the ring, but Ambrose blasted "The Beast" with a fire extinguisher he'd found under the ring. Ambrose then hit Lesnar with a series of chair shots. After getting a two count on Lesnar, Ambrose again left the ring, and tossed several more chairs into the ring. Lesnar looked to finish Ambrose off with an F5, but Ambrose reversed it into a DDT, securing another two count. Sensing he was close to victory, Ambrose brought in his final weapon, a baseball bat wrapped in barbed wire. Lesnar avoided being hit with the bat and, instead, nailed Ambrose with another suplex and an F5 onto the pile of chairs, earning the pinfall victory over Ambrose.

A New Women's Championship

During the *WrestleMania* pre-show, WWE Hall of Famer Lita made a special announcement—the Divas Championship was being retired and, in its place, the women Superstars of WWE would be competing for the WWE Women's Championship. *WrestleMania 32* would feature a Triple Threat Match for this title featuring three standouts from the recent Women's Revolution—Becky Lynch, Sasha Banks, and current WWE Divas Champion Charlotte Flair. The three women knew each other well, having clashed in NXT before joining WWE. Familiarity had definitely bred contempt among the trio; each of them wanted to show the fans she was the class of the WWE Women's Division.

The match started with a flurry of attempted pinfalls. Sasha was knocked to the outside, leaving Charlotte and Becky alone in the ring. Becky took early control with an inverted DDT, but Charlotte kicked out. Sasha rejoined the match, dumping Becky out of the ring. Charlotte and Sasha traded moves without either gaining an advantage. Their back-and-forth gave Becky time to recover and reinsert herself into the match

Charlotte locked her Figure 8 submission move on Becky, but before Lynch tapped out, Banks broke the hold by hitting Charlotte with a frog splash off the top turnbuckle. Charlotte kicked out of the pinfall attempt at two, frustrating Banks. The three-way battle continued out of the ring; Becky dove onto Sasha, but Sasha pulled Charlotte's father, Ric Flair into Becky's path and "The Irish Lass Kicker" accidentally took out "The Nature Boy." Charlotte saw her chance and executed a moonsault off the top rope onto both Sasha and Becky.

Charlotte and Becky battled to the top rope and Sasha tossed Becky off the turnbuckle and started raining blows on Flair. Becky did not stay down long, leaping back onto the ring and dropping Sasha into a Tree of Woe. She then nailed Flair with a Becksploder Suplex, forcing Flair out of the ring. Becky went to slam Sasha, but "The Boss" reversed it into a Backstabber and locked Lynch in her Bank Statement submission move. Flair re-entered the ring, tossing Banks out onto the floor and then put Becky into her Figure 8. Sasha tried to break the hold, but Ric Flair grabbed hold of her and Becky was forced to submit, making Charlotte Flair the first-ever WWE Women's Champion.

▶ *Charlotte Flair launches a top-rope moonsault onto both Becky Lynch and Sasha Banks.*

Hell to Pay for Shane

After a more than six-year absence, Shane McMahon made a shocking return to WWE in February 2016. He confronted his father and sister in the ring, telling Mr. McMahon that he was back and looking for control of *RAW*. Mr. McMahon agreed to give Shane an opportunity to earn what he wanted—all Shane had to do was win a match at *WrestleMania 32*. Shane agreed, but realized he had a tough task ahead when his father revealed that Shane's opponent would be Undertaker and the match would be Hell in a Cell. To ensure that "The Deadman" was fully motivated, Mr. McMahon promised that if Undertaker lost, he would never compete at *WrestleMania* again.

Shane arrived ringside accompanied by his three sons and glanced nervously at the ominous cage. Undertaker followed, and the cage was sealed tight on the two competitors. Shane quickly demonstrated he was not intimidated, attempting to trade blows with Undertaker until he leveled Shane with a ferocious hit. Undertaker went for an early pin, but Shane surprised him by putting him in a triangle chokehold, which Undertaker had to struggle to fight out of.

Undertaker brought the ring steps to the ring and tried to put Shane away by chokeslamming him onto them, but Shane managed to kick out at two. Undertaker tried to drop an elbow on Shane while he was draped across the steps, but Shane moved at the last minute and Undertaker hit the steps with his full weight. The two swapped submission moves, with Undertaker locking Shane into his Hell's

▶ *Shane McMahon risks everything by diving off the top of the cell onto Undertaker.*

Gate, and Shane eventually reversing it into a painful Sharpshooter. Neither man would submit. Shane wowed the WWE Universe by hitting a Coast to Coast move, driving a garbage can into the face of "The Deadman," but, to Shane's chagrin, Undertaker kicked out. Shane then retrieved a bolt cutter from under the ring and cut some of the bolts holding the cell together. The move backfired on Shane, however, as Undertaker grabbed him and drove him through the panel and outside of the cell.

Undertaker once again tried to finish Shane off with a Tombstone onto the announcers' table, but Shane blocked the move by putting a Sleeper Hold on "The Deadman." The two crashed through the table and Shane recovered first. He grabbed a toolbox and hit Undertaker with it twice and then nailed "The Deadman" with a television monitor, leaving Undertaker prone on another table. Shane then climbed onto the top of the cell and leaped off, looking to drop a devastating elbow on Undertaker. Undertaker moved at the last second and Shane took the entire brunt of the fall, crashing through a table. Undertaker carried his opponent back into the ring, delivered a Tombstone Piledriver, and pinned Shane to win the match.

▶ *Two of the world's largest athletes, NBA Hall of Famer Shaquille O'Neal and Big Show, square off.*

Welcome to the Ring: Shaquille O'Neal!

The third annual André the Giant Battle Royal got off to a surprise start when the final entrant was revealed. The 20th competitor turned out to be none other than Shaquille O'Neal, stunning the WWE Universe. The other Superstars in the match were just as amazed as the basketball Hall of Famer entered the ring. The previous year's winner, Big Show, immediately confronted the NBA star. Kane tried to attack both men, but received a double chokeslam. After Big Show eliminated Fandango, O'Neal matched him by taking out Damian Sandow. The two titans then attacked each other. This was a mistake, as the other competitors joined forces to eliminate both giants.

In a blast from the past, Diamond Dallas Page eliminated Viktor from the Ascension, but his partner, Konnor, got revenge by dumping DDP out of the ring. NXT callup Baron Corbin, making his WWE debut, eliminated three other Superstars, including "The Big Red Monster" Kane, becoming the third-ever André the Giant Battle Royal Champion.

▶ *NXT standout Baron Corbin throws Kane out of the ring in his WWE debut.*

▶ *The Rock hits Bray Wyatt with a Rock Bottom.*

The Rock Takes on The Wyatt Family

When it comes to making *WrestleMania* moments, few have been as successful as "The Most Electrifying Man in Sports Entertainment"—The Rock. Once again, "The Great One" delighted the WWE Universe by coming to *WrestleMania*, and he brought the world-famous Dallas Cowboys Cheerleaders with him. The Rock was honored to announce that the WWE Universe had set an attendance record with a crowd 101,763 strong. Before The Rock could go any further, he was interrupted by Bray Wyatt and The Wyatt Family. "The Eater of Worlds" Bray Wyatt came out to threaten The Rock, so The Rock challenged a member of the Wyatt Family to a match. Erick Rowan responded, and soon wished he hadn't. The Rock gave him a Rock Bottom and pinned Rowan in just six seconds, breaking yet another *WrestleMania* record for the all-time shortest match.

The Wyatt Family didn't take kindly to The Rock setting a *WrestleMania* record at their expense, so the trio surrounded the ring, ready to dispense a three-on-one beatdown on "The Great One." Three on one became three on two when John Cena arrived to help his two-time *WrestleMania* rival. They quickly dispatched the three members of The Wyatt Family and celebrated with the crowd.

Rebelling Against The Authority

For Roman Reigns, the path to the top of WWE seemed to be continually blocked by The Authority. It didn't have to be that way—Stephanie McMahon and Triple H, a.k.a. The Authority, were happy to have Reigns be WWE Champion and the face of the company, as long as he did their bidding. Twice they told him that if he played ball, they would make his path to the championship an easy one. Reigns refused to compromise his integrity and won the title through sheer hard work, overcoming a number of challenges put in his way by The Authority to defeat Sheamus for the WWE Championship.

Triple H and Stephanie McMahon were not done stacking the deck against "The Big Dog," however. Generally, the Royal Rumble Match is used to determine who would challenge the WWE Champion at *WrestleMania*. However, Reigns was forced to defend his title in the 2016 Rumble Match. As entrant #1, he put on an amazing show, making it to the final three participants. However, the man who entered as #30—Triple H himself—won the match and became the WWE Champion. At least Reigns earned the number one contender's spot, enabling him to challenge "The Game" for the title in *WrestleMania 32*'s main event.

Early in the match, Triple H lived up to his "Cerebral Assassin" moniker, getting under the skin of Reigns in hopes that "The Big Dog" would let his anger lead to a mistake. Reigns refused to take the bait, and mocked Triple H with a D-Generation X Crotch Chop. Reigns backed up his taunts with a couple of clotheslines and some meaty blows. The Champ looked in trouble, until Stephanie McMahon distracted the official, allowing Triple H to hit Reigns with a low blow.

The illegal move changed the momentum of the match, and Triple H kept wearing down Reigns, hitting him with a series of inverted Atomic Drops and a Spinebuster. The action spilled out of the ring, with Triple H bouncing Reigns' head off an announce table. Reigns launched a comeback that Triple H short-circuited by tossing Reigns over the announce table. The champion continued to dismantle Reigns until Roman nailed Triple H with a surprise blow. The match continued to build in intensity, with each man disregarding his own safety to punish his opponent. One particularly brutal moment occurred when Reigns speared Triple H through a barricade surrounding the ring, damaging himself as well.

Triple H tried to slow things down with a series of submission moves focused on Reigns' left arm. Twice Reigns used his unbelievable strength to lift "The Game" and slam him to the mat, forcing Triple H to relinquish his holds. Reigns nailed Triple H with a wicked spear, but before the official could complete his three count, Stephanie McMahon pulled him out of the ring to argue matters. She continued to berate the official and was accidentally speared by Reigns when Triple H ducked out of the way. A downed Stephanie still managed to insert herself into the match when she handed Triple H his signature sledgehammer to finish off the challenger. However, Triple H never got the chance to use it: Reigns hit the champion with two Superman Punches and a Spear to pin him and win the WWE World Heavyweight Championship for the third time in his career.

▶ *Roman Reigns takes out his frustration with The Authority on its leader, WWE Champion Triple H.*

WRESTLEMANIA 33

CAMPING WORLD STADIUM – ORLANDO, FLORIDA

April 2

2017

Attendance

75,245

ANNOUNCERS
Michael Cole, John Bradshaw Layfield, Corey Graves, Tom Phillips, David Otunga, Jim Ross, Jerry "The King" Lawler, Byron Saxton

RING ANNOUNCERS
JoJo, Greg Hamilton, Al Roker

SPECIAL MUSICAL GUESTS
Stephen Marley, Pitbull, Flo Rida, LunchMoney Lewis, The New Day

Event Card

MAIN EVENT—NO HOLDS BARRED MATCH
- Roman Reigns defeated Undertaker

UNIVERSAL CHAMPIONSHIP MATCH
- Brock Lesnar w/ Paul Heyman defeated Goldberg (Champion) to become new Champion

UNITED STATES CHAMPIONSHIP MATCH
- Kevin Owens defeated Chris Jericho (Champion) to become new Champion

FATAL 4-WAY ELIMINATION MATCH FOR THE RAW WOMEN'S CHAMPIONSHIP
- Bayley (Champion) defeated Nia Jax, Sasha Banks, and Charlotte Flair

NON-SANCTIONED MATCH
- Seth Rollins defeated Triple H w/ Stephanie McMahon

FATAL 4-WAY LADDER MATCH FOR THE WWE RAW TAG TEAM CHAMPIONSHIP
- The Hardy Boyz (Matt & Jeff) defeated Cesaro & Sheamus, Enzo Amore & Big Cass, and Luke Gallows & Karl Anderson (Champions)

to become new Champions
- John Cena & Nikki Bella defeated The Miz & Maryse

SIX-PACK CHALLENGE FOR THE SMACKDOWN WOMEN'S CHAMPIONSHIP
- Naomi defeated Alexa Bliss (Champion), Becky Lynch, Carmella w/ James Ellsworth, Mickie James, and Natalya

ANDRÉ THE GIANT MEMORIAL BATTLE ROYAL
- Mojo Rawley defeated Adam Rose, Bo Dallas, Curtis Axel, Damien Sandow, Darren Young, Fandango, Diamond Dallas Page, R-Truth, Tatanka, Tyler Breeze, Goldust, Heath Slater, Jack Swagger, Kane, Konnor, Mark Henry, Viktor, Big Show, and Shaquille O'Neal

CRUISERWEIGHT CHAMPIONSHIP MATCH
- Neville (Champion) defeated Austin Aries

INTERCONTINENTAL CHAMPIONSHIP MATCH
- Dean Ambrose (Champion) defeated Baron Corbin

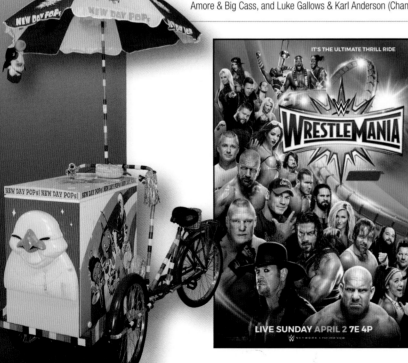

"You don't get many moments like this, if ever, in your life."

—Roman Reigns

Furor, Frenzy, and Fun in Florida

For the first time since 2008, WrestleMania returned to Orlando for the "Ultimate Thrill Ride." The first WrestleMania event to be held since the 2016 brand split between SmackDown and RAW saw eight championships contested, including a WrestleMania rematch that had been 13 years in the making.

▶ *Neville defies gravity with his Red Arrow move to finish off Austin Aries.*

The Cruiserweights Return

A Cruiserweight Championship was set to be defended for the first time since *WrestleMania XX*. Current champion Neville was looking to deliver a royal beatdown to number one contender Austin Aries. Neville showed little respect for Aries, but the challenger pushed Neville to his limit with a deep arm drag, a dropkick, and an elbow off the second rope. Aries attempted to keep up his momentum with a dive outside the ring, but Neville was ready and dropped his opponent with a vicious kick.

Neville tried to finish off Aries by climbing to the top rope, but Aries followed him and executed a perfect top-rope Hurricanrana that sent the champion flying across the ring. Aries rolled Neville into his Last Chancery chokehold submission move, and the desperate champion raked Aries across his recently surgically repaired eye sockets to escape the hold. Neville then hit Aries with his Red Arrow move to secure the pinfall and retain his championship.

Last Men Standing

The fourth annual André the Giant Memorial Battle Royal featured Superstars from *SmackDown*, *RAW*, and NXT. The chances of a repeat winner seemed strong at first, as 2015 winner Big Show dominated, until Braun Strowman amazed the WWE Universe by dumping Show out of the ring. Realizing that Strowman was now the favorite to win, most of the remaining competitors worked together to eliminate him.

Eliminations were fast and furious. American Alpha tag team took out three competitors, and the rest of the field eliminated Jordan and Gable. History was made when Tian Bing, the first Chinese competitor to appear in a WWE match, eliminated both members of Breezango, but Dolph Ziggler took him out. The final three were two *SmackDown* competitors, Mojo Rawley and Jinder Mahal, as well as NXT's Killian Dane. Mahal was stomping on Rawley outside the ring and taunting Rawley's friend, New England Patriot tight end Rob Gronkowski, who was watching ringside. When Mahal tossed a drink in Gronk's face, the NFL star followed Mahal into the ring and dropped him with a shoulder tackle. This allowed Rawley to eliminate both Dane and Mahal, winning the match. Mojo and Gronk celebrated the victory inside the ring.

Dirty Deeds Beat Dirty Tricks

Dean Ambrose entered *WrestleMania 33* as Intercontinental Champion. His challenger, Baron Corbin, had previously done everything he could to soften up Ambrose leading into his WrestleMania title defense by sneakily attacking the champion with a lead pipe and a forklift, damaging the ribs of "The Lunatic Fringe" in the process. Corbin targeted those ribs early in their match with a couple of brutal clotheslines, following up with a trio of shots that drove Ambrose's back into the ring post. The two showed their vicious sides by taking the battle out of the ring, slamming each other into the ring barricades. Ambrose finally turned the momentum of the contest by dodging a pair of Corbin attacks: the first resulted in "The Lone Wolf" smacking into the ring post; the second led Corbin to collide with the ring steps. Increasingly frustrated at his inability to keep the champion down, Corbin resorted to his signature End of Days finishing move. But Ambrose brilliantly reversed the move into a Dirty Deeds DDT to pin Corbin and retain the Intercontinental Championship.

▶ *Dean Ambrose drops an elbow onto his Intercontinental Championship challenger, Baron Corbin.*

Who Rules SmackDown?

The 2016 WWE brand split between *RAW* and *SmackDown* put Shane McMahon in charge of *SmackDown*. One of his top Superstars, former WWE Champion AJ Styles, claimed that Shane had deprived him of a title opportunity and launched Shane into a car window. *SmackDown* General Manager Daniel Bryan wanted to fire Styles, but McMahon wanted revenge by facing Styles at *WrestleMania*. Styles jumped at the idea, eager to embarrass McMahon in the ring.

Wary of Shane's punching prowess, Styles tried to make the match a more technical contest, but Shane surprised him with a variety of maneuvers. Styles decided to mock Shane by attempting one of the *SmackDown* Commissioner's signature moves—the Coast to Coast. However Shane was ready and tossed a can into Styles midair. Shane then showed Styles how it was done by executing his own Coast to Coast. McMahon looked to finish Styles off by driving an elbow into him from the top rope, but Styles countered by jumping out of the way and letting Shane crash through the table. Styles then rolled out of the path of Shane's Shooting Star Press move then leapt from the top rope to land a Phenomenal Forearm and a pinfall victory.

▶ *AJ Styles tries to finish off Shane McMahon with a Phenomenal Forearm.*

Former Best Friends Collide

Chris Jericho had been the best possible friend for Kevin Owens, helping Owens retain his Universal Championship over several months. But at Chris Jericho's Festival of Friendship, Owens made it abundantly clear he was only using Jericho to remain as champion. Owens emphasized this point by beating Jericho down. Jericho was able to gain a measure of revenge by costing Owens the Universal Championship, so Owens decided to take Jericho's United States Championship at *WrestleMania 33*.

The two began their bout hammering each other with punches. Jericho shocked Owens with an early Walls of Jericho move, but Owens forced a break by reaching the ring ropes. Jericho kept his momentum going early, but Owens soon took control with a Cannonball into the corner and by tossing Jericho out of the ring. Owens wasn't satisfied with physical domination; he also mocked Jericho with a barrage of insults. The two competitors traded blows and moves with neither able to keep his opponent down. Owens tried to end the match by hooking in Jericho's own Walls of Jericho submission move, but Y2J was able to counter. Owens nearly won the match with a Pop-up Powerbomb, but Jericho kicked out of the pinfall right before the three count.

Owens went for a trademark Pop-up Powerbomb, only to see Jericho reverse it into a Codebreaker. An exhausted Jericho climbed over to cover Owens for a three count, but Owens managed to get a single finger on the ring rope to stop the count. Owens then rolled out of the ring, and as Jericho followed, Owens kicked Y2J and then executed a painful Powerbomb into the ring apron. He then rolled Jericho back into the ring and pinned him, capturing the United States Championship for the first time in his career.

▶ *Chris Jericho nails his former best friend Kevin Owens with a Lionsault.*

▶ *Bayley slams her elbow down on Charlotte.*

Four-way Championship Scrap

After Bayley achieved her lifetime dream of winning the *RAW* Women's Championship, there was no shortage of contenders looking to step up and challenge her for the title at *WrestleMania 33*. The Superstar Bayley beat for the title, Charlotte Flair, felt that she was owed a rematch, and three-time champion Sasha Banks thought that she deserved a shot as well. Nia Jax, the most powerful woman on the *RAW* roster, was also looking to give the championship a permanent home around her waist. With all three having valid claims, Bayley was put in the unenviable position of defending her title in a Fatal 4-Way Elimination Match.

Jax opened the match by overpowering Charlotte Flair. She then turned her attention to Sasha and Bayley, tossing them around like rag dolls. Jax's brute strength led the other three combatants to temporarily set aside their rivalries and work together. For a time, this tactic didn't seem to work and Jax continued to dominate, but eventually the trio managed to pull a Triple Powerbomb on Jax and all three covered her to keep her shoulders down for the three count.

Now down to three competitors, Flair was initially content to let Bayley and Banks slug it out. But after the two started battling outside the ring, Flair nailed the pair with a perfectly executed Corkscrew Moonsault. Charlotte rolled Sasha back into the ring and went to hit her trademark Natural Selection move, but Banks countered with her Bank Statement submission hold. After escaping the maneuver, a frustrated Flair removed the padding from the second turnbuckle and then launched Banks headfirst into it, securing the pinfall and eliminating her.

So the match was down to the reigning champion Bayley and the four-time title holder Flair. Bayley was favoring her left knee, which had been injured earlier in the contest. Charlotte wrapped Bayley's legs into a Figure Four Leglock, but before she could bridge it into her signature Figure Eight, Bayley reached the ring ropes, forcing a break. Charlotte decided to punish Bayley's knee further, hanging the champion in a Tree of Woe and kicking the knee some more, but Bayley was able to reverse the attack into a top-rope suplex. Flair decided to dive at Bayley's knee, but the champion moved and Charlotte rammed her own head into the steel of the turnbuckle she had exposed earlier in the match. Bayley dropped an elbow on Flair from the top rope and pinned her, thus successfully defending her title on her first *WrestleMania* appearance.

Return of The Hardy Boyz

RAW Tag Team Champions Luke Gallows and Karl Anderson were set to defend their titles in a Ladder Match against two teams—the duo of Sheamus & Cesaro and the team of Enzo Amore & Big Cass. The New Day were the hosts of *WrestleMania*, and when they came out before the match they had an exciting announcement—there would be a fourth team, the returning Hardy Boyz.

While the Hardys had not competed in a WWE match in almost seven years, they showed no signs of rust, taking the battle to the Champs while Cesaro & Sheamus and Enzo & Big Cass fought outside the ring. Both Gallows and Anderson were the recipients of the Hardys' signature Poetry in Motion double-team move. Matt Hardy then introduced the first ladder to the ring, which he used as a weapon against the other teams. Big Cass got his team back in the match by delivering big boots to both Jeff and Matt Hardy. Sheamus and Cesaro demonstrated their potent offense by nailing the two champions with a simultaneous swing from Cesaro on Anderson and a rhythmic beating of Gallow's chest by Sheamus. Enzo and Big Cass tried to climb the ladder and retrieve the championships, but Sheamus and Gallows worked together to slam Big Cass into another ladder. Enzo thought this left him a clear path up the ladder, but Anderson dropped him off the ladder into Sheamus' European Uppercut.

With bodies strewn about the ring, Jeff Hardy took out both Sheamus and Cesaro by dropping them both with a Swanton Bomb off the top of a 20-foot (7-meter) ladder. With all their competitors down, Matt Hardy was able to scale the ladder and retrieve the tag team titles. The Hardys were back in WWE and they were back as champions.

▶ *The Hardy Boyz make a triumphant return at WrestleMania.*

▶ *Nikki Bella and John Cena deliver dual moves to Maryse and The Miz.*

A Win and a Proposal

In the months leading into *WrestleMania 33*, The Miz and his wife Maryse had numerous issues with John Cena and his girlfriend, Nikki Bella. The Miz thought that Cena was a hypocrite for embarking on a Hollywood career after criticizing The Rock for the same thing. The Miz and Maryse also felt that Cena's relationship with Nikki was a fake affair for the cameras and that they, in fact, were WWE's "It" couple. Cena and Nikki challenged The Miz and Maryse to settle things in the ring at *WrestleMania 33*, and a Mixed Tag Team Match was set.

Nikki Bella was set to start the match against Maryse, but after the two circled each other in the ring, sizing up their opponents, Maryse tagged in The Miz, forcing Nikki to leave the ring and Cena to come in. The mind games continued, with The Miz posing for the crowd every time Cena tried to begin the match. When the physical stuff finally started, The Miz took control, dropping Cena with blows and a Diving Double Ax Handle off the top rope. The Miz kept Cena prone on the mat with a series of kicks, after which he showboated for the crowd. Miz managed a two count after nailing Cena with a DDT. Miz then taunted Nikki with Cena's own "you can't see me" gesture, receiving a slap for his trouble. As The Miz staggered back, Cena hurled him out the ring. Nikki finally tagged in, dropped Maryse with a spear and, when Maryse fled the ring, threw herself over the top rope to flatten The Miz. She then followed Maryse back into the ring and dropped her with a right hook. Cena slammed Miz and he and Nikki simultaneously hit Maryse and The Miz with 5-Knuckle Shuffles. Cena finished off The Miz with an Attitude Adjustment, while Nikki nailed Maryse with the Rack Attack. Both The Miz and Maryse were pinned at the same time, giving the win to Cena and Bella.

During their victory celebration, Cena grabbed a mic and congratulated Nikki for her year-long comeback from a broken neck to compete in the ring again. He also produced a ring box, got down on one knee and asked Nikki for her hand in marriage. A stunned Bella said "yes" and the WWE Universe roared their approval for the newly engaged couple.

Long Live the "Kingslayer"

Throughout the second half of 2014 and for much of 2015, Seth Rollins was Triple H's protégé and The Authority's hand-picked face of WWE. In November 2015, that all came crashing down, as a devastating knee injury forced Rollins to relinquish the WWE Championship and spend more than nine months sidelined from competition. When he finally returned, it seemed at first that he would still be the darling of The Authority, but instead Triple H attacked him, allowing Kevin Owens to become Universal Champion. Rollins spent the next several months calling out "The Game" and challenging him to a match. Triple H finally agreed, as long as it was an unsanctioned bout and Rollins could not sue him or WWE. Rollins agreed, ready to add a new nickname to his collection—"Kingslayer."

Rollins started the match on fire, raining blows down upon Triple H and physically dominating him both in and out of the ring. Rollins nailed Triple H with a pair of suicide dives, and tried to finish him off with a Pedigree onto the German announcer's table, but Triple H countered it into a spike DDT. It was then that Triple H's gameplan became apparent as Triple H focused most of his offense on Rollins' surgically repaired knee. The blows to the knee became so brutal that the announcers wondered if Rollins would receive career-threatening damage. Rollins was able to stem Triple H's momentum, but when he tried a Sunset Flip off the top rope, his knee suddenly gave way and he collapsed.

Grinning deviously, Triple H attempted to finish off his former protégé with a Pedigree, but Rollins countered the move into a Buckle Bomb. Rollins took a risk by hitting a splash off the top rope onto Triple H outside the ring, and the move seemed to do additional damage to his own knee. Rollins looked to plaster Triple H with a chair, but Triple H once again targeted Rollins' knee. "The Game" twice had Rollins in submission moves that hyperextended his knee and he looked to finish him off with his sledgehammer. Rollins fought back and grabbed the sledgehammer himself. Triple H's wife, Stephanie McMahon, managed to swipe the weapon from Rollins and "The Game" then nailed his opponent with his Pedigree finisher, which he assumed would end the match; however, Rollins kicked out of Triple H's follow-up pinfall attempt. "The Game" attempted a second Pedigree off the second rope, but Rollins reversed it into a Back BodyDrop and then followed that with a Phoenix Splash off the top rope. Rollins went for the win, but Triple H kicked out at two.

Stephanie once again inserted herself in the match by grabbing Rollins on the ring apron. That proved a disastrous mistake. Rollins kicked Triple H and "The Game" fell into his wife, sending her crashing through a ringside table. Distracted by his wife's plight, Triple H fell victim to a Pedigree and a three count. "The Kingslayer" had finally won.

▶ *Seth Rollins stuns his former mentor Triple H with a textbook-perfect dropkick.*

▶ *Bray Wyatt falls victim to Randy Orton's devastating RKO.*

Orton's Challenge

By winning the 2017 Royal Rumble Match, Randy Orton earned the right to challenge for the WWE Championship at *WrestleMania 33*. However Bray Wyatt was WWE Champion and Orton, a member of The Wyatt Family, initially claimed that he wouldn't challenge Bray for the title. Eventually this was revealed to be mind games; Orton was trying to lower Wyatt's guard in order to take the WWE Championship.

Orton started off strong, nailing Wyatt with a Thesz Press and peppering him with numerous blows. He then executed a perfect powerslam and, clearly looking for a quick ending to the contest, attempted an RKO. Wyatt blocked the move and bailed out of the ring to gather himself. Orton rolled Wyatt back into the ring, but Wyatt blasted Orton with a punch and a shoulder block to drop "The Viper." Wyatt then played mind games of his own as the arena darkened and an image of hundreds of maggots was projected onto the ring. Wyatt repeated the trick twice more with worms and roaches.

Orton halted Wyatt's momentum with an RKO outside the ring, but Wyatt was able to kick out. Wyatt tried another Sister Abigail, but Orton reversed it into a back breaker and a draping DDT. Orton once again tried an RKO, but Wyatt countered it into another Sister Abigail. Orton barely got his shoulder up before the official counted three. Just as Wyatt pulled Orton up to attack him again, Orton executed an RKO out of nowhere, pinning Wyatt and becoming WWE Champion for the 13th time.

"The Beast" in Championship Form

Brock Lesnar had left a trail of destruction through WWE since his debut in 2002. His list of victims included some of WWE's greatest Superstars, but there was one man Lesnar had never defeated: Goldberg. The two had clashed twice, at *WrestleMania XX* in 2004 and *Survivor Series* in 2016, and both times Goldberg had beaten "The Beast." Lesnar hoped the third meeting would change that, particularly because Goldberg's Universal Championship would be on the line.

The match started, as most Lesnar matches do, with "The Beast" sending the champion to Suplex City, delivering a trio of German suplexes. Lesnar posed for the crowd after his third suplex, only to turn around into a Spear from Goldberg. The champion then hit Lesnar with a second Spear, and Lesnar rolled out of the ring to halt the champion's momentum. But Goldberg would not relent and he followed Lesnar out and speared him a third time, sending "The Beast" crashing through a ringside barricade.

The champion brought Lesnar back into the ring and set him up for his Jackhammer finisher. Lesnar floated out of the move and attempted to give Goldberg an F5, but instead Goldberg hit his fourth Spear of the match. Goldberg followed that up with a Jackhammer, but Lesnar managed to kick out before the three count. Goldberg attempted a fifth Spear, but Lesnar leaped over the charging champion, sending Goldberg into the ringpost. Lesnar tossed Goldberg with seven additional German suplexes, completing Goldberg's estruction with an F5 for the pin, and became the new Universal Champion.

A Hometown Win

SmackDown's Women's Championship picture was a crowded affair, so General Manager Daniel Bryan set up a Six Pack Challenge for the title. Champion Alexa Bliss would be defending against Becky Lynch, Naomi, Mickie James, Natalya, and Carmella. The first Superstar to gain a pinfall or submission would be crowned champion. Naomi in particular was looking for a big night as *WrestleMania 33* was being held in her hometown of Orlando, Florida.

Things started off chaotically, with all six women fighting in the ring simultaneously. Soon only Lynch and James remained there, and Lynch pummeled James with a kick that sent her outside the ring. Lynch then delivered Bexploder Suplexes to both Natalya and Carmella. Carmella's ally, James Ellsworth, tried to interfere in the match, so he received a Bexploder as well. Mickie James then hit Becky with her knees off the top rope, but Bliss broke up the pinfall attempt. Naomi almost pinned Natalya with a Sunset Flip and then Natalya tried to put Naomi in her signature Sharpshooter. Carmella broke the hold, so Natalya put both Naomi and Carmella in a Double Sharpshooter. Before either could submit, James broke things up with a Mick Kick to Natalya.

It seemed like no one would get a clean finish, until Naomi cleared the field with an over-the-top-rope dive on all the other competitors. She then rolled Bliss back into the ring and forced the champion to submit, making Naomi the WWE SmackDown Women's Champion for the second time.

▶ *Naomi feels the glow of her hometown title victory.*

▶ *Roman Reigns tries to level Undertaker with a powerful Superman punch.*

"The Big Dog" Claims His Yard

For the first time in eight years, Undertaker entered 2017's Royal Rumble Match with designs on winning and claiming a championship opportunity at *WrestleMania 33*. Things did not go Undertaker's way thanks to Roman "The Big Dog" Reigns, who eliminated Undertaker and told him that the WWE ring was his yard now. Undertaker did not take this challenge kindly, and vowed to claim Roman's soul at *WrestleMania 33*.

Undertaker looked to set the young upstart straight right away, pummeling Reigns with clubbing blows and dumping him out of the ring multiple times. Reigns made it clear that he belonged by knocking the Undertaker around and then throwing him out of the ring. As the two men battled outside, Undertaker seized the momentum with a few timely headbutts. He seemed to be setting Reigns up for a Tombstone through the announcer's table; however Reigns countered by spearing Undertaker through the table instead.

As the contest moved back to the ring, Reigns peppered Undertaker with rights and lefts. Reigns taunted "The Deadman" and got a Last Ride for his trouble. Undertaker was amazed when Reigns kicked out at two and, taking advantage of the match's No Holds Barred stipulation, seized a steel chair. Undertaker and Reigns fought over the chair, slamming each other repeatedly with the unforgiving steel. Undertaker chokeslammed Reigns onto the chair, but once again Reigns kicked out at two. The WWE Universe were stunned when Reigns also kicked out following Undertaker's Tombstone piledriver. Reigns then retrieved the steel chair and repeatedly nailed Undertaker. He speared him twice, but Undertaker kicked out of two pinfall attempts. Reigns then hit Undertaker with his fifth Superman Punch of the match and speared "The Deadman" for the three-count victory— only the second loss for Undertaker in his illustrious *WrestleMania* career.

After celebrating his win, Reigns left up the ramp while the sellout crowd saluted "The Deadman," chanting "Thank you 'Taker!" Sensing that a WWE era was ending, Undertaker slowly removed his fighting gloves, overcoat, and hat to the solemn strains of Chopin's "Funeral March" and left them in the center of the ring before he departed the stadium.

▶ *Undertaker's gear is left the ring, leading the WWE Universe to speculate about his retirement.*

WRESTLEMANIA 34

MERCEDEZ-BENZ SUPERDOME – NEW ORLEANS, LOUISIANA

April 8
2018

Attendance
78,133

ANNOUNCERS
Michael Cole, Corey Graves, Jonathan Coachman, Tom Phillips, Byron Saxton, Vic Joseph, Nigel McGuinness, Jim Ross, Jerry "The King" Lawler, Beth Phoenix, Paige

RING ANNOUNCERS
JoJo, Greg Hamilton, Lilian Garcia

Event Card

MAIN EVENT – UNIVERSAL CHAMPIONSHIP MATCH
■ Brock Lesnar (Champion) w/ Paul Heyman def. Roman Reigns

WWE CHAMPIONSHIP MATCH
■ AJ Styles (Champion) def. Shinsuke Nakamura

MIXED TAG TEAM MATCH
■ Ronda Rousey & Kurt Angle def. Stephanie McMahon & Triple H

FATAL 4-WAY MATCH FOR THE UNITED STATES CHAMPIONSHIP
■ Jinder Mahal def. Randy Orton (Champion), Rusev w/ Aiden English, and Bobby Roode to become new Champion

RAW WOMEN'S CHAMPIONSHIP MATCH
■ Nia Jax def. Alexa Bliss (Champion) w/ Mickie James to become new Champion
■ Daniel Bryan & Shane McMahon def. Kevin Owens & Sami Zayn

WWE RAW TAG TEAM CHAMPIONSHIP MATCH
■ Braun Strowman & Nicholas def. The Bar (Sheamus & Cesaro) (Champions) to become new Champions

TRIPLE THREAT MATCH FOR THE INTERCONTINENTAL CHAMPIONSHIP
■ Seth Rollins def. The Miz (Champion) and Finn Bálor to become new Champion
■ Undertaker def. John Cena

SMACKDOWN WOMEN'S CHAMPIONSHIP MATCH
■ Charlotte Flair (Champion) def. Asuka

TRIPLE THREAT MATCH FOR THE SMACKDOWN TAG TEAM CHAMPIONSHIP
■ The Bludgeon Brothers (Luke Harper and Erick Rowan) def. The Usos (Jimmy and Jey) (Champions) and The New Day (Kofi Kingston and Big E) w/ Xavier Woods to become new Champions

5TH ANNUAL ANDRÉ THE GIANT MEMORIAL BATTLE ROYAL
■ Matt Hardy def. Karl Anderson, Curtis Axel, Shelton Benjamin, Tyler Breeze, Primo Colon, Baron Corbin, Apollo Crews, Bo Dallas, Scott Dawson, Tye Dillinger, Aiden English, Fandango, Chad Gable, Luke Gallows, Goldust, Curt Hawkins, Kane, Mike Kanellis, Konnor, Titus O'Neil, R-Truth, Mojo Rawley, Rhyno, Zack Ryder, Sin Cara, Heath Slater, Viktor, Dash Wilder, and Dolph Ziggler

MATCH FOR THE VACANT CRUISERWEIGHT CHAMPIONSHIP
■ Cedric Alexander def. Mustafa Ali to become new Champion

WOMEN'S BATTLE ROYAL
■ Naomi def. Sasha Banks, Bayley, Bianca Belair, Dana Brooke, Carmella, Taynara Conti, Kavita Devi, Sonya Deville, Mickie James, Dakota Kai, Lana, Sarah Logan, Becky Lynch, Liv Morgan, Natalya, Ruby Riott, Mandy Rose, Peyton Royce, and Kairi Sane

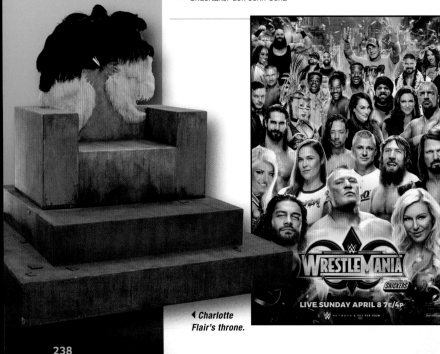

◀ *Charlotte Flair's throne.*

> **"I had no idea what I was in for, but I was in for it all the way now."**
>
> —Ronda Rousey

Return to New Orleans

For the second time in five years *WrestleMania* was located in New Orleans. The last time the city hosted the show, Brock Lesnar shocked all by ending a hallowed WWE record: Undertaker's 21-0 undefeated streak. Lesnar returned, this time defending the Universal Championship against Roman Reigns. Daniel Bryan also returned to competition after a two-year absence.

▶ *Chaos rules the ring in the early portions of the André the Giant Battle Royal.*

The 5th André the Giant Battle Royal

The *WrestleMania 34* pre-show opened with the 5th André the Giant Memorial Battle Royal. Thirty Superstars attempt to burnish their resume with an impressive victory. The final five came down to Dolph Ziggler, Matt Hardy, Baron Corbin, Mojo Rawley, and Kane. "The Showoff" Ziggler jumped on the back of the "Big Red Monster" Kane in an attempt to eliminate him, but Kane shrugged Ziggler off his shoulders and dumped him out of the ring, eliminating Ziggler. Corbin took advantage and sent Kane over the ropes and on to the floor, leaving Matt Hardy and the last two André Battle Royal winners. With the crowd squarely behind Hardy, the other two decided to form an alliance and remove their common enemy. Before the two could finish off the Woken One, the lights went out and Hardy's longtime rival Bray Wyatt appeared in the ring. Wyatt, "The Eater of Worlds", had not been seen since Hardy tossed him in his "Lake of Reincarnation." Now reborn, Wyatt worked to help Hardy eliminate the last two competitors and win the 5th Annual André the Giant Battle Royal.

Crowning a New Cruiserweight Champion

The Cruiserweight Championship had been vacated in January, and new *205 Live* General Manager Drake Maverick launched a 16-man tournament to crown a new champion. With the final match scheduled to take place at *WrestleMania 34*, both Cedric Alexander and Mustafa Ali had won three matches in the tournament to advance to the winner-take-all finale.

The two shook hands to start the match in a sign of mutual respect competitors don't often give each other before championship bouts. The two opened the match showing off their technical skills, but soon began to hammer each other with hard punches and kicks. Ali thought he had the match won when he hit in succession a reverse Hurricanrana, a tornado DDT off the top rope, and his patented 054 Splash. But Alexander managed to get his foot on the rope to halt the three count. Ali tried to hit another 054, but Alexander moved out of the way before nailing Ali with a trio of back elbows and a devastating Lumbar Check move to keep Ali's shoulders pinned to the mat for the three count and his first Cruiserweight Championship.

▶ *Mustafa Ali demonstrates some theatrics on his way to the ring.*

A Battle Royal for the Women

For the first time in history, the women would have a *WrestleMania* Battle Royal of their own. Twenty competitors from *RAW*, *SmackDown*, and NXT would each try to claim the distinction of the first battle royal winner in the next step of the Women's Evolution. The current Money in the Bank winner, Carmella, lorded her Money in the Bank briefcase over the field, but that only encouraged all 19 other combatants to work together to oust her from the match. After Dana Brooke was eliminated by the pack, the NXT women showed why they were a viable threat, working together to take down a number of WWE Superstars. The three members of the Riott Squad worked together effectively to eliminate a number of WWE and NXT competitors.

With a seeming final six of the Riott Squad, Natalya, Bayley, and Sasha Banks, the on-and-off friends Bayley and Sasha decided to work together to eliminate Natalya, Liv Morgan, Ruby Riott, and Sarah Logan. The two went to celebrate, but Bayley tossed Banks. Thinking she'd won the match, Bayley was shocked to learn Naomi had yet to be eliminated. *SmackDown*'s queen of the glow tossed Bayley out of the ring to become the first-ever *WrestleMania* Women's Battle Royal winner.

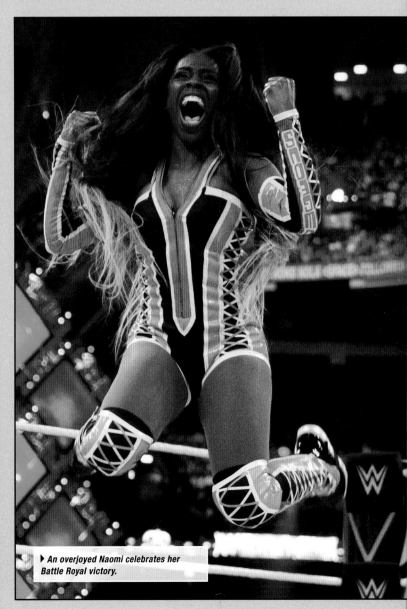

▶ *An overjoyed Naomi celebrates her Battle Royal victory.*

Triple Threat for the Intercontinental Championship

The Miz used every opportunity to tell the WWE Universe that the WWE Intercontinental Championship was more prestigious than the WWE Universal Championship and that was completely due to his efforts. The Miz demanded suitable competition at *WrestleMania* and both Seth Rollins and Finn Bálor made their cases for being his opponent by beating The Miz in non-title matches. Rather than pick one as most worthy, *RAW* General Manager Kurt Angle set a Triple Threat match at *WrestleMania 34* where The Miz would face both challengers.

The trio began the match at a frenetic pace, with a series of rollups designed to garner an early pinfall, but no man would stay down. Bálor executed a daring suicide dive onto both of his rivals outside the ring, but once in the ring, The Miz showed a previously unseen intensity to his in-ring moves, securing an early two count against Bálor with a Neckbreaker and an almost-pin on Rollins with a DDT. The Miz then locked Bálor in a painful Figure 4, but before he could secure a tapout, Rollins wiped out The Miz with a Frog Splash from the top rope.

Bálor thought he had the match won when he dropped Miz with a combination of a Slingblade, dropkick, and a Coup de Grâce, but just as he went to pin the champion, Rollins stomped him onto The Miz's back. Rollins then executed a second Stomp, this one on The Miz, to pin the Awesome One and win the Intercontinental Championship for the first time in his career.

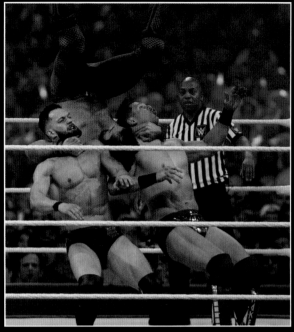

▶ *Seth Rollins attempts to take out Finn Bálor and The Miz with a single move.*

▶ *SmackDown Women's Champion Charlotte makes a grand entrance.*

Flair Faces Undefeated Asuka

Asuka had been undefeated in singles competition since her debut at NXT in October 2015. Her success continued in WWE where she won the Women's Royal Rumble match, allowing her to select her opponent at *WrestleMania*. In a bold move, Asuka chose to put her 914-day undefeated streak against Charlotte's *SmackDown* Women's Championship.

The two immediately traded arm drags, each escaping the other through sheer athleticism. Charlotte used her power advantage, peppering Asuka with vicious chops, but Asuka sent her sprawling to the outside with a hip attack. Charlotte was driven into the ring barricade and began tending her left shoulder, so Asuka targeted that side of her body. Charlotte stunned Asuka with a Spanish Fly off the top rope, but the challenger kicked out at two. Charlotte followed up with a Natural Selection move, but Asuka turned it into a submission move. Finally, Charlotte grabbed the upper hand with a devastating spear, then locked Asuka in a Figure 8. Asuka had no choice but to submit, allowing "the Queen" to successfully retain her title.

Four Men, One Championship

Randy Orton had defeated Bobby Roode for the United States Championship at *Fastlane* in early March, so Roode invoked his contractual rematch at *WrestleMania 33*. But both Jinder Mahal and Rusev felt they had proven themselves worthy of challenging for the title as well, so the match became a Fatal 4-Way. Roode tossed Mahal out of the ring to start the match and Rusev sent Orton out as well, leaving Roode and Rusev in the ring together. Rusev kept rolling with a drop kick onto Roode and then a flip onto both Orton and Mahal outside the ring. The champion made his way back into the match and crunched Roode's bones with a superplex off the top rope.

The action spilled outside the ring with Orton dropping Rusev's back on the ring barricade. He continued to punish Rusev inside the ring, planting him with a draping DDT and administering RKOs to both Rusev and his hype man Aiden English. He dished out an RKO to Jinder Mahal as well when Mahal broke up the pinfall attempt, but before Orton could pin Mahal, Bobby Roode nailed Orton with his Glorious DDT move. Mahal broke up that pinfall, only to fall to a roundhouse kick from Rusev. Rusev almost punctuated a perfect Rusev day by making Mahal submit to an Accolade move, but Jinder's second, Sumil Singh, distracted Rusev long enough for Mahal to recover and plant Rusev with his Khallas signature slam and pin, granting Mahal the United States Championship.

◀ *Jinder Mahal overcomes three competitors to win the United States Championship.*

Welcome to WWE, Ronda Rousey

Former UFC Champion Ronda Rousey shocked the WWE Universe when she debuted at the 2018 *Royal Rumble*. While it appeared that Stephanie McMahon and Triple H were happy to add Rousey to the roster, Kurt Angle revealed the truth—ever since Rousey embarrassed them at *WrestleMania 31*, the pair were dying to get Rousey into WWE so they could control her. However, as part of her contract, Rousey could select her *WrestleMania* opponent, and she selected Stephanie and Triple H in a mixed tag match against her and Angle.

The WWE Universe were pumped to see Rousey make her in-ring debut, but after pie-facing Rousey and pulling her down by her hair, Stephanie was content to let her husband Triple H start the match with Angle. Stephanie and Triple H took advantage of Rousey's inexperience by double-teaming Angle every time the official was engaged with Rousey. The duo cut the ring in half, preventing Angle from reaching his partner. Angle was finally able to reach his corner thanks to a suplex, but Stephanie had pulled Rousey off the apron, preventing a tag.

A desperate Angle tossed Triple H out of the ring and finally made the tag everyone wanted to see. Stephanie was reluctant to enter the ring, so Rousey pulled her in by her hair, tossing McMahon around and relishing the chance for revenge. Rousey tried to lock McMahon in the arm bar, but Stephanie blocked the move, then drove a thumb into Rousey's eye. Worried that his wife would be hurt, Triple H pulled Stephanie out of the ring. Rousey peppered Triple H with punches, then pulled him up on her shoulders, but Stephanie saved her husband.

Triple H tried to powerbomb Rousey, but Rousey countered it into a Hurricanrana move that she linked into an armbar. Stephanie broke up the submission hold on her husband, only to be locked into her own Rousey armbar. Triple H tossed Angle into Rousey, ending the hold, then threw Angle into a ring post, followed by Stephanie doing the same to Rousey. The couple geared up to execute stereo Pedigrees on their opponents, but each countered the move into a back body drop. Triple H went sprawling out of the ring and Angle followed him, leaving Ronda and Stephanie. Rousey locked McMahon in an armbar. With no one able to save her, Stephanie was forced to tap out to the painful move.

▶ *Harper and Rowan show some surprising agility when nailing Jimmy Uso.*

Bludgeoning Their Way to the Titles

Since the 2016 brand split, The New Day and The Usos were the two dominant figures in the *SmackDown* tag team division. From March 2017 through *WrestleMania*, the two teams were the only squads to hold the Tag Team Championship, with three reigns by The Usos and a pair by The New Day. The veteran teams had a terrifying new opponent in the Bludgeon Brothers. Luke Harper and Erick Rowan lived up the their name, decimating anyone that got in their way. All three would be in the ring together for a Triple Threat Match for the *SmackDown* Tag Team Championship at *WrestleMania 33*.

The match began with The Usos and The New Day working together to take out the Bludgeon Brothers, but the tactic failed. Instead, Harper and Rowan disposed of all three members of The New Day and performed some double team moves on Jimmy Uso, including tossing him into the ring steps. An injured Woods took the battle to the Brothers, but they tossed him into a ring post, removing him from the equation. The Usos regrouped and dumped Rowan out of the ring, focusing their double-team moves on Harper. They did manage to get a two count on him. Rowan slammed Kingston and then his partner Powerbombed Kofi off the second rope to earn a three count and become the new *SmackDown* Tag Team Champions.

◀ *Ronda Rousey has bad intentions for Triple H on her shoulders.*

Cena Calls Out The Dead Man

John Cena did not have a championship match or marquee rivalry to take him to *WrestleMania*, so he decided to rectify this by calling out Undertaker. Undertaker had not been seen since his loss to Roman Reigns at *WrestleMania 33*, but Cena challenged Undertaker to return and face him. Cena didn't receive a response, so he watched the matches at *WrestleMania* from the crowd until an official came out with a message that sent Cena backstage.

Excited, Cena returned to the ring, ready for a confrontation with Undertaker. In typical Undertaker fashion, the lights in the arena went off, but instead of The Dead Man, Elias emerged, mocking Cena. Cena dispatched of Elias before getting ready to leave. However, the lights went off a second time and when they returned, Undertaker's ring gear was in the center of the ring. Lightning bolts struck the clothing, which then disappeared. Undertaker's ominous entrance theme hit and he appeared at the top of the entrance ramp.

Once in the ring, Undertaker delighted the WWE Universe by performing his Old School maneuver on Cena before nailing him with a pair of clotheslines, a Snake Eyes, and a big leg drop across Cena's chest. Undertaker tried to hit Cena with a chokeslam, but he countered the move into a side slam. Cena was prepared to follow up with a Five-Knuckle Shuffle, but The Dead Man sat up, stunning Cena, then chokeslamming him to the mat. Undertaker then delivered a textbook Tombstone Piledriver on Cena and recorded the three count for the pinfall victory.

▶ *Undertaker chokeslams John Cena on his successful return to the ring.*

▶ *Daniel Bryan leaps through the air to deliver a missile dropkick onto Sami Zayn.*

Fighting for Their Jobs

Kevin Owens made it impossible for the *SmackDown* Commissioner, Shane McMahon, to remain impartial when he attacked Shane's father, Mr. McMahon. The two battled several times before Owens and his friend Sami Zayn brutally attacked Shane and General Manager Daniel Bryan. Rather than fire them, Bryan suggested a match with him and Shane at *WrestleMania*, with the duo's employment on the line.

Before the match even started, Zayn and Owens snuck up and attacked their opponents. It looked like Bryan would be unable to compete so Shane started alone, allowing Kevin and Zayn to seize the momentum.

Owens managed to put Shane down with a top-rope frog splash. However, Owens' attempted pinfall was broken up by Bryan's dramatic return to the match. Both Owens and Zayn tried to prevent Shane from tagging Bryan into the match, but Bryan eventually was tagged in to roars of approval from the WWE Universe.

Bryan eventually slammed Zayn with a series of "Yes!" Kicks then dropped Zayn with a high running knee before putting Sami in a "Yes!" Lock. Zayn tapped out, giving Bryan a win in his return to the ring and unemployment for Owens and Zayn.

Bliss Gets What's Coming to Her

RAW Women's Champion Alexa Bliss wanted no part of a one-on-one match with powerful Nia Jax, so Bliss tried to claim that they were friends. This worked until Bliss was caught on camera mocking Jax. Enraged, Jax was ready to make the bully pay at *WrestleMania 34*, and take her title.

First, Jax eliminated any ringside interference from Bliss' ally Mickie James, planting her with a Samoan Drop. Jax then turned her attention to the champion. The bell rang and Bliss tried to escape the ring, but Jax caught her and tossed her around the ring before lifting her above her head and tossing Bliss down to the mat. Again Bliss tried to run, but Jax clotheslined her. Bliss was finally able to stop Jax's momentum with an illegal poke in the eye and attacking her knee before slamming her with a Twisted Bliss from the top rope to outside the ring.

Bliss covered Jax to try and retain her title, but Jax kicked out before the three count. Bliss tried to add insult to injury by mocking the challenger while slapping her, but Little Miss Bliss had pushed her opponent too far. Jax slammed the champion to the mat and then tossed Bliss into a pair of corners and followed each with a splash. Jax slammed her opponent to the mat once again and then performed a Samoan Drop off the second rope to pin Bliss and win the *RAW* Women's Champion.

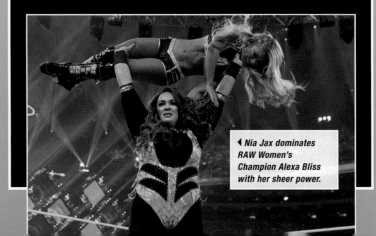

◀ *Nia Jax dominates RAW Women's Champion Alexa Bliss with her sheer power.*

The Dream Match Turns to a Nightmare

After he won the 2018 men's Royal Rumble Match, Shinsuke Nakamura earned the right to challenge a champion of his choosing to a match at *WrestleMania 34*. The WWE Universe were delighted when he chose WWE Champion AJ Styles.

The two circled each other to start the match, neither man wanting to make the first mistake and give his opponent an opening. Nakamura proved that he had done research, blocking Styles' attempted suplex. Styles kept his advantage with several kicks and a chin lock to wear down the challenger.

The two combatants traded moves and near falls. A frustrated Nakamura thought he had the match won when he drove his knee into the back of Styles, but the champion kicked out. Nakamura tried to finish off Styles with his Kinshasa move, but Styles countered it into a Styles Clash and a three count to retain his championship. After celebrating, Styles helped his rival to his feet. It seemed like a humbled Nakamura was paying tribute to a worthy rival, kneeling to present the title to Styles, but it was a ruse. Nakamura nailed Styles with a low blow.

▶ *A victorious Braun Strowman raises the hand of his fellow RAW Tag Team Champion, Nicholas.*

▶ *Shinsuke Nakamura demonstrates why he is called the King of Strong Style, nailing WWE Champion AJ Styles with a high knee.*

The Monster Among Men and The Kid

To set the match for the *RAW* Tag Team Championship at *WrestleMania 34*, *RAW* General Manager Kurt Angle set up a tag team battle royal, where the winning squad would earn a championship opportunity against the reigning champs The Bar. Braun Strowman entered the match and decimated the tag teams in it, winning the match on his own. Angle told Strowman he would receive the title shot as long as he had a partner.

At the event, The Bar was stunned when Strowman announced that a child named Nicholas would be his tag partner. Strowman told Nicholas to just stand in the corner and he would do the rest. First Strowman tossed Sheamus out of the ring and then he slammed Cesaro. But The Bar used double-team maneuvers to take control of the match. Strowman knocked down both the champs with a cross body before tagging in Nicholas. Before Cesaro could attack the boy, Strowman tagged back in, powerslammed Cesaro and won, making him and a 10-year-old boy *RAW* Tag Team Champions.

Lesnar vs. Reigns, Round 2

For the second *WrestleMania* in the past four years, "The Beast" Brock Lesnar was defending a World Championship against Roman Reigns in the main event of a *WrestleMania*. After the two combatants opened the match exchanging blows, Lesnar used a common tactic from his playbook, nailing Reigns with three consecutive German suplexes. But Reigns made it clear to the champion that it wouldn't be that easy as he countered with a trio of Superman Punches, with the last occurring outside the ring. Reigns went for a fourth Superman Punch outside the ring, but Lesnar caught him and reversed the move into a belly-to-belly suplex. Lesnar brought Reigns back into the ring and executed two German suplexes followed by two belly-to-belly suplexes.

Lesnar looked ready to finish off Reigns, setting up him up for an F5 onto an announcer's table outside the ring. However, the challenger reversed the move and slammed Lesnar into the ring post, then tossed him over the announcer's table. Knowing he had to get Lesnar into the ring to win the match, Reigns dragged the champ back in the ring and delivered another Superman Punch and a pair of Spears. But Lesnar kicked out of the pinning combination before the count of three. A frustrated Reigns tried to land another spear, but Lesnar drove a knee into the challenger's face, getting a two count of his own. Lesnar hit an F5 on Reigns, but again, The Big Dog kicked out of the pinfall. Lesnar hit the move two more times, but Reigns kicked out each time. Lesnar hit a fourth F5, but this one sent Reigns crashing through the announcer's table. A bloodied Reigns speared Lesnar twice, but he could not keep the champion for a three count. Reigns attempted another spear, but Lesnar caught the challenger, delivered a sixth F5, and pinned The Big Dog to retain his Universal Championship.

▶ *Roman Reigns endures multiple F5 maneuvers from Brock Lesnar.*

THE BIG DOG'S YARD

Since his debut as one third of The Shield, Roman Reigns has been a staple at the "Showcase of the Immortals." His first two appearances at *WrestleMania* were as part of The Shield, with the trio defeating Big Show, Randy Orton, and Sheamus at *WrestleMania 29* and beating Kane and The New Age Outlaws at *WrestleMania 30*. The following year began the first of four consecutive *WrestleMania* events that would see "The Big Dog" Roman Reigns close the night in the main event. Three times he would compete for a World Championship, and once he would face the most dominant force in *WrestleMania* history over whose yard the *WrestleMania* ring truly was…

WrestleMania 31

A year after he was the runner up, setting a record with 12 eliminations, Reigns returned to the 2015 *Royal Rumble* and eliminated six other competitors on his way to winning the match and earning a guaranteed WWE Championship Match in the main event of *WrestleMania 31*. Reigns got the right to challenge "The Beast" Brock Lesnar. After withstanding Lesnar's power in the ring, it seemed like Reigns was ready to overcome The Beast and become WWE Champion for the first time in his career. But Seth Rollins crashed the party, cashing in his Money in the Bank Championship opportunity to make the match a Triple Threat. Rollins won the match and became the WWE Champion over his former Shield running buddy.

◀ *Roman Reigns looks to deck WWE Champion Triple H with a Superman punch.*

◀ *Roman Reigns floors Brock Lesnar with his patented Spear.*

WrestleMania 32

Roman Reigns finally became the WWE Champion, but The Authority did everything they could to take the title from "The Big Dog". Triple H and Stephanie McMahon made Reigns defend the title in the 2016 Royal Rumble Match, and Triple H won the bout, becoming the new champion. But Reigns earned the right to challenge Triple H at *WrestleMania*. Reigns managed to defeat the "Cerebral Assassin" and become a three-time WWE Champion.

WrestleMania 33

While Reigns did not challenge for the WWE or Universal Championships at *WrestleMania 33*, he did face a significant challenge—competing against Undertaker. For years, Undertaker said that the ring was his yard, and his 23-1 record at *WrestleMania* backed up his claim. But Reigns was ready to own the yard, even if it meant going through Undertaker. In one of the most brutal matches in the history of the event, Reigns put Undertaker down, handing him his second loss in 25 appearances. The result was so shocking that Undertaker would not be seen in WWE rings for another year.

▶-Roman Reigns forces Undertaker to stay down.

▶ *Brock Lesnar and Roman Reigns stare each other down before their match.*

WrestleMania 34

The Big Dog wanted to correct the one blemish on his *WrestleMania* record by defeating "The Beast" Brock Lesnar and taking the Universal Championship at *WrestleMania 34*. The two traded verbal barbs and vicious beatdowns in the weeks leading to the event and the match itself was a slugfest with each man thinking he'd earned the victory multiple times after hitting his signature moves. After a brutal match, Lesnar was finally able to pin Reigns and deny him the Universal Championship.

WrestleMania 35

While Reigns did not compete in the main event of *WrestleMania 35*, he entered the event having recorded the most impressive victory in his career—overcoming leukemia. Reigns had to relinquish the Universal Championship in October 2018 to begin treatment for the disease but was in remission by February 2019. He was able to square off against Drew McIntyre in his first one-on-one encounter in more than six months, defeating the "Scottish Psychopath" and demonstrating that the WWE ring was still the Big Dog's yard.

▶ *Roman Reigns proves his returned strength in his match against Drew McIntyre.*

WRESTLEMANIA 35

METLIFE STADIUM — EAST RUTHERFORD, NEW JERSEY

April 7
2019

Attendance
82,625

ANNOUNCERS
Michael Cole, Corey Graves, Renee Young, Tom Phillips, Byron Saxton, Vic Joseph, Nigel McGuinness, Aiden English, Percy Watson, JBL, Jerry "The King" Lawler, Paige, Booker T, Shawn Michaels

RING ANNOUNCERS
Lilian Garcia, Greg Hamilton, Mike Rome

HOST
Alexa Bliss

MUSICAL GUESTS
Joan Jett & the Blackhearts, Yolanda Adams, Elias

Event Card

MAIN EVENT — WINNER TAKES ALL TRIPLE THREAT MATCH FOR THE RAW AND SMACKDOWN WOMEN'S CHAMPIONSHIPS
- Becky Lynch defeated Ronda Rousey (*RAW* Women's Champion) and Charlotte Flair (*SmackDown's* Women Champion) to become new Champion of both

UNIVERSAL CHAMPIONSHIP MATCH
- Seth Rollins defeated Brock Lesnar (Champion) w/ Paul Heyman to become new Champion

WWE CHAMPIONSHIP MATCH
- Kofi Kingston w/ Big E & Xavier Woods defeated Daniel Bryan (Champion) w/ Erick Rowan to become new Champion

FAREWELL MATCH FOR KURT ANGLE
- Baron Corbin defeated Kurt Angle

UNITED STATES CHAMPIONSHIP MATCH
- Samoa Joe (Champion) defeated Rey Mysterio

FATAL FOUR-WAY MATCH FOR THE WOMEN'S TAG TEAM CHAMPIONSHIP
- The Ilconics (Billie Kay & Peyton Royce) defeated The Boss 'n' Hug Connection (Sasha Banks & Bayley) (Champions), Nia Jax & Tamina, and Beth Phoenix & Natalya to become new Champions

NO HOLDS BARRED MATCH
- Triple H defeated Batista

WWE RAW TAG TEAM CHAMPIONSHIP MATCH
- Zack Ryder & Curt Hawkins defeated The Revival (Dash Wilder & Scott Dawson) (Champions) to become new Champions

INTERCONTINENTAL CHAMPIONSHIP MATCH
- Finn Balor defeated Bobby Lashley (Champion) w/ Lio Rush to become new Champion

FALLS COUNT ANYWHERE MATCH
- Shane McMahon defeated The Miz
- Roman Reigns defeated Drew McIntyre
- AJ Styles defeated Randy Orton

FATAL 4-WAY MATCH FOR THE SMACKDOWN TAG TEAM CHAMPIONSHIP
- The Usos (Jimmy and Jey) (Champions) defeated Aleister Black & Ricochet, The Bar (Sheamus & Cesaro), and Rusev & Shinsuke Nakamura w/ Lana

6TH ANNUAL ANDRE THE GIANT MEMORIAL BATTLE ROYAL
- Braun Strowman defeated Mustafa Ali, Karl Anderson, Andrade, Curtis Axel, Shelton Benjamin, Tyler Breeze, Michael Che, Apollo Crews, Bo Dallas, Lince Dorado, EC3, Chad Gable, Luke Gallows, Jeff Hardy, Matt Hardy, Luke Harper, Colin Jost, Jinder Mahal, Gran Metalik, Kalisto, Konnor, No Way Jose, Titus O'Neil, Otis, Rhyno, Bobby Roode, Heath Slater, Tucker, Viktor

CRUISERWEIGHT CHAMPIONSHIP MATCH
- Tony Nese defeated Buddy Murphy (Champion) to become new Champion

WOMEN'S BATTLE ROYAL
- Carmella defeated Asuka, Dana Brooke, Nikki Cross, Sonya Deville, Mickie James, Maria Kanellis, Lana, Candice LeRae, Sarah Logan, Ember Moon, Liv Morgan, Naomi, Ruby Riott, Mandy Rose, Kairi Sane, and Zelina Vega

"I feel like I'm in a dream, and I don't want to wake up."

—Kofi Kingston

Women Take Over

WrestleMania returned to the New York area for the sixth time in 35 years as MetLife Stadium served as host venue for the second time in six years. And for the first time in WWE history, the main event would be a women's match. Becky Lynch hoped for her biggest win, but she would have to beat *RAW* Women's Champion Ronda Rousey, who had never lost a singles match in WWE, and 8-time Women's Champion Charlotte Flair, who seemed to shine brighter when the stage got bigger.

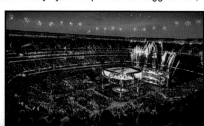

Tony Nese Gets His Moment

Long Island's own Tony Nese, "The Premier Athlete," wanted to capture his first-ever Cruiserweight Championship in his backyard. To do so, Nese won an eight-man tournament that earned him a match against reigning champion Buddy Murphy. But Murphy had no desire to end his six-month championship run.

Nese got off to a strong start, raining blows on the champion and countering a few of Murphy's patented moves to keep his momentum going. However, when Nese went to the top rope for a high-flying move, Murphy was able to drop Nese across the top turnbuckle and take control of the match. Murphy began to wear Nese down and tried to end the match with a leaping DDT, but Nese was able to reverse the move into a suplex into the corner turnbuckles. The two traded punches and kicks and then the Nese hit a moonsault for the first near fall of the match. Murphy almost won the match by combining a superkick of Nese on the top turnbuckle with a running slam, but Nese was able to kick out at two. Nese regained control with a reverse hurricanrana. The Premier Athlete nailed the Juggernaut with a 450 splash, but the champion would not stay down for three. For the second time in the match, Nese tossed Murphy into the turnbuckle with a suplex, but this time he followed it up with a Running Nese move to pin the champion and capture the Cruiserweight Championship for the first time in his career.

'Mella is Money

Female Superstars from *SmackDown*, *RAW*, and NXT competed in a Battle Royal for the second straight year. After Ember Moon eliminated Maria Kanellis, Asuka took out her frustration over recently losing the *SmackDown* Women's Championship by eliminating both Candice LeRae and Nikki Cross. Moon ensured that there would be a new winner by knocking the previous winner Naomi out of the match before Lana shocked the WWE Universe by eliminating Moon.

The Riott Squad, realizing that there was strength in numbers, began to work together, eliminating Lana and Kairi Sane as well as beating down Asuka and Carmella. Dana Brooke stunningly took out both Ruby Riott and Liv Morgan. The numbers continued to dwindle and Asuka found herself fighting the makeshift alliance of Sonya Deville and Sarah Logan. Asuka eliminated Deville, but Logan then knocked Asuka out. Logan temporarily thought she had won the match, but Carmella had not yet gone over the top rope and the two battled at the ropes, almost eliminating each other several times, before the Staten Island Princess claimed the match by Superkicking Logan off the ring apron.

▶ *Carmella tries to toss the last remaining competitor, Sarah Logan, out of the ring.*

The End of a Bad Streak

Curt Hawkins had seen his career stall in the most embarrassing way, running up a gargantuan losing streak that hit 269 matches. Longtime friend Zack Ryder wanted to help Hawkins, reminding him that as a pair they had been Tag Team Champions in the past, and perhaps they could recapture that magic by facing *RAW* Tag Team Champions The Revival at *WrestleMania*.

Hawkins started the match against Scott Dawson, who taunted his opponent, asking why Ryder wasn't in the match when he was the better Superstar, getting under his skin before Hawkins could tag his partner in. The Revival used teamwork to work over Ryder, but Zack was able to stem the tide with a top-rope missile dropkick. The Champs isolated Ryder, preventing

▶ *Ryder and Hawkins bask in the glory after capturing the RAW Tag Team Championship.*

him from tagging in his partner. Dash Wilder and Dawson continued to pound down Ryder, but Ryder reversed a tag-team suplex into a double neckbreaker. Dawson knocked Hawkins off the ring apron before Ryder could tag him in.

Hawkins finally re-entered the match and seemed to take out all his frustration from his losing streak on the champs, peppering them with punches and two well-placed dopkicks. The four competitors were almost counted out, but Dawson rolled Hawkins back in the ring after a Brainbuster move for what he thought would be an easy pin. But Hawkins was playing possum. He caught Dawson in a Small Package move to earn the win and the *RAW* Tag Team Championship.

Rollins Slays The Beast

Most of the WWE Universe was excited to see a women's main event *WrestleMania* for the first time ever; two men, however, were not. Brock Lesnar's advocate Paul Heyman explained that if his client was not going to close the show, he wanted to compete first, so he could leave the stadium and celebrate. Lesnar attacked Rollins before he could even get in the ring, pummeling the challenger with knees, punches, and an F5. The match had not even started when Lesnar tossed Rollins over the announcer's desk and through a sign. The official finally rang the bell and Lesnar made it seem like it would be a quick bout, tossing Rollins with a pair of German suplexes and aiming to finish off the challenger with an F5. Rollins was able to float out of the move and shoved Lesnar toward the official. While the referee slid out of the ring to avoid a collision, Rollins took advantage with a low blow. Rollins downed Lesnar with a kick and then delivered three consecutive Stomps to pin Lesnar and win the Universal Championship.

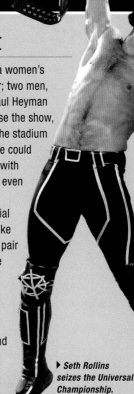

▶ *Seth Rollins seizes the Universal Championship.*

▶ *Braun Strowman throws Jinder Mahal over the ropes.*

Braun's Not Joking Around

The "Monster Among Men" Braun Strowman was not in a good mood. *Saturday Night Live* cast members Colin Jost and Michael Che were special *WrestleMania* correspondents, but Jost had enraged Strowman by making disparaging remarks. Strowman entered the André the Giant Memorial Battle Royal and the duo was forced to join him in the match.

Jost and Che wisely hid under the ring at the start of the match, while Strowman tossed several competitors out of the ring. Strowman faced off with Luke Harper, before the other competitors jumped the two in an attempt to remove them from the match, but both men fought on. Both Mustafa Ali and Andrade claimed multiple eliminations, but Strowman continued to dominate, eliminating both members of Heavy Machinery, Jinder Mahal, Harper, and Ali. The Hardys had Strowman on the ropes when Che and Jost emerged and attempted to help get Strowman over the top rope. Once Strowman tossed The Hardys out of the ring, he turned his attention to the *SNL* duo. Jost tried to defuse the situation by bringing out his therapist, but Strowman was not having it, beating down the therapist and eliminating both Che and Jost to win the match.

A Phenomenal Battle with The Viper

AJ Styles and Randy Orton were on a collision course to determine the true face of *SmackDown*. Orton tried to end the match early with a quick RKO, but Styles was able to block the move. Orton seized control of the match with a thumb to the eye, a dropkick, and several stomps and uppercuts. The two traded control before Styles almost made a fatal error when he went for a Phenomenal Forearm that Orton was set to counter into an RKO. Luckily for Styles, Orton missed his move, crashing to the mat. Styles then executed a perfect 450 move on Orton for a two count. Orton almost won the match when he nailed Styles with a top-rope superplex and then followed that up with a draping rope DDT. He wanted to finish the match with an RKO, but Styles blocked it and turned it into an enziguri. Orton did manage an RKO, but Styles, incredibly, managed to kick out. Frustrated, Orton attempted a top-rope RKO, but Styles countered it with a Pelé kick. Styles then delivered a pair of Phenomenal Forearms on Orton before pinning the Viper to win the match.

▶ *AJ Styles flies over the top rope to nail Randy Orton with a Phenomenal Forearm.*

A Female Revolution

The Women's Evolution continued in WWE in 2019 with the introduction of the Women's Tag Team Championship. Sasha Banks and Bayley were the first to hold the new championship and were set to defend the titles at *WrestleMania* against three squads: Tamina and Nia Jax, the Ilconics, and Natalya and Beth Phoenix.

Bayley and Tamina started the match, but all four squads quickly took advantage of the no disqualification stipulation by battling in and out of the ring. The official regained control of the match and the Champs used some smooth teamwork on Natalya and Phoenix. Kay tagged herself in and the Ilconics also showed some excellent tag team maneuvers. Not to be ignored, Natalya and Phoenix executed moves once perfomed by the Hart Foundation before Natalya almost recorded a submission when she put both Bayley and Banks into the Sharpshooter. However, Tamina managed to break up the pin and she and Jax delivered a wicked double headbutt to Phoenix and Samoan Drops in stereo on the Ilconics. Tamina and Jax tried to end the match with a double top-rope splash, but Phoenix shoved Jax off the top onto the floor below. The champions hit Phoenix with a one-two punch and a Bayley top-rope elbow, followed by a Banks frog splash, but Phoenix managed to kick out at two. The champions set Phoenix up on the top turnbuckle, but Phoenix reversed things and hit them with a top-rope Glam Slam. But Phoenix did not realize that Kay had tagged herself in. Kay pinned Bayley instead to win the Women's Tag Team Championship for the Ilconics.

▶ *Natalya locks both Sasha Banks and Bayley in her signature Sharpshooter.*

Joe Dominates Mysterio

The United States Championship was set to be defended at *WrestleMania 35*, with Rey Mysterio challenging the dominant champion Samoa Joe. There had been some question earlier in the week if the match was even going to happen after Rey was injured in a match with Baron Corbin at *RAW*. Not only did Mysterio set those fears aside, but he got off to a flying start, countering a slam with a DDT and then nailing Joe with a 619. He tried to continue his run with a top-rope maneuver, but Joe caught him and locked him in the Coquina Clutch, forcing Mysterio to pass out. Joe made a statement win, taking Mysterio out in about a minute.

▶ *Samoa Joe scoops up Rey Mysterio en route to a dominating title defense.*

Punishing The Usos

SmackDown Tag Team Champions The Usos defied Mr. McMahon by refusing to help him keep Kofi Kingston out of the WWE Championship match. As punishment, the boss forced them to defend their titles against three other teams. The odds of The Usos keeping their titles seemed slim as they faced down 5-time champions The Bar, the powerful combo of Rusev and Shinsuke Nakamura, and the NXT upstarts Ricochet and Aleister Black.

Jey Uso and Black started out, but Sheamus soon tagged in to battle Black. The Bar seized control when Cesaro starting spinning Ricochet around while Sheamus pounded the chests of Rusev, Nakamura, Jey, and Black. Cesero tried to force Ricochet to submit to a sharpshooter, but Jimmy Uso broke the hold and The Usos and The Bar spilled out of the ring. Rusev and Nakamura worked on Black and Ricochet, but couldn't gain a three count. The Bar, The Usos, and Rusev and Nakamura tried a massive superplex on Ricochet, but he managed to land on his feet. With bodies strewn outside of the ring, The Usos hit Sheamus with an array of kicks and a double top-rope splash to pin Sheamus and retain their titles.

▶ *Both Usos come flying down on Sheamus to finish off the Celtic Warrior.*

▶ *The Miz risks everything to suplex Shane McMahon off a camera platform.*

It Gets Personal for The Miz

The Miz thought he had the perfect tag team partner in Shane McMahon, and the two even captured the SmackDown Tag Team Championship. But after they lost the titles, and a rematch, Shane betrayed The Miz and not only beat him down, but also put his hands on The Miz's father at ringside. The Miz sought revenge at *WrestleMania* in the form of a brutal Falls Count Anywhere Match.

Shane tried to get the Miz emotional by again putting his hands on The Miz's father, and the plan worked, allowing Shane to pepper the Awesome One with a series of lefts and rights. Outside the ring, Shane nailed The Miz with a monitor and was ready to deliver a crushing elbow from the top rope when The Miz's father got in the way. Shane invited The Miz's father into the ring and instructed him on how to set a defensive stance while fighting before he began pummeling the man. That set off The Miz, who sprinted into the ring and began beating on his opponent, clubbing Shane repeatedly. While Shane was down, The Miz attended to his father, demanding that officials help his dad out.

Shane and The Miz then began brawling throughout the arena, with The Miz driving McMahon into a support structure and then Shane returning the favor, before following that up with a DDT for a two count. Shane introduced a chair to the match, blasting Shane's ankle and back with it repeatedly. The two fought into the row of international announcers and then The Miz tossed Shane over a guardrail and onto a golf cart below. Surprisingly, McMahon managed to kick out of several pins and then climbed up to a camera platform to escape, but The Miz followed him. Ignoring McMahon's pleas for mercy, The Miz superplexed Shane off the platform but Shane landed on top of The Miz, allowing Shane to steal a pinfall victory.

Kofimania is Running Wild!

Kingston's WWE career had massive momentum in early 2019, however Mr. McMahon was not impressed, and continued to place obstacles in the way of Kingston and his New Day compatriots. But Kingston would not be denied, and he earned a match at *WrestleMania* against Daniel Bryan for the title he had long yearned to hold, the WWE Championship.

The two traded holds early on in an environment where the WWE Universe was squarely in Kingston's corner. Kingston took early advantage when he drop-kicked the champion out of the ring and then dove onto him. Bryan stemmed Kingston's momentum and locked him in a painful Surfboard move. After escaping the hold, Kingston fired back at Bryan with a Boom Drop. The challenger tried to follow up with a dive outside the ring, but Bryan moved and Kingston crashed into the announcer's table.

Bryan began to seize control of the bout, methodically working over Kingston, alternating blows and holds. The camera panned to the back where practically the whole locker room was watching the match on a monitor and cheering Kingston on. Bryan punished Kingston with a painful Boston Crab hold, but Kingston reached the ropes. The two continued their back-and-forth with Kingston getting a near fall with an SOS and Bryan almost forcing a submission with a LaBell Lock move. Bryan rolled out of the ring seeking help from his manager, Erick Rowan, but Big E and Xavier Woods took Rowan. Back in the ring, Bryan hit his patented running knee, but Kingston somehow kicked out. Finally, Kingston fought out of one more LaBell Lock, softened the champion up with a series of stomps, and delivered a Trouble in Paradise move for the three count and the WWE Championship victory.

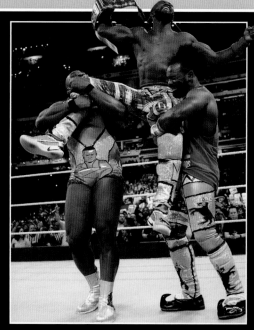

▶ *Kofi Kingston celebrates finally capturing the WWE Championship with the rest of The New Day.*

▶ *Roman Reigns completes his inspirational comeback by decking Drew McIntyre with a Superman punch.*

Reigns' Triumphant Return

Roman Reigns' world came crashing down in October 2018 when he had to relinquish the Universal Championship and step away from WWE to fight leukemia. The WWE Universe supported him and reacted ecstatically to the news in February 2019 that he was in remission and cleared to return to action. One competitor did not share that joy: Drew McIntyre. McIntyre felt Reigns shouldn't have returned and planned to end his career at *WrestleMania*.

Reigns got an early two count in the bout with a Samoan Drop and tried for a spear that McIntyre countered into a Spinebuster and a two count of his own. They continued to trade the advantage, with McIntyre testing Reigns' in-ring stamina with some painful stretches and submission holds. Reigns attempted to nail McIntyre with a Drive By, but McIntyre dodged it. McIntyre briefly took over the match, but Reigns began to dominate, hitting McIntyre with a Drive By and a Samoan Drop on the floor outside the ring. Reigns went for a Superman Punch, but McIntyre was initially able to dodge it. McIntyre could not avoid the second one, and Reigns was able to then spear and pin McIntyre to win his first singles match in six months.

The Doctor of Thuganomics Ruins Elias' Big Show

Elias had promised the WWE Universe an unforgettable, uninterrupted musical interlude at *WrestleMania*. Perhaps that was a promise that Elias should not have made. As he performed, a video chronicling Babe Ruth's famous "called shot" from the 1932 World Series began playing in the background. A bewildered Elias looked on as the video changed to "Basic Thuganomics," John Cena's original theme music, and out emerged the "Doctor of Thuganomics" himself. Wearing a throwback Ruth Yankees jersey and hat, Cena stormed to the ring and eviscerated Elias with a blistering freestyle rap. Cena did not limit his attack to words either; he delivered an Attitude Adjustment to Elias, although he called it by the move's original name "the F-U," to the delight of the capacity crowd.

▶ *John Cena brings back the F-U move to drop Elias.*

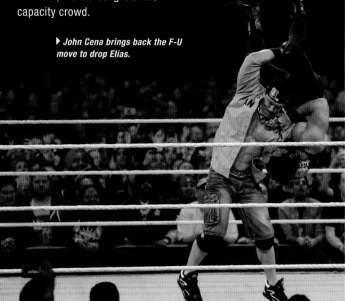

▶ *Kurt Angle hits Baron Corbin with an Olympic Slam.*

Farewell to a Legend

Kurt Angle knew that his in-ring days were coming to an end, but he planned to go out on his own terms. He was given permission to pick his opponent for his last match at *WrestleMania*. Angle's choice of Baron Corbin did not sit well with the WWE Universe, but Angle wanted an opportunity to shut Corbin up in the ring after all the trouble Corbin had given him during his tenure as *RAW* General Manager.

Angle started off strong, landing several blows on Corbin and then tossing him with an overhead suplex. Corbin dropped Angle with a series of punches and then took the time to taunt the WWE Universe for its love of the "Olympic Hero." He tried to hit Angle with a blow off the second turnbuckle, but Angle dodged the attack and then nailed Corbin with a trio of German suplexes. Angle tried to hit the Angle Slam, but Corbin countered it with a big kick. Corbin managed to get a two count after a spinning slam off Angle, and Angle also came close to winning twice—first with an Angle Slam and then with an Ankle Lock. Corbin kicked out of the submission move, but Angle then executed three more German suplexes. Angle decided to wow the WWE Universe one last time by attempting a Moonsault, but Corbin moved before Angle landed and finished Angle off with his End of Days move, leaving the crowd stunned that Angle's last match had ended as a loss.

Batista Returns

The WWE Universe hadn't seen Batista for almost five years, but he returned and set his sights on Triple H. Batista insisted that Triple H put his in-ring career on the line for a match, which Triple H agreed to, as long as it would be a No Holds Barred Match.

Both Superstars circled each other before Batista tossed Triple H into a corner, delivering a series of shoulder tackles and a punch that briefly leveled Triple H. Batista then threw Triple H over a barricade. Triple H found a toolbox that he nailed Batista with and its contents scattered, including a chain and several pairs of pliers. Triple H whipped Batista with the chain and then using one pair of pliers to crush Batista's fingers and a set of needlenose pliers to rip the nose ring off Batista's face. Batista attempted a pinfall, but Triple H kicked out at two. Triple H recovered enough to attempt a Pedigree, but Batista was able to counter it into a slam. Batista then attempted a Batista Bomb through a table, but Triple H countered that into a back body drop. He then speared Batista through another table. Hunter then produced a sledgehammer, but Batista speared Triple H before he could use it. Desperate, Triple H managed to Powerbomb Batista on the steel steps and followed that up with a Pedigree, but Batista managed to kick out at two. Ric Flair emerged to give Triple H a new sledgehammer and taunted Batista long enough to distract him while Triple H slammed him with it. One Pedigree later, and Triple H had pinned Batista, preserving his in-ring career.

Bálor Dominates Lashley

Finn Bálor promised that his alternate persona "The Demon" would appear at his fight with Lashley for the Intercontinental Championship. Lashley seem unconcerned, so Bálor let his actions speak for him, opening the match with a spinning heel kick and a leg drop. He followed that with a driving dropkick and a dive onto Lashley outside the ring. Lashley was able to buy himself some time by chokeslamming Bálor, following that up with a pair of suplexes and a lariat. After a brief Demon comeback, Lashley speared Bálor twice for a two count. Bálor fought out of a Lashley powerbomb and then stunned the WWE Universe by delivering a powerbomb of his own. Bálor then climbed to the top turnbuckle and hit Lashley with a Coup de Grace, pinning the champion to capture the Intercontinental Championship.

▶ *Finn Bálor crushes Intercontinental Champion Bobby Lashley with a top-rope Coup de Grace.*

Lynch Takes it All

Ronda Rousey, Charlotte Flair, and Becky Lynch had made some of the biggest impact as part of the Women's Evolution. While they shared common goals, they also had a deep enmity for each other and their battles in the ring and on social media made their Triple Threat Match for both the *RAW* and *SmackDown* Women's Championships one of the most anticipated in *WrestleMania* history.

At the start of the match, each woman eyed her two opponents, deciding who to attack first. Both Lynch and Flair advanced on Rousey, but then Flair backed off, allowing Rousey and Lynch to go at it. After peppering Lynch with a series of punches that sent her out of the ring, Rousey turned her attention to Flair and managed to kick her out of the ring as well. Lynch and Flair combined forces to attack Rousey. With Rousey temporarily out of commission, Charlotte took control of the match, punching Lynch repeatedly. Charlotte went to the top rope for a moonsault, but Lynch caught her and turned it into a Dis-Arm-Her. Luckily for Flair, Rousey returned to the ring and broke up the submission move before Flair could tap out.

Rousey attempted to put both Lynch and Flair in her arm bar maneuver, but Lynch escaped, and Flair countered the move into a Boston Crab. Lynch broke up the latter hold with a bulldog on Flair and then she delivered DDTs to Rousey and Flair at the same time. The competitors began taking more risks by hitting top-rope moves, with Becky delivering a top rope Becksploder Suplex on Flair and then Rousey nailed both Lynch and Flair with a high cross body. The trio continued to punish each other, but no one could get a three-count. Lynch introduced a table to the match, and Lynch and Rousey worked together to hip toss Flair through the table. Rousey looked to finish Lynch off with a Piper's Pit, but Lynch countered it to keep Rousey down for a controversial three count that earned Lynch both Women's Championships.

▶ *Becky Lynch shows off her two Championships.*